The Elder Scrolls IV
SHIVERING ISLES

PRIMA Official Game Guide

Prima Games
A Division of Random House, Inc.
3000 Lava Ridge Court, Suite 100
Roseville, CA 95661

D0992729

www.primagames.com

ISBN: 978-0-7615-5549-0
Library of Congress Catalog Card Number: 2007922920
Printed in the United States of America

07 08 09 10 LL 10 9 8 7 6 5 4 3 2 1

TABLE OF CONTENTS

INTRODUCTION

"Oblivion is a place composed of many lands, thus the many names for which Oblivion is synonymous: Couldharbour, Quagmire, Moonshadow, and others. It may be supposed that one prince rules each land of Oblivion. The princes whose names appear over and over are the aforementioned Sanguine, Boethiah, Molag Bal, Sheogorath, Azura, Mephala, Clavicus Vile, Vaermina, Malacath, Hermaeus Mora, Namira, Jyggalag, Nocturnal, Mehrunes Dagon, and Peryite."

—*On Oblivion*, by Morian Zenas

"The fearful obeisance of Sheogorath is widespread, and is found in most Tamrielic quarters. Contemporary sources indicate that his roots are in Aldmeri creation stories; therein, his is 'born' when Lorkhan's divine spark is removed. One crucial myth calls him the 'Sithis-shaped hole' of the world."

—*Varieties of Faith in the Empire*, by Brother Mikhael Karkuxor of the Imperial College

You are headed to a very strange place.

The Shivering Isles is the private realm of Sheogorath, the Daedric Prince of Madness—his own little slice of Oblivion. It exists because he wills it to. Its nature reflects his nature, divided and mercurial. Dementia and Mania. Madness and Creativity. Sheogorath embodies both, and therefore so does the Shivering Isles.

Granted, on the surface, things operate here much as they do in Cyrodiil. Guards make their rounds and respond to crimes. Folks get up in the morning and open their shops. Business as usual. However, scratch that surface a bit and a something odd is bound to seep out. The Isles is arguably an open-air asylum. Everyone here is at least a bit "touched by Sheogorath," but some hide it better than others.

And yet this isn't a case of the inmates running the asylum. Sheogorath may come off as madder than a March Hare in conversation, but his mind is dominated by practical concerns. He's facing an event called the Greymarch—an invasion by the forces of Order—and he's looking for a champion. That's you.

You can enter the Shivering Isles at any time. As soon as you escape from the Imperial Dungeon, you can find the mysterious statue on the strange island east of Bravil. The Shivering Isles are equally accessible and challenging for heroes that have attained great power and stature in Cyrodiil. Once inside, you find that you can come and go as you please. Sheogorath doesn't seem to mind, if he even notices.

Should you choose to explore, the Shivering Isles is a big place. There are dozens of dungeons and many new creatures to test your mettle. The city of New Sheoth is a large, complex place, filled with intrigue and conflict. There are many smaller stories waiting to be told, waiting for a hero of their own.

Adventuring in the Shivering Isles, you discover there is method in the madness, and madness in the methods. You learn something of the nature of a broken mind. You learn the deepest, darkest secrets of the Realm of Madness. And be warned, you are rewarded greatly.

Strange events, some of them. For you're headed to a very strange place.

ALCHEMY

INGREDIENTS AND FLORA

Ingredient	Plant/Creature Name	Effect 1	Effect 2	Effect 3
Alocasia Fruit	Alocasia	Damage Magicka	Light	Restore Fatigue
Ashen Remains	Alkanet	Damage Luck	Fortify Fatigue	Silence
Aster Bloom Core	Aster Bloom	Burden	Dispel	Restore Agility
Black Tar	Mushroom Tree Sapling & Black Tar	Damage Speed	Damage Fatigue	Damage Health
Blister Pod Cap	Blister Pod	Fortify Magicka	Invisibility	Nighteye
Bone Shard	Shambles	Damage Luck	Damage Magicka	Frost-Shield
Congealed Putrescence	Putrid Gigantea	Damage Health	Fire Damage	Restore Strength
Elytra Ichor	Elytra	Burden	Chameleon	Restore Magicka
Feldew	—	Felldew Effect	—	—
Flame Stalk	Flame Stalk	Fire Damage	Frost-Shield	Invisibility
Fungus Stalk	Fungus Stalk	Fortify Health	Restore Strength	Restore Magicka
Gnarl Bark	Gnarl	Damage Health	Fire Shield	Restore Endurance
Greenmote	—	Greenmote Rapture	—	—
Grummite Eggs	Grummite Egg Mound/Sac	Chameleon	Damage Magicka	Dispel
Hound Tooth	Skinned Hound	Burden	Cure Poison	Detect Life
Hunger Tongue	Hunger	Cure Disease	Cure Poison	Fire Damage
Hydnum Azure Giant Spore	Hydnum Azure	Detect Life	Fortify Health	Frost Shield
Knight Heart	Knights of Order	Jyggalag's Favor	—	—
Letifer Orca Digestive Slime	Letifer Orca Planta	Damage Fatigue	Damage Health	Damage Magicka
Red Kelp Gas Bladder	Red Kelp	Cure Disease	Fortify Magicka	Restore Speed
Rot Scale	Rot Scale	Burden	Damage Health	Paralyze
Scalon Fin	Scalon	Burden	Damage Health	Shock Damage
Screaming Maw	Screaming Maw	Chameleon	Detect Life	Restore Willpower
Shambles Marrow	Shambles	Damage Health	Damage Magicka	Frost Damage
Smoked Baliwog	—	Damage Fatigue	Feather	Restore Fatigue
Swamp Tentacle	Swamp Tentacle	Fortify Health	Restore Personality	Water Breathing
Thorn Hook	Thorn Hook	Damage Luck	Damage Health	Fortify Health
Unrefined Greenmote	—	Drain Intelligence	Drain Fatigue	Drain Health
Void Essence	Flesh Atronach	Fortify Speed	Fortify Endurance	Fortify Health
Watcher's Eye	Watcher's Eye	Fortify Magicka	Light	Restore Intelligence
Water Root Pod Pit	Water Root Pod	Fire Shield	Restore Health	Resist Fire
Wisp Core	Root Stalk	Burden	Chameleon	Light
Withering Moon	Withering Moon	Cure Disease	Restore Magicka	Reflect Spell
Worm's Head Cap	Worm's Head	Fortify Fatigue	Nighteye	Paralyze

Effect 4	# of Plants	Commonly Location	Concentration Location	Harvest Chance
Restore Health	314	Mania	Hale & Bliss	80%
Weakness to Fire	21	Cylarne and Ebrocca (in urns)	Cylarne	100%
Shield	118	Mania	Mania Palace Garden	80%
Shock Damage	904	Dementia (saplings have reduced harvest chance)	—	Varies
Restore Magicka	310	Dementia	Deepwallow	66%
Restore Willpower	4	—	—	100%
Restore Magicka	195	Dementia	New Sheoth Graveyard	66%
Silence	—	—	—	—
—	—	Dunroot Burrow	—	—
Restore Health	817	Mania	Dunroot Burrow	33%
Water Walking	817	Dementia, Rendil Drararas house	Gloomstone Passage	50%/33%
Shield	—	—	—	—
—	—	Greenmote Silo	—	—
Silence	1,036	Dementia	Xilera	33%/80%
Invisibility	—	—	—	—
Fortify Magicka	—	—	—	—
Restore Endurance	439	Mania	Camp Hopeful	66%
—	—	—	—	—
Restore Fatigue	223	Dementia	Split	66%
Water Breathing	673	Mania	Dunroot Burrow	50%
Silence	97	Dementia	Swampgas Hole	33%/25%
Water Breathing	—	—	—	—
Restore Health	123	Mania	Gloomstone Passage	66%
Paralyze	—	—	—	—
Restore Health	—	—	—	—
Water Walking	150	Dementia	Xedilian	80%
Restore Magicka	84	Dementia	Swampgas Hole	33%
Drain Magicka	—	Greenmote Silo	—	—
Restore Health	—	—	—	—
Reflect Spell	54	Mania	Knotty Bramble	80%
Water Breathing	171	Dementia	Fellmoor	80%
Restore Intelligence	858	Everywhere	Swampgas Hole	25%
Shield	1,079	Dementia	Swampgas Hole	33%/25%
Restore Luck	414	Mania	Dire Warren	80%/66%

EQUIPMENT

LIGHT ARMOR

Type	Weight	Health	Price	Armor	Enchantment
Impure Amber Boots	1.9	130	5	2.25	Fortify Acrobatics: 2
Impure Amber Cuirass	6.3	130	25	5.75	Fortify Agility: 2
Impure Amber Gauntlets	1.3	65	5	2.25	Fortify Marksman: 1, Fortify Hand to Hand: 1
Impure Amber Greaves	3.8	100	15	3.5	Fortify Speed: 2
Impure Amber Helmet	1.3	65	5	2.25	Fortify Intelligence: 2
Impure Amber Shield	2.5	100	15	6.75	Reflect Spell: 5
Lesser Amber Boots	2.5	110	20	2.75	Fortify Acrobatics: 4
Lesser Amber Cuirass	8.3	215	65	7	Fortify Agility: 4
Lesser Amber Gauntlets	1.7	110	20	2.75	Fortify Marksman: 2, Fortify Hand to Hand: 2
Lesser Amber Greaves	5	160	30	4.25	Fortify Speed: 4
Lesser Amber Helmet	1.7	110	20	2.75	Fortify Intelligence: 4
Lesser Amber Shield	3.3	160	30	8.25	Reflect Spell: 6
Amber Boots	3	190	45	3.25	Fortify Acrobatics: 6
Amber Cuirass	10	375	160	8.25	Fortify Agility: 6
Amber Gauntlets	2	190	45	3.25	Fortify Marksman: 4, Fortify Hand to Hand: 4
Amber Greaves	6	280	80	5	Fortify Speed: 6
Amber Helmet	2	190	45	3.25	Fortify Intelligence: 6
Amber Shield	4	280	80	9.75	Reflect Spell: 7
Fine Amber Boots	3.6	340	115	3.75	Fortify Acrobatics: 8
Fine Amber Cuirass	12	680	415	9.5	Fortify Agility: 8
Fine Amber Gauntlets	2.4	340	115	3.75	Fortify Marksman: 6, Fortify Hand to Hand: 6
Fine Amber Greaves	7.2	510	205	5.75	Fortify Speed: 8
Fine Amber Helmet	2.4	340	115	3.75	Fortify Intelligence: 8
Fine Amber Shield	4.8	510	205	11.25	Reflect Spell: 8
Grand Amber Boots	4.2	560	335	4.5	Fortify Acrobatics: 10
Grand Amber Cuirass	14	1,115	1,200	11.25	Fortify Agility: 10
Grand Amber Gauntlets	2.8	560	335	4.5	Fortify Marksman: 8, Fortify Hand to Hand: 8
Grand Amber Greaves	8.4	835	600	6.75	Fortify Speed: 10
Grand Amber Helmet	4.5	560	335	4.5	Fortify Intelligence: 10
Grand Amber Shield	5.6	835	600	13.5	Reflect Spell: 9
Perfect Amber Boots	4.7	735	590	5.25	Fortify Acrobatics: 12
Perfect Amber Cuirass	15.5	1,470	2,100	13.25	Fortify Agility: 12
Perfect Amber Gauntlets	3.1	735	580	5.25	Fortify Marksman: 10, Fortify Hand to Hand: 10
Perfect Amber Greaves	9.3	1,080	1,200	8	Fortify Speed: 12
Perfect Amber Helmet	3.1	735	580	5.25	Fortify Intelligence: 12
Perfect Amber Shield	6.2	1,080	1,200	15.75	Reflect Spell: 10

HEAVY ARMOR

Type	Weight	Health	Price	Armor	Enchantment
Impure Madness Boots	9.8	200	35	4.25	Fortify Athletics: 2
Impure Madness Cuirass	32.5	400	135	10.75	Fortify Strength: 2
Impure Madness Gauntlets	6.5	200	35	4.25	Fortify Blade: 1, Fortify Blunt 1
Impure Madness Greaves	19.5	300	65	6.5	Fortify Endurance: 2
Impure Madness Helmet	6.5	200	35	4.25	Fortify Willpower: 2
Impure Madness Shield	13	300	65	12.75	Reflect Damage: 5
Lesser Madness Cuirass	37.5	650	290	12	Fortify Strength: 4
Lesser Madness Gauntlets	7.5	325	80	4.75	Fortify Willpower: 4
Lesser Madness Greaves	22.5	490	145	7.25	Fortify Endurance: 4
Lesser Madness Helmet	7.5	325	80	4.75	Fortify Blade: 2, Fortify Blunt 2
Lesser Madness Shield	15	490	145	14.25	Reflect Damage: 6
Lesset Madness Boots	11.3	325	80	4.75	Fortify Athletics: 4
Madness Shield	17	750	335	15.75	Reflect Damage: 7
Madness Helmet	8.5	500	190	5.25	Fortify Willpower: 6
Madness Greaves	25	750	335	8	Fortify Endurance: 6
Madness Gauntlets	8.5	500	190	5.25	Fortify Blade: 4, Fortify Blunt 4
Madness Cuirass	42.5	1,000	670	13.25	Fortify Strength: 6
Madness Boots	12.8	500	190	5.25	Fortify Athletics: 6
Fine Madness Boots	14.6	775	400	5.75	Fortify Athletics: 8
Fine Madness Cuirass	48.8	1,550	1,420	14.5	Fortify Strength: 8

HEAVY ARMOR CONT.

Type	Weight	Health	Price	Armor	Enchantment
Fine Madness Gauntlets	9.8	775	400	5.75	Fortify Blade: 6, Fortify Blunt: 6
Fine Madness Greaves	29.3	1,165	710	8.75	Fortify Endurance: 8
Fine Madness Helmet	9.8	775	400	5.75	Fortify Willpower: 8
Fine Madness Shield	19.6	1,165	710	17.25	Reflect Damage: 8
Grand Madness Boots	16.9	1,150	940	6.75	Fortify Athletics: 10
Grand Madness Cuirass	56.3	2,300	3,350	17	Fortify Strength: 10
Grand Madness Gauntlets	11.3	1,150	940	6.75	Fortify Blade: 8, Fortify Blunt: 8
Grand Madness Greaves	33.8	1,725	1,625	10.25	Fortify Endurance: 10
Grand Madness Helmet	11	1,150	940	6.75	Fortify Willpower: 10
Grand Madness Shield	22.5	1,725	1,675	20.25	Reflect Damage: 9
Perfect Madness Boots	18.6	1,450	1,545	8	Fortify Athletics: 12
Perfect Madness Cuirass	61.9	2,900	5,525	19.75	Fortify Strength: 12
Perfect Madness Gauntlets	12.4	1,450	1,555	8	Fortify Blade: 10, Fortify Blunt: 10
Perfect Madness Greaves	37.1	2,175	2,915	11.75	Fortify Endurance: 12
Perfect Madness Helmet	12.4	1,450	1,555	8	Fortify Willpower: 10
Perfect Madness Shield	24.8	2,175	2,915	23.75	Reflect Damage: 10

AMBER/MADNESS WEAPONS

Type	Weight	Value	Health	Speed	Reach	Damage	Enchantment
Impure Amber Hammer	35	95	225	0.7	1.3	15	Damage Health: 2
Impure Amber Mace	17	30	165	0.9	1	11	Damage Health: 2
Impure Amber/Madness Sword	22	35	165	1	1	11	Damage Health: 2
Impure Madness Axe	14	25	135	1.1	0.8	9	Damage Health: 2
Impure Madness Claymore	25	60	195	0.8	1.3	13	Damage Health: 2
Unpolished Amber Hammer	44	165	290	0.7	1.3	17	Damage Health: 5
Unpolished Amber Mace	21	85	220	0.9	1	13	Damage Health: 5
Unpolished Amber Sword	26	85	220	1	1	13	Damage Health: 5
Unpolished Madness Axe	18	50	190	1.1	0.8	11	Damage Health: 5
Unpolished Madness Claymore	31	105	255	0.8	1.3	15	Damage Health: 5
Lesser Amber Hammer	53	315	360	0.7	1.3	19	Damage Health: 7
Lesser Amber Mace	25	125	285	0.9	1	15	Damage Health: 7
Lesser Amber/Madness Sword	30	165	285	1	1	15	Damage Health: 7
Lesser Madness Axe	22	115	250	1.1	0.8	13	Damage Health: 7
Lesser Madness Claymore	36	220	325	0.8	1.3	17	Damage Health: 7
Madness Axe	26	255	315	1.1	0.8	15	Damage Health: 10
Amber Mace	29	280	360	0.9	1	17	Damage Health: 10
Amber/Madness Sword	34	310	360	1	1	17	Damage Health: 10
Madness Claymore	41	455	400	0.8	1.3	19	Damage Health: 10
Amber Hammer	62	615	440	0.7	1.3	21	Damage Health: 10
Fine Amber Hammer	71	1,150	530	0.7	1.3	23	Damage Health: 12
Fine Amber Mace	33	565	440	0.9	1	19	Damage Health: 12
Fine Amber/Madness Sword	38	630	440	1	1	19	Damage Health: 12
Fine Madness Axe	30	530	390	1.1	0.8	17	Damage Health: 12
Fine Madness Claymore	47	875	485	0.8	1.3	21	Damage Health: 12
Very Fine Amber Sword	42	1,270	525	1	1	21	Damage Health: 15
Very Fine Hammer	80	2,150	625	0.7	1.3	25	Damage Health: 15
Very Fine Mace	37	1,125	525	0.9	1	21	Damage Health: 15
Very Fine Madness Axe	34	1,080	475	1.1	0.8	19	Damage Health: 15
Very Fine Madness Claymore	53	1,675	575	0.8	1.3	23	Damage Health: 15
Grand Amber Hammer	89	3,900	730	0.7	1.3	27	Damage Health: 17
Grand Amber Mace	41	2,350	620	0.9	1	23	Damage Health: 17
Grand Amber/Madness Sword	46	2,400	620	1	1	23	Damage Health: 17
Grand Madness Axe	38	2,275	570	1.1	0.8	21	Damage Health: 17
Grand Madness Claymore	59	3,100	675	0.8	1.3	25	Damage Health: 17
Perfect Amber Hammer	98	6,100	840	0.7	1.3	29	Damage Health: 20
Perfect Amber Mace	45	4,050	720	0.9	1	25	Damage Health: 20
Perfect Amber/Madness Sword	50	5,800	720	1	1	25	Damage Health: 20
Perfect Madness Axe	42	3,925	665	1.1	0.8	23	Damage Health: 20
Perfect Madness Claymore	65	4,900	780	0.8	1.3	27	Damage Health: 20

AMBER/MADNESS BOWS

Type	Weight	Value	Health	Damage	Enchantment
Impure Bow	9	20	130	9	Damage Health: 2
Unpolished Bow	11	45	160	10	Damage Health: 5
Lesser Bow	13	105	200	11	Damage Health: 7
Amber/Madness Bow	15	260	240	13	Damage Health: 10
Fine Bow	17	550	290	15	Damage Health: 12
Very Fine Bow	19	1,145	340	17	Damage Health: 15
Grand Bow	21	2,375	390	19	Damage Health: 17
Perfect Bow	23	4,025	450	21	Damage Health: 20

 Unlike other materials, Amber and Madness magic armor and weapons are available at the same level as the mundane versions.

AMBER/MADNESS ARROWS

Type	Weight	Value	Damage	Enchantment
Impure Arrow	0.10	2	9	Damage Health: 2
Unpolished Arrow	0.10	3	10	Damage Health: 5
Lesser Arrow	0.10	4	11	Damage Health: 7
Amber/Madness Arrow	0.10	6	12	Damage Health: 10
Fine Amber Arrow	0.10	10	13	Damage Health: 12
Very Fine Amber Arrow	0.15	16	14	Damage Health: 15
Grand Arrow	0.23	28	15	Damage Health: 17
Perfect Arrow	0.28	43	16	Damage Health: 20

Armor	Available at PC Level
Impure	1
Lesser	4
Amber/Madness	8
Fine	12
Grand	17
Perfect	23

Weapons	Available at PC Level
Impure	1
Unpolished	3
Less	5
Amber/Madness	8
Fine	10
Very Fine	14
Grand	18
Perfect	23

SPELLS

Name	Skill	Range	Effect
Glimpse of Death	Apprentice	Touch	Drain Health (60 points for 3 seconds)
Snow Flare	Novice	Target	Fire Damage (7 point), Frost Damage (5 points)
Hail Fire	Apprentice	Target	Fire Damage (15 points), Frost Damage (10 points)
Icy Blaze	Journeyman	Target	Fire Damage (25 points), Frost Damage (20 points)
Salve	Novice	Self	Restore Fatigue (10 points), Restore Health (15 points)
Remedy	Apprentice	Self	Restore Fatigue (20 points), Restore Health (10 points)
Rejuvenate	Journeyman	Self	Restore Fatigue (40 points), Restore Health (20 points)
Revive	Expert	Self	Restore Fatigue (75 points), Restore Health (35 points)
Rejuvenate Friend	Journeyman	Target	Restore Fatigue (20 points), Restore Health (10 points)
Remedy Friend	Apprentice	Touch	Restore Fatigue (20 points), Restore Health (10 points)
Summon Flesh Atronach	Apprentice	Self	Summon Mangled Flesh Atronach (25 seconds)
Summon Flesh Atronach	Journeyman	Self	Summon Torn Flesh Atronach (25 seconds)
Summon Flesh Atronach	Expert	Self	Summon Stitched Flesh Atronach (25 seconds)
Summon Flesh Atronach	Master	Self	Summon Sewn Flesh Atronach (25 seconds)
Summon Hunger	Apprentice	Self	Summon Hunger (20 seconds)
Summon Hunger	Journeyman	Self	Summon Gluttonous Hunger (20 seconds)
Summon Hunger	Expert	Self	Summon Ravenous Hunger (20 seconds)
Summon Hunger	Master	Self	Summon Voracious Hunger (20 seconds)
Summon Shambles	Journeyman	Self	Summon Decrepit Shambles (30 seconds)
Summon Shambles	Expert	Self	Summon Shambles (30 seconds)
Summon Shambles	Master	Self	Summon Replete Shambles (30 seconds)

CREATURES

HUMANOID ENEMIES

HERETICS

Found primarily in Mania, Heretics are wandering, mad Mages. They believe that Sheogorath is a man passing himself off as a god or Daedric Prince. They refuse to recognize his rule and avoid the cities and towns. Heretics and Zealots have opposite but equally fanatical beliefs, and hate each other with a passion.

They summon Hungers to do their bidding. Heretics are fond of Destruction spells and will use a Dispel against you. They prefer war axes but do not wear armor. Instead, they wear special robes and hoods by which they know each other. If you wear both the robe and hood, most Heretics will not recognize you as an enemy unless you get too close. Then the jig is up. However, Heretic bosses will always recognize you as an imposter regardless of how far away you are, assuming they have detected you.

Rank	Level Range
Heretic Novitiate	1–5
Heretic Soldier	6–10
Heretic Crusader	11–15
Heretic Warpriest	16–20
Transformed Heretic	20 and up

ZEALOTS

Zealots are also mad Mages and can be found primarily in Dementia. They believe that Sheogorath is a god and worship him fervently. They kill anyone they find that does not believe likewise, which is just about everyone. Zealots hate Heretics for obvious reasons.

While their melee combat skills are not as good as those of the Heretics, Zealots are superior wizards. They can summon Flesh Atronachs to do battle. Like Heretics, they are well stocked with Destruction spells. However, they also have a 15 percent Spell Absorption ability. Zealots prefer short swords and daggers. Similar to the Heretics, they have special robes. When you wear both the robe and the hood, a Zealot will not recognize you as an enemy unless you get too close. Zealot Bosses will always know you are an imposter, regardless of how far away you are, assuming they have detected you.

Rank	Level Range
Zealot Neophyte	1–5
Zealot Missionary	6–10
Zealot Proselytizer	11–15
Zealot Patriarch/Matriach	16–19
Ascended Zealot	20 and up

GOLDEN SAINTS

For the most part, Golden Saints are not your enemies. However, there are several quests where you are forced to fight them. Primarily they serve as guards for the lands of Mania and its Duke, Thadon. They patrol the roads and the district of Bliss, and will arrest wrongdoers.

Golden Saints wear unique heavy armor that is all one piece, although the helmet and shield are separate. They carry a sword and bow for weapons. Saints reflect 15 percent of all spells, but have a 50 percent Weakness to Poison. In addition to a set of normal Restoration and Destruction spells, they have a Lesser Power of Disintegrate Weapon (100 points). You will occasionally run into specialist Saints that have stronger spellcasting abilities.

DARK SEDUCERS

Like Golden Saints, Dark Seducers are not usually opponents, except in special circumstances. They serve as the guards for the lands of Dementia and its Duchess, Syl. They patrol the roads and the district of Crucible, and will arrest wrongdoers.

Dark Seducers wear unique light armor that is all one piece, although the helmet and shield are separate. They carry a war axe and bow for weapons. Seducers have a 15 percent Spell Absorption ability, but have a 50 percent Weakness to Frost. In addition to a set of normal Restoration and Alteration spells, they have a Lesser Power of Absorb Health (1 point for 60 seconds). You will occasionally run into specialist Seducers that have stronger spell casting abilities.

PRIESTS OF ORDER

Normal people of the Shivering Isles (if such a term can be used) are sometimes swayed to take the side of Order. When they join with Jyggalag, they become Priests of Order and are granted certain spells and powers. Chief among these is the ability to activate an Obelisk. Once activated, an Obelisk can spawn Knights of Order to join the priest in combat. The priests have a Bound Dagger spell as their only melee weapon. Fortunately, they do not wear armor. Some Priests of Order carry crystal staffs of lightning.

KNIGHTS OF ORDER

Knights of Order are not human, yet they're not creatures. They look like men in armor, hence the term Knight. That said, if you were to open that armor, you would find it empty. They are basically walking tanks with no spellcasting ability at all. They do have a moderate Sneak skill and are, therefore, able to detect you even when you are sneaking if you are not careful. Knights of Order are 50 percent resistant to poison. Their magic resistance varies with their level.

CREATURES

BALIWOGS

Rank	Level Range
Young Baliwog	1–3
Baliwog	6
Venomous Baliwog	9

YOUNG BALIWOG

Type: Creature	Combat Skill: 25
Level: 1–3	Magic Skill: 90
Health: 10–30	Stealth Skill: 5
Magicka: 0	Attack Damage: 8
Fatigue: 50–150	Weapons: None
Soul: Petty	

Advantages: Water Breathing, Automatically heal 1 point per second when swimming in water
Weaknesses: None
Ingredient: None
Ranged Magic: None
Melee Magic: Swampfever disease 15%

BALIWOG

Type: Creature	Combat Skill: 25
Level: 6	Magic Skill: 5
Health: 130	Stealth Skill: 5
Magicka: 0	Attack Damage: 12
Fatigue: 120	Weapons: None
Soul: Lesser	

Advantages: Water Breathing, Automatically heal 1 point per second when swimming in water
Weaknesses: None
Ingredient: None
Ranged Magic: None
Melee Magic: Swampfever disease 15%

VENOMOUS BALIWOG

Type: Creature	Combat Skill: 50
Level: 9	Magic Skill: 5
Health: 180	Stealth Skill: 5
Magicka: 0	Attack Damage: 19
Fatigue: 200	Weapons: None
Soul: Common	

Advantages: Water Breathing, Automatically heal 1 point per second when swimming in water
Weaknesses: None
Ingredient: None
Ranged Magic: None
Melee Magic: Swampfever disease 15%

ELYTRA

Elytra have a disturbing tendency in melee to often block by turning their claws almost sideways. Like a water spider, they can walk on the water.

Rank	Level Range
Elytra Hatchling	1
Elytra Drone	4
Elytra Soldier	9
Elytra Noble	14
Elytra Matron	19 and up

ELYTRA HATCHLING

Type: Creature	Combat Skill: 25
Level: 1	Magic Skill: 5
Health: 24	Stealth Skill: 40
Magicka: 10	Attack Damage: 5
Fatigue: 50	Weapons: None
Soul: Petty	

Advantages: Water Walking, Resist Poison 50%
Weaknesses: Weakness to Magic 20%
Ingredient: Elytra Ichor
Ranged Magic: None
Melee Magic: None

ELYTRA DRONE

Type: Creature	Combat Skill: 25
Level: 4	Magic Skill: 20
Health: 120	Stealth Skill: 50
Magicka: 20	Attack Damage: 8
Fatigue: 150	Weapons: None
Soul: Lesser	

Advantages: Water Walking, Resist Poison 50%
Weaknesses: Weakness to Magic 20%
Ingredient: Elytra Ichor
Ranged Magic: None
Melee Magic: Damage Health 1 point for 10 seconds

ELYTRA SOLDIER

Type: Creature	Combat Skill: 50
Level: 9	Magic Skill: 45
Health: 210	Stealth Skill: 60
Magicka: 20	Attack Damage: 12
Fatigue: 250	Weapons: None
Soul: Common	

Advantages: Water Walking, Resist Poison 50%
Weaknesses: Weakness to Magic 20%
Ingredient: Elytra Ichor
Ranged Magic: None
Melee Magic: Damage Health 2 points for 10 seconds, Damage Magicka 1 point for 10 seconds

ELYTRA NOBLE

Type: Creature	Combat Skill: 75
Level: 14	Magic Skill: 70
Health: 275	Stealth Skill: 70
Magicka: 20	Attack Damage: 18
Fatigue: 320	Weapons: None
Soul: Greater	

Advantages: Water Walking, Resist Poison 50%
Weaknesses: Weakness to Magic 20%
Ingredient: Elytra Ichor
Ranged Magic: Damage Health 3 points for 12 seconds, Damage Magicka 2 points for 12 seconds
Melee Magic: None

ELYTRA MATRON

Type: Creature	Combat Skill: 100
Level: 19+	Magic Skill: 98+
Health: 266+	Stealth Skill: 80+
Magicka: 19+	Attack Damage: 25+
Fatigue: 323+	Weapons: None
Soul: Grand	

Advantages: Water Walking, Resist Poison 50%
Weaknesses: Weakness to Magic 20%
Ingredient: Elytra Ichor
Ranged Magic: Damage Health 3 points for 15 seconds, Damage Magicka 2 points for 15 seconds
Melee Magic: Once-a-day power—Damage Health 1 point for 100 seconds, Damage Magicka 1 point for 100 seconds

FLESH ATRONACHS

Fast and agile, the Flesh Atronach has a variety of special combat moves.

Rank	Level Range
Mangled Flesh Atronach	1–3
Torn Flesh Atronach	6
Stitched Flesh Atronach	11
Sewn Flesh Atronach	16
Mended Flesh Atronach	21 and up

MANGLED FLESH ATRONACH

Type: Daedra	Combat Skill: 42–46
Level: 1–3	Magic Skill: 6–8
Health: 16–48	Stealth Skill: 6–8
Magicka: 0	Attack Damage: 10–11
Fatigue: 130–390	Weapons: None
Soul: Petty or Lesser	

Advantages: Immune to poison, Resist Fire 30%, Resist Magic 30%, Water Breathing
Weaknesses: Weakness to Shock 30%, Stunted Magicka
Ingredient: Void Essence
Ranged Magic: None
Melee Magic: None

TORN FLESH ATRONACH

Type: Daedra	Combat Skill: 40
Level: 6	Magic Skill: 5
Health: 80	Stealth Skill: 30
Magicka: 0	Attack Damage: 18
Fatigue: 500	Weapons: None
Soul: Lesser	

Advantages: Immune to poison, Resist Fire 30%, Resist Magic 30%, Water Breathing
Weaknesses: Weakness to Shock 30%, Stunted Magicka
Ingredient: Void Essence
Ranged Magic: None
Melee Magic: None

STITCHED FLESH ATRONACH

Type: Daedra	Combat Skill: 40
Level: 11	Magic Skill: 40
Health: 125	Stealth Skill: 5
Magicka: 10	Attack Damage: 24
Fatigue: 600	Weapons: None
Soul: Common	

Advantages: Immune to poison, Resist Fire 30%, Spell Absorption 30%, Water Breathing, Restore Health (50 points)
Weaknesses: Weakness to Shock 30%, Stunted Magicka
Ingredient: Void Essence
Ranged Magic: None
Melee Magic: None

SEWN FLESH ATRONACH

Type: Daedra	Combat Skill: 50
Level: 16	Magic Skill: 45
Health: 180	Stealth Skill: 5
Magicka: 10	Attack Damage: 30
Fatigue: 750	Weapons: None
Soul: Greater	

Advantages: Immune to poison, Resist Fire 30%, Spell Absorption 30%, Water Breathing, Restore Health (50 points)
Weaknesses: Weakness to Shock 30%, Stunted Magicka
Ingredient: Void Essence
Ranged Magic: None
Melee Magic: Damage Health (20 points)

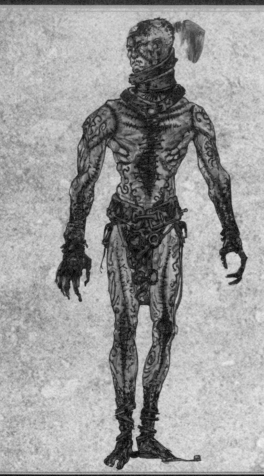

MENDED FLESH ATRONACH

Type: Daedra	Combat Skill: 75+
Level: 21 and up	Magic Skill: 70+
Health: 210+	Stealth Skill: 43+
Magicka: 21+	Attack Damage: 36+
Fatigue: 1,050+	Weapons: None
Soul: Grand	

Advantages: Immune to poison, Resist Fire 30%, Reflect Spell 25%, Spell Absorption 30%, Water Breathing, Restore Health (50 points)
Weaknesses: Weakness to Shock 30%, Stunted Magicka
Ingredient: Void Essence
Ranged Magic: Fire Ball (25 points, 10-foot radius)
Melee Magic: Damage Health (20 points)

GNARLS

Gnarls have a special magical defense system. When struck by elemental magic (fire, frost, shock), they are damaged normally but absorb some aspect of the spell for 16 seconds. They physically grow larger, which allows them to do more damage and resist normal damage 20 percent. They gain a short-term 70 percent resistance to that element and a 50 percent weakness to the other two elements.

The ideal strategy with Gnarls is to keep hitting them with alternating elemental magic. Each spell will do 50 percent more damage than the one before. If that isn't possible, avoid using spells against them at all.

Rank	Level Range
Germinal Gnarl	1–3
Gnarl Sapling	6
Gnarl Rootbender	11
Verdant Gnarl	16
Elder Gnarl	21 and up

GERMINAL GNARL

Type: Creature	Combat Skill: 27–31
Level: 1–3	Magic Skill: 12–16
Health: 15–45	Stealth Skill: 22–26
Magicka: 10–30	Attack Damage: 4–5
Fatigue: 15–45	Weapons: None
Soul: Petty	

Advantages: None
Weaknesses: None
Ingredient: Gnarl Bark
Ranged Magic: —
Melee Magic: —

Germinal Gnarls are devoid of any special powers.

GNARL SAPLING

Type: Creature	Combat Skill: 50
Level: 6	Magic Skill: 50
Health: 90	Stealth Skill: 30
Magicka: 12	Attack Damage: 15
Fatigue: 200	Weapons: None
Soul: Lesser	

Advantages: None
Weaknesses: None
Ingredient: Gnarl Bark
Ranged Magic: Damage Health (15 points), Silence (20 seconds)
Melee Magic: —

GNARL ROOTBENDER

Type: Creature	Combat Skill: 50
Level: 11	Magic Skill: 50
Health: 250	Stealth Skill: 40
Magicka: 15	Attack Damage: 22
Fatigue: 250	Weapons: None
Soul: Common	

Advantages: None
Weaknesses: None
Ingredient: Gnarl Bark
Ranged Magic: Damage Health (20 points), Silence (25 seconds)
Melee Magic: —

VERDANT GNARL

Type: Creature	Combat Skill: 60
Level: 16	Magic Skill: 59
Health: 300	Stealth Skill: 50
Magicka: 18	Attack Damage: 26
Fatigue: 300	Weapons: None
Soul: Greater	

Advantages: None
Weaknesses: None
Ingredient: Gnarl Bark
Ranged Magic: Damage Health (20 points), Silence (25 seconds)
Melee Magic: —

ELDER GNARL

Type: Creature	Combat Skill: 92+
Level: 21+	Magic Skill: 91+
Health: 357+	Stealth Skill: 82+
Magicka: 21+	Attack Damage: 32+
Fatigue: 315	Weapons: None
Soul: Grand	

Advantages: None
Weaknesses: None
Ingredient: Gnarl Bark
Ranged Magic: Damage Health (25 points), Silence (30 seconds)
Melee Magic: —

GRUMMITES

In addition to the Grummites mentioned here, you can run into Grummite Shamans and Grummite Archers. They are like normal Grummites, but they specialize in spells and bows respectively.

Rank	Level Range
Grummite Whelp	1–3
Grummite Beater	6
Grummite Painbringer	11
Grummite Torturer	16
Grummite Deathdealer	20 and up

GRUMMITE WHELP

Type: Creature	Combat Skill: 22–26
Level: 1–3	Magic Skill: 12–16
Health: 15–45	Stealth Skill: 13–16
Magicka: 0	Attack Damage: 4–5
Fatigue: 135–405	Weapons: Grummite dagger
Soul: Petty	(10 damage)

Advantages: Water Breathing, Resist Frost 50%
Weaknesses: Weakness to Fire 25%
Ingredient: Grummite Eggs 25%
Ranged Magic: None
Melee Magic: Random poison potions

Grummite Whelps regenerate 1 point per second in water. However, they also regenerate an additional 1 point per second in the rain.

GRUMMITE BEATER

Type: Creature	Combat Skill: 40
Level: 6	Magic Skill: 20
Health: 125	Stealth Skill: 20
Magicka: 0	Attack Damage: 6
Fatigue: 135	Weapons: Crude Grummite
Soul: Lesser	mace (13 damage), 50%
	chance of shield

Advantages: Water Breathing, Resist Frost 50%
Weaknesses: Weakness to Fire 25%
Ingredient: Grummite Eggs 25%
Ranged Magic: None
Melee Magic: Random poison potions

Grummite Beaters regenerate 1 point per second in water. However, they also regenerate an additional 1 point per second in the rain.

GRUMMITE PAINBRINGER

Type: Creature	Combat Skill: 50
Level: 11	Magic Skill: 20
Health: 200	Stealth Skill: 30
Magicka: 0	Attack Damage: 9
Fatigue: 200	Weapons: Grummite mace
Soul: Common	(17 damage), 50% chance of
	shield

Advantages: Water Breathing, Resist Frost 50%
Weaknesses: Weakness to Fire 25%
Ingredient: Grummite Eggs 25%
Ranged Magic: None
Melee Magic: Random poison potions

Grummite Painbringers regenerate 2 points per second in water. However, they also regenerate an additional 1 point per second in the rain.

GRUMMITE TORTURER

Type: Creature	Combat Skill: 65
Level: 16	Magic Skill: 50
Health: 325	Stealth Skill: 40
Magicka: 5	Attack Damage: 12
Fatigue: 400	Weapons: Crude Grummite
Soul: Greater	cleaver (19 damage), 50%
	chance of shield

Advantages: Water Breathing, Resist Frost 50%
Weaknesses: Weakness to Fire 25%
Ingredient: Grummite Eggs 25%
Ranged Magic: None
Melee Magic: Random poison potions

Grummite Torturers regenerate 2 points per second in water. However, they also regenerate an additional 1 point per second in the rain. Torturers also have a once-a-day power to restore 25 points of Health and 50 points of Fatigue.

GRUMMITE DEATHDEALER

Type: Creature	Combat Skill: 75+
Level: 20+	Magic Skill: 65+
Health: 500+	Stealth Skill: 70+
Magicka: 20+	Attack Damage: 12
Fatigue: 50+	Weapons: Grummite cleaver
Soul: Grand	(21 damage), Grummite
	shield

Advantages: Water Breathing, Resist Frost 50%
Weaknesses: Weakness to Fire 25%
Ingredient: Grummite Eggs 25%
Ranged Magic: None
Melee Magic: Absorb strength (10 points for 20 seconds)

Grummite Deathdealers regenerate 3 points per second in water. However, they also regenerate an additional 1 point per second in the rain. Painbringers also have a once-a-day power to restore 25 points of Health and 50 points of Fatigue.

HUNGERS

Hungers are fast. If the Absorb Fatigue attack pushes you below zero, you will be knocked down.

Rank	Level Range
Starved Hunger	1
Hunger	4
Gluttonous Hunger	9
Ravenous Hunger	14
Voracious Hunger	19

STARVED HUNGER

Type: Daedra	Combat Skill: 25
Level: 1	Magic Skill: 25
Health: 40	Stealth Skill: 25
Magicka: 25	Attack Damage: 9
Fatigue: 100	Weapons: None
Soul: Petty	

Advantages: Resist Fire 33%
Weaknesses: Weakness to Shock 25%
Ingredient: Hunger Tongue
Ranged Magic: None
Melee Magic: Absorb Fatigue (5 points for 5 seconds)

HUNGER

Type: Daedra	Combat Skill: 45
Level: 4	Magic Skill: 35
Health: 100	Stealth Skill: 25
Magicka: 30	Attack Damage: 14
Fatigue: 160	Weapons: None
Soul: Lesser	

Advantages: Resist Fire 33%
Weaknesses: Weakness to Shock 25%
Ingredient: Hunger Tongue
Ranged Magic: None
Melee Magic: Absorb Fatigue (8 points for 5 seconds)

RAVENOUS HUNGER

Type: Daedra	Combat Skill: 60
Level: 14	Magic Skill: 60
Health: 360	Stealth Skill: 40
Magicka: 60	Attack Damage: 33
Fatigue: 300	Weapons: None
Soul: Greater	

Advantages: Resist Fire 33%
Weaknesses: Weakness to Shock 25%
Ingredient: Hunger Tongue
Ranged Magic: None
Melee Magic: Absorb Fatigue (12 points for 5 seconds)

GLUTTONOUS HUNGER

Type: Daedra	Combat Skill: 50
Level: 9	Magic Skill: 50
Health: 200	Stealth Skill: 40
Magicka: 50	Attack Damage: 23
Fatigue: 230	Weapons: None
Soul: Common	

Advantages: Resist Fire 33%
Weaknesses: Weakness to Shock 25%
Ingredient: Hunger Tongue
Ranged Magic: None
Melee Magic: Absorb Fatigue (10 points for 5 seconds)

VORACIOUS HUNGER

Type: Daedra	Combat Skill: 70
Level: 19	Magic Skill: 70
Health: 400	Stealth Skill: 10
Magicka: 50	Attack Damage: 40
Fatigue: 350	Weapons: None
Soul: Grand	

Advantages: Resist Fire 33%
Weaknesses: Weakness to Shock 25%
Ingredient: Hunger Tongue
Ranged Magic: None
Melee Magic: Absorb Fatigue (14 points for 5 seconds)

SCALON

Scalon are very slow out of the water. However, they have a leaping attack that covers a lot of distance. Some Scalon (25 percent) can turn invisible for 60 seconds. They use this power to ambush their targets.

Rank	Level Range
Diseased Scalon	7
Scalon	12
Hulking Scalon	17

DISEASED SCALON

Type: Creature	Combat Skill: 40
Level: 7	Magic Skill: 5
Health: 125	Stealth Skill: 50
Magicka: 11	Attack Damage: 18
Fatigue: 100	Weapons: None
Soul: Lesser	

Advantages: Water Breathing
Weaknesses: None
Ingredient: Scalon Fin
Ranged Magic: None
Melee Magic: 25% Scalon Fever disease

SCALON

Type: Creature	Combat Skill: 50
Level: 12	Magic Skill: 5
Health: 175	Stealth Skill: 70
Magicka: 11	Attack Damage: 22
Fatigue: 100	Weapons: None
Soul: Common	

Advantages: Water Breathing
Weaknesses: None
Ingredient: Scalon Fin
Ranged Magic: None
Melee Magic: 25% Scalon Fever disease

HULKING SCALON

Type: Creature	Combat Skill: 75
Level: 17	Magic Skill: 5
Health: 320	Stealth Skill: 90
Magicka: 11	Attack Damage: 28
Fatigue: 200	Weapons: None
Soul: Greater	

Advantages: Water Breathing
Weaknesses: None
Ingredient: Scalon Fin
Ranged Magic: None
Melee Magic: 25% Scalon Fever disease

SHAMBLES

Rank	Level Range
Decrepit Shambles	7
Shambles	12
Replete Shambles	18 and up

Upon their death, Decrepit Shambles explode with a Frost attack, 10 points with a radius of 12 feet.

DECREPIT SHAMBLES

Type: Undead	Combat Skill: 65
Level: 7	Magic Skill: 25
Health: 150	Stealth Skill: 15
Magicka: 20	Attack Damage: 16
Fatigue: 180	Weapons: None
Soul: Lesser	

Advantages: Water Breathing, Resist Paralysis 100%, Resist Poison 100%, Resist Frost 70%
Weaknesses: None
Ingredient: Shambles Marrow or Bone Shard
Ranged Magic: None
Melee Magic: None

SHAMBLES

Type: Undead	Combat Skill: 70
Level: 12	Magic Skill: 35
Health: 300	Stealth Skill: 35
Magicka: 20	Attack Damage: 23
Fatigue: 250	Weapons: None
Soul: Common	

Advantages: Water Breathing, Resist Paralysis 100%, Resist Poison 100%, Resist Frost 70%
Weaknesses: None
Ingredient: Shambles Marrow or Bone Shard
Ranged Magic: None
Melee Magic: Frost (15 points)

Upon their death, Shambles explode with a Frost attack, 15 points with a radius of 12 feet.

REPLETE SHAMBLES

Type: Undead	Combat Skill: 75
Level: 18+	Magic Skill: 70
Health: 360+	Stealth Skill: 40
Magicka: 18+	Attack Damage: 35
Fatigue: 180+	Weapons: None
Soul: Greater	

Advantages: Water Breathing, Resist Paralysis 100%, Resist Poison 100%, Resist Frost 70%
Weaknesses: None
Ingredient: Shambles Marrow or Bone Shard
Ranged Magic: None
Melee Magic: Frost (25 points in a 10-foot area)

Upon their death, Replete Shambles explode with a Frost attack, 25 points with a radius of 12 feet.

SKINNED HOUNDS

Skinned Hounds are very fast.

Rank	Level Range
Skinned Hound	1–5
Greater Skinned Hound	12

SKINNED HOUND

Type: Undead | Combat Skill: 42–50
Level: 1–5 | Magic Skill: 52–60
Health: 20–100 | Stealth Skill: 42–50
Magicka: 3–15 | Attack Damage: 10–12
Fatigue: 50–250 | Weapons: None
Soul: Petty or Lesser |

Advantages: Water Breathing, Resist Disease 100%, Resist Frost 30%
Weaknesses: Weakness to Fire 50%
Ingredient: Hound Tooth
Ranged Magic: None
Melee Magic: None

GREATER SKINNED HOUND

Type: Undead | Combat Skill: 65
Level: 10 | Magic Skill: 5
Health: 225 | Stealth Skill: 80
Magicka: 35 | Attack Damage: 19
Fatigue: 300 | Weapons: None
Soul: Common |

Advantages: Water Breathing, Resist Disease 100%, Resist Frost 30%
Weaknesses: Weakness to Fire 50%
Ingredient: Hound Tooth
Ranged Magic: None
Melee Magic: None

CREATURES

Main Quest

A Door in Niben Bay

To open a path to the Shivering Isles, simply wait two days after you load the expansion pack or two days after you leave the Imperial Dungeon where you generated your character. You get a journal entry reporting a rumor that a door has appeared on a small island in Niben Bay.

It's a portal, rather than a literal "door," but the rumor is true. Make this your active quest and consult your map—you discover that "A Strange Door" has turned up on an island located just east of Bravil, where no island previously existed. Fast-travel to the Bay Roan Stables north of Bravil, make your way east-southeast to the shore, and swim like you mean it. You soon come to a rocky island dotted with large mushrooms. Follow one of the ramps on the island's near corner to the upper level, where a glowing purplish cloud revolves within a mouthlike enclosure. This is the entrance to something called The Fringe.

The two NPCs near the door won't say much. The guard, Gaius Prentus, is too preoccupied with the door's ominous sounds. The Khajiit is too crazy to talk. Evidently she's already been through the door and back again, and it's messed her up a bit inside.

Well, if they're not going to explain themselves, check things out yourself. Head for the door.

When you move close to the portal, a third NPC, Belmeyne Dreleth, appears beside it. He's crazy, too. Also violent. He'll attack Prentus. Prentus, being a guard and 10 levels above your own, makes short work of him and then advises you to keep your distance from the door.

Once the guard has said his piece, you'll get another journal entry…and someone beyond the door begins to talk. No one tells you so at this stage, but this is the Daedric Prince Sheogorath, on whose behalf you may already have performed a very strange errand in the Khajiit village of Border Watch.

 That daedric quest for Sheogorath has been adjusted slightly to accommodate the events in the *Shivering Isles* quest line. See the last paragraph of the "Sheogorath" entry in the "Daedric Quest" chapter for a rundown on the changes.

Sheogorath's key point is: "Bring me a champion! Rend the flesh of my foes. A mortal champion to wade through the entrails of my enemies!" That would be you. Once the speech is done, you're free to activate the door. Do so and you'll find yourself alone in a dark, quiet room with a sarcastic bald man named Haskill and a metronome (just to emphasize the quiet). Haskill invites you to sit down, and he won't get down to business until you do, so have a seat and speak to him.

Haskill then reveals that he's chamberlain to Sheogorath, that you're in an antechamber to that lord's private Realm, that the doorway on the Niben Bay island is an invitation to the would-be champions alluded to in Sheogorath's speech, and, somewhat obliquely, that madmen like Dreleth were "ill-prepared" for their experience in the Isles and are, thus, beyond cure.

Talking to Haskill carries no obligations. You can simply use the door to get back to the Niben Bay island and return to Haskill whenever you wish. Or you can agree to proceed across

The Fringe to the Gates of Madness. "If you can pass them, perhaps the Lord Sheogorath will find a use for you," says Haskill.

If you agree to make the attempt, Haskill suggests you "mind the Gatekeeper. He dislikes strangers to the Realm." Then he stands and vanishes. You'll see him again soon. The room dissolves into hundreds and thousands of butterflies, and you find yourself outdoors at the west end of a large walled enclosure.

You're on your way.

THROUGH THE FRINGE OF MADNESS

Finding the Gates won't be difficult; the path from the butterfly room leads directly there, and a high stone wall around The Fringe reins in exploration. But getting through the Gates is quite another matter.

You won't have full freedom of action in the Isles until you pass the Gates.

Make your way down the steep path to the east. In the shallow pool at the bottom you find a live Grummite and a dead Baliwog, courtesy of the Grummite.

The Fringe includes a pair of fortresslike enclosures: Xeddefen to the south and the Gardens of Flesh and Bone to the northwest. You can't get inside either installation yet, but you can clear out enemies in their exterior (Grummites in the former case and Skeletons in the latter).

Follow your quest target east to find a third Fringe location: the village of Passwall. Here you can head straight up the stairs on the eastern path to reach the Gates of Madness, where the Gatekeeper is about to demolish a party of adventurers. Or you can chat first with the self-appointed mayor, Shelden, and the hypochondriac, Felas Sarandas.

You'll find that everyone in Passwall is a little nuts, just like these two. In fact, everyone on the Shivering Isles suffers from some form of insanity.

However, the most efficient route is to simply head east to the Gates to see what all the fuss is about.

You arrive at the top of the hill to find the battle already underway. It is one-sided. The Gatekeeper, a great tattooed giant with a huge blade, kicks the adventurers' butts with ease. This has some advantages. If you're just starting out in *Oblivion*, you can loot a full steel suit of armor, plus a steel claymore, warhammer, and mace from the bodies.

Once the battle is over and the adventurers' Orc captain has fled, you get another journal entry suggesting you consult the residents of Passwall before taking on the Gatekeeper.

Depending on who's talking, you'll be referred to either Relmyna Verenim or Jayred Ice-Veins, who will, in turn, cough up two of the three options for killing the Gatekeeper. Either of the first two options will make the Gatekeeper weaker. You can use all three to make the Gatekeeper the easiest possible fight. Your options are as follows:

1. You can consult "Mayor" Shelden right away, as he and Felas Sarandas are on hand to watch the battle. Ask him about "Gatekeeper" and he'll tell you that Jayred wants to kill the giant.

In fact, check in with Shelden repeatedly for comic relief. He offers a running commentary on Main Quest events—with most of his comments centering on himself.

Sounds to us like you have a potential ally. Find Ice-Veins. His home is south of the inn, but he only sleeps there. At other times he is wandering around The Fringe. Just follow your quest target to find him.

When you find Ice-Veins, ask after "Gatekeeper" and he proposes you help each other. You'll pick the lock to the Gardens of Flesh and Bone. Easy enough, and Jayred even provides a pick. He says he'll collect the bones of the dead Gatekeeper within and use them to create special arrows to take the current Gatekeeper down. Agree, and he'll lead the way up the hill to the Gardens.

Pick the one-tumbler lock and then, if you wish, stand back and let Jayred tackle the three skeletal baddies who move in from the corners of the exterior courtyard. After the bad guys are taken care of, Jayred claims the bones from the dead Gatekeeper's body. Jayred asks you to find him in "a few hours," and returns to his house on the south side of Passwall.

Give Jayred two hours and then ask him about "bone arrows." He gives you 20 and keeps 10 for himself, then he suggests you head off to do the deed...which proves fairly simple: just keep your distance and keep firing.

2. Talk to Relmyna Verenim about "Gatekeeper," then say, "Then I must kill the Gatekeeper" and, "I will find a way." She tells you go bug Nanette Don. And, in case you read this as a blow-off, that's exactly what it is. Alternately, you can read the Letter to Sheogorath on the little table in Relmyna's room or go directly to Nanette.

As Relmyna suggested, Nanette's a blabbermouth and she spills it all—if you first coax her Disposition up to 70. The Gatekeeper has an Achilles heel: Relmyna's tears hurt him. And however improbable it may sound—Relmyna was as hard as coffin nails in your encounter—the monster brings out a soft side in his "mother." To see how weepy she truly is, Nanette suggests you follow Relmyna to a rendezvous with the Gatekeeper at midnight.

Do it. Wait outside The Wastrel's Purse. A little after 11:00 p.m. you see Relmyna leave the building and make her way up the hill toward the Gates. Follow her—it doesn't matter if she's aware of you or not—and get close enough to overhear her heartfelt monologue without also setting off the monster. Don't step onto the stone circle where Relmyna meets her child. At the end, you learn from a journal that Relmyna has dropped a handkerchief full of her tears. Run up, or sneak up, and grab it.

The handkerchief is converted to three potions of Relmyna's Tears in your inventory. This poison can then be applied to your current weapon. It removes some of the Gatekeeper's special abilities: his Restore Health ability, 75 percent Resistance to Magic, and Immunity to Paralysis. His Lesser Powers remain in effect, however. The giant can still cure poison, damage your Health and Fatigue, and Restore Health once per day. However, Relmyna's Tears still set him up perfectly for an immediate follow-up assault using the bone arrows or a potent weapon.

3. You can fight fair—meaning conventionally. The Gatekeeper is very tough, but he isn't invincible. If you have a powerful character and a potent weapon imported from Cyrodiil, and you hit the giant often and hard enough to overcome his Health regeneration, you can kill him without outside assistance. Unsurprisingly, the Wabbajack

staff you can liberate from Sheogorath in the parent game doesn't work on Relmyna's bouncing baby boy.

However, be advised that, like virtually everything else in the game, the Gatekeeper and most of his abilities and powers are adjusted to your current level. As you get tougher, he gets tougher.

And that does it. Depending on which route you've taken, the results will be a little different. Ice-Veins offers his congrats and voices his determination to pass through the Gates before heading off toward them. If Relmyna is still nearby when you kill the Gatekeeper, she speaks to her dead "child." It's rather touching.

Take the two keys from the giant's body. This kicks off another tier of local reactions...and another appearance by Haskill. He tells you a bit about the Isles' capital, New Sheoth—consisting of Bliss, Crucible, and Palace districts—and the distinctive lands beyond the Gates.

Does it matter which Gate you choose? Yes and no. The two lands are not divided from each other as The Fringe is separated from the Shivering Isles, and you can move freely from one region to the other. However, each door gives you a different power. The Dementia door gives you the Blessing of Dementia, which allows you to cast a powerful area effect, Demoralize. The Mania door gives you the Blessing of Mania, which allows you to cast an equally powerful area effect spell, Frenzy.

Either way, Jayred follows you through, though he won't remain under your influence. He embarks on his own adventures, wandering across the Isles and fighting wilderness creatures. These adventures may get him killed or they may not. Either way, you'll be heading northeast on foot to New Sheoth.

There are two paved roads to the capital: Overlook Road—a long loop over high ground on the north side of the Isles—and The Low Road across the lakelands closer to the island's center. The latter is a much more direct route, but you still have to do a good deal of fighting, including fighting with: a Mage at Hardscrabble Camp near the junction of Overlook and Low Road; Grummites outside Blackroot Lair to the southeast; a Skinned Hound where the road draws near to the water for the first time; another Grummite in a rocky defile east of the junction with Pinnacle Road; and four selections from a smorgasbord of possible creatures both southwest and northeast of the first bridge, east of the second bridge, and southeast of the New Sheoth Graveyard.

 Make sure you get Blackroot Lair added to your map. You'll be able to use it as a fast travel shortcut to the dungeon Xedilian for the next quest.

If you take Overlook Road, you enter New Sheoth in the Crucible District on the city's south side. To reach the Palace District, simply climb the steps to the northwest and north, then turn east at the gate to the Bliss District and climb the three flights of stairs at the end. It's a short hop across the grounds to the Palace proper and then to the throne room, where you find the snake-eyed Daedric lord and his chamberlain. Talk to Sheogorath and he rewards you with the Charity of Madness amulet, which has leveled Fire, Frost, and Shock resistance enchantments, for having made it this far. Talk to him some more and learn you're the sought-after champion.

Naturally, he has a job for his champion.

 The pedestals around the throne room are designed for artifacts recovered in your travels. You may have missed it in the shadows on the south side of the room, but there's already one here: a replica of the Gatekeeper's head! This one, and all but the last, are purely representational and can't be used by you.

Something or someone called the Greymarch is coming. You must prevent its arrival in the Isles. The Daedric Prince won't describe it yet—"it would just cloud your little mind"—but he does say, "There are those that have other ways into my Realm, and they're on the move." He sends you off to activate a location called Xedilian—"a little place I use to take care of unwanted visitors"—with a Manual of Xedilian and the Attenuator of Judgment.

You're the dungeon repairman. Sheogorath tells you to talk to Haskill on the fine points, but just read the manual—it's pretty comprehensive—and you'll put it all together. As the headline suggests, Xedilian is a trap for unwelcome adventurers. It sucks them in with the Resonator of Judgment, then tortures them in three chambers that either kill the adventurers outright or drive them mad. You won't get a quest target to Xedilian until you read the book.

However, Xedilian is not working. Speak to Haskill about "Xedilian" and he directs you to find the three Focus Crystals and place them in their respective Judgment Nexuses to power up the installation.

Does he tell you where to find them? No, of course not. And no one else will, either. This may seem baffling at first, but it just means the crystals are already at Xedilian and you don't need special instructions.

But we're getting ahead of ourselves. If you marked Blackroot Lair earlier, you can fast-travel there now, or you can travel back to the Gates of Madness. If not, you have to hoof it at least part of the way. You encounter a wilderness critter or two as you move south—not to mention two Grummites outside Xedilian itself.

Yup, the Grummites have made Sheogorath's torture chamber their home and appropriated the crystals for their own use. Your first duty here is to clear 'em out. This is not a small endeavor because there are a dozen Grummites on the upper of the two levels and 11 more in the Hall of Judgment. But ultimately it's a rewarding endeavor. The crystals found on the staffs of the first three Grummite Shamans are Focus Crystals. You can find the first crystal on the Shaman southwest of the entry-level door. The Nexus is nearby. Just activate it to put the Focus Crystal in place. This also opens the metal gate to the south.

Don't worry about the inaccessible doors that turn up on your map, including one near the dungeon entrance. You can't reach them now—they're on an inaccessible upper tier—and you divine their purpose soon enough.

The passage beyond the metal gate leads down to a bonfire and a switch. The switch opens a pit beneath you. Drop down to find the second Shaman, the second crystal, and the second Nexus. Place this crystal to open the gate to the east and the path to the Halls of Judgment. Here you find the third Shaman, third crystal, third Nexus, and third newly opened gate (this one just north of the Nexus). At the bottom, at the west end of the long east–west chamber, you find a crystalline formation. This is the Resonator of Judgment. Just activate it with the Attenuator of Judgment in your inventory to tune it and ba-da-bing: You get a journal suggesting you return to New Sheoth to report your success, and the gate just to the north raises.

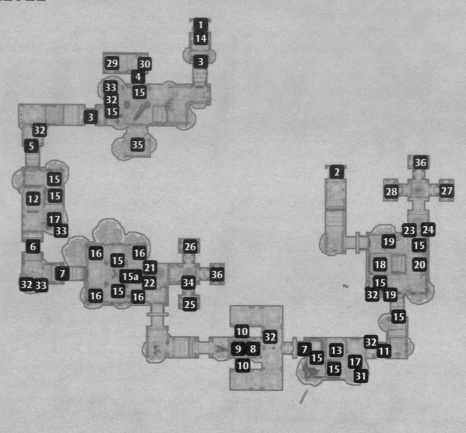

Xedilian: Entry Level

1. Exit to the dungeon exterior.

2. Entrance to Halls of Judgment.

3. Gate: Opened by pressing a nearby button.

4. Gate: Closed initially. Opens automatically after you complete your main business in Xedilian.

5. Gate: Open initially. Closes automatically after you complete your main business in Xedilian.

6. Gate: Opens after you place a Focus Crystal in the Judgment Nexus at #12.

7. Metal door.

8. This button…

9. …opens this pit.

10. Inoperable gate: There's nothing back there to find anyway! The urn (#32) that appears just to the east is actually on the lower level.

11. Gate: Opens when you place the second Focus Crystal at #13.

12. The first Judgment Nexus: Place the first Focus Crystal here.

13. The second Judgment Nexus: Place the second Focus Crystal here. Everybody got that?

14. Three Knights of Order sucked in by the Resonator appear here after you claim your reward.

15. Grummites.

15a. On your first run-through, this is the location of a Grummite. However, when you revisit the level as dungeon master, you find here the pint-sized Mania Gnarl through which you meet three adventurers. Mess with them. Push the button at #20 to make the Gnarl appear as big as the Gatekeeper and drive adventurer Lewin Tilwald bonkers.

16. Or push the button at #21 to introduce eight additional Mania Gnarls onto the scene—two at each location. They kill Lewin.

17. Grummite Shaman: The two on this level have the Focus Crystals you need to use at #12 and #13.

18. On your first run-through, there's a flawless topaz on this platform. As dungeon master, watch the two surviving adventurers deal with a cage full of faux treasure.

19. Push the button at #23 to shoot fireballs from these statues at adventurer Syndelius Gatharian. They punt him into the next life. Note that the southern statue has a conventional Grummite loot chest on its western side.

20. Or push the button at #22 to dump a torrent of keys here. This drives Syndelius mad.

21. In the dungeon master portion of the level, this button makes the little Gnarl at #15a appear to grow to giant size. This drives adventurer Lewin nuts.

22. This button introduces two additional little Gnarls at each #16 location. They attack and kill Lewin. It's just not Lewin's day.

23. This button deposits a storm of identical keys at #20.

24. And this one fires fireballs from the statues at #19.

25. After tuning the Resonator, when you teleport in from #4 in the Halls of Judgment, you appear here.

26. Once you finish tormenting the three adventurers in the big room to the southwest, teleport to #27 using this pad.

27. You appear here after teleporting from #26.

28. After tormenting the two surviving (or sane) adventurers in the big room to the south, use this pad to teleport out to #13 on the Halls of Judgment level.

29. When you teleport out from #14 in the Halls of Judgment (after wrapping up your dungeon master business), you appear here. Kiliban Nyrandil (#33) is here, too. Talk to him for the first part of your reward.

30. This chest contains spoils from the dead/gone-cuckoo adventurers. It's a "boss" container with better than boss container odds. You get a nice Talisman of Abetment with leveled Detect Life,

Feather, and Water Breathing enchantments; a ring; gold; a scroll; two gems; and three healing potions—and you have 25 percent chances of receiving up to four lockpicks and repair hammers.

31. Grummite boss chest: These generally have nice stuff. It always contains mediocre gold and a piece of Madness Ore, which pops up in the Miscellaneous Quest "The Antipodean Hammer," with a 40 percent chance of either a second ore sample…or a mold for making an item from the ore. In addition, you get 25 percent shots at additional gold, a gem, a poison potion, a flawless pearl, two repair hammers, and three lockpicks; 10 percent chances of jewelry, a soul gem, a piece of magic or conventional armor, or a conventional weapon; and a five percent shot at a magic weapon.

32. An urn with one or two Restoration (i.e. healing) items and a 10 percent shot at a repair hammer.

33. Conventional Grummite loot chest: And yet not so conventional. You always get gold. A quarter of the time, you find a pearl and up to two lockpicks. Same deal with the Madness Ore described in #30. And you have 10 percent shots at jewelry, a repair hammer, arrows, a piece of conventional armor, and a conventional weapon. But here's the unconventional part: *two* percent of the time you find one of six items that can be used in the Miscellaneous Quest "The Museum of Oddities."

34. Kiliban Nyrandil: Xedilian's caretaker, a rather long-winded source of information on its operation, and bestower of the best part of your reward.

35. If you settled for making the adventurers crazy, they turn up in here when you're done.

36. Just as a matter of academic interest, you can't reach these two pads. The western one isn't hooked up to anything. The eastern connects to a likewise inaccessible pad at #21 in the Halls of Judgment.

However, you can't return directly to the Palace; the gate back to the upper level has closed behind you. The teleport pad beyond the gate leads to "Xedilian"—the first of three sections of an otherwise inaccessible upper layer of the dungeon's entry level. Activate it to meet caretaker Kiliban Nyrandil. He explains (eventually) that you'd ordinarily have been teleported to the pad near the entrance and that your presence here means adventurers are already entering the newly activated dungeon. Kiliban refers you to the owner's manual for details but can also describe your task and options himself. Hey, the guy likes to talk.

This kicks off the second phase of the quest, Baiting the Trap, in which you're the dungeon master. That sounds nicer than "torturer."

Belly up to the balcony around the corner to the west to trigger the release of the three adventurers into the first room. You may notice a subtle change from when you cleared the Grummites out of it: the square room is now occupied by a single, smaller-than-usual Gnarl. (The Chamber of the Gnarl mentioned by Kiliban corresponds to the Chamber of Conversion in the Xedilian manual.)

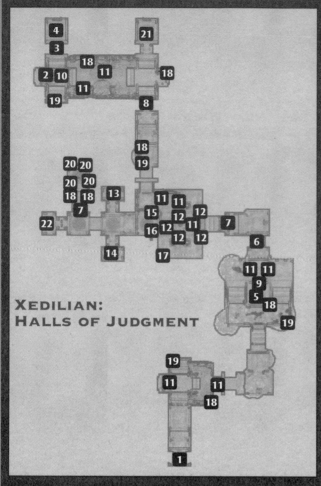

XEDILIAN: HALLS OF JUDGMENT

1. Exit to Xedilian entry level. This becomes inaccessible, owing a gate at #8, once you've tuned the Resonator at #2.

2. The Resonator: Activate this crystal formation (which will become extremely familiar with time) to tune the device and complete the first stage of your work in Xedilian. It sends out a siren call that summons a range of unwanted visitors, opens the gate at #3, and closes one at #8—cutting off your retreat.

3. This gate opens when you tune the Resonator at #2, giving you access to the teleport pad at #4.

4. This teleport pad zaps you back to #25 on the upper tier of Xedilian's entry level.

5. The third Judgment Nexus: Place the Focus Crystal extracted from the third Grummite Shaman at #9 here to open the gate at #6.

6. Gate: Open it by placing the Focus Crystal taken from the Grummite Shaman at #9 in the Judgment Nexus at #5.

7. Metal door.

8. Gate: This one closes when you tune the Resonator at #2, cutting off your retreat. To get out of Xedilian, use the teleport pad at #4.

9. Grummite Shaman: It holds the final Focus Crystal, which you need to use in the third Judgment Nexus at #5 to open the gate at #6.

10. A second Grummite Shaman: This one has no Focus Crystal.

11. Grummites: These grunts and the two Shaman are in place on your first pass through the level.

12. Zombies: These show up only later, when you're running Xedilian as dungeon master—and then only if you press the button at #15 to resurrect them. They then kill Grommok gro-Barak—the lone remaining adventurer.

13. Teleport pad: When you teleport out from #28 on the dungeon's entry level, you appear here.

14. Teleport pad: Once you've decided the fate of poor Grommok, use this pad to zap back to Xedilian's entry level. You appear at #29 on that map.

15. This button resurrects the five zombies (#12) around adventurer Grommok gro-Barak. They kill him.

16. This button supplies another illusion—making Grommok think he's died. Though dying without a fight seems to be the actual issue for the big Orc. He's back in his own body after a few seconds, but no longer in his right mind.

17. Grummite boss chest: Like the one at #30 on the entry level. But how to get up there? The brazier at the center of the room to the north is a good diving board. Even so, you probably need an expert-level Acrobatics skill.

18. Urn: See #31 on the entry level.

19. Chest: See #32 on the entry level.

20. These two shelves and two cupboards are home to the first significant library specific to the Shivering Isles. In Kiliban Nyrandil's quarters, you find copies of An Elytra's Life, Fall of Vitharn, From Frog to Man, Guide to New Sheoth, Heretical Thoughts, The Living Woods, Myths of Sheogorath, The Prophet Arden-Sul, Saints and Seducers, Wabbajack, and Zealotry. Note that there's also a two percent chance that the cupboard to the southwest (with From Frog to Man on top) contains an item useful in the Miscellaneous Quest "The Museum of Oddities."

21. Inaccessible teleport pad linked to the eastern of the two #36 pads on Xedilian's entry level.

22. Inoperable, and inaccessible, teleport pad.

Don't rush things here. Hang out and listen to the adventurers for a while. They have a fair amount of entertaining incidental dialogue both before and after your decision.

Once the adventurers reach their positions in the middle of the room, two buttons are activated on the north and south sides of the balcony. The button to the north introduces onto the floor below a swarm of mini-Gnarls, which attack the adventurers and kill the Breton rogue, Lewin Tilwald. The south button pipes in a hallucinogen that makes them think the single mini-Gnarl is as big as a house. That drives Lewin insane—by the time the creature fades away, he's a gibbering wreck—and the other two adventurers (the Dunmer Syndelius Gatharian and Orc Grommok gro-Barak) leave him behind.

Behind you, you find the gate across from the entry teleport pad is open. Use this teleport pad to reach the Chamber of Avarice. The balcony here overlooks a chamber not so subtly changed since your last visit: a big cage full of treasure sits atop the stairs on the west side of the room. (No, don't even think about it. The treasure is just a mockup and the cage has no lock.) The east button springs a fire trap that kills Syndelius. The west button drops a hailstorm of keys on the foot of the stairs that sends him over the brink. Grommok is on his own.

Activate the newly available teleport pad to enter the final room—this one above the Hall of Judgment. Here you find the jittery Orc in a chamber strewn with decomposing corpses. The north button on the balcony reanimates them and they kill Grommok. The south one makes Grommok think he's joined them; briefly, he turns into a ghost. By the time the illusion lapses and he's back in his own form, the strain has sent him around the bend into madness.

Talk to Kiliban again. He instructs you to activate the teleport pad to the south and meet him in the reception room—the teleport room near Xedilian's entrance—to collect your earnings. First up: a Focus Crystal. This non-interactive souvenir will be sent to Sheogorath's Palace and placed in the main hall. Second, a "most unusual weapon" extracted from Grommok. It's two enchanted swords in one—Dawnfang from 6 a.m. to 6 p.m. and Duskfang from 6 p.m. to 6 a.m. The former has a leveled Fire Damage enchantment, the latter a leveled Frost Damage enchantment.

You may also notice a curious unleveled enchantment on each version of sword. You get a good explanation of this Nourish Blade in Grommok's accompanying journal. Each sword counts its kills. Once that count reaches 12, it converts into a superior version of same weapon, with Dawnfang gaining an additional leveled Absorb Health enchantment and Duskfang an additional leveled Absorb Magicka enchantment.

And finally, you can take what you wish from the Recovery Chest at the east end of the room. The contents vary, but it always contains a Talisman of Abetment amulet with Detect Life, Feather, and Water Breathing enchantments, along with a ring, gold, scroll, gems, healing potions, lock picks, and repair hammers.

All set to leave? Well, you're not quite done. When you leave the reception room, you are attacked by three leveled Knights of Order. Kill them—it shouldn't be too hard with your new sword—and take any Hearts of Order you find on their bodies. (You can't escape Xedilian until the Knights are dead. A Resonator-like crystal formation blocks the exit.) Granted, the Knights have at least a 20 percent Resistance to Magic as well as a 50 percent Resistance to Poison, but all are four levels below your own.

After the Knights are dead, speak to Kiliban. (The Knights can knock him out but can't kill him.) The caretaker says the Knights are "soulless abominations" of legend, not native to the Isles, who haven't appeared in the Isles in centuries. Why are they at Xedilian? They're drawn to Obelisks scattered throughout the Isles, similar to the one from which the Resonator of Judgment was created. You learn more about them from Haskill a bit later. You're to return to Sheogorath and report their appearance.

And with that, Kiliban marches into the teleport pad and vanishes from the game. That also goes for any of the three NPCs you've reduced to insanity. In theory, they become residents of the Shivering Isles, but you won't meet them again. The lower portion of the dungeon is shut off to you as well.

Fast-travel back to New Sheoth's Palace District and talk to Sheogorath. He provides yet another reward: a new Lesser Power that summons Haskill to your aid within the Shivering Isles. (Try to use it back in Cyrodiil and you get a message on the spell's limitations.) "He knows a lot," says the Madgod. "More than he knows." The Daedric Prince insists you try the power out a couple of times before he'll proceed (and you can do it a great number of times, with Haskill growing more exasperated with each successive summoning).

Poor fellow. Why does he put up with you?

Here you reach a kind of plateau in the quest line and the pace drops off a bit. (You don't get a new quest in the dying breath of the last one.) This would be a good time to take a time-out and familiarize yourself with the layout of and services available within this strange city.

Knight of Order

Talk to Sheogorath again. He now refers to defeating the Knights' master—Jyggalag, the Daedric Prince of Order—and stopping the Greymarch. It turns out this is "an apocalypse of sorts" which occurs at the end of each era—a ritual invasion of Sheogorath's Realm by the forces of Order. But he quickly shifts gears, recognizing that you're still a stranger in a strange land. Sheogorath is all about shifting gears—usually without pushing in the clutch first.

"We're going to give you a taste of where you've found yourself," he says. "You're going to learn." In theory, you're supposed to learn about madness at the feet of Thadon, the Duke of Mania and Syl, the Duchess of Dementia. Meeting and greeting these illustrious individuals and doing their bidding is the stuff of the next two quests, Addiction and The Lady of Paranoia, which can be tackled in any order. At the same time, you also get the ostensible quest, Understanding Madness. However, it's just an in-game signpost that you've completed the other two.

 From this point on, make sure to talk to Sheogorath and Haskill between each quest. They each have fun and informative things to say about the story that's unfolding.

Thadon's right in the Palace complex. He's up with the sun at 6 a.m. to practice his dancing and painting at the east end of the Halcyon Conservatory (i.e., the House of Mania's garden). From Sheogorath's throne room, simply use the eastern of the two doors in the north wall, cross the hall beyond, and follow the passage on the far side north, east, and south.

Talk to Thadon. He blathers on for a bit—many of the crazies in the Isles do—but finally comes round to a quest. A former lover has made off with his favorite toy: a Chalice of Reversal that, in combination with a substance known as Felldew, made the Duke's world brighter and more cheerful. Thadon doesn't make getting it back any easier; he won't name the suspected thief but identifies her as a member of Syl's court. So you're going to have to ask around a bit.

Two characters can give you the Chalice's location with varying perspectives and degrees of accuracy, plus a quest target: Wide-Eye, and Syl's own steward, Kithlan. These two send you off to Dunroot Burrow northeast of the city. At a Disposition of 60, Kithlan reveals the Chalice is actually in the ruined tower above that dungeon, and he explains that the Elytra (i.e., giant bugs) that inhabit it produce Felldew.

In dialogue, they're divided over how much you should have to do with Felldew. Wide-Eye makes it sound like a necessity. You have to pump her Disposition up to 70 for her to refer to the dangers that attend Felldew's use. Kithlan needs no such coaxing to be frank to the point of bluntness: It's a poison and it'll kill you.

However, whichever way you get to your destination, your journal makes it clear that Felldew is needed for safe passage through the dungeon. The point is to make you balance the consequences of its use with the requirements of the task at hand.

The quickest route to the Burrow is through the city gate in the northwest corner of the Bliss district. Follow the winding path up the mountainside to the northwest. This leads you past an eastern side road to Fain, Frenzied Camp, and Camp Hopeful. From Camp Hopeful, a path leads east to the entrance to the ruins. Alternately, just past the Fain side road, you find safe passage west, up a grassy ridge and over the mountaintop. Just be careful on the north side; it's very steep.

You may think, at first, that your magic map has goofed and directed you to the wrong place. The entrance to the little stone blockhouse called the Sanctum of Decadence requires a key and you don't have one. This is the tower to which Thadon referred. To enter the Burrow, follow your quest target to a second entrance below the giant tree stump on higher ground to the west. You know you're in the right place when you're attacked by a Felldew-producing Elytra. Eat the Felldew—this grants a 20-point boosts in Strength, Intelligence, and Agility, plus access to the lair—and then activate both the Barrier Membrane and root door within.

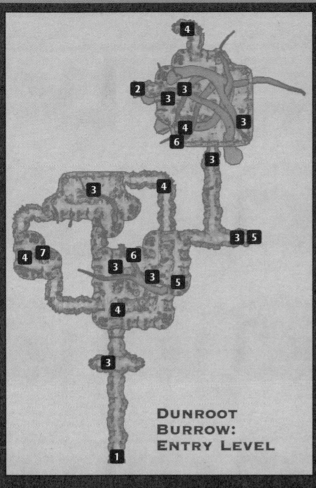

DUNROOT BURROW: ENTRY LEVEL

7. Hollowed Amber limb: Contains Amber, of course. This turns up in the Miscellaneous Quest "The Antipodean Hammer." How much Amber? Well, you're guaranteed one piece and you've got three 50 percent chances at additional ones. And there's a one percent chance you come up with a unique piece of Amber—it's shaped like Sheogorath—which plays into the Miscellaneous Quest "The Museum of Oddities."

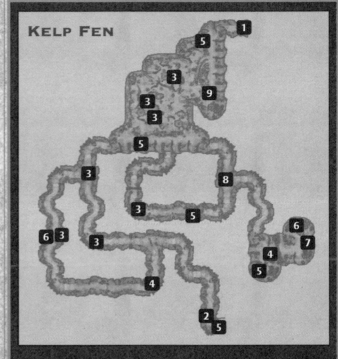

KELP FEN

1. Exit to dungeon exterior.
2. Entrance to Kelp Fen.
3. Standard Elytra: This variety has no Felldew.
4. Felldew-bearing Elytra: Take this drug periodically as you pass through this dungeon to avoid the stat-destroying symptoms of withdrawal.
5. Hollowed stumps: One, and possibly two, Restoration-related items.
6. Hollowed stumps: These look just like the #5 hollowed stumps, but the contents are wholly different. They're more like chests. Gold is the only given, and your best bets for additional booty are a gem and a sample of Amber (25 percent chances). The odds on everything else are no better than 10 percent, but there's such a richness of possibilities—for instance you have four 1-in-10 shots at different arrays of armor and a 1-in-20 shot at magic heavy armor—that you're likely to come up with *something*. Other 10 percent chances include arrows, jewelry (conventional and magic), a potion, a scroll, a soul gem, and a weapon. And there's a two percent chance of an item from the Miscellaneous Quest "The Museum of Oddities."

1. Exit to Dunroot Burrow entry level.
2. Exit to the Drone Tunnels.
3. Standard Elytra.
4. Felldew-bearing Elytra: Just two on this and each of the next two levels.
5. Hollowed stumps: Just like the #5 hollowed stumps from the entry level.
6. Hollowed stumps: And just like the #6s from the entry level.
7. Hollowed Amber stumps: And, despite said stumpiness, just like the #7 hollowed Amber stumps from the entry level.
8. Watch yourself around the little mushroom-y patch on the ground here. It's the trigger for three spike traps in the tunnel ceiling.
9. Spore cloud trap: If you set it off, it casts a leveled area-effect spell that paralyzes you briefly and drains your Agility to feed your Speed. Note that a spell or arrow sets it off as easily as your presence!

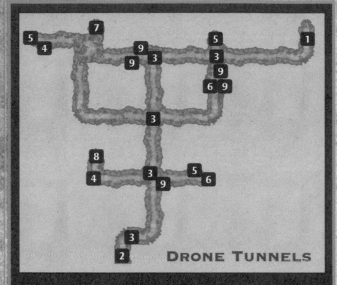

DRONE TUNNELS

1. Exit to Kelp Fen.

2. Exit to Bramble Halls.

3. Standard Elytra.

4. Felldew-bearing Elytra.

5. Hollowed stumps: The ones with the healing supplies.

6. Hollowed stumps: These ones are more like chests. The northern of the two stumps has a worm trap directly above it!

7. Hollowed Amber limb: This one's hanging down from above.

8. Spike trap.

9. Worm traps.

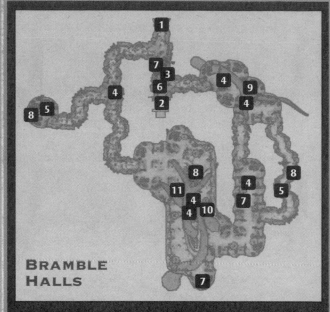

BRAMBLE HALLS

1. Exit to Drone Tunnels.

2. Exit to Sanctum of Decadence.

3. And you thought you were just going to walk from #1 to #2 in a straight line? Nuh-uh. Roots block your progress here. Go west, young whatever-you-are.

4. Standard Elytra: The ones that appear to be up on root bridges are in fact on ground level.

5. Felldew-bearing Elytra.

6. Elytra boss: …*if* you've reached Level 19. If you haven't, it's just plain old Elytra.

7. Hollowed stump: The healing balms variety

8. Hollowed stump: The everything-under-the-sun variety.

9. Hollowed stump: The boss chest variety! Only a piece of Amber is guaranteed to appear, but the odds of other nice stuff appearing are sometimes significantly higher than usual. There's a 50 percent chance of an item that could be a second piece of Amber (which is probable) or a mold for a manufacture of an Amber item (which you put to use in the Miscellaneous Quest "The Antipodean Hammer"). You've got two 50 percent shots at scrolls, a potion, and pocket change gold; 25 percent chances of magic jewelry, a gem, and a more significant helping of gold; and 10 percent chances for alchemical equipment, armor (heavy, light, and magic), a staff, a magic weapon, and each of two soul gems.

10. The trigger point for the spike traps in the south and east walls.

11. Spore cloud trap.

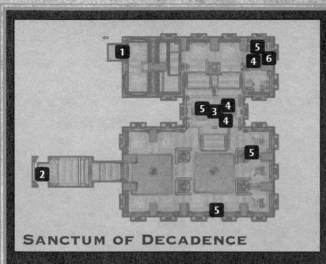

SANCTUM OF DECADENCE

1. Exit to Bramble Halls.
2. Exit to the dungeon exterior outside the "tower" entrance.
3. Chalice of Reversal: What you're here to grab. So grab it already. This kills the Felldew withdrawal symptoms, fixes your wrecked stats, and transforms future Felldew use into a stat-buffing experience.
4. Felldew addicts.
5. Felldew.
6. Another little Shivering Isles library: *Bark and Sap*, *The Blessings of Sheogorath*, *An Elytra's Life*, *Myths of Sheogorath*, *The Prophet Arden-Sul*, *Saints and Seducers*, *The Shivering Bestiary* and *The Standing Stones*. There's also a copy of *The Lusty Argonian Maid* hidden behind a bedstead farther south.

And here it gets tricky. This Elytra lair is extremely dark in places. It has five levels and these levels have more than one tier. It's populated by lots and lots of Elytra—including a boss in the Bramble Halls level if you've hit Level 19. And they're not all the same: some of these critters won't be aggressive toward you if you're under the influence of the euphoric effects of the drug. These are the five green-tinged, Felldew-bearing Elytra in the entry level and two each in the Kelp Fen, Drone Tunnels, and Bramble Halls levels. However, when the bad effects of Felldew kick in, even these critters attack.

The effects of the Felldew you took to get in here don't last. The attribute boosts drop to 10 points and wear off entirely after a short while. Withdrawal effects follow swiftly and worsen quickly. Initial five-point hits to Strength, Agility, and Intelligence are followed by additional 10-point hits to the same attributes, with further 10-point hits to Willpower, Endurance, and Speed. Then Willpower, Endurance, and Speed get bashed by another 10 points and Fatigue by 50. Finally Magicka and Health take 30-point hits.

By that time, will there be anything left to hit? Yes…if you've eaten more Felldew to anticipate or counteract the withdrawal effects. Addiction indeed. Hence, your trip through the Burrow is very much a balancing act. On one hand, you

want to get to the Chalice quickly. Grabbing it counteracts all the bad effects of addiction. On the other, you want to stay alive long enough to get there by killing the right kind of Elytra (to claim their Felldew) and avoiding battles with the wrong kind. The latter are a waste of time, and time is one thing you don't have in great supply.

It helps to know the way, as the dungeon can seem mazelike even when it's at its most linear. Always keep an eye on your quest target, and look at your local map frequently. At the bend in the entry corridor, kill the Elytra for its Felldew. Wiggle your way north and east through the trench in the first large chamber. In the corridor to the north, kill a second Felldew-bearing Elytra. In the second big room, climb the huge root to the upper level and the make your way south and east across the bridge over the trench. After the bridge, make your first left and follow the northbound corridor to a third large room. Head north-northeast, climb another root to the upper level, and then make your way west-northwest to the entrance to the Kelp Fen.

This sprawling level is slightly tricky, too. Make your way south, descend to the floor of the large room to the west, and enter the corridor at the center of its south side. This loops back to an east-west passage on the south side of the afore-mentioned big room—but make sure you also follow the eastside corridor en route to find one of the level's two Felldew-bearing Elytra. Watch out for spike traps at this junction. At the west end of the passage, just head south and east to the exit to the Drone Tunnels. You find the other Felldew Elytra at the south end of a long connecting tunnel.

Drone Tunnels is simple if you're making good time and have stockpiled Felldew. Just make your first two lefts to reach the exit. Unfortunately, if you need Felldew, neither of the Felldew Elytra can be found along this path. Each is located near the end of a dead-end corridor—one west of the final intersection on your way to the exit, and the other in the level's far northwest corner. Keep an eye out for worm traps.

In Bramble Halls, the exit is just south of the entrance, but your direct route is blocked by roots. Instead, you need to follow a loop to the west. You find the first Felldew Elytra in a cul-de-sac west of this corridor. In the big room at the end of the hall, climb the root at its south end—watch for spore and spike traps on the room's east side—and follow the hall at the top north and west to exit to the Sanctum of Decadence. You find the second Felldew Elytra at the south end of a parallel passage to the east.

Whew. You made it.

However, you're not done fighting. The Sanctum's been taken over by three combative Felldew junkies—two of them generic and two levels below your own, and one called Joofy the Brown who's one level above you. Kill 'em all (not hard, since they have no weapons or armor), grab the Chalice to both cure your addiction and set your stats to rights, and make your exit up the stairs in the southwest corner.

Reward? You find eight portions of Felldew on the addicts and a six more laying around loose in the Sanctum. You'd be within your rights to consider it more curse than reward. But after activating the Chalice you find Felldew's effect has changed. The Chalice turns off the withdrawal effects. The drug now bumps up Strength, Agility, and Intelligence by 5 points

and Health and Magicka by 20. Moreover, on the bookshelves against the east wall at the top of the entry stairs, you find several of the 23 conventional books specific to the Shivering Isles: *Bark and Sap*, *The Blessings of Sheogorath*, *Myths of Sheogorath*, *The Prophet Arden-Sul*, *Saints and Seducers*, *The Shivering Bestiary*, *The Standing Stones*, and *Wabbajack*.

Some of these are just for fun, but a few (notably, *The Shivering Bestiary* and *The Standing Stones*) have a useful purpose. And *The Prophet Arden-Sul* anticipates your next mission.

Perhaps you will learn something after all.

The actual reward? On your return, Thadon appoints you "Courtier of Mania, with all of its entitlements. Which is to say, none." And an inoperable version of the Chalice appears on the pedestal across from the Focus Crystal.

THE LADY OF PARANOIA

Lots of folks discourage you from taking a direct approach with this lady. Haskill suggests a delicate hand in your dealings with the woman Sheogorath calls "ever wary, ever worried." And, if you coax his Disposition up to 70, Kithlan suggests you buttonhole Syl in the Dementia gardens around midnight.

It's all different flavors of red herring. Whatever you've heard about her wary nature, the Duchess of Dementia doesn't need to be handled with kid gloves, and you won't need a special appointment to see her. (Indeed, you can't get into the garden without a key, which won't become available until much later in the quest line.) She's plenty accessible—emerging from her private garden into Dementia's main hall to hold court at 8 a.m. and remaining there until midnight.

On the strength of your Sheogorath connection (and her belief that everyone she already knows is out to get her), Syl immediately takes you into her confidence—appointing you Grand Inquisitor in charge of rooting out the spies she believes surround her—and sends you off to talk to Herdir in the torture chamber. Just follow the passage south from the main hall and make your first right. Herdir's always there. Introduce yourself and ask what you're supposed to do; he proposes a trek through the city's southern Crucible district.

Herdir is doubtful about the purported conspiracy; he's just going along for the ride because he likes torturing people. (Torture is a barbaric practice, but in the Shivering Isles, it does work—albiet at the sacrifice of the torturee's good disposition.) But just because Syl's paranoid doesn't mean no one's out to get her. You won't have to visit Crucible to pick up the whiff of a plot.

There are a few ways to get at the information. Either boost the steward Kithlan's Disposition to 80 or authorize Herdir to torture him a couple of times, and he notes that courtier Anya Herrick seems nervous or scared. Stammering, Herrick denies any knowledge of a plot, but let Herdir work his magic on her for a bit and she gives up Ma'zaddha. (You can also go to Herrick directly, or pick up her name from Ushnar gro-Shadborgob, who lives in the upper portion of the Crucible district.)

You don't need to talk to Ma'zaddha at this stage. You can persuade, bribe, and torture the Khajiit all you like, but he won't reveal a thing—though he hints that he might talk if you present him with actual evidence.

Instead, have Herdir physically abuse other Crucible residents. The merchant, Cutter; the skooma addict, Caldana Monrius; the publican, Sickly Bernice; and beggar, Bhisha, all reveal that Ma'zaddha's been seen meeting at night with Nelrene—the head of Syl's Dark Seducer guards.

Shh! We are not alone! It's not safe to speak. Go, before someone sees us.

However, that's not in itself evidence of wrongdoing—it's just evidence of a conversation—and neither Ma'zaddha nor Nelrene give up any information. But talk to Herdir about "other things" and "investigation," and he suggests you eavesdrop on their chat for leverage. If you summon Haskill, he notes that Herdir's a rather obvious fellow—meaning you should leave him behind for this stage of the quest. He's right. Send the sadist back to the Palace. You won't need him for a while.

Follow Ma'zaddha from his house, about halfway up the west side of Crucible's main drag, or follow Nelrene from the Palace; it doesn't matter. They meet around 1 a.m. in southern Crucible in a cul-de-sac on the west side of Brithaur's house. The crates nearby provide an excellent hiding place. Be sure you are sneaking to maximize your chances of them not detecting you. From what you overhear, they're *clearly* tied to a plot to depose Syl.

When the conversation ends, you get a journal suggesting you confront Ma'zaddha with this evidence. (You don't have enough to break Nelrene the disciplined). You can do this as soon as the Khajiit walks away from the rendezvous. He discloses that Nelrene is taking orders from an unidentified third party and agrees to get this person's name by midnight of the next day. (He can also reveal the whole reason for the plot: Syl has been dallying with the Duke of Mania!) You're to meet Ma'zzadha at his house just north of the rendezvous point. Use the entrance up the ramp in the rear to avoid detection when picking the two-tumbler lock.

Uh-oh. When you show up, you find Ma'zaddha lying dead on the ground floor. He's not holding a smoking gun, but he does have in his pocket the key to a cupboard in the northwest corner of the second floor bedroom. Within, you find Nelrene's Ceremonial Shortsword and Ma'zaddha's Crinkled Note. The latter reveals that the sword was to be the assassination weapon (in Anya's hands) and that a certain Muurine is behind the plot. When you mention the sword to Nelrene, she confirms Muurine's involvement.

And Muurine? You have to track down this High Elf mage, and that takes you back to the Crucible district. She lives diagonally across the street from Ma'zaddha. You can enter the house directly via the front door (two tumblers) or upstairs via a bridge from the Things Found shop (three tumblers at the shop's end of the bridge and two more at Muurine's). Or you can wait for her to leave her house, which she does several times a day.

Talk to her about "conspiracy," and she promptly fesses up. However, she doesn't fight or try to buy you off. She recognizes the plot has failed, and simply awaits the natural consequences.

Oddity: Muurine's Uncle Leo, a zombie, staggers around harmlessly upstairs. Evidently Muurine is a Necromancer!

Things move quickly now. Tell Syl what you learned. She asks you to meet her in the torture chamber. Muurine appears in that chamber's central cage instantly. Syl enters, pronounces sentence, and pushes the button at the base of the right-hand column to electrocute Muurine. Syl is happy with your work,

makes you a Courtier of Dementia, and rewards you with the bow, Ruin's Edge. This bow randomly casts one of six spells when fired: a strong or weak Paralyze spell, Silence, Demoralize, Frenzy, or Burden. It is your friend; use it often.

Then, simply pop over to Sheogorath's court for an acknowledgment of your achievement, another trophy (a model of the Inquisitor's Cage)…and another quest.

Make sure you search Muurine's body afterward. You find her house key and also a curious Duelist's Key and a slim book called *Liturgy of the Duelists*. This ties in with an odd hobby. It's the rules of an exclusive Duelists club—one with membership rolls greatly diminished by this quest. See the "Freeform" section for details.

THE COLD FLAME OF AGNON

1. Entrance to Cylarne dungeon (main passage).
2. Entrance to Cylarne dungeon (Underdeep).
3. Gate to Dark Seducer camp: You get the gate key—

indeed, the key to the whole shebang—from either of the gate wardens (Vik at #6 and Chuna at #7).
4. Gate to the Golden Saints camp: Ditto.

5. You retrieve the Flame of Agnon from the base of this tower after the fire is ignited at the Altar of Despair.

6. Vik: Dark Seducer gate warden. She supplies the key to the gates at #4 and #5 and directs you to see Dark Seducer leader Ulfri in the main passage (i.e. through the door at #1). Typically, she's the first casualty of the Saints attack. But if she somehow survives, she redeploys to the Underdeep to oppose a sneak attack in the Underdeep.

7. Chuna: The Golden Saints' gate warden. She supplies the same key as Vik and directs you to see Saints leader Kaneh at #8. And she joins in whichever of the attacks you select.

8. Aurmalz Kaneh: The Golden Saints leader. She's holding out for a traditional attack down the main passage (through the door at #1), but her lieutenant, Mirel (#9), is pushing for a surprise attack through a lightly defended region called the Underdeep (reached via the door at #2). If you scout the Dark Seducer positions, you can persuade Kaneh to see the light—at which time you can betray the Saints by tipping Seducer leader Ulfri to the plan. (You can also triple-cross the Seducers by diverting their forces to the Underdeep and then going with Kaneh's original main-passage assault.)

9. Mirel: Kaneh's lieutenant has a plan for an attack via the Underdeep, but Kaneh's having none of it. Scouting out Seducer positions in the Underdeep (#2) and main passage (#1) will change her mind.

10. Generic Golden Saints. They all join in whichever of the attacks you select.

11. These NPCs appear only after the quest is over. Depending on which side won the battle for the Altar of Despair, they are either generic Golden Saints or Dark Seducers.

12. Chest: Gold, as usual. You find heavy armor 25 percent of the time (and magic heavy armor another 10), a lockpick (15 percent), and a repair hammer, arrows, a stealthy potion, a scroll, and a weapon (10 percent). The leveled lock has one to five tumblers.

13. Obelisk: Inert when you approach the complex, this great crystal (#15 on the Obelisks map in the "Freeform" section) is activated and churns out a pair of Knights of Order once you light Cylarne's flame.

14. A patrolling Knight of Order five levels beneath your own. This one doesn't appear until the third set of patrols is added at the end of the Main Quest mission "Ritual of Accession."

15. Wilderness critter: Depending on your level, this could be a Baliwog, Gnarl (starting at Level 4), Scalon (Level 9), or Hunger (Level 11).

16. This one's a Baliwog or a Scalon (again starting at Level 9).

17. And this one an Elytra, Gnarl, Hunger (all starting at Level 1), Skinned Hound (Level 4), or Shambles (Level 9).

18. Altar of Rapture: You may find Kaneh (#8) praying here when you return to her to recommend an attack route. And you find it burning with a golden flame once the ritual at the Altar of Despair is complete.

"Now to the meat of the endeavor," says Sheogorath. "The reason for your being here and the likely cause of your death."

In time, you're to take Sheogorath the Madgod's place while he makes himself scarce during the Greymarch. And a first step in that direction is restoring the flame to the Great Torch that's supposed to burn over New Sheoth's Sacellum Arden-Sul—and is ritually extinguished with each new Greymarch—to keep his Mad People in line. For this purpose, you're to visit the ruins at Cylarne, in the far northwest corner of the Isles, and recover the Flame of Agnon.

"Oh, and take care with my minions," Sheogorath adds. "In their eternal quest to please me, they're constantly fighting over Cylarne."

Start with Haskill. Sheogorath has given you only part of the story. The Flame of Agnon isn't currently burning. It has to be lit first by the Saints or Seducers using the altars of Rapture and Despair. Ordinarily, Sheogorath would just command them to do this, but you don't have that authority. "I'm afraid you may have to be a little clever," says the chamberlain.

If you took the long route to New Sheoth from the Gates of Madness via Overlook Road, your journey to Cylarne can be comparatively short. Just fast-travel to Camp Tall Trees or Milchar and make your way northwest. If not, you can still shorten it by fast-traveling back to the Gates of Madness and then heading north on Overlook. From here, follow the path northwest.

Sheogorath

At the fork, head west. You quickly run into an Obelisk and its attendants. You may as well shut it down, per Haskill's earlier instructions. See the "Freeform" section for details on Obelisks.

Cylarne's just off the northwest coast on the Isle of Flame; it recalls in appearance the Gardens of Flesh and Bone from The Fringe. On the descending entry stairs, you get a journal directing you to talk to the commanders of the Saints and Seducers on how to relight the Flame of Agnon. Start with either Chuna, the Saint guarding the east gate, or Vika, the Seducer guarding the west gate. Tell them you're here at Sheogorath's behest and they change their haughty tone pronto.

Does it matter which one? No. For the most fun, talk to 'em both. Chuna and Vika each surrender a Cylarne Key that gives you access to the whole place.

There are four potential paths through this quest, two siding with the Saints, and two with the Seducers. Each has a straightforward attack or defend option. You attack with the Saints and defend with the Seducers. There is also a sneak attack through the Underdeep option with the Saints and an option to betray the sneak attack for the Seducers.

GATHERING INFORMATION FROM THE SAINTS

You eventually have to choose side, but until that point, it's safe to gather information. Neither side attacks either you or each other until you have chosen.

Chuna explains that the Saints can't light the flame until they liberate the underground Altar of Despair from the Seducers (whom they call "Mazken"). You're to speak to the newly arrived Aurmazl Kaneh (commander of the Aureals, as the Saints call

themselves) in the encampment at the Altar of Rapture.

When you approach, you find Kaneh already involved in a confab with her lieutenant, Mirel. Listen in. The latter is urging on the commander an attack along a lightly defended route known as the Underdeep, rather than the planned attack route along the heavily defended main passage. But he doesn't shake Kaneh's resolve—the commander worries that it's a trap—and your journal suggests you question Mirel about the Underdeep. It sounds like a good idea. Perhaps you could find a way to persuade Kaneh.

Try Kaneh on "Flame of Agnon" and "Battle Plans." She's happy to do your bidding with respect to the Flame once the Altar of Despair is back in Saint hands, and she asks for your help in the coming battle. You can respond in at least three ways: agree to join in the main corridor assault, propose to scout the Seducer positions, or tell her you don't want to get involved. If you talked to Mirel on the "Underdeep" topic, you have a fourth option: ask about the Underdeep proposal.

Kaneh still won't buy into it; she seems to think it's a guy thing. But if you choose the "scout" option and follow up with explorations of the Underdeep and Cylarne levels, you can talk her into it later. You see, the Seducers don't yet regard you as an enemy—you haven't committed to the Saints cause yet—and won't attack you as you wander through these regions. (The patrolling Seducer lieutenant, Stela, challenges you if you encounter her, but you just have to throw Sheogorath's name at the problem for it to go away.)

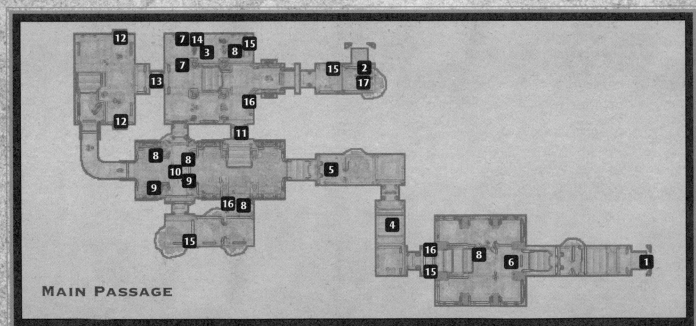

MAIN PASSAGE

1. Exit to dungeon exterior.
2. Exit to Altar of Despair.
3. Dark Seducers leader Grakedrig Ulfri. If you agree to help the Seducers fight off a Main Passage assault, she orders you to follow her south to a position on the bridge (#10) once the Saints' attack begins. If you lead the

Saints into an ambush in the Underdeep, she redeploys there and takes up position at #5 on that map.
4. Stela: Ulfri's lieutenant. In the Main Passage, she patrols to #5 and #6. If you send the Saints through the Underdeep without first warning Ulfri, she redeploys to #6 on that level.

5. and 6. The area that Stela patrols.

7. Ulfri's bodyguards: If you propose leading the Saints into an ambush in the Underdeep, they redeploy to the Underdeep and take up positions in the western and north parts of that level.

8. In the event of a redeployment, these five Dark Seducers (four of them are archers) hold their positions in the Main Passage.

9. On the other hand, these two archers redeploy to the Underdeep and take up positions along the Saints' initial approach.

10. If the Saints launch an assault down the Main Passage, Ulfri leads you to this spot on the bridge. Moreover, once the Seducers in the area have been killed, the Saints hold up at roughly this spot *beneath the bridge* and leader Kaneh sends you ahead alone to open the closed gate…

11. …here.

12. To get to the button on the north side of that gate, you have to get past these two trapped statues, which fire Damage Health spells…

13. …and then through this gate to deal with the three additional Seducers that appear at #17.

14. Hit this button to disable the trapped statues at #12.

15. Urns and a chest: These each contain one or two Restoration-related items.

16. Urns and a chest: Gold for sure. Fair shots (25 percent) at a piece of light armor and a repair hammer, and poor shots (10 percent each) at a gem, jewelry, light magic armor, arrows, a combat-related potion, a scroll, and a weapon.

17. Three additional Dark Seducers. These blue ladies are enabled only if you opt for a Main Passage assault against the preexisting Seducer forces, assuming the Seducers don't redeploy to the Underdeep. They appear when you make your move to open the gate at #11.

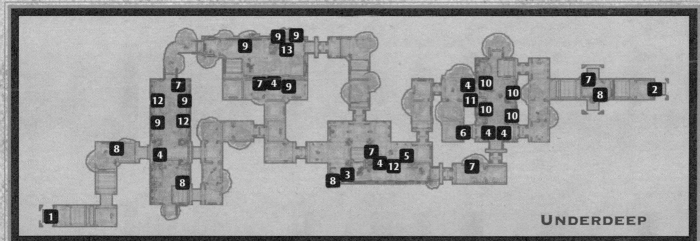

UNDERDEEP

1. Exit to the Altar of Despair.

2. Exit to the dungeon exterior, the Underdeep entrance within the Saints' surface enclosure.

3. This is the lone Seducer present during your reconnaissance of this level.

4. If you indicate to Ulfri that you'll lead the Saints into an ambush in the Underdeep, she redeploys her two bodyguards, two additional Seducers from the Main Passage (those at #9), and the two from the Altar of Despair into the Underdeep. These troops take up these positions along the Saints route…

5. …while Ulfri herself moves here.

6. If you *don't* alert Ulfri to the Saints' Underdeep assault, things work a bit differently once the Saints enter the level. In that case, the #4 and #5 don't appear. Seducer lieutenant Stela, Ulfri's two

bodyguards, and gate warden Vika head for this location in an attempt to intercept the attackers.

7. Urns: These contain one of two Restoration-related items.

8. Urns and chests: Gold for certain, fair shots at a repair hammer or armor (25 percent), and poor shots (10 percent) at a gem, jewelry, a piece of magic light armor, arrows, combat-related potion scroll, or weapon.

9. Trapped statues: Working on proximity triggers once the attack starts, these fire Damage Health spells. Even the fallen top portion of the westernmost statue in the long room on the north side of the level serves as a trap!

10. Dart traps: They're turned on by a button on a pedestal…

11. …here. The Seducer nearby turns it on.

12. Collapsing-column trap.

13. Falling-ceiling trap.

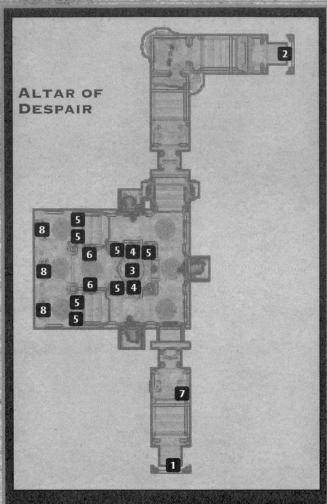

ALTAR OF DESPAIR

1. Exit to Main Passage.

2. Exit to Underdeep.

3. Altar: The site of the flame-lighting ceremony at mission's end. The leader of the side you've taken sacrifices herself as her comrades kneel in prayerful attitudes nearby.

4. Dark Seducers: These two guards redeploy to the Underdeep if you indicate to Ulfri that you'll lead the Saints into an ambush on that level.

5. Golden Saint defensive positions: The Altar is the focal point for a likely battle royale between Golden Saint units defending a conquered Altar and Seducer units counterattacking from whichever path the Saints didn't follow. As long as the Saints' assault is underway and there are live Seducer enemies still out there, the Saints trigger this mass redeployment when they reach the Altar (for this purpose, a large square area at the center of the level). If they've survived, the six generic Saints soldiers and lieutenant Mirel will take up predetermined defensive positions both around the Altar itself and atop the two adjacent flights of stairs. Bring it on, sister.

6. Aurmalz Kaneh's positions: The Saints' leader occupies slightly different positions depending on whether the Saints approached from the southern Main Passage or from the north via the Underdeep.

7. Urn: Contains one or two Restoration-related items.

8. Cremation urns: At each of the three locations, you find five urns. They're guaranteed only to hold Ashen Remains, but a gem and jewelry could turn up in each. (The ashes are an ingredient. In the dungeon Ebrocca, you find a way to manufacture them yourself!)

State your business. Cylarne is holy ground, unfit for mortals.

Vika

You find the entrance to the Underdeep on the north side of the Saints' camp. There's virtually no one down here. You find just a single Seducer in the middle portion of the ruins. Just follow the green map marker and you eventually kick off a journal entry confirming Mirel's report that the Underdeep is lightly defended and urging you to check the main passage.

To reach it, use the entrance to the Altar of Despair in the level's far southwest corner, then exit to the Cylarne level south of the Altar. Explore this region for a journal that the main passage is indeed held in strength. You find archers on high ground in positions that aren't immediately accessible. If questioned, Ulfri also reveals the presence of a number of traps. Currently inactive, these are found in statues that fire leveled Damage Health spells.

GATHERING INFORMATION FROM THE SEDUCERS

The gatekeeper Vika sends you off to meet with the Grakedrig (Seducer for "commander"), Ulfri, about rekindling Agnon's flame. Make your way west through the gate and down into Cylarne's dark underground section. Ulfri is easy to find—she's in the gated room that leads to the Altar entrance—and eager to help. But, naturally, she wants your help in beating down an anticipated Golden Saint assault on the Altar of Despair.

Via the "Battle plans" topic, you get three choices: help with the Altar's defense as requested, non-involvement, or chatting up the Saint commander, Kaneh, for her own plans. Ulfri especially likes the deviousness of that last one.

You find Kaneh at the Saints' surface encampment, across the way from the Cylarne gate. Events proceed as described previously in "Gathering Information from the Saints." The key this time around is to talk to Saints lieutenant Mirel. He gives you the skinny on a lightly defended back door into the Altar of Despair called the Underdeep. This gives you a third option when you return to the Ulfri: "I'll lead the Saints into an ambush." Ulfri then redeploys the lion's share of her forces into the Underdeep section and reduces the Seducer complement in the main passage (Cylarne) to five soldiers.

PLAYING FOR THE SAINTS

After your reconnaissance, return to the Saints' camp and propose the Underdeep route to Kaneh. Now she's persuaded. The eight soldiers—Kaneh, Mirel, and six generic Saints—promptly storm into the entrance and make short work of the Seducers therein before heading on to the Altar.

 You have to accompany the soldiers. If you tarry, or use the other entrance, they wait for you on the first landing.

To be sure, you find more troops here than during your earlier visit. The Seducer lieutenant Stela, who's two levels above your own; Ulfri's two bodyguards, each one level above yours; and the gate warden Vika (if she survives) all head into the Underdeep once the attack begins.

Then again, maybe you want to get right down to business. The main passage assault is doable, too: it's just more work. The odds there are more or less even and your presence on point is required. (Of course, you can also adjust the odds in advance by using your free ride through the Seducer lines to kill off the more remote troopers. The downside is that hostilities haven't begun—you haven't declared yourself—so, if witnessed, these attacks may count against you as murders.)

In this case, just tell Kaneh you'll help her with her planned assault. The Saints go marching in, only to find that a closed gate up the stairs on the north side of the east-west corridor prevents access to the Altar level…and that a pair of traps up the corridor to the north threaten to cut the party to pieces. Once the Seducers in the immediate area are dead (and this can take a while, as some of the archers have cover), Kaneh speaks to you: the Saints will hold position here while you get the gate open.

It's easy. Just loop north and east to a second gate—this one with an accessible button on the south wall beside the portal. The traps to the north and south target spots just west of the gate, and there's plenty of time between their shots to get through. The gate Kaneh wants open is just to the southeast. (The button is beside the gate on the east wall.) And yet, for all your good work, the Saints may not use this gate after all and simply pile through the freshly opened one, beat down the three newly spawned Seducers in the room beyond, and follow the trench to the Altar entrance.

In either case, you face the remaining Seducers at the Altar—including the leader, Ulfri, who is five levels above your own. When Ulfri drops, you get a message to clear out the remaining Seducers. When they're gone, the surviving Saints gather near the Altar and Kaneh (who can't be killed) speaks to you: she's going to sacrifice herself to relight the flame. And, with that, she walks onto the Altar, raises her arms, and vanishes with a grunt in a gout of greenish flame.

A third option is a triple-cross: get the details on the Underdeep from Mirel and tell Seducer chief Ulfri that you'll lead the Saints into an ambush there. (You find this described in the Seducer section below.) But, instead, send the Saints down the now lightly defended main passage. They roll right over the Seducers, they don't have to deal with the traps or the closed gate, and they take possession of an undefended Altar. To be sure, they have to deal with counterattacking Seducers trickling back in from the Underdeep, but the Saints can bring a lot more force to bear than the strung-out Seducers, and you're there to help out with the combat math.

THE ART OF SEDUCTION

You can follow through on your arrangement with Ulfri and double-cross the Saints by lying to persuade Kaneh to follow the dangerous Underdeep route. Or you can triple-cross the Seducers by directing the Saints into an attack down the lightly defended main passage. (See the previous "Saints" section.)

Altar of Arden-Sul

If double-crossing the Saints, you don't have to first scout out the Seducer positions in Cylarne and the Underdeep, but you do have to accompany the attackers and you may bear the brunt of the Saints anger when they discover you've screwed them over. (Like Ulfri and Stela, Kaneh and Mirel are respectively five levels and two levels above your own.)

From here on in, things proceed as they did with the Saints. You get a journal when Kaneh goes down and another when the last of the Saints is bumped off. The surviving Seducers trek through the dungeon to the Altar of Despair. Just talk to Ulfri (who can't die in this version of the battle) to learn she'll sacrifice herself to relight to the flame.

Finally, there's the straight-up defense of the main passage. Ulfri's request that you go with her is followed immediately by a report that the Saints' assault has started. The blue soldier dons her helmet and runs south to the bridge above the approach route. Equip that nice new Ruin's Edge bow and join her if you like; it's a good (though exposed) vantage point for gunning down the attackers. However, the Saints take their sweet time making their way in from the east and you can use that extra time to shut the east-west gate in this room before you do. Otherwise, you may find the Saints charging up the stairs into the Seducers rear areas. Once the gate is closed, the Saints won't open it and this leaves them exposed to the withering fire from the traps in the statues that flank the door. (Don't hit the north-wall button near Ulfri, as this disables the trap outside the gate.)

CARRYING A TORCH

Either way, once the Altar is lit, you simply have to retrieve the flame from the base of the tower in Cylarne's entry courtyard…by, uh, stepping into it and setting yourself on fire. Be the torch. It's painless and impresses the folks back in New Sheoth to no end.

Fast-travel back to that city's Bliss or Crucible district, follow the map marker to the southwest corner of the former or the northwest of the latter, and enter the Sacellum Arden-Sul.

You have one more side to choose before you're done. At the top of the stairs, you run into the priests Arctus (who represents Dementia) and Dervenin (who represents Mania). Each asks you to light the Great Torch on behalf of their cause and district. If you tell them you're thinking of doing so for the other side, they offer some enticement—previews of their respective rewards. Light the Torch for Mania, and you get the Raiment of Arden-Sul—full-body clothing with a leveled Fortify Intelligence, Fortify Willpower, Resist Paralysis, and Shield enchantments. Light it for Dementia to collect the Raiment of Intrigue, with leveled Fortify Speed, Luck, Security, and Sneak enchantments.

Your decision in conversation with the respective priests opens one of the two Fire Gates at the west end of the nave. Just as you stepped into the flame to acquire it, step through the gate to light the torch, talk to the priest to collect the reward, and get a journal entry to report your achievement to Sheogorath.

You won't have far to go. Sheogorath knows. He's sitting in the Sacellum's pews, applauding like a proud poppa, and, at length, offering up a new quest. (Back at the Palace, you find a new trophy on the northside of the hall: Ulfri's or Kaneh's helmet.)

THE RITUAL OF ACCESSION

To establish you as an authority figure in the Realm, you're going to replace either the Duke of Mania or the Duchess of Dementia. There are strange ways of handling the succession process in this strange place, and Sheogorath sends you to talk to the priests Arctus and Dervenin for the details.

So which one goes—the junkie or the paranoid?

Talk to Arctus for the "ritual of accession" for dumping the present Duchess: You have to cut out her heart and bring it to the Sacellum's altar. Arctus will declare you Duke, and Sheogorath has to sign off on the arrangement. (In fact, this sign-off is a formality; you just have to talk to him.)

The Mania side comes from Dervenin. Thadon chooses his successor from among the members his court. He throws a big party for that individual and, at its height, drinks three potions of a drug called Greenmote to burst his own heart. The successor then gathers the blood, brings it to the temple altar, and gathers similar stamps of approval.

Gross, either way.

Once you've consulted the priests, save your game, consult Sheogorath again on the topic "decision," and chose your target.

Does it matter? Absolutely. The nobleperson you replace changes the complexion of a number of future missions in ways large and small. And this one not least among them.

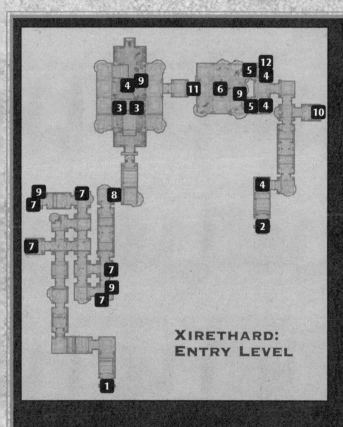

XIRETHARD:
ENTRY LEVEL

1. Ladder up to the southeast corner of the House of Dementia's gardens.
2. Exit to the Depths level.
3. Dark Seducer archers.
4. Dark Seducer melee fighters. When the secret doors at #5 open, the three fighters east of these doors all rush into the room west of the doors.
5. Secret doors: These open when you cross an invisible line that curves through the middle of the room, just west of the central column…
6. …here. (At the same time, the door at #11 closes.)
7. Trapped statues: They fire leveled Damage Health spells.
8. This button turns off the traps.
9. Urns and a chest: These contain one or two items of healing supplies.
10. An urn, two barrels, and five crates. The barrels hold two torches each and the crates hold only clutter, but the urn contains gold for certain, maybe a piece of light armor and a repair hammer (25 percent chances of each), and possibly magic light armor, arrows, a combat-related potion, a scroll, a weapon, a gem, and jewelry (10 percent chances of each).
11. This door closes when you cross the invisible line referenced in #5. It opens again when you push the button at #12.
12. This button re-opens the door at #11.

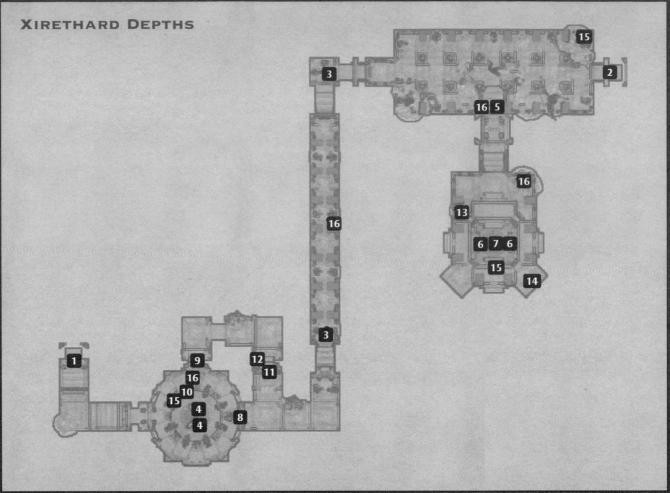

Xirethard Depths

1. Exit to Xirethard entry level.

2. Exit to Subterrane level.

3. Patrolling Dark Seducers: As they follow their routes, these two trade places.

4. Dark Seducer archers operating from behind a barricade. This barricade seems to have been erected in a hurry; notice they didn't put away the silverware first.

5. Dark Seducer door guard.

6. Syl's bodyguards.

7. The Duchess of Dementia.

8. This exit is blocked.

9. This is a secret door.

10. To open the secret door at #9, press the button at the base of the statue.

11. The secret door takes you back into the main hallway.

12. This button opens the secret door at #11.

13. Madness Ore deposit: There's a fellow who can make equipment from this stuff in the Miscellaneous Quest "The Antipodean Hammer."

14. Boss chest: You're guaranteed only a sample of Madness Ore and up to 10 gold. (Sigh.) But you probably (75 percent chance) get 20–745 more. (Woo-hoo!) Other potential nice stuff: jewelry, heavy armor, a stealth-related potion, and up to three lockpicks, all 25 percent chances. Additional nice stuff, only with less potential, includes a stealth skill book, magic weapon and heavy armor, a regular weapon, a mold for an item made from Madness Ore (used in the Miscellaneous Quest "The Antipodean Hammer"), and a soul gem or two.

Now for how to get to the boss chest….Odds are you can't. It's on the upper level of the sanctum. You have to be a Master of Acrobatics *and* enhance the skill magically to reach the low edge of the upper level. Two items come equipped with a 10-point Fortify Acrobatics enchantment: the Flowing Greaves and the Grand Ring of Acrobatics. A second ring, Ring of Acrobatics, gives you another eight points. (Alas, these are available only in leveled loot.)

15. Two chests and an urn: The potential contents of these are the same as the urn mentioned in #10 in the entry-level map descriptions. The first you encounter has a level lock of one to five tumblers.

16. Urns: One or two healing items.

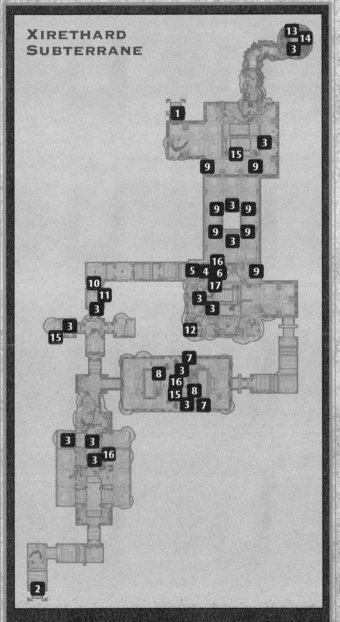

XIRETHARD SUBTERRANE

1. Exit to Depths.

2. Exit to dungeon exterior.

3. Shambles…unless you haven't reached Level 9, in which case these are all Skeletons. If Shambles, remember: they go out with a bang!

4. Zealot Mage: Note that this room is on a higher level than the rooms that appear immediately around it. (On the lower level, this is the location of one of the trapped statues at #9.)

5. Floor trap, operated by a button on the pedestal…

6. …here.

7. Falling-ceiling trap.

8. Collapsing-column trap.

9. Trapped statues. (The two northernmost are on a lower level than it appears here.)

10. Secret door…

11. …and the button that opens it.

12. Dark Chest of Wonders: Yes, that's really its name. It has a leveled lock of two to five tumblers and contains the Ring of the Oceanborn, with Nighteye and Water Breathing enchantments.

13. Hollowed Amber limb: A sample of Amber, three 50 percent chances of additional pieces, and a one percent chance of a piece of Amber that looks like Sheogorath (which comes into play in the Miscellaneous Quest "The Museum of Oddities").

14. Hollowed stump: Gold is a given. There are 25 percent chances you pick up a gem and an item that could be either Amber or equipment made from Amber. You've got five different shots at armor: heavy, light, general armor, general magic armor (all 10 percent), and magic heavy armor (five percent). Other 10 percent shots are jewelry, a soul gem, arrows, a potion, a scroll, and a weapon. There's also a 1-in-50 shot at an oddity from #13.

15. Two chests and an urn: Gold's a definite. An ingredient, jewelry, and arrows are possible (25 percent chances). Lockpicks come in at 15 percent; and a potion, torch, weapon, and up to two pieces of Armor at 10.

16. Urns: Healing supplies (one or two items) and maybe a torch (10 percent chance) just to keep you guessing!

17. The Zealot Mage's "boss" chest: It could contain a piece of Madness Ore and a little gold. But it's a safe bet you get a lot more gold (75 percent chance) and some combo of jewelry, heavy armor, a stealthy potion, and up to three lockpicks (25 percent chances for each), plus a stealthy skill book, magic heavy armor, magic and non-magic weapons, Amber equipment, and up to two soul gems (10 percent).

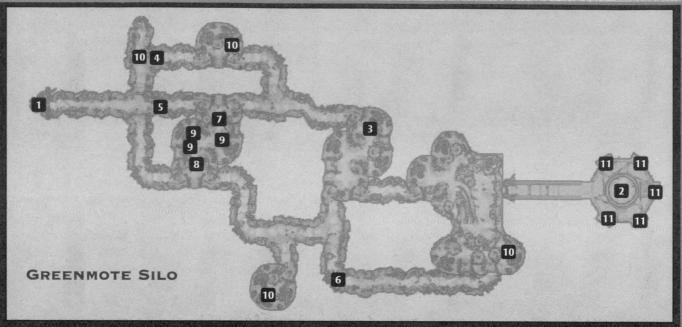

GREENMOTE SILO

1. Ladder up to the Palace courtyard.

2. Big pile of Greenmote. Activate it twice and you've got the stuff to send Thadon to his grave.

3. The routes of three of the four Golden Saint guards start here.

4. One of them heads west-northwest to this spot…

5. …another straight west to this spot…

6. …and the third south to this one.

7. The fourth guard starts here…

8. …and patrols south-southwest to here. Is she lazy? No, she's guarding the silo's low-rent treasure room (three chests; see #9). She's easy to avoid as she's not interested in the hall to the south and heads back north without due diligence. Your only obstacle is the guard who patrols from #3 to #6.

9. Gold for sure, with a repair hammer and light armor possible and a gem, magic light armor, arrows, combat-related potion, scroll and weapon all conceivable (though unlikely).

10. Hollowed stump: Must be a *biiig* stump, too, as there's potentially a ton of stuff in here. Gold (always); a gem and Amber (25 percent of the time); jewelry, four different shots at armor, a soul gem, arrows, magic jewelry, a potion, a scroll, and weapon (all 10 percenters); magic heavy armor (five percent); and a tidbit to feed the Miscellaneous Quest "The Museum of Oddities" (two percent).

11. Around the edge of the room, there are no fewer than 18 urns of Unrefined Greenmote. There are also three loose potions on the table on room's east side. This is The Wrong Stuff for this quest, but it combines with Nirnroot (if you have any left over from the Miscellaneous Quest "Seeking Your Roots") to make a fair little poison. You'll have to be an Apprentice-level alchemist.

MAIN QUEST

DUKE'S QUARTERS

(map with numbered markers: 19, 9, 5, 18, 3, 18, 2, 18, 14, 17, 14, 20, 18, 13, 11, 12, 7, 8, 17, 15, 14, 19, 17, 16, 20, 1, 6, 10, 4)

1. Exit to the Halcyon Conservatory (a.k.a. House of Mania gardens). This door has a leveled lock with two to five tumblers and can also be unlocked using the House Mania Key pickpocketed from the duke, his steward Wide-Eye, or servant Gundlar.

2. Thadon's meal: Activate it to poison it with the Greenmote you took from the silo.

3. Ditto with Thadon's wine. (It's the big bottle on the left side of the middle shelf.)

4 and 5. Don't let the two Golden Saint guards catch you in the act. The patrol route of the southern guard takes in #4, #6, #7, #8, #9, and #10. The route of his northern buddy consists of #5, #9, #11, #12, #11 again, and #9 again.

6–12. Waypoints for guard patrol routes (see #4 and 5)

13. Another nice little library. This one includes the Acrobatics skill book *The Black Arrow, v 1* and (on the top shelf of the southern bookshelves) and the Sneak skill book *Sacred Witness* (on the bottom shelf of the northern bookshelves)—both imported from Cyrodiil—and the non-skill books *The Blessings of Sheogorath*, *Fall of Vitharn*, *Guide to New Sheoth*, *Heretical Thoughts*, *Myths of Sheogorath*, *The Prophet Arden-Sul*, *Wabbajack* and *Zealotry*. These latter books are all specific to the Shivering Isles and have appeared in previous Main Quest libraries. However, there's also one new volume here: the first of three volumes of the rare *16 Accords of Madness* (this one Vol. XII).

14. Two chests and an urn: Each contains gold. You have a 25 percent chance of finding heavy armor; a 15 percent chance of a lockpick; and 10 percent chances of magic heavy armor, a repair hammer, arrows, a stealthy potion, a scroll, and a weapon.

15. A sapphire, a ruby, five lockpicks, and two additional books: *The Liturgy of Affliction* and a second copy of *The Blessings of Sheogorath*

16. A full set of alchemy equipment; lesser and petty soul gems; three samples of Alocasia Fruit, Blister Pod Cap, Flame Stalk, and Screaming Maw; two samples of Red Kelp Gas Bladder; and one each of Aster Bloom Core, Congealed Putrescence, and Digestive Slime. (Thadon didn't throw up on his alchemy table; the Putrescence and Slime are extracted from the Putrid Gigantea mushroom and Letifer Orca Planta, respectively.)

17. Ingredients: In each of these containers, you have five 75 percent chances of nailing one of 20 ingredients specific to the Shivering Isles.

18. In each of the three kitchen urns, you find one portion of Unrefined Greenmote. There's also one portion loose on Thadon's nightstand.

19. The eight crates at these two locations contain mostly useless stuff. But there's a chance (okay, just a 10 percent chance) that each contains a repair hammer, and a slightly less than 15 percent chance that each contains either a bit of gold, a lockpick, or a common ingredient.

20. There's a two percent chance these clothing cupboards contain an item needed in the Miscellaneous Quest "The Museum of Oddities."

RITUAL OF MANIA

Going after Thadon, eh? We don't blame you. You're probably still peeved about the reward he provided when you returned his Chalice.

You can't get him to voluntarily select you as his successor, so no party for you. Your journal suggests asking around in New Sheoth for a way to trick Thadon into overdosing on Greenmote. Any number of folks in town suggest speaking to his steward, Wide-Eye. Seek her out. That may take a while, as she's a busy lady. She wanders the Mania side of the Palace for most of the day, takes her dinner at 8 p.m. in the Mania hall until midnight, and then makes for bed.

Ask about "Thadon" and she mentions he's already using the stuff. Evidently every night is party night in the house of Mania. Boost her Disposition to 60 and ask about "Daily Routine." She discloses that she runs a "special errand" at noon, dinner is at 8 p.m., and chef Gundlar spices up Thadon's food with "just a hint of Greenmote." It's hidden in a special silo, and she won't provide its location for love or money.

So follow her on that noon errand. A little after noon, Wide-Eye makes her way from the Halcyon Conservatory to the Palace grounds—heading south to the stairs, west, north, and finally east into a nondescript niche. You get a journal entry here urging you to watch her. (In fact, you can't very well do anything else, as you're frozen in place.) She activates the bust at the east end to reveal a secret entrance, then descends into the silo. You get another journal entry: you need to collect two portions of Greenmote and you're not to get caught in the collecting. Play it safe and stay in sneak mode the whole way.

Nevertheless, this is slightly tricky, as the narrow tunnels are patrolled by four Golden Saints. They arrest you if they spot you—Wide-Eye attacks you if she spots you—and the whole thing gets messy. Happily, there's a good deal of concealing darkness en route, and the guards' routes make them easy to evade—especially if you follow the southernmost passage, where you have to dodge just one guard. On the east side of the dungeon, you find a paved corridor descending to a large round room with a great green mound at its center. Activate this mound twice to collect the required Greenmote portions—the unrefined Greenmote in the surrounding urns, in the dungeon's 28 mushroom tree saplings, and on the alchemy table on the east side of the room won't do. You get a journal entry instructing you to visit Thadon's kitchen before 8 p.m. and sneak extra Greenmote into Thadon's meal and wine. Make your way back to the dungeon entrance with the same caution you exercised on the way in, and return to the House of Mania.

You probably saw a good deal of this place in "Addiction," but nothing like a kitchen. That's because it's in the northeast corner of Thadon's locked quarters. You have to pickpocket the key from Wide-Eye, Gundlar, or Thadon himself, or pick the leveled lock and then either kill or sneak around the two Golden Saint guards within.

The sneaking is a bit tricky. The guards appear to be directly in your path, but each follows a long patrol route that takes them well out of your way. There's a good sized window where you can slip in and out of the kitchen undetected, plus a nice hiding place behind the kitchen containers if you're in need of extra time. Use the big columns that run down the middle of the room to good effect, and you'll soon be looking down at Thadon's dinner—a tray on the northern table against the kitchen's south wall. Activate it once to drug the food.

Thadon's Wine

And what about the wine? The bottle on the adjacent table isn't for Thadon. The bottle you want, conveniently marked "Thadon's Wine," is on the left side of the middle shelf just west of the tables. Activate this one and you get another journal entry directing you to watch the results at tonight's feast. Then wait until the guards' backs are turned and make your way back out, again, using the columns for cover, and head for the Mania dining hall. A little after 8 p.m., Thadon rises, reads a bit of his new soliloquy, clutches his heart, and drops dead. Activate his body to collect his blood, then a second time to claim his Diadem of Euphoria crown (with leveled Fortify Speechcraft, and Magicka and Resist Magic enchantments). Head for the Sacellum. Activate the altar; Thadon's tainted blood fills the bowl, a fountain of fire rises above it, and then vanishes with a boom. Dervenin now appears in his pulpit and names you the Duke of Mania.

RITUAL OF DEMENTIA

Syl thinks everyone's out to get her. Now she's actually right.

This is a more or less straightforward assassination. However, you can't just waltz into the House of Dementia and whack the Duchess. She is nowhere to be found in the House's public areas. You need the key to the private ones.

As with Thadon, ask around New Sheoth. Pretty much anyone kicks you over to Dementia courtier Anya Herrick and steward Kithlan—with the additional intelligence (at a Disposition of 55) that Herrick's been more loyal than ever following the events of "The Lady of Paranoia" and that Kithlan's now "disillusioned" about his boss.

Nevertheless, each requires persuasion to betray the Duchess and each can make your job easier. Get their respective Dispositions up to 60 and they're yours. Ask about "Replaced" and tell them you need to get close to the Duchess. Herrick agrees to distract at least two of the Dark Seducer guards and Kithlan provides a key to Syl's private quarters.

Go get Syl. Kithlan's key lets you into Syl's private garden through the locked door east of the throne. Here you have to fight two Royal Guards at your own level—the two additional guards Herrick distracts would ordinarily appear in Syl's bedroom—and then make your way east into the Duchess's quarters.

Here you get the impression that someone's done your work for you. Syl lies dead on her bed.

Syl

Wrong. Kithlan appears and reveals this is just a doppelganger; the real Syl has already escaped through a secret entrance. She didn't leave her heart in her sock drawer, so you have to pursue her. The escape hatch is opened by activating the bust of Sheogorath just south of the door to Syl's private quarters. Activate the ladder below to enter the dungeon Xirethard.

You won't find any enemies in the initial section, but the statues at the ends of the corridors send a lot of fireballs your way. Use the alcoves to stay clear of them until you reach the switch that turns them off (well northeast of the entrance).

Just north and east of that switch, you find a metal door. North of that door, the battle is joined in earnest. You run into three of the level's six Dark Seducer defenders—two archers up on the bridge and a melee fighter down below. Once you've cleared them out, climb the stairs to the west, cross the bridge, and enter the large square room to the east. When you advance halfway across it, a gate closes behind you, doors open in the room's northeast and southeast corners, and three melee fighters enter. Use ranged weapons and magic here. Just keep backing and shooting; don't let them box you in. Once they're dead, exit to the east and head south to the entrance to the Xirethard Depths. Syl waits for you here.

At the bottom of the stairs, you find two Seducer archers holed up behind a barricade and the apparent exit to the east hopelessly blocked. Ah, fell for it, did you? The actual exit is a secret door in the northern niche. The trigger is a hard-to-spot button on the side of the pedestal just left of the niche. The passage beyond loops east and south to another not-so-secret door, a metal door, and a long north–south passage with two more Seducers. This leads to a huge pillared chamber with a third Seducer up the stairs to the south, plus Syl and two more Royal Guards like the ones from the Palace just beyond the metal door behind her. This is nasty—Syl's five levels above your own—but quite doable. Once she's dead, perform emergency surgery, take her heart and Nerveshatter hammer (with leveled Weakness to Shock and Shock Damage enchantments), and make your way back to the surface. Back in the Sacellum, activate the Altar to place Syl's heart in the bowl. This time, the flaming fountain burns green and it's Arctus who swears you in.

There are two ways to the surface. One is back the way you came. The other is deeper in the dungeon. Much deeper. See the Subterrane map for details.

MEANWHILE, BACK AT THE RANCH...

Once you've been named a Duke or Duchess, speak to Sheogorath. He's tickled by your success and is about to take up another matter when you hear a familiar voice. If you took out Thadon, it is Syl, accompanied by two Seducer bodyguards, protesting against the killing and your elevation to the ducal throne. If you performed an impromptu heart transplant on Syl, it is Thadon and two Saint bodyguards with a similar complaint—albeit one phrased in crazier language. In each case, the noble reveals that the forces of Order have taken over The Fringe and, at the end, asserts that he or she will take the side of Jyggalag against Sheogorath as a Priest of Order.

The Daedric Prince is a bit put out—treachery at the ducal level is unprecedented—but says simply that "we'll see how this plays out." (It plays out in the "The Roots of Madness" quest.) In any event, he gives you the power to summon Dark Seducers (if you replaced Syl) or Golden Saints (if you replaced Thadon) and turns over the Ring of Lordship. If you're the new Duke of Dementia, this carries with it leveled Chameleon, Fortify Endurance, and Resist Poison enchantments. If Mania, then the enchantments are Fortify Personality, Resist Disease, and Shield. And back at the Palace, a new trophy decorates Sheogorath's throne room: Syl's heart or a flask of Thadon's blood.

RETAKING THE FRINGE

Ask Sheogorath about The Fringe, and he acknowledges the truth of what the angry noble just asserted: Order has invaded that region. Sheogorath's forces are already on the scene, but you're to help them and prevent Jyggalag from using this antechamber as a staging area for a broader assault.

Sheogorath's army *needs* your help. Fast-travel back to the Gates of Madness and make your way down the hill into Passwall. You can't help but notice the redecorating Jyggalag has done to The Fringe. You find a small force fighting a Knight of Order. Once the Knight is no more, the leader—the Dark Seducer, Grakendo Udico, or the Golden Saint, Aurig Desha—speaks to you.

The news is pretty much all bad. An Order spire in the middle of The Fringe has become active, transformed the land around it with crystalline formations—which block access to each of the buildings in the hamlet—and started spitting out Knights. And the Saints/Seducers are losing. While each Knight Jyggalag's men kill is replaced by another, the Madgod's forces are being inexorably ground down. Something has to be done to redress the balance.

Udico/Desha does have a plan to slow down the enemy but says there's not enough time before the next attack wave. Dealing with that wave is the next order of business. She offers you the option to position the defenders—a benefit of your new title—or she can do it herself. Frankly, there aren't enough troops remaining (just four) to call it an army, and your most significant choice is bow vs. melee for each of them. If you let her do it, she sets up three of them as frontline troops and the fourth as an archer in the rear. Help them kill off the three waves of attackers from the south—nine Knights in total—and then consult with your lieutenant again. If you have a Heal Other spell, use it between the waves to help keep your little unit intact.

When you speak with Udico/Desha again, she reports that the forces of Order have effectively tipped their hand. The entrance to Xeddefen—a fortresslike ruin you may have explored on your initial trip to Passwall—has lately been unsealed and Knights now guard the place. Udico/Desha suggests you search there for the Spire's power source while she holds down the fort at Passwall.

Xeddefen is almost straight south from the hamlet, and the exterior is indeed defended. The Grummites you may have found here earlier have been replaced by as many as a half-dozen Knights of Order (three of them reinforcements from the interior ruin who move outside when the fighting starts). Clear them out and wind your way to the door on the south side of the surface ruin.

Inside, you should find a pile of dead Grummites, the dead scout referenced by your lieutenant, a pair of Priests of Order, and three clusters of three Knights each. Get the Xeddefen key from one or the other of the priests; it unlocks the doors to the north. Make sure to collect Hearts of Order whenever you can as you fight the Knights. You need them at the bottom of the dungeon.

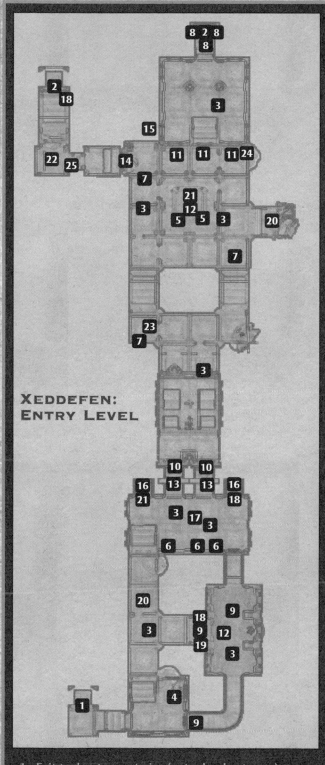

XEDDEFEN: ENTRY LEVEL

1. Exit to dungeon exterior (entry level entrance).

2. Exits to Fain level.

3. Grummites: There are two Xeddefens, the one before the forces of Order occupy the dungeon in the "Retaking The Fringe" mission, and the one after. The Grummites appear on this level should you visit the dungeon before that quest kicks off.

4. This is what's left of the Grummites after the arrival of the Order: three dead bodies. Each is guaranteed to hold a weapon. In addition, on each corpse, there's a 1-in-4 chance of Madness Ore, a poison potion, and up to two lockpicks, plus a 15 percent chance of minor items, like small amounts of gold and additional lockpicks.

5. Knights of Order: These two remain on station at these locations.

6-8. Knights of Order: These fine fellows—three waves of three Knights each, triggered by your entry into certain zones—truck on out of the dungeon. The first wave appears at #6, the second at #7, and the third at #8. You can fight them—a nasty business—or, if you're stealthy, you can just let them truck on by. They make for Passwall and start hammering your Saint/Seducer lieutenant who, mercifully, cannot be killed.

9-11. Trigger points of the three waves of Knights: #9 for the first wave, #10 for the second, and #11 for the third.

12. Priests of Order: They've got something extra in this dungeon. Trigger the appearance of a wave of Knights and then watch the priest on the Knights' path out of the dungeon. You see him cast an area-effect spell on the Knights. It's called Jyggalag's Embrace, it bumps their health by 30 points for 30 seconds and, if you can sneak close enough, you can get the benefit of that bump as well.

13. Locked doors: In the Grummite version of the dungeon, you have to pick these two- to five-tumbler locks. In the Order dungeon, you can open them with the Xeddefen Key found on the Priests of Order at #12. The second door unlocks automatically once you pass the first.

14. This secret door…

15. …is opened with the button here. Note that this button isn't accessible—there's an intervening wall—until Order takes over the dungeon.

16. Statues. No traps at all. We promise.

17. You'll recall that Udico/Desha mentioned sending a scout into Xeddefen. Here she is—a Golden Saint or Dark Seducer, depending on your affiliation with Mania or Dementia in "The Ritual of Accession." And, in either case, quite dead. You can get armor off her—iron for Golden Saint and fur for Dark Seducer.

18. Two urns and a chest: Healing supplies—one or two items—with a 10 percent chance of a repair hammer.

19. "Boss" urn: It contains a drop of gold and a sample of Madness Ore. There's a 40 percent chance of either a second piece of ore or equipment made from it, with the odds of equipment improving at Level 9. One-in-four odds are attached to a more significant payout in gold, a gem, poison potion, pearl, and up to two repair hammers and three lockpicks. For jewelry, armor, soul gems, and weapons, the odds drop to 1-in-10, and to 1-in-20 for a magic weapon.

20. Madness Ore deposit.

21. One chest and one urn: Each has gold. The rest is sketchier. Maybe a pearl, Madness Ore, or equipment made from it, and up to two lockpicks. (The chance of each is 25 percent.) A smaller maybe for weapons, armor, arrows, jewelry, and repair hammers (10 percent). And the smallest maybe for an item useful in the Miscellaneous Quest "The Museum of Oddities."

22. Remove the floor here by pushing the button just to the east. You drop into the water below and can then reach the secret entrance to the Fain level.

23. A bit of loose loot: a flawed diamond.

24. And another: a single gold piece—technically hidden by the debris from the nearby fire, but nevertheless grabbable.

25. This button removes the floor at #22 and closes the nearby gate.

At various times as you delve deeper into Xeddefen, Knights of Order come running at you. Well, not really at you. They're headed to the surface to pillage The Fringe. You can attack them or let them pass. In most cases you can stay hidden from them and avoid the combat, if that's your wish.

You may also escape (or just defer) some of these encounters by using a secret passage. Just after you pass the low dais where you come upon the second priest, you find a north–south alcove against the west wall. Press the button below the crystalline formation in the alcove's north wall. This opens a panel in the west wall. Follow this hall west as far as you can. In the last room, a gate closes behind you, the floor rolls back, and you drop into a shallow pool with a Grummite egg room to the south and a second entrance to Fain to the north. Just bear in mind that some or all of your pursuers may, nevertheless, follow you into Fain.

Fain is big, but you can ignore the east and west wings and make your way straight up the central stairs to the entrance to the Great Chamber. En route, you have to deal with trapped statues and two waves of two Knights each—not to mention a mini-boss Knight three levels above your own on a central landing.

At the base of the Great Chamber's entry stairs, you learn from a journal entry that the spire is amplifying the power of an Obelisk. You have to shut it down. We discuss Obelisks

extensively in the "Freeform" section, and the rules that apply to Obelisks in general apply to this one as well: you need to overload it by feeding it three Hearts of Order found on the bodies of the Knights.

But first things first: from the stairs, head east, and who do you find emerging from a secret hideaway but Shelden—the obnoxious former "mayor" of Passwall. After the Order's attack, he and Passwall resident Felas Sarandas hid down here to stay out of the way. Needless to say, it didn't work out that way: they jumped from the frying pan into the fire, and Felas seems to have made a second jump into the Order's service. (You run into him later in "Rebuilding the Gatekeeper.") Now Shelden wants out and asks you to escort him back to Passwall.

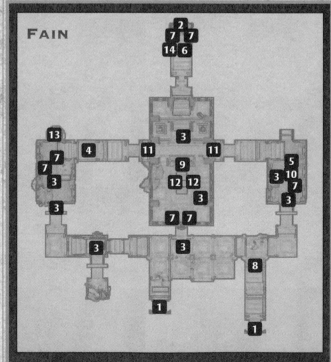

FAIN

1. Exits to Xeddefen's entry level.
2. Exit to the Great Chamber: However, if you haven't reached the "Retaking The Fringe" mission in the Main Quest, this door is blocked by a cave-in.

MAIN QUEST

3. If you haven't reached "Retaking The Fringe" in the Main Quest, there are Grummites at these locations.

4. This is a patrolling Grummite. If "Retaking The Fringe" is live, this is a patrolling Knight of Order.

5. In either case, he moves to this point. Note that the intervening gates at #11 are added for "Retaking The Fringe." They open automatically to admit the passing Knight, but are closed to you unless you can slip in behind a Knight.

6. Grummite boss.

7. If the Main Quest mission "Retaking The Fringe" is running, there are Knights of Order at these locations. Many of these are turned on, in two waves of two Knights each, only when you enter certain zones.

8. The first of these waves is triggered near the bottom of these stairs…

9. …and the second in the middle of your climb to the exit to the Great Chamber. Which also happens to be the location of a Knights of Order boss three levels above your own.

10. Priest of Order.

11. Gates: You can't get through on your own…but the patrolling Knight of Order can.

12. Trapped statues.

13. Madness Ore deposit.

14. Boss chest: Just like the boss urn at #13 on the entry level.

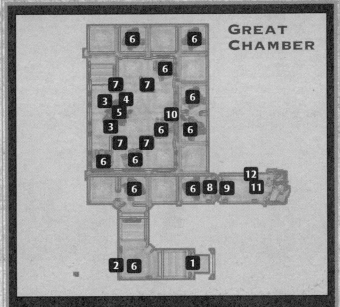

GREAT CHAMBER

1. Exit to the Fain level. Once you shut down the obelisk at #5, the place begins to fall apart and this exit is blocked by a cave-in.

2. Exit to the Felles level. At the same time the cave-in blocks access to #1, access to this level is opened up.

3. Knights of Order.

4. Priest of Order.

5. Obelisk: Overload it by inserting three Hearts of Order. This event triggers the collapse of the spire and much of Xeddefen, with debris falling both directly onto the obelisk from the spire above…

6. …and from the ceilings above these locations throughout the level.

7. These columns come down, too.

8. A secret door, from which emerges…

9. …Passwall's self-proclaimed mayor Shelden! He asks you to shepherd him to safety. Agree and he follows you. Precollapse, you can extract him via Fain—entered at #1—and the entry level. Postcollapse, take him through Felles at #2. Decline, and he runs off on his own to get dead.

10. Crystal chest: You need a Heart of Order to open it. Inside, there's a soul gem and quite possibly a healing potion and a spot of gold (50 percent chances). Other stuff that might turn up includes more gold, alchemical equipment, a scroll or weapon (25 percent chances), jewelry, a repair hammer, magic and regular armor, magic arrows (!), and a potion (10 percent chances).

11. A sack, beside the bedroll, containing a healing potion.

12. Grain sack: Contains not grain, but an ingredient that could be common or uncommon.

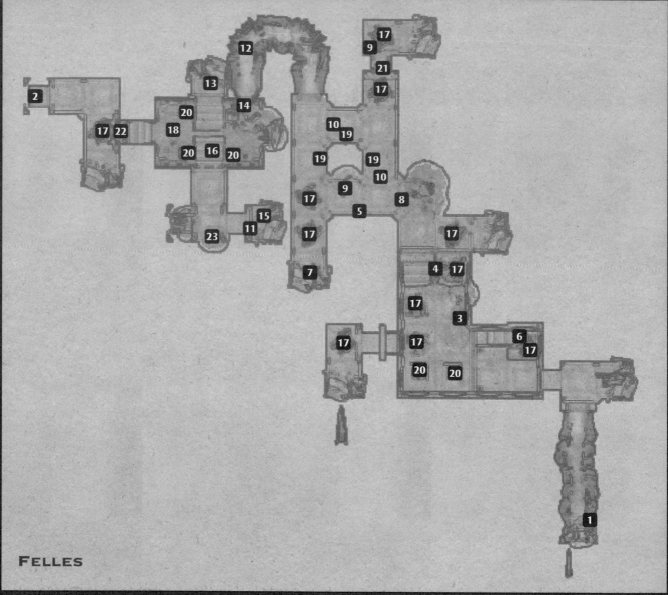

Felles

1. Exit to Great Chamber.

2. Exit to Fales level.

3. Knight of Order. Don't worry about him. He's a sacrificial lamb for the trapped statue…

4. …here. Don't worry about the statue either. When it kills the Knight, it shoots its bolt.

5. Knight of Order, two levels above your own.

6. Trigger for Knight of Order at #5: Trigger zones are a reason to move slowly through this level and Fales. The first time the player pulls a trigger, a Knight is sent running to the trigger location. This is at once a bad thing and a good thing. The bad thing is that a Knight's coming after you. The good thing is it's coming after you through levels loaded with traps. The Knight often sets these traps off along the way, meaning you can't set those traps off

yourself, and the traps may kill (or at least weaken) the Knight in question, thus saving you from the burden of fighting the Knight yourself. In the later stages of this level, you take on the Knights in straight up combat, so make sure you set only one off at a time.

7. Knight of Order.

8. Trigger for Knight at #7.

9. Knight of Order, Level 1.

10. Triggers for Knight at #9.

11. Knight of Order, two levels below your own.

12. Trigger for Knight at #11.

13. Knight of Order, two levels below your own.

14. Trigger for Knight at #13.

15. Knight of Order, two levels below your own.

MAIN QUEST

16. Trigger for Knight at #15.

17. Falling-ceiling trap.

18. Falling-rock trap.

19. Additional trapped statues.

20. Collapsing-column traps.

21. Gate: Nah, you're not getting in. The button to open the gate is on its inaccessible north side. And, anyway, there's nothing behind it except unpleasant things.

22. Gate: Yeah, you're getting in. This gate is opened with the button at #13. If Shelden is following you, or even just waiting for you elsewhere, the irate Passwall mayor runs off to find his own way home. You run into him again in the Fales level.

23. This button opens the gate at #12.

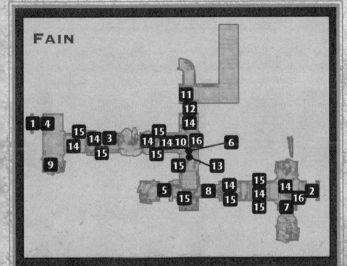

FAIN

1. Exit to Felles level.

2. Exit to dungeon exterior (waterside exit).

3. Knight of Order.

4. Trigger for Knight of Order at #3.

5. Knight of Order, two levels below your own.

6. Trigger for Knight of Order at #5.

7. Knight of Order.

8. Trigger for Knight of Order at #7.

9. Urn: One or two healing items and a 10 percent shot at a repair hammer.

10. You should start to hear Shelden talking when you reach this point…

11. …and you find the man himself here…

12. …behind this impassable gate. You can have a one-sided "chat" with him by walking up to the gate…

13. …or elicit an alternate comment by heading in the opposite direction instead. Belly up to the gate after he delivers this line for another alternate remark.

14. Falling-ceiling trap.

15. Collapsing-column trap.

16. Trapped statues.

If you prefer stealth play, don't let Shelden come with you. He just gets in the way. If you prefer to meet your challenges head on, go ahead and invite him to join you. In your company, Shelden can't be killed—just rendered unconscious. (If you turn him down, the idiot runs off on his own. Now the Knights can kill him…and probably will. Shelden's not an important character, but he delivers some colorful lines later on if you keep him alive long enough to say 'em.)

You can either shepherd him out of the dungeon now (he makes his way back to Passwall on his own once you leave Xeddefen), have him wait here (the best option), or have him follow you on down into the Obelisk enclosure. Beat down the priest and two Knight guards (plus any others the Obelisk pumps out before you're done), then move out. The place is collapsing about your head, and the whole level has turned into a trap. The collapse has also blocked the exit stairs…but a new entrance to a level called "Felles" has appeared just west of the blockage.

The "root door" notwithstanding, this is part and parcel of Xeddefen and it's collapsing, too. The good news is that it's collapsing on the Knights, and because they're beaten down, some are significantly easier to defeat than their comrades. There is only one path out now. All side passages quickly dead end. In the first room, use the western stairs and move cautiously through the hallways to the northwest, where a U-shaped root tunnel deposits you in a large east–west chamber. The gate up the stairs at the west end is closed, but the switch to open it is on a pedestal up the south stairs.

But wouldn't you know? The moment you step through the open gate, it closes behind you. Condemning you as "the worst escort in history," Shelden runs off to find his own way home, leaving you to explore the final collapsing level on your own. He gets in a final taunt: Toward the end of the east–west corridor at the beginning, you hear a voice. Turn north at the corner, and you see Shelden behind a closed gate, gloating that he found "the easy road."

You can't get through this gate, and there's nothing to find beyond the gate in any case. Your path lies south and east—through another heavily trapped hall that's also home to the last three Xeddefen Knights. Two of them are wussies. Kill 'em in a straight-up fight or bury 'em in rocks. Outside, you find yourself in Shelden's company by the water's edge between Xeddefen and Passwall. Talk to Mayor Putz and he says he's going to stay and rebuild the community. "These fools need me." Yeah, they'd have to be fools to need him!

Head north to find the spire in ruins and Udico/Desha wandering in the Passwall area. Seek her out. She's amazed at your survival, and notes that even with the tower's destruction,

The Fringe remains full of Knights of Order. You're to return to Sheogorath to sort out how to deal with them. (You also find Dredhwen, Passwall's eternally tired innkeeper, somewhere in the area. She doesn't have anything to say initially, but leave The Fringe and return to elicit her brief take on recent events.)

 Talk to Udico or Desha a second time for her take on rebuilding the village and how the spire's collapse brought on the collapse of Xeddefen itself. Most of the collapse, anyway. Should you return to the door you used to enter the dungeon, you find Xeddefen and Fain levels are still accessible, and any critters or treasures you left undisturbed are still there for your killing/grabbing pleasure. However, the exit from Fain to the Great Chamber is now blocked by debris. You can still enter the easternmost nub of Fales via the waterside exit, but you can't go far. Another cave-in blocks the passage west.

Use the Gates of Madness to reenter the Realm and then fast-travel to the Palace. You find a new trophy in the throne room: a Knight of Order helmet. Talk to Sheogorath and he promptly sends you off to reestablish contact with an unlikely ally.

REBUILDING THE GATEKEEPER

Now to make the Gates of Madness secure again. You're to pay a call on Relmyna Verenim to enlist her aid in creating a replacement for her late "child," the Gatekeeper. "Tell her you're working for me," says Sheogorath. "She'd do anything for me, that little minx."

Relmyna and protégé Nanette Don, formerly of Passwall, have removed to Xaselm—a deep hole in the ground northeast of the Gates of Madness. If you ask Haskill about Relmyna and then Xaselm, and tell him you like painting by numbers, he marks the location on your map and you can fast-travel there directly. If not, or if you tell him you're a DIY sort of bloke, it's easily reached on foot after you fast-travel to the Gates, Hardscrabble Camp to the south-southwest, or Blackroot Lair to the south. The exterior is guarded by two undead creatures, and you find the entrance up the stairs on the mountainside to the south.

Relmyna's been busy here. Also kinda sloppy. Scattered around the top level, you find five "Failed Experiments." Three of the critters are in a nook off a looping lairlike passage on the east side of the level, and another two under bridges at the northwest end of the second large room. They look like dead zombies, and most of them stay dead on your approach. However, one of the three in the nook is very much alive. it rises from the ground and attacks on your approach. You'll find these throughout the dungeon.

The entry level is pretty straightforward. Blast the 11 undead critters—four guaranteed to be either Shambles or Skeletons—from a healthy distance. Do not let the many trapped statues hit you with their Damage Health spells. There's just one closed gate, and the "open" button is right next to it.

 You can turn off traps by pushing the four buttons under the two bridges at the northwest end of the second large room.

MAIN QUEST

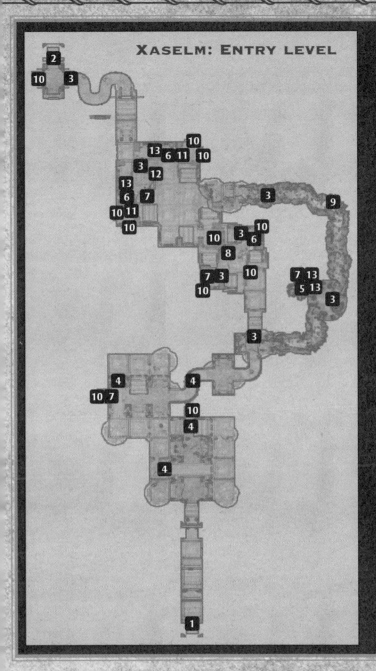

XASELM: ENTRY LEVEL

1. Exit to dungeon exterior (main entrance).

2. Exit to Experiment Chambers.

3. Flesh Atronach, a Skeleton, or a Skinned Hound.

4. Skeleton (if you haven't yet reached Level 9) or a Shambles.

5. Most of the Failed Experiments (#13) are just dead zombies. This one's still ticking.

6. Urn: One or two healing items and a 10 percent shot at a torch.

7. Three urns and a chest: You can count on gold. You can count on every fourth finger for ingredients, jewelry, and arrows, and every tenth finger for a potion, torch, weapon, and up to two pieces of armor. And since the whole finger thing is already getting kind of tired, we'll just say there's a 15 percent chance of finding a lockpick.

8. Madness Ore deposit.

9. #6…only in a hollowed stump and without the torch.

10. Trapped statues: They're turned off by the four buttons…

11. …at these two locations.

12. Three pieces of Mort Flesh. You also find this on the four dead failed experiments (#13) and the one live one (#5).

13. Dead Failed Experiments.

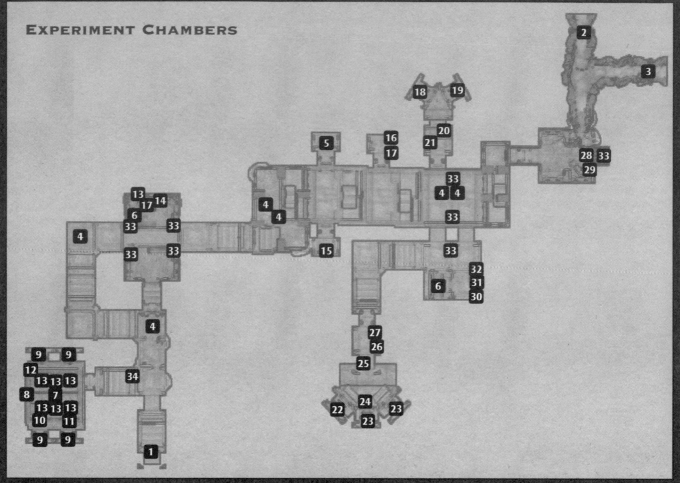

EXPERIMENT CHAMBERS

1. Exit to Xaselm's entry level.

2. Exit to Corpse Pit.

3. Exit to Sanctum of Vivisection.

4. Flesh Atronaches, Skeletons, or Skinned Hounds.

5. This corpse storage room contains four Failed Experiments—one of which rises from the ground on your approach and attacks!

6. More "live" Failed Experiments.

7. The inaccessible lower level is an arena where Relmyna Verenim is pitting two Shambles and a Skinned Hound against a Hunger. The young Altmer lady who appears on this spot is designed to make the Hunger fight more fiercely. You can't free the maiden, so go ahead: Hit the button at #8 and watch the results.

8. This button on the upper level opens the gate to the four cells on the north and south sides of the arena below.

9. The cells: The Hunger appears in the northwest one, the Shambles in the northeast and southwest, and a Skinned Hound in the southeast.

10. This button activates the six dart traps (#13) in the ceiling above the arena.

11. And this one removes the arena floor for a quick cleanup.

12. The scroll on this table lays out the experiment in detail.

13. Statues: The untrapped variety.

14. Down in this trench, Relmyna's running tests with the dart trap just to the west. Push the button here to activate it. This takes out the Failed Experiment just to the southwest.

15. Another storeroom, with five hanging corpses...and five bowls carefully arranged to catch their drippings. Each corpse contains a bone, a bit of gold, or other minor loot.

16. A full set of alchemy equipment.

17. Urn: One or two healing items and a 10 percent chance of a torch.

18. Skinned Hound.

19. Shambles.

20. This button releases both the Skinned Hound at #18 and the Shambles at #19 from their cells so they can have at it.

MAIN QUEST

21. Two log entries in scrolls on this table lay out the experiment. Here, Relmyna has been messing with the Hound's blood.

22. Scalon.

23. Baliwogs.

24. Evidently, a rather pudgy Breton.

25. This button opens all three cells to the south. The Scalon kills everything in sight…

26. …despite the fraternal bond alluded to in this log entry.

27. Chest: It contains gold and, in decreasing order of likelihood, an ingredient, jewelry, and arrows; a lockpick; or a potion, torch, and up to two pieces of armor.

28. A "boss" Flesh Atronach, guaranteed to be up to your own level.

29. Boss chest: What sorts of things does a Flesh Atronach collect? Gold, and a 75 percent chance of a lot more gold. That's pretty much a universal. They like jewelry (50 percent chance) and magic jewelry (10 percent), even if they don't wear it out in public. They dig armor and scrolls—25 percent chances of up to two pieces of each. There's also a 10 percent chance of magic armor. And, in small ways, they like combat-related skill books, alchemical equipment, staffs, both magic and conventional weapons, and soul gems (10 percent each, with two shots at the soul gems).

30. On this table, there are three samples of Mort Flesh and a mortar and pestle.

31. This bookshelf holds four samples of Void Essence, most of an alchemical kit (the missing alembic's just to the north), three healing potions, and two Restore Strength potions.

32. And this table holds two portions of Bonemeal, an alembic, and mortar and pestle.

33. Trapped statue.

34. An emerald!

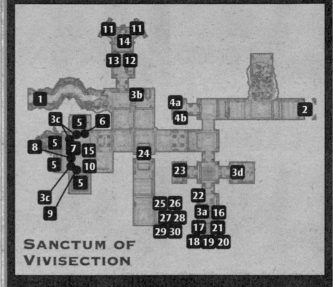

SANCTUM OF VIVISECTION

1. Exit to the Experiment Chambers.

2. Exit to dungeon exterior (back entrance): Relmyna supplies the key.

3a-3d. Relmyna Verenim: You deal with her twice here—once to get an assignment to collect four ingredients, and once to report their collection from the Gardens of Flesh and Bone. She's always around, though we can't say where with authority. Her location depends on the time of day, where you are in the "Rebuilding the Gatekeeper" mission, and whether you've done a little side quest. But she doesn't wander far. Just follow your quest target. When you return to her with the four ingredients for the creation of the new Gatekeeper, she should be at #3b. And once a day she worships at the small shrine to Sheogorath at #3d.

4a-4b. Nanette Don: Not a party to this quest, but Relmyna's big-mouthed student is here, too. Once the "Through the Fringe of Madness" mission is complete, she migrates from Passwall to Xaselm, where she eats, sleeps, and works through the day.

5. The guinea pigs in Relmyna's pain experiments. She tortures them with spells, then asks how they feel about it, and brings them back to life when they die. Somehow, we doubt that all the necessary permission slips have been signed for this trip to Hell. You can save the victims from further torment by sacrificing yourself to a stat-damaging spell from Relmyna. The prisoners vanish from the cells on your next visit to the Sanctum. Or you can participate in the torture by pushing the buttons at #6 through #10.

6. This button sets off dart traps above the cell to the north.

7. This button sets off spike traps in the cell to the west.

8. These two buttons fire Damage Health spells from the two statues at the rear of the cell to the west (top button for the left statue, bottom for the right).

9. This button activates dart traps in the cell to the south and opens up the floor afterward to clean up the mess.

10. This one opens the ceiling to admit a body falling from the tower above and then opens the floor. Alone among the prisoners, this one is not tortured by Relmyna.

11. Live Flesh Atronaches.

12. This button opens their cages. Needless to say, they fight.

13. And this one activates the three dart traps above the central portion of the enclosure to the north…

14. …here.

15. Another of Relmyna's log entries on the table here…

16. …and one here. Also on this table: a flawless topaz, a pearl, a ruby, and a jewelry box. This contains one to three items of jewelry (with a 10 percent chance of a magic one) and possibly a potion (also a 10 percent chance).

17. A mortar and pestle, two portions of Shambles Marrow, and one each of Bonemeal and Scalon Fin.

18. Three healing and two Restore Strength potions, plus two pieces of alchemical equipment (a calcinator, and a retort). On an adjacent stand, there's a copy of *The Shivering Bestiary*.

19. A little library: *The Blessings of Sheogorath*, *From Frog to Man*, *The Liturgy of Affliction*, *The Living Wood*, *Myths of Sheogorath*, *The Shivering Apothecary*, and *Zealotry*.

20. Two Hound Teeth, two portions of Void Essence, an alembic, and two more books: *Bark and Sap* and *An Elytra's Life*.

21. A clothing cupboard—worth mentioning only because of the itsy-bitsy chance you come up with an item needed in the Miscellaneous Quest "The Museum of Oddities."

22. Relmyna's Skinned Hound: Pet…or just another unfortunate victim? We're unsure. All we can say is that, predictably, it's dead.

23. Dumping ground for Failed Experiments and Mort Flesh.

24. This passage doesn't open up until after you return to the Sanctum with the ingredients Relmyna needs to fire up the new Gatekeeper. You visit the room at the end to select body parts. Note that these control the "gift" you can receive from the Gatekeeper once it's on station at the Gates of Madness.

25. The two selectable heads.

26. The two hearts.

27. The two sets of legs…

28. …and torsos.

29. The three left arms…

30. …and three right arms.

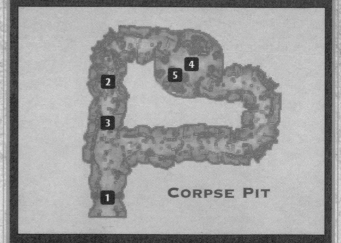

CORPSE PIT

1. Exit to the Experiment Chambers.

2. A hole in the corridor floor allows you to drop down to this small level's innermost recess…:

3. …and the Hollowed Amber Limb therein. Note that this appears on the lower level—not the upper, as displayed here. This limb contains one piece of Amber for sure and as many as four additional pieces, with 50 percent chances for three of them and a one percent chance for the fourth. It's an odd-shaped piece connected to the Miscellaneous Quest "The Museum of Oddities."

4. This level's filled with 18 dead bodies—16 Failed Experiments and 2 Test Subjects. However, an additional three Failed Experiments are still alive and kicking. They're clustered here.

5. Boss chest: Identical in potential contents to the one at #29 on the Experiment Chambers level.

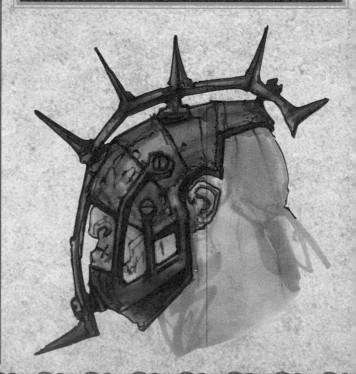

Gardens of Flesh and Bone:
Entry level

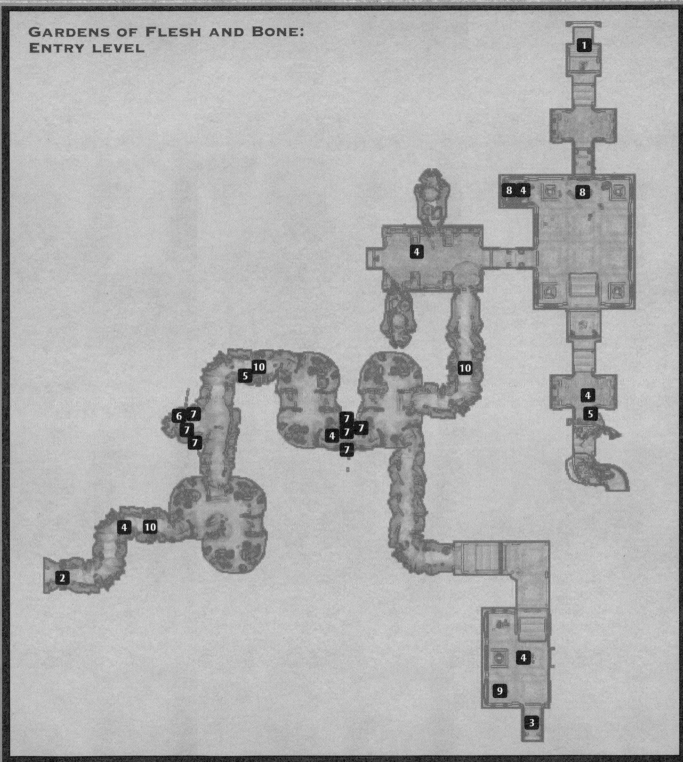

MAIN QUEST

1. Exit to dungeon exterior
2. Exit to Natatorium of Wound Bled Tears. You won't use this door until you're on your way out of the dungeon.
3. Exit to the Conservatorium Corpusculum.
4. Flesh Atronach, Skeleton, or Skinned Hound.
5. Hollowed stump and an urn: Gold, always. Some

kind of armor or magic armor is also likely. You get four 10 percent shots at it and a 5 percent shot at magic heavy armor. You get a gem and Amber a quarter of the time; jewelry or magic jewelry a fifth of the time; a 10 percent shot at a soul gem, arrows, a potion, a scroll, and a weapon; and a two percent chance at an item needed in the Miscellaneous Quest "The Museum of Oddities."

6. Hollowed stump: One or two healing-related items.

7. Spike trap: There are more of these in the western cluster than appear here; we couldn't fit them all in!

8. Falling-ceiling trap.

9. Trapped statue.

10. Root gate: You can get through the first of these on your way south to the Conservatorium Corpusculum. However, the pull pods that open the other two are inaccessible until you reenter the level from the Natatorium of Wound Bled Tears on your way out on the dungeon.

You soon find yourself at the entrance to the "Experiment Chambers." This isn't a particularly difficult level. If you want to just hustle through, use the northern of the two corridors to the west as you enter the level, cross the bridge, and drop down the successive tiers to the east. En route, you face a half-dozen guards—all either Skeletons, Skinned Hounds, or Flesh Atronachs. The last enemy, a boss waiting in the ruined chamber at the level's eastern extremity, is a leveled Flesh Atronach. North of the boss, the tunnel splits. The east branch goes to the Sanctum of Vivisection, where you find Relmyna and Nanette, and the north route goes to the Corpse Pit. Here, in a looping corridor, you find 19 more "Failed Experiments" and two "Test Subjects." Be warned: three of the experiments aren't quite dead.

If you do hustle through Experiment Chambers, you skip over much of the fun here—reading Relmyna's four coolly clinical research documents and playing around with her undead toys. Current studies in the Chambers include: the effects of a dart trap at a (dead) headless zombie; what passes between a starving Scalon and Baliwog once pudgy prey is introduced into their enclosure; a battle between a juiced-up Skinned Hound and a Shambles; and down the first hall to the west, another between two Shambles and a Hunger aroused to ferocity by the presence of fresh meat (in the form of the Altmer lady).

The button to the west on the player's level opens the four gates down in the pit, the western of the two buttons to the south fires darts down into the enclosure, and the eastern opens the pit floor.

In the Sanctum, you may well hear screams. If so, this means Relmyna is in the west wing experimenting on three test subjects. "Sadist" doesn't quite describe her. She's brutal, but utterly passionless. She'll kill a caged victim with spells, resurrect her, and then ask calmly, "Please indicate on a scale of one to ten, how much pain you are feeling at this moment."

If she's not there, you find her either asleep in her east-wing quarters (midnight to 6 a.m.), praying to Sheogorath at the altar just down the hall, or checking on the dead Atronach on the slab just east of the Sanctum entrance.

If you want to participate in this "research," you can. (cough) Heartless bastard. (cough) The buttons outside the cells supply additional sources of pain—darts, spikes, fire balls—and in two cells, trapped floors open to clean up the mess. Or you can put a stop to it in a side quest. Heal up first, for the pain of Relmyna's victims shortly becomes your pain.

Ask Relmyna about "victims," and she's claim they're "volunteers of one sort or another." Riiight. You can then back off or order Relmyna to knock off the torture. She replies like an intelligent lunatic, but acquiescing—provided you're willing to accept the suffering yourself. Agree and she promises not to experiment on "*these* people" (meaning she plans to sign up new victims), and she tears into you with an Exalted Pain spell that takes five points off your Strength, Agility, Willpower, and Endurance attributes, plus knocks down Health and Magicka by 50. (Back out now, and you won't get another opportunity to persuade her to release the prisoners.) Now try out the "exalted pain" topic and she provides you with the Manacles of Pain, which boost your Strength and Willpower by five points but drain Endurance and Intelligence by 10.

You want to get fixed up before the next phase of your mission, so visit the Sacellum Arden-Sul and activate the altar. The Blessing of Arden-Sul restores all eight attributes and Magicka, and cures disease. You have to repair your Health on your own. When you return to the Sanctum, you find the cells empty.

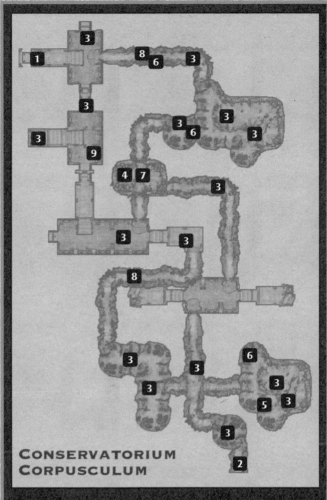

CONSERVATORIUM CORPUSCULUM

1. Exit to Gardens of Flesh and Bone (entry level).

2. Exit the Caverns of Susurration.

3. Leveled Flesh Atronach, Skinned Hound, Shambles, or Skeleton.

4. Dermis Membrane: Activate to collect this ingredient for Relmyna Verenim.

5. Osseous Marrow: Ditto.

6. Three hollowed stumps and an urn: See #5 on the entry level map.

7. Hollowed stump: See #6 on the entry level map.

8. Root gates: The one east of the level entrance can't be opened initially—the adjacent pull pod is on the far side—but the one south-southeast of the entrance can.

9. Okay, whose bottle of beer is this? Ordinarily, we wouldn't mention it, but it's the only discrete item on this big level…and Relmyna doesn't seem like the type to throw back a brew.

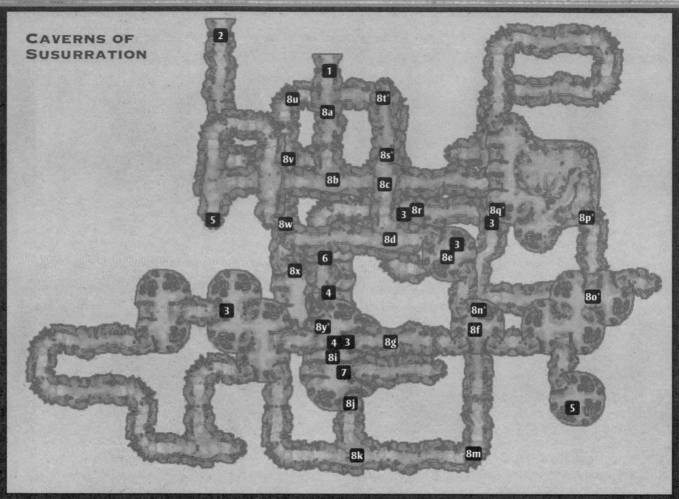

CAVERNS OF SUSURRATION

1. Exit to the Conservatorium Corpusculum.

2. Exit to the Natatorium of Wound Bled Tears.

3. Hunger.

4. Also Hungers, but these appear on a lower level than displayed here.

5. Hollowed stumps: See #5 on the entry level map.

6. A "boss" hollowed stump: Surprise! Gold is not a metaphysical certainty here. You have a 50 percent chance of a small sum and a 25 percent chance of an additional 20–745 in leveled gold. The only certainty is Amber, with a 50 percent chance of a second piece or a piece of equipment made from Amber. You also have 50 percent shots at a potion and each of two scrolls; 25 percent chances at a gem and magic jewelry; and 10 percent chances at armor (heavy, light, and magic), a piece of alchemical apparatus, a staff, a magic weapon, and up to two soul gems. Note that this stump is on a level lower than advertised.

7. Essence of Breath: What you're here to get. It's a two-stage affair. Activate it, wait a moment or two while the invisible pharmacist bottles it up for you, and then activate the little bottle that appears to collect this component for Verenim. This, too, is on a lower level than it appears here.

8a-8y: To prevent you from getting lost in this maze, use the nice fog—which is accompanied by a whispering sound (the "susurration")—that leads you from the level entrance to the Essence. In this book, you have to settle for breadcrumbs—8a, 8b, and so forth—with an asterisk to denote those portions of the path on lower levels than pictured here. The four root gates along this path all open automatically on your approach.

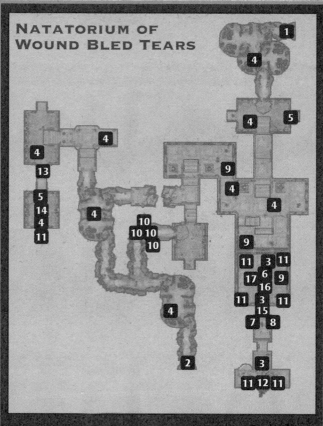

NATATORIUM OF WOUND BLED TEARS

1. Exit to Gardens of Flesh and Bone (entry level).

2. Exit to the Caverns of Susurration.

3. Flesh Atronach.

4. Leveled Flesh Atronach, Skinned Hound, Shambles, or Skeleton.

5. Chests: See #3 in the Conservatorium Corpusculum. The western of the two has a one- to five-tumbler lock.

6. Conceivably, this chest is empty. It's not likely, but none of the dozen types of potential loot is guaranteed to appear. Gold, the two scrolls and the single potion have a 50 percent chance of showing up. A gem, ingredient, and magic jewelry all have a 25 percent chance; and the alchemical apparatus, staff, magic armor, and weapons, or two soul gems all have 10 percent shots.

7. An urn containing one or two healing items.

8. A boss urn with the same potential contents as the stump at #6 in the Caverns of Susurration.

9. Falling-ceiling trap.

10. Spike traps: The trigger's the little mushroom-y patch on the floor.

11. Trapped statues.

12. Blood Liqueur.

13. This room is a trap. When you approach the chest at #5 to the south, the door all of a sudden gets very

locked (all five tumblers) and the statue at the south end starts blasting. And then there's the undead critter at #4. To unlock the door, hit the button at #14.

14. This button unlocks the door at #13.

15. This door is opened…

16. …by the button here.

17. But not by this button, which gets you pounded simultaneously by all four of the surrounding trapped statues…

18. …Or by this one, which dumps the ceiling on your head

Talk to Relmyna. You can adopt different tones with her and extract different responses, but bottom line, she agrees to help create a replacement Gatekeeper. However, she's still mourning the old one and unwilling to return to his "womb" in the Gardens of Flesh and Bone. That's your job. Relmyna provides a laundry list of the required components—Blood Liqueur, Osseous Marrow, Dermis Membrane, and Essence of Breath—and a key that works with both the Gardens' interior and a private surface entrance to the Sanctum that connects directly with the surface. Use the exit at the east end of the Sanctum, and you find yourself in a valley northwest of Xaselm. Off you go. Fast-travel to the Gates of Madness and then make your way on foot through Passwall and west-northwest to the Gardens.

The first level may seem a puzzle. Once you've cleared the large room south of the entrance and the smaller chamber to the west, where can you go? Try the passage that leads south from the western room. Yes, it's blocked by roots, but the roots function as a gate and the pod on the passage's right side is an unconventional pull cord. The trapped passage to the west ends with more blocking roots—no pod this time—so make your way south again to another stone chamber. At the south end, you find a metal door to the Conservatorium Corpusculum.

Once out in the main corridor, head south and then east. Just before you turn climb stairs at the east end of the hall, turn north and climb the slope into a lairlike tunnel. Drop off the bridge just ahead, and activate any one of the four Dermis Membrane plants here to retrieve that ingredient. Follow the passage east and south to another stone room and head briefly west and then south, up the slope, into another lairlike passage. Follow the first passage east and, in the room at the end of the hall, climb the root to the upper level and an Osseous Marrow plant. Activate this as well to collect the requested sample. Now backtrack to the last intersection and head south to the Caverns of Susurration.

The last part of the Conservatorium only looked like a maze. The Caverns really are one—but only if you miss the clues to the correct path. The builders have dropped a bunch of breadcrumbs for you—not only a rail of Withering Moon plants but a cloud of fog that shushes you as it moves along the correct path to a glowing Essence of Breath plant. It'd almost be too easy if it wasn't for the seven leveled Hungers that inhabit this level. They're tough little critters who can resist Fire attacks, but they're weak against Shock.

Activate the plant and a little flask appears. Wait a moment or two and then activate the flask. Now you just need the Blood Liqueur. That's down on the final level: The Natatorium of Wound Bled Tears. To find the entrance, just retreat to the last intersection and follow the passage west and north.

In the Natatorium, at the branch in the corridor, head north and follow the corridor east and south, down the stairs to a chamber guarded by a pair of Flesh Atronachs. The door is remotely operated, but the remote's just a short ways away—on the south side of the bier at the center of the room. In the flooded room beyond, you face a boss-level Atronach…and find the Blood Liqueur plant bursting through the south wall. Take a sample and you get a journal entry bumping you back to Relmyna. And, no, you don't have to trek all the way back through the preceding levels. You also have a new map marker. Just follow it north and east to an entrance the dungeon's top level and then northeast again to its exit. Fast-travel to Passwall, hoof it through the Gates of Madness, and fast-travel again to Xaselm's secret entrance.

Within, seek out Relmyna at the usual locations—minus the cells, if you did the little self-sacrifice side quest above—to learn that in your absence she's created different versions of various body parts: a pair of legs, left and right arms, torso, head, and heart. They're laid out in a newly accessible section of the Sanctum—south of the dead Atronachs—and you get to choose which ones appear in the final version. "Artist's prerogative," says the necromancer.

Just trot down there and select one of each for a journal recommending you trot back to Relmyna. The heads Angry Mind and Helm of Power invest the giant with the Ability to bump up its respective Willpower and Strength stats, and the Legs of Nimbleness and Legs of Fortitude its respective Agility and Endurance. The hearts of Spell Turning and Wound Sharing provide respective Reflect Spell and Reflect Damage abilities. The three left arms offer shields against Fire, Frost, and Shock, while the three right arms provide boosts in the Blade skill (the Arm of Slashing) or Blunt skill (the Arms of Chopping and Bashing). Finally, the torsos Breast of Life and Breast of Magic carry with them 50-point Fortify Health and Fortify Magicka abilities.

 If you change your mind about any or all of these components, just return to this room before finalizing things with Verenim and swap out the body parts by selecting new ones.

Does it make a difference which parts you choose? Not in terms of the critter's job as Gatekeeper. He has one Main Quest encounter with the Order—he can go up against gangs of adventurers once the Main Quest is complete—and, however equipped, he's going to knock down all comers like so many bowling pins.

Then again, think of the body parts in terms of powers you'd like to have yourself. Once the new Gatekeeper goes live, you're able to augment your own powers based on the ones you've given him. (Read on for details.)

Once you've spoken to her, Relmyna asks you to meet her at Sheogorath's statue in The Fringe—that's the huge bust just on the other side of the Gates of Madness—and then heads for the Sanctum's secret exit. Walk with her or fast-travel. Either way, talk to the lady again when she arrives and ask her to begin the ceremony. She instructs you to place the Gatekeeper's body into the Cistern of Substantiation—the mystical pool that just now appeared before the statue. Activate it and all six parts appear in the pool and sink from view. Relmyna begins her incantation and, in sequence, instructs to you place the Dermis Membrane, Blood Liqueur, Osseous Marrow, and Essence of Breath into the cistern. A Flesh Atronach now appears and walks into the middle of the swirling pool. (Don't bother trying to play Marco Polo with this critter; it just stops the ceremony until you're clear of the Cistern.)

Then it vanishes. A great light rises from the water. There's an explosion—it knocks you down, but you're undamaged—and a greater monster steps forth. You're greater, too: you now have a new Greater Power—the ability to summon a Flesh Atronach for two minutes. Relmyna gives the creature its task and then makes herself scarce. You can, too…or you can stick around and watch the show. Four Knights of Order are headed up the hill from Passwall, followed by none other than Felas Sarandas in his new role as Priest of Order. Yeah, he's dead. They're all dead.

And, no, you've nothing to fear from Gatekeeper II—unless you attack it. Which doesn't get you anything; you can't kill this one. However, activate its body for a new Greater Power. (Activate it repeatedly to cycle through the seven available choices; each replaces the one before it.) If you gave a power to the Gatekeeper, he gives it back to you now. These 14 "gifts" are all time-limited versions of the new Gatekeeper's abilities, with a one-minute durations for head, leg, right arm, and torso powers, and 30-second durations for the heart and left-arm powers. All but two of the gifts have the same magnitudes as the Gatekeeper's abilities. The exceptions are the two for the torso, which both have magnitudes of 100.)

Return to the Palace. Check out your new trophy—the new Gatekeeper's melee weapon—and talk to Sheogorath. He's delighted about your achievement. But his delight doesn't last long.

And, in fact, neither does Sheogorath himself.

The Lord discloses what you may already have guessed: Sheogorath is Jyggalag. During the Greymarch, the former fades out and the latter fades in. This process can't be stopped, but your intercession can prevent the god from permitting his darker side from destroying his own Realm.

In the middle of your exchange with the Daedric Prince, a messenger appears and runs up to Sheogorath. If the messenger is a Golden Saint (meaning you killed Syl back in "The Ritual of Accession"), she reports an assault by the Order on the Saints' stronghold at Brellach. If a Seducer, he reports a similar attack on the Seducer base at Pinnacle Rock. In either case, you're expected to hook up with the commander of the surviving forces that are waiting outside the stronghold, then sortie to the relief of the Saints/Seducers chief in one of two virtually identical dungeons.

Haskill clarifies that this won't be easy: If the Order's attacking a stronghold, its forces must be strong. They are. In each case, you face a total of 29 Knights and 11 or 12 Priests of Order.

On the Saints side, you find Brellach well north-northwest of New Sheoth on the north side of a peninsula known as Saints Watch. The closest locations discovered during the Main Quest are Dunroot Burrow to the southwest and Frenzied Camp to the south, and they're not all that close. You trim some cross-country footwork if you've located the Heretic Mage stronghold of Cann, or the village of Highcross at the peninsula's southern base. On the stairs just north of the entrance, you find commander Issmi and two generic Saint warriors. Issmi explains that Thadon betrayed the fortress and that Saints' chief Staada is being held in the base near the waters of the Wellspring. (Remember Staada? You may have killed her in the Daedra goddess Azura's quest in *Morrowind*. But Daedra eventually come back, and so has Staada—only to become a victim again.)

If you're working with Seducers, you face a long haul. Pinnacle Rock's near the tip of the southern peninsula known as Madgod's Boot. The closest you can get by fast travel is Xedilian (from the "A Better Mousetrap" quest), and you still face a long trek southwest through a spartan (and then increasingly lush) countryside. En route, you pass Backwash Camp, the heretic-mage dungeon, Xiditte, Lost Time Camp, Corpserot Prison, and an Obelisk (west of the prison). You meet Adeo and two generic Seducers on a little bridge south of the fortress entrance. Adeo reports that Syl betrayed the base and that Seducer-in-chief Dylora has been captured by the Order and imprisoned within.

GOLDEN SAINTS: BRELLACH

BRELLACH: HALL OF HONOR

[Map with numbered markers: 12d, 12d, 12b, 12b, 12c, 2, 11, 10, 12, 12a, 9, 6, 7, 4, 3, 5, 7, 11, 6, 5, 8, 10, 5, 5, 4, 5, 6, 5, 1]

1. Exit to dungeon exterior.

2. Exit to Hall of Reverence.

3. Exit to Font of Rebirth. This door is unlocked once you complete your business on the Font level.

4. Closed gates: Don't worry, you open them on your way out of the dungeon.

5. Knights of Order.

6. Priests of Order.

7. Crystalline walls: Break them down by ringing the chime at #8.

8. Chime: Bang the gong and the crystalline walls at #7 shatter, giving you access to the Crystal Chest at #9.

9. Crystal Chest: Like others of its type, this chest requires a Heart of Order to open. Inside, there's a soul gem, perhaps a modest amount of gold, and a

healing potion. There are also fair shots at alchemical equipment, a scroll, a weapon, and additional gold. Less likely are jewelry, a repair hammer, armor, magic arrows, and an additional potion. The trick is getting to the chest. The crystalline walls at #7 block the way and you're not directed to the solution (ringing the chime at #8) until you meet Staada at #8 in the Hall of Reverence level.

10. An urn containing one or two healing items

11. Chest and an urn: Gold. You know that. However, the chances for other loot are poor. 25 percent for heavy armor, 15 percent for a lockpick, and 10 percent for a repair hammer, magic heavy armor, arrows, stealthy potion, scroll, or weapon. The urn, near the Hall of Reverence exit, has a leveled lock with one to five tumblers.

12-12d. Reinforcements? Depends. Your companion Issmi can't be killed in combat, but the two Golden Saint warriors accompanying her can. If they're still intact when you hit the trigger at #12, you won't find anything in the room at #12a. However, if you've lost one or both warriors, you encounter one or two replacements at #12b and a single Knight of Order at #12c. Talk to one of the replacements—if there's just the one, he's shielded from the view of the Knight by the column—and they take your orders. They're not as good as the originals—these Saints are "inferior males" four levels below your own—but if you lose them in the battle, you're compensated with an additional one or two Saints who appear at #12d.

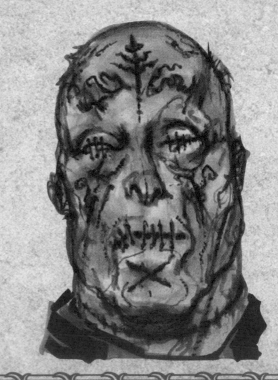

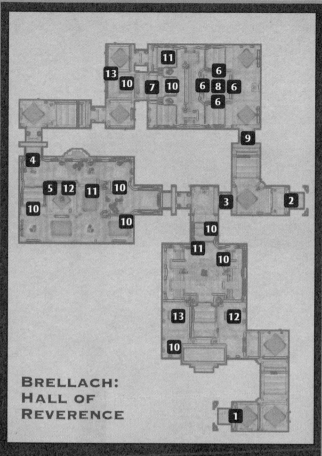

BRELLACH: HALL OF REVERENCE

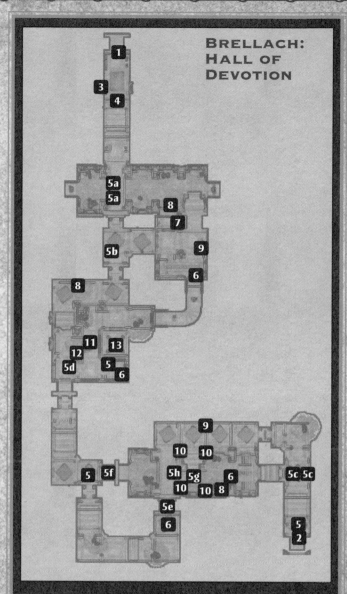

BRELLACH: HALL OF DEVOTION

1. Exit to the Hall of Honor.

2. Exit to the Hall of Devotion.

3. Closed gate: You can't open this from the east side until you free Staada at #8.

4. However, this gate can be opened by pushing the button…

5. …here.

6. Crystalline walls: As in the Hall of Honor, these can be broken down by ringing the chime…

7. …here.

8. This frees Golden Saint leader Staada, who joins the party and unlocks the previously locked door…

9. …here.

10. Knights of Order.

11. Priests of Order.

12. Chest and an urn: Each holds one or two Restoration-related potions.

13. Chest and an urn: Just like the containers at #11 in the Hall of Honor. The southern of the two has a leveled lock of one to five tumblers.

1. Exit to the Hall of Reverence. It's also here that Staada utters some halting words about the forces of Order stopping up the Wellspring and, with the other Saints, drops to the floor. You're on your own. We don't mean to be unsympathetic, but this would be a good time to take Staada's Golden Longsword—a nice, unenchanted, one-handed blade.

2. Exit to the Font of Rebirth.

3. Ring this chime…

4. …to shatter the crystalline wall here

5. Knights of Order.

5a-5b. These two Knights begin their patrol when you approach the bridge. Starting under the bridge, they make their way east to the stairs, south up the stairs, and west down the corridor to #5b. That makes it easy to snipe one of 'em or simply avoid them both. What's your pleasure?

5c-5h. These Knights start their patrol when you enter the western half of the big room to their west. They head west through the gate, north up the stairs, cross the bridge, and then wind their way west and north…all the way to #5d. This clears them out of your path to the level exit. If you're sneaky, trigger their patrol by entering the gate at #5e, then backtrack to the gate at #5f and avoid them altogether. If you're feeling combative, wait until the Knights advance to #5g and then hit the button at #5h. This triggers the trapped statues at #10.

6. Priests of Order.

7. Crystal Chest: Just like the one at #9 back in the Hall of Honor.

8. An urn with one or two Restoration-related items.

9. Still like the containers back at #11 in the Hall of Honor.

10. Trapped statues.

11. Falling-ceiling trap.

12. Collapsing-column trap.

13. Ignore the other six other chimes you find on this level, four of which are in the corners of this small room. They're inaccessible.

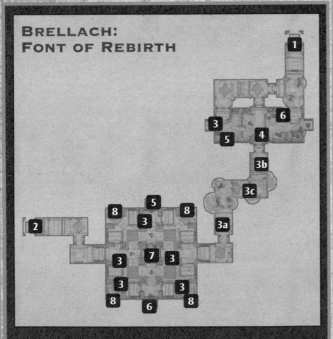

BRELLACH: FONT OF REBIRTH

1. Exit to the Hall of Devotion.

2. Exit to the Hall of Honor, which is locked up tight until the Wellspring flows again.

3. Knights of Order.

3a-3c. #3a is a patrolling Knight of Order. Once you reach #3b, the Knight starts to move to #3c—

meaning you're going to run right into him as you head west around the corner.

4. Priest of Order: Easy target for a snipe.

5. Urn containing one or two Restoration-related items.

6. Chests: #11 from the Hall of Honor revisited. The northern of the two has a leveled lock of one to five tumblers.

7. The Wellspring: Remove the Order's crystal plug by ringing the chimes (#8) in the room's four corners

8. Chimes: Ring each to shatter the plug blocking the Wellspring at #7. Then hook up with Staada and head west to the exit to the Hall of Honor.

DARK SEDUCERS: PINNACLE ROCK

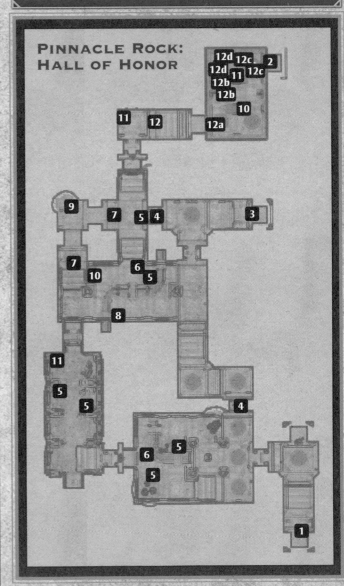

PINNACLE ROCK: HALL OF HONOR

MAIN QUEST

1. Exit to dungeon exterior.

2. Exit to Hall of Reverence.

3. Exit to the Font of Rebirth: This door is unlocked once you complete your business on the Font level.

4. Closed gates: You can open these from the other side on your way out of the dungeon.

5. Knights of Order.

6. Priests of Order.

7. Crystalline walls: Ring the chime at #8 to make them shatter.

8. Chime: Activate it, and the crystalline walls at #7 splinter into crystal shards, giving you access to the Crystal Chest at #9.

9. Crystal Chest: Like others of its type, this requires a Heart of Order to open. Inside is a soul gem, perhaps a modest amount of gold, and a healing potion. Plus, there are fair shots at alchemical equipment, a scroll, a weapon, and additional gold. Less likely are jewelry, a repair hammer, armor (conventional and magic), magic arrows, and an additional potion. The trick is getting to the chest. The crystalline walls at #7 block the way and you're not directed to the solution (ringing the chime at #8) until you meet Dylora at #8 in the Hall of Reverence level.

10. Chest and an urn: Each holds healing items.

11. Urns: Gold (always), a repair hammer or light armor 25 percent of the time, and a gem, jewelry, magic light armor, arrows, a combat-related potion, scroll, and weapon 10 percent of the time. The one in the hallway leading to the Hall of Reverence exit room has a leveled lock of one to five tumblers.

12-12d. Reinforcements? It depends. Your companion Adeo can't be killed in combat, but the two Dark Seducer Warriors accompanying her can. If they're still intact when you hit the trigger at #12, you won't find anything in the room at #12a. However, if you've lost one or both warriors, you encounter one or two replacements at #12b and two Knights of Order at #12c.

Replacements appear within easy striking distance of the new Knights, and it's entirely possible to lose them before you can recruit them. While the Knights are the standard leveled ones that appear throughout this dungeon, the Dark Seducers are "inferior males" four levels below your own. The good news: You're compensated for these additional losses with an additional one or two Seducers who appear at #12d. Talk to the replacements and they follow your orders. The female warriors aren't answerable to you.

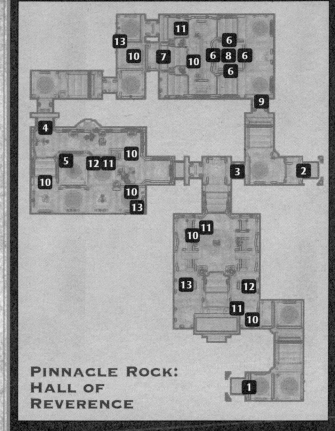

PINNACLE ROCK: HALL OF REVERENCE

1. Exit to the Hall of Honor.

2. Exit to the Hall of Devotion.

3. Closed gate: You can't open this from the east side until you free Dylora at #8.

4. However, this gate can be opened by pushing the button…

5. …here.

6. Crystalline walls: As in the Hall of Honor, these can be broken down by ringing the chime…

7. …here.

8. This frees Dark Seducer leader Dylora, who joins the party and unlocks the previously locked door…

9. …here.

10. Knights of Order.

11. Priests of Order.

12. Chest and an urn: Each holds one or two healing-related potions.

13. Two chests and an urn: Just like the containers at #11 in the Hall of Honor. The one on the bier west of the stairs descending into the first big room has a leveled lock of one to five tumblers.

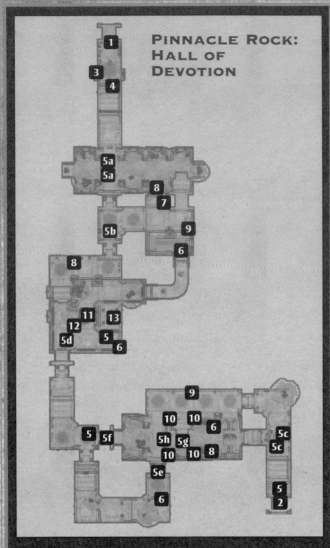

PINNACLE ROCK: HALL OF DEVOTION

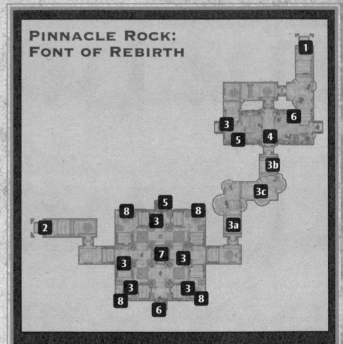

of your path to the level exit. If you're sneaky, trigger their patrol by entering the gate at #5e, then backtrack to the gate at #5f and avoid them altogether. If you're feeling combative, wait until the Knights advance to #5g and then hit the button at #5h. This triggers the trapped statues at #10.

6. Priests of Order.

7. Crystal Chest: Just like the one at #9 back in the Hall of Honor.

8. An urn with one or two Restoration-related items.

9. Still like the containers back at #11 in the Hall of Honor. The northern of the two has a leveled lock of one to five tumblers.

10. Trapped statues.

11. Falling-ceiling trap.

12. Collapsing-column trap.

13. Ignore the other six other chimes you find on this level, four of which are in the corners of this small room. They're all inaccessible.

PINNACLE ROCK: FONT OF REBIRTH

1. Exit to the Hall of Reverence. It's also here that Dylora utters some halting words about the forces of Order stopping up the Wellspring and, with the other Seducers, drops to the floor. You're on your own.

2. Exit to the Font of Rebirth.

3. Ring this chime…

4. …to shatter the crystalline wall here

5. Knights of Order.

5a-5b. These two Knights begin their patrol when you approach the bridge. Starting under the bridge, they make their way east to the stairs, south up the stairs, and west down the corridor to #5b. That makes it easy to snipe one of 'em or simply to avoid them both. What's your pleasure?

5c-5h. These Knights start their patrol when you enter the western half of the big room to their west. They head west through the gate, north up the stairs, cross the bridge, and then wind their way west and north…all the way to this spot. This clears them out

1. Exit to the Hall of Devotion.

2. Exit to the Hall of Honor: Locked up tight until the Wellspring flows again.

3. Knights of Order.

3a-3c. #3a is a patrolling Knight of Order. Once you reach #3b, it starts to move to #3c—meaning you're going to run right into it as you round the corner to the west (unless you back off a bit).

4. Priest of Order: Easy target for a snipe

5. Urn containing one or two Restoration-related items

6. Chests: #11 from the Hall of Honor revisited. The northern of the two has a leveled lock of one to five tumblers.

7. The Wellspring: To remove the Order's crystal plug, ring the chimes (#8) in the room's four corners.

8. Chimes: Ring each of the four to shatter the plug blocking the Wellspring at #7. Then hook up with Dylora and head west to the exit to the Hall of Honor.

Either way, give the commander the go-ahead and move in with the three allies in tow. Slow and steady wins this race here. You'll want to methodically clear out the Knights and Priests of Order. Keep your little band close to you for mutual support—you maintain numerical superiority throughout these levels—and give them a chance to heal up before you move on again. Don't worry about most of the gates you can't immediately open. The only one you have to pass through is in the northwest corner of the Halls of Reverence's first section. To find the button, head south from the gate, up the stairs, and make a U-turn at the top into an alcove. The button is on the right side of the left-hand pedestal.

Beyond the gate, a hall leads to a large room. Staada/Dylora is imprisoned at its center. Talk to her through the gap on the east side of the enclosure. She explains that you can't break through the barrier and asks you to ring the chime to shatter it. What chime? No one explains further at this stage, but you now have a new map marker for the location atop the stairs just west of Staada's prison. It's more like a temple gong! Activate it to give it a bang, and the sympathetic vibration breaks the Saint/Seducer chief out of the slammer.

Talk to her again. She signs on with the party, elaborates on the treachery that led to her imprisonment, and stresses the importance reaching the Wellspring. It's the Saints/Seducers connection between the Waters of Oblivion (where Daedra go when they "die") and the Shivering Isles, and its destruction would mean their destruction.

The door in the southeast corner of the room is now unlocked. Follow the corridor beyond to the entrance to the Hall of Devotion. You no sooner enter than your party members drop dead—Staada/Dylora with some parting remarks about the Order having stopped up the Wellspring. You have to un-stop it on your own.

Start by un-stopping this passage—activating the chime on the west wall to shatter the barrier blocking the way south. You have to clear out seven more Knights and four priests to reach the Font of Rebirth to the southeast. We recommend sneaking, because a number of enemies here are vulnerable to ambush.

Follow the flowing water. In the Font, make your way south-southeast until you find a large room with a pyramid at its center. As you descend the stairs, you get a journal entry that this is the Wellspring and that you need to destroy its frosting of Order crystals to get it flowing again. The simple part: you need to activate the chimes in the room's four corners. The not-so-simple part: the room is defended by five Knights. However, with Nighteye, successful sneaking (stay out of the light at the tops of the stairs), and good aim, you can take most of them down from a distance.

Once the Wellspring flows again, you get a journal entry advising you to chat up Staada/Dylora. But isn't she…dead? Yeah. But evidently the Wellspring is running at peak efficiency today and everyone who died at the beginning of the Hall of Devotion has been recycled back into action. (Your three original comrades are even following you again temporarily.) The chief Saint/Seducer is somewhere around the Wellspring. Just track her down by her map marker for her thanks, a Summon Golden Saint or Dark Seducer spell, and leveled Golden Saint or Dark Seducer Armor (unenchanted heavy and light armor, respectively). Exit through the passage west of the Wellspring to enter a previously inaccessible section of the Hall of Honor and the dungeon exit.

SYMBOLS OF OFFICE

Damn. There's no proper reward when you get back to the Palace. However, one of the chimes from Brellach/Pinnacle Rock should be installed in the throne room as a trophy. And Sheogorath seems depressed. He's out of time—about to be taken over by Jyggalag—and advises you to run for your life, lest he kill you the next time you meet. He'd *planned* to make you a gift of his staff, but the power's gone out of it. It's dead. And Sheogorath says he's dead, too. He crunches down, as if in pain, then grows to giant size and vanishes in a blaze of light.

Your journal suggests you turn to Haskill. And the chamberlain, in turn, suggests you take Sheogorath's place on the Isles throne—provided you can remake his now-drained staff. To do so, you need to recover the lost secrets of its construction from the remainder of Juggalag's library within the ruin at Knifepoint Hollow. He provides its location—just northwest of the city in the Isles' central "lakes" region—and a crystal that opens the library door. Should you speak to him again, he provides a name not previously mentioned: "Hurry to Dyus. Do as he asks. No danger is too great."

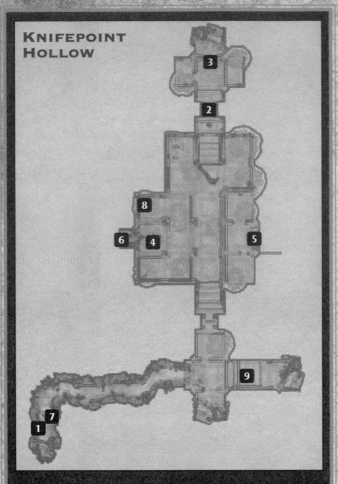

KNIFEPOINT HOLLOW

1. Exit to dungeon exterior.

2. Ancient door: Activate it with the Knifepoint Crystal in your inventory. The door crumbles and you get to meet…

3. …an interesting fellow named Dyus of Mytheria. He instructs you on where to find the components for Sheogorath's remade staff.

4. Through the arch on this lower tier, you find the entrance to Chantry. It doesn't have a part to play in your Main Quest mission, but does contain an item needed for an undocumented quest on the The Hill of Suicides. Note that once you descend, you can't return without traversing Chantry first.

5. Secret door: Opened only on the east side, this allows the player who has traversed the Chantry level to re-enter Knifepoint Hollow.

6. Chest: This contains gold for certain, with 25 percent chances of an ingredient, arrows, and jewelry; a 15 percent chance of a lockpick; and 10 percent chances of a potion, torch, weapon, and two pieces of armor

7. Hollowed stump: Again with the gold. This time, you have 25 percent chances of heavy armor and arrows; a 15 percent chance of a lockpick; and 10

percent chances of a repair hammer, stealthy potion, scroll, torch, and weapon.

8. Madness Ore deposit.

9. Undead boss. A plain old Skeleton at Level 1, a low-level Flesh Atronach boss at Level 2 and progressively nastier variations on Skinned Hounds, Flesh Atronaches and Shambles (Shambleses?) up to Level 21.

Fast-travel to the Bliss district, make your way out the city gate to the northwest, and make your way around the southern end of the mountain. You find the root door into Knifepoint Hollow below a great tree on the western shore of the central of three small lakes.

You don't have much to worry about here. Only one enemy can be found on the upper of the two levels. It's an undead boss, ranging from a Skeleton at Level 1 to one of the nastiest of the Flesh Atronachs at Level 21, and it's straight ahead of you as you leave the lairlike entry passage and enter the stone ruin. Once it's gone, simply activate the ancient door at the north end of the big room and the door crumbles. Within, you find not a library, but a prison cell.

Talk to the solitary man in the chair, and he identify himself as Dyus of Mytheria. He knows your errand, all of it, and he'll help (though his immortality seems to have robbed him of any strong feeling for this task). Dyus makes the physical staff, but you have to go out into the world and collect the "divine essence" that gives it power: the Eye of Ciirta from the Howling Halls of Mania and a branch from the Tree of Shades in Milchar.

 Knifepoint Hollow is only the upper level of this dungeon. Down below is Chantry, reached through an archway on the lower tier of the Hollow, just west of the path north to Dyus. You can explore this Heretic Mage lair freely—killing the 10 mages and single boss and claiming their middling loot. Just note that, once you've dropped down to the entry level, you can't get out again and need to find a second exit back to the Hollow.

Is there anything else here? Naturally. On your way to the exit, you find a little chapel off to the east. Push the button on the north side of the northern pedestal to open a secret door east of the altar. This is a treasure room of sorts. But the most interesting item is Gadeneri Ralvel's skull atop the chest in the northeast corner. Take it. This is part of an undocumented quest. For details, see "The Hill of Suicides" in the Freeform section.

You now have map markers for the Howling Halls and Milchar. You can visit these locations is any order you please. (The latter site is closer to the Hollow, so we'll head there first.) You are able to shorten your trip by fast-traveling first to Fetid Grove to the southeast, Dreamwalk Camp to the northeast, the village of Hale to the northwest, or Camp Tall Trees to the southwest. Note, too, that this ruined fortress has no fewer than four entrances: to Xetrem in the southeast, to Tieras in the northeast, to Sufflex in the southwest, and a root door down to Nexus roughly in the middle, beneath a great tree. You want the last of these.

Milchar: Nexus

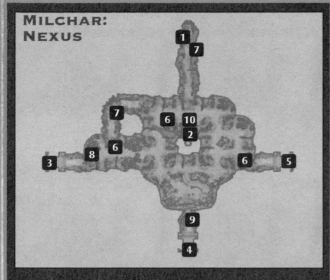

1. Exit to dungeon exterior. Nexus is a hub for four of the five other levels. The exception: Chatterhall, which is reached only via Tieras (#5). However, you need to visit only Nexus and the Grove of Reflection for this mission.

2. Exit to Grove of Reflection.

3. Exit to Sufflex.

4. Exit to Xetrem.

5. Exit to Tieras.

6. A leveled Baliwog, Elytra, Scalon, or Gnarl.

7. Hollowed stump: Gold, naturally. Somewhat less naturally: armor of some sort (four 10 percent chances and one five percent chance); a gem and a piece of Amber (25 percent chances); jewelry, a soul gem, arrows, a potion, a scroll, and a weapon (10 percent chance). Once in a blue moon there's an item from the Miscellaneous Quest "The Museum of Oddities."

8. Hollowed stump: One or two Restoration-related items.

9. Chest: The same potential contents as the stumps at #7.

10. You appear here when you activate the teleport pad at #3 in the Grove of Reflection.

Milchar: Grove of Reflection

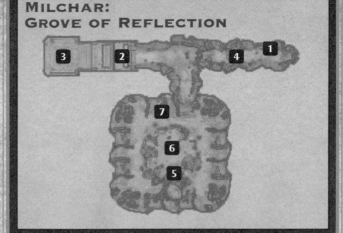

1. Exit to Nexus.

2. A not-so-secret secret door. You can't open it until you have a branch from the Tree of Shades at #5.

3. A teleport pad: This zaps you back to #10 in the Nexus.

4. A hole in the floor: This drops you down onto the level's lower tier.

5. Tree of Shades: Once you've eliminated the doppel-ganger (see #6 and #7), activate the tree to break off a branch for Dyus.

6. Standing stone: When you approach this monument, you create an unfriendly double of your character…

7. …that appears here. It attacks. This is one of the nastier battles you face in the Shivering Isles.

By levels—it has six, all told—this is one of the biggest dungeons in the Shivering Isles. However, you need to traverse only two: Nexus and the Grove of Reflection. When you enter Nexus, just make your way straight south to find the Grove entrance. When you enter, you get a journal entry reminding you that you have to reveal "your true self" to the tree before you can take a branch.

While pondering this, head west, drop down the hole, and head west and south to a small pool with a standing stone at its center. Approach the stone—you don't have to activate it—and a shadowy creature appears on the north side of the pool and attacks.

Suddenly, you have your hands full…with you. Based on a snapshot of your character taken when you entered the Grove, this doppelganger is potent enough to kill you quickly and hardy enough to survive your own attacks for a good while. It has twice your Health. And, irrespective of what you're holding when you pose for the snapshot, it has Shadowrend, a two-handed sword or axe (depending whether your Blade or Blunt skill is higher) with leveled Damage Health and Weakness to Magic enchantments.

How to beat it? Play on the differences between the copy and your character. See, it's not a *perfect* copy. The doppelganger doesn't have many of the stomping big weapons from *Oblivion*, though it can inherit most of your weapons from *Shivering Isles*, *Knights of the Nine*, and the downloadable plugins. Hence, you can out-weapon it—even make a clone of this clone with the Skull of Corruption—or out-spell it. The doppelganger can't cast advanced Summoning spells—though it casts low-level ones—

while you can bring a Dremora Lord or Xivilai to the party.

Finally, the doppelganger has only half your Speed. If you fight the thing in the open areas, you could conceivably evade its attacks and wear it down with ranged weapons and more conventional magic while staying out of its reach.

Once it's dead, take Shadowrend, activate the Tree of Shades on the south side of the pool to take the branch, push the button at the west end of the entry corridor to open the secret door, activate the teleport beyond to return to the Nexus level, and return to the surface.

 And the other four Milchar levels? They're not related to your mission. But you come back here twice—in the Miscellaneous Quest "The Coming Storm" for the Amulet of Distregration (on the Chatterhall level below Tiera), and for a skull in the Xetrem level that plays into the undocumented quest "The Hill of Suicides."

On to the Howling Halls. It's on the peninsula called Heretics Horn—more specifically, on a high hilltop southeast of the village of Deepwallow (which is, in turn, southeast of New Sheoth). If you popped in here earlier, you found a generic Zealot Mage dungeon, with most of it shut off by an impassable locked door. Now it's transformed into the home of Ciirta's odd cult.

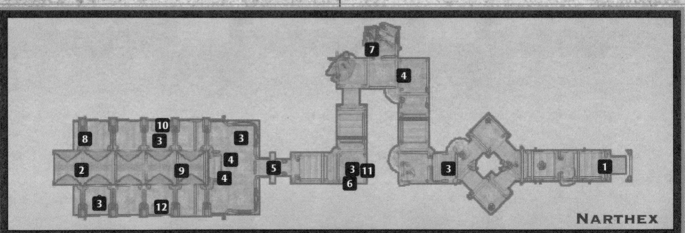

NARTHEX

1. Exit to dungeon exterior.
2. Exit to Congregation Chambers.
3. Zealot Mages/Flesh Atronaches: If you hit the Howling Halls before undertaking the "Symbols of Office" segment of the Main Quest, you find a different dungeon. In that case, it's inhabited by leveled Zealot Mages—some of whom may be replaced by Flesh Atronaches if you've reached Level 9. However, note that you won't face more than two of these, as you're pulled up short by the locked door at #5. The key only appears on apostles during "Symbols of Office."
4. Apostles: Then again, when you visit the dungeon during "Symbols of Office," you find Ciirta's apostles

instead. The easiest route is to whack the easternmost of these and take his key, robes, and dagger. The first gets you through the door at #5; the second prevents most of the inhabitants from recognizing you as an outsider. The two apostles west of the door at #5 have a little chat right in front of you, and a third in the Congregation Chambers level helps you arrange Ciirta's assassination.
5. Locked door: You can get through it only with the Howling Chamber Key found on each apostle during the "Symbols of Office" segment of the Main Quest.
6. Then again, if you don't like killing innocents, you can pickpocket the key from the apostle and swipe a couple of loose robes from this table.

7. **Urn:** One or two healing items and a 10 percent chance of a torch.

8. **Alms Collection Chest:** Supplied with a two- to five-tumbler lock, this chest contains a load of gold and possibly jewelry (25 percent of the time), weapons (conventional and magical), up to two soul gems, and a matrix from the Miscellaneous Quest "The Antipodean Hammer" (all 10 percent).

9. **Collection basket:** Well, if you're going to steal from the Alms Collection Chest, we don't suppose you'd stop at the collection plate. So here goes: four flawed diamonds, four flawed rubies, four topazes, and twelve gold nuggets.

10. Three gold nuggets, two samples of Aster Bloom Core, and one each of Gnarl Bark and Withering Moon.

11. **Shambles skull:** Foreshadowing. This skull is useless, but intended to suggest that other bones you find in the dungeon might not be....

12. Propped against the bust is a copy of *The Madness of Pelagius*. Incidental item, or more foreshadowing?

CONGREGATION CHAMBERS

1. Exit to Narthex.
2. Exit to Antechamber.
3. **Ra'kheran:** You're not the only one who wants Ciirta dead. This fellow already has a conspiracy up and running, but he needs someone to collect daggers to administer the coup de grace. Once that's done, he meets fellow conspirators (#4) at #5 and heads off into the Antechamber for a showdown with Ciirta.
4. These two guys are involved in the plot as well. If you throw your lot in with Ra'kheran, avoid killing them. Once you've collected the daggers, they meet Ra'kheran (#3) at #5 before heading into the

Antechamber to confront Ciirta. (Otherwise, you find them following a basic eat/sleep/wander routine.)

5. Once you've collected the daggers required by Ra'kheran, the three conspirators meet here and then head off in the Antechamber to do the deed. Et tu, Ra'kheran?

6. Regular apostles, not involved in the plot against Ciirta. It's worth following them around a bit as their elaborate routines touch on locations with useful or interesting items—notably, the shrine to Pelagius at #10, the library at #12, and the alchemy table at #13.

7. **Chests:** One hundred percent chance of gold, 25 percent chance at light armor and arrows, 15 percent chance at a lockpick, and 10 percent chances at a repair hammer, stealthy potion, scroll, torch, and weapon. Plus two items from the Miscellaneous Quest "The Museum of Oddities."

8. Just like the chests at #7, except that these two have leveled locks of one to five tumblers.

9. **Clothing cupboards:** Notable mainly for the two percent chance that they contain an item of use in the Miscellaneous Quest "The Museum of Oddities."

10. A little shrine to the mad Tamriel emperor Pelagius. On this table, there's a sapphire, a flawed topaz, a flawed ruby, seven gold coins, another copy of *The Madness of Pelagius*...and a locked (one to five tumblers) glass display case containing the Pelvis of Pelagius—an item you need in the Miscellaneous Quest "The Museum of Oddities."

11. If you don't want to kill folks to collect daggers for Ra'kheran, there's a loose dagger here, along with another robe.

12. **The Howling Halls library:** The biggest one you've come across to date in the Main Quest. On and around these two sets of shelves, and on the little table nearby, you find 70-odd volumes. Admittedly, most of the selections are from back in Cyrodiil and there's a good deal of repetition, but you find three of the rarest books in the Shivering Isles: volumes VI, IX, and XII in the *16 Accords of Madness* series. They're all together on the left side of the bottom shelf of the right-hand shelves.

13. **An alchemist's station:** You find most of the alchemical apparatus (no mortar and pestle); two healing potions; and one each of Alacrity (speed), Catastrophe (a luck-draining poison), and Insulation (fire resistance). Plus there are three portions of Fungus Stalk; two each of Thorn Hook and Withering Moon; and one each of Black Tar, Blister

Pod Cap, Digestive Slime, and Rot Scale.

14. Some wit has hidden a pair of Fire Ball scrolls and a Fortify Agility potion on the crossbeam here.

15. An ingredient cache: three portions of Thorn Hook, two of Congealed Putrescence, and one of Digestive Slime.

16. If you've taken the undercover route—you killed only one of the apostles—you may have the sense from dialogue that these are nice gentle folks. If so, here's where that illusion is punctured. You find four corpses hanging from the ceiling; one that's been tied to the wall; and a skeleton, Bonemeal, and Shambles Marrow down below.

17. A scroll of Lake Stride (Journeyman-level Water Walking) lies on the floor beside the bed.

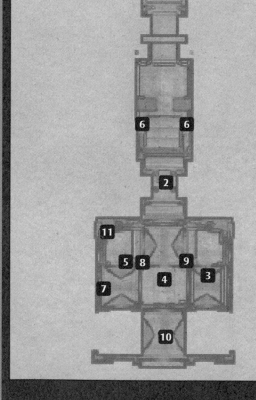

ANTECHAMBER

1. Exit to Congregation Chambers.

2. Locked door to Ciirta's quarters. This four- or five-tumbler lock can be picked or unlocked with the Howling Chamber Key, which can be pickpocketed from any apostle.

3. Ciirta: You either have to kill her for her Eye or assist in Ra'kheran's conspiracy and claim the Eye after the assassination.

4. If you take the latter approach, the confrontation between the plotters and Ciirta takes place here.

5. Luminary Kaz: Ciirta's lieutenant, we suppose.

6. Urns holding one or two Restoration-related items…with a 10 percent chance of a torch.

7. A jewelry box holding one to four items of jewelry, with a 10 percent chance of an item of magic jewelry among them. (There's also a 25 percent shot at a potion.) Nearby, there's Madness Ore, a second loose dagger (for use in Ciirta's assassination, oddly enough)…and the only loose Heart of Order in the game!

8. A flawless diamond, two flawless pearls, and a jewelry box containing one to three items of jewelry, with a 10 percent chance that one of them has magic. There's also a 10 percent chance in holds a potion. Reach this roof beam cache, and the one at #9, by jumping atop the rampways in the room's northeast and northwest corners.

9. Two sacks of gold and common and petty soul gems.

10. Ciirta's chest: Gold and Madness Ore, yes. More gold, probably. Jewelry, heavy armor, a stealth-related potion, and up to three lockpick, maybe. A stealth-related skill book, magic heavy armor, a magic or conventional weapon, a matrix for the Miscellaneous Quest "The Antipodean Hammer," and up to two soul gems—unlikely. All this good stuff is protected by a three- to five-tumbler lock, which can be unlocked with Ciirta's Key, recovered from her body.

11. A 22-volume library. Nothing new—though it's conceivable you haven't seen *The Predecessors*, which last appeared in the Main Quest in Jayred Ice-Veins' and Nanette Don's houses in Passwall.

You can get the Eye of Ciirta two ways:

1. Kill Ciirta yourself and just take it. There are two approaches to this as well.

   A. The power-gamer approach: Whack everyone in your path. Hell, whack even those that aren't remotely in your path. This keeps you only moderately busy. There are three apostles on the Narthex level and seven in the Congregation Chambers, while Ciirta and her lieutenant, Luminary Kaz, wait in the Antechamber. Each of the apostles is two levels below your own—save for Ra'kheran, who is at your level—while Kaz is at your level and Ciirta is three above it.

   Talk to Ciirta first if you like—you get her whole story—or just attack and send her whizzing down the cosmic drain. 'Tain't that hard. She has access to a wide array of Heretic and Sorcerer spells. But she's a spell-caster, usually unarmored and unarmed (unless she has Bound equipment), and you're already too close for a spellcaster to feel comfortable.

B. Whack the first Apostle you find and take his cute little costume and Howling Chamber Key. Then wear the robe. It gets you through the base without being recognized as an outsider. (You learn this if you call in Haskill for a consult.) The key unlocks the difficult door to the Antechamber. You reach Ciirta with a minimum of fuss.

2. Enlist co-conspirators to kill Ciirta for you. This requires some work.

Hang a quick left after you enter the Congregation Chambers and talk to Ra'kheran. Lie to him or tell him the truth about Sheogorath; it doesn't matter. You learn he's unhappy with Ciirta's focus on revenge against Sheogorath and has designs on her position. Help him, and he and his allies knock off the leader. "Then you can take whatever you need and go," he says.

Ra'kheran needs weapons to do the deed. He can't gather them himself—a suspicious Ciirta has forbidden the Khajiit and his pals from carrying weapons—but you could. Bring him three Apostle daggers and you're good to go, provided you observe certain niceties along the way: wear an Apostle's robe (he provides one) and don't kill Ra'kheran's two allies (they're the ones without daggers).

In fact, you probably don't have to kill anyone else. Two daggers are lying around loose—one of them on the Congregation Chambers level. Climb the stairs to the west and make your way north along the east side of the raised area to a metal door. Beyond, the passage continues north and east. In the first room, you find the dagger atop a cupboard to the left of the bed.

The other dagger is on the Antechamber level. Backtrack to the room with the raised area, and enter the archway in the west wall south of the stairs. A U-turn north and east takes you up to the raised area (where you find a dining room table set for eight). Then proceed north to the Antechamber's entrance. Here you may be stymied unless you grabbed the Howling Chamber Key from your victim earlier. The passage leads south to metal door with a four- or five-tumbler lock.

Beyond the door, you find Ciirta's quarters and an evidently high-ranking Apostle, Luminary Kaz. Don't talk to Ciirta. It's a one-way door to a fight. Just take the dagger (and the nearby Heart of Order, if you like) from the table in the southwest corner. Zip back to Ra'kheran, talk to him about "Daggers" and turn 'em over to him. He immediately runs off to meet his two co-conspirators atop the raised area, and the three then make their way north into the Antechamber. Follow them to watch the final scene unfold.

The downside is that you're then seen as a participant and may come under attack from Kaz.

It's also conceivable (though not likely) that Ciirta will survive the assault. In that event, you get a journal entry telling you that you have to finish the job yourself.

Either way, take Ciirta's Eye, Robe, and key. The robe has leveled Shield, Fortify Health, and Fortify Destruction enchantments. The key gives you free access to the boss-level chest at the foot of her bed.

 What happens at the Howling Halls now? Ra'kheran takes over as the cult's chief and remains in the Antechamber. His two co-conspirators file back to the Congregation Chambers and take up their old routines. The Apostles not involved in the assassination plot seem a bit lost—the more so if both Ciirta and Ra'kheran are dead.

Return to Dyus with the Eye and branch. He takes them and create the requested staff—which appears in your inventory as the Incomplete Staff of Sheogorath—and instructs you to soak it in the Font of Madness in Sheogorath's throne room.

And your throne room souvenir? A book from the now-defunct library of Jyggalag: *The Prophetic Deduction, Vol. 34,857.* (No, you can't read it. You'd be lost, not having read the previous 34,856 volumes.)

THE ROOTS OF MADNESS

Needless to say, it isn't that easy. Activate the Font with the staff in your inventory—it's just behind the throne—and you find that it's iced over with the Order's crystals. Talk to Haskill to learn that Jyggalag's agents (presumably aided by Thadon or Syl) have poisoned its water by poisoning the feeder pools of Mania and Dementia. You need to enter the Fountainhead through the door (formerly sealed) behind Sheogorath's throne and root out the source of the contamination.

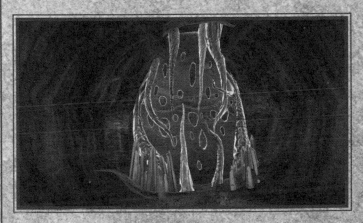

The top level is big and mazelike, but your job here is pretty simple: reach the Pool of Mania level to the west and the Pool of Dementia to the east and kill their attendant priests.

However, the Order has been busy down here, and obstacles have been placed in your way. It has sealed six doors and six containers with its crystals. It has poisoned the four minor pools: in the northeast and southeast corners of the level, in the south central portion, and at the west end. And the pools, in turn, have twisted the tail of this dungeon's peaceful brand of Gnarl. Six have been poisoned and attack you on sight.

That doesn't include the one you find moving in from a side passage to the west just after you enter the dungeon. This one

is peaceful…and useful. Ignoring you, it turns south down the hallway and promptly opens a door sealed with the Order's crystals. Now you can explore to east and west of the T-junction to the south.

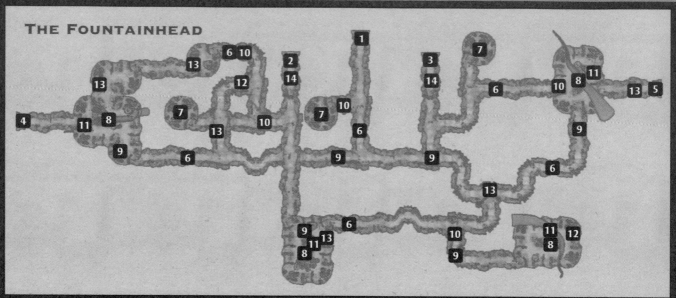

THE FOUNTAINHEAD

1. Exit to Sheogorath's throne room, soon to be *your* throne room.

2. Exit to the Pool of Mania: Note that this is on an upper tier inaccessible from within the rest of The Fountainhead. You can use this as a shortcut back to The Fountainhead after completing the Pool of Mania. Until you do, it's equipped with a five-tumbler lock.

3. Exit to the Pool of Dementia. Ditto, except for the Pool of Dementia.

4. Lower tier entrance to the Pool of Mania.

5. Lower tier entrance to the Pool of Dementia.

6. These doors have been locked down with the Order's crystals. You need either a peaceful Gnarl or a Shard of Order, obtained from the bodies of the Priests of Order at #11, to get through.

7. Gnarl Chrysalis: Gnarl Cultivators are produced when you activate these three toothy hanging sacks. They can open crystal-locked doors and unseal crystal-blocked containers.

8. In Order hands, these four pools convert peaceful Gnarls that drink from them into hostile "Ordered" Gnarls. In your own hands, they do the reverse…and heal you as well! Once the quest is complete, all pools are converted to healing pools.

9. These six Gnarls are already working for the Order when you start the level…

10. …while these five are still peaceful.

11. Priests of Order: Liberate an Order pool by killing its attendant priest. Use their Shards of Order to unlock the crystal-locked doors and open crystal-blocked containers.

12. Hollowed Amber stump and limb: These hold one to five pieces of Amber. Three of the four pieces that aren't built-ins have 50 percent shots at appearing, while the fourth Sheogorath-shaped piece has but a one percent chance! Note that containers (both #12 and #13) work like the crystal-encased doors; they're inaccessible until a friendly Gnarl clears away the crystals or you use a Shard of Order to open them.

13. Hollowed stumps: Gold always, Amber a quarter of the time, and everything else an iffy 10 percent: gems, jewelry, armor, soul gems arrows, potions, scrolls, and weapons.

14. Holes in the floor where you, after exiting the respective pool levels, can drop down to The Fountainhead's lower tier.

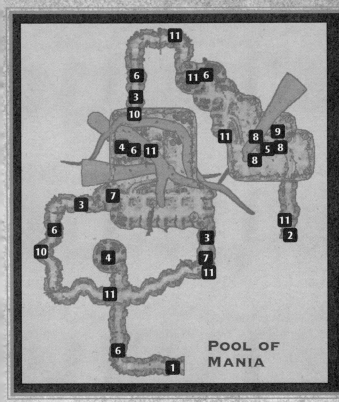

POOL OF MANIA

1. Exit to the lower tier of The Fountainhead (#4 on that map).

2. Exit to the upper tier of The Fountainhead (#2 on that map).

3. Crystal-locked doors.

4. Gnarl Chrysalis.

5. Pool.

6. "Ordered" Gnarls.

7. Peaceful Gnarls.

8. Priests of Order.

9. If you tackle this Pool second, the traitor—Syl or Thadon—appears here. If you tackle it first, you face just the Priests.

10. Hollowed Amber limbs: Same contents as in The Fountainhead and the same problems in getting at them. Note that the northern of the two limbs hangs high on the wall. Climb the great root to the south to reach it.

11. Hollowed stumps: Ditto. Note that the stump at the center of the large central room appears, not up on a root, but on the lower level.

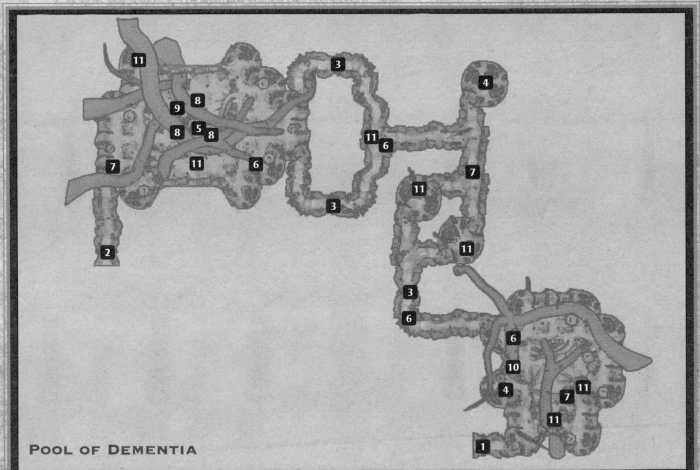

POOL OF DEMENTIA

1. Exit to lower tier of The Fountainhead (#5 on that map).
2. Exit to the upper tier of The Fountainhead (#3 on that map).
3. Crystal-locked doors.
4. Gnarl Chrysalis.
5. Pool.
6. "Ordered" Gnarls.
7. Peaceful Gnarls.
8. Priests of Order.
9. If you tackle this Pool second, the traitor—Syl or Thadon—appears here. If you tackle it first, you face just the Priests.
10. Hollowed Amber stump. Like the other Amber containers in The Fountainhead dungeon.
11. Hollowed stumps: Like the ones at #13 in The Fountainhead level. Note that the stumps that appear here on roots are in fact on ground level below.

Check the side passage for the Cultivator's source. You find a Gnarl Chrysalis. Order hasn't touched these, and they're your ace in this hole. When activated, each of the three Chrysalis pods—in the central, west, and northeast sections of the level—spits out a Gnarl Cultivator. This woody critter then goes on its merry way, opening sealed doors, seeking out poisoned pools, removing the crystals encasing containers, or following you (if you are entering new territory).

However, as their name suggests, the Cultivators are not soldiers of the line but facilitators for your operations. They do not attack the Ordered Gnarls on their own. You still have work to do here.

Strictly speaking, you aren't tasked with cleaning up the Fountainhead level, and you can do as much as you're comfortable doing. But securing the four pools by killing their attendant priests—best done from a distance—is a good idea. It turns them into healing spas for the player, which can then serve as a base of operations. A liberated pool also restores a peaceful disposition to poisoned Gnarl who drinks from it—as the Gnarls do, periodically—while poisoned pools do the reverse. And the priests' bodies supply four Shards of Order that can be used to open those crystal-locked doors either in Fountainhead or the two Pool levels. However, a better use for them is to open the crystal-locked chests that you find scattered though the dungeon.

At the Pool of Mania, follow either the east or west path to a large room, drop down to the floor, and use the great root in the northwest corner of the room to climb to the upper level. Use a Shard to open the door at the top or you can spawn a Cultivator at the Chrysalis near the base of the ramp. At the Pool of Dementia, follow the passage west from the northwest corner of the first large room. If you're in a hurry, it takes as many as two Shards to reach the Pool room. But have patience. A Gnarl may open the first door for you, and a Chrysalis in the level's northeast corner can help you deal with the second. Exits back to the north-central section of the Fountainhead are reached through the south side of the Mania room and a corridor on the upper level in the southwest corner of the Dementia room.

At each of these sites, you face three priests a level lower than your own. Sneak-attack one with a ranged weapon from high ground and then make two survivors come up to you; in each case they have only one route of approach, you are able to administer additional whacks and, depending on the window you provide, the cliff's edge intercepts many of their spells.

At whichever Pool you choose to tackle last, you face the traitor Thadon or Syl. Both are redoubtable opponents—five levels above your own and now armed with a boss-level short blade and a priest staff. One approach is to guide the traitor and priests back up one of the tunnels where you can bring area-effect spells to bear. Also, it is possible to get them to attack the otherwise peaceful Gnarls. The Gnarls soften the priest up for you.

Once Thadon/Syl and the priests are all down, return to the Font and try the staff again. Ta-da! The staff now casts a Voice of Sheogorath wide area-effect paralysis spell that freezes opponents at a distance of up to 75 feet for 15 seconds—but doesn't damage them.

You've received a new trophy: a Shard of Order. And you can now sit on Sheogorath's throne. Up to now, you've been turned down if you tried. Not that it does anything special, but it's good to be king.

However, you've no quarter to enjoy the moment. Seconds later a messenger appears in the throne room and summons you to meet with Autkendo Jansa (if the messenger is a Seducer) or Aurmazl Zudeh (if a Saint) on a matter of "the gravest import to the security of the realm."

Three Saints or Seducers gather by one of the Palace's western exits (Saints to the north, Seducers to the south). Approach, and their leader speaks to you: An Obelisk has activated on the lower level of the Palace grounds. Your troops have engaged the forces of Order. The commander speculates that this is the final assault and that Jyggalag may even appear. You can then opt to lead the defense of the Palace yourself, in which case the three troopers follow you, or commit them to battle, in which case they take off on their own.

It doesn't really matter. You don't need to micromanage the battle and you can't win it on the backs of the Saints and Seducers. The key to victory is your new staff. Equip it now. Then check your inventory for Hearts of Order; you need six to shutdown the two Obelisks. Yes, two—a second Obelisk goes live to the north of the first. If there's a deficit, you can make it

up from the bodies of dead Knights of Order. Then make your way down to the Obelisk, zap the area with the Staff of Sheogorath to freeze enemies, and place the three Hearts. Reapply as needed to deal with new arrivals, and repeat at the second Obelisk. But don't overuse the staff: it only has 20 charges.

My Lord! Autkendo Jansa sent me to find you. She requests your immediate assistance.

Dark Seducer

Moments after the priests hang the "out of order" sign on the second obelisk, there's an event: All living Knights on the battlefield are swept up into the sky. A bright star appears over the grounds between the two Obelisks. Then the star flows to the earth below and explodes, killing any surviving allied troops, and in its place is Jyggalag.

Uh-oh.

This leveled monster has a whole raft of abilities. It has the standard Knight of Order resistances to Magic and Poison. It regenerates its Health. Its area-effect Touch of Order spell knocks you down, absorbs your Health, and does Frost Damage, while its ranged spell, Jyggalag's Supremacy, administers a nasty shock. Oh, and you can't paralyze it. Your Staff of Sheogorath seems useless here.

Well, not quite useless. It doesn't freeze Jyggalag in place, but it does cut off his Health regeneration for 15 seconds. You can then wear him down much more quickly—especially if you use ranged magic, thus keeping the staff equipped, and maintaining a decent speed to keep you out of range. (Jyggalag's is just 16.) Make him chase you down the long hallways along the sides of the Palace grounds while keeping up a steady stream of spells and he eventually gives up the ghost and fades away.

Of course, being a Big Bad Guy, Jyggalag's pale, vaporous essence is contractually entitled to make an exit speech. It's an interesting one, too: As you'd figure, he concedes and declares that the Greymarch is at an end. But then he offers up some history: Sheogorath is the newcomer. Once upon a time, Jyggalag ruled the Isles and more—so much, that the other Daedric Princes, jealous of his power, finally placed a curse of Madness upon him. Hence, the inception of Sheogorath, "a broken soul living in a broken land," and the eternal cycle of re-conquest and damnation renewed.

But you've broken the curse—you are Sheogorath—and Jyggalag has been released into the "voids of Oblivion." Somehow, we suspect we have not seen the last of him.

"I will take my leave, and you will remain here, mortal," he says. "Mortal…? King? God? It seems uncertain. This Realm is yours. Perhaps you will grow to your station."

Perhaps you will. As Sheogorath, you have the opportunity to do so in small ways.

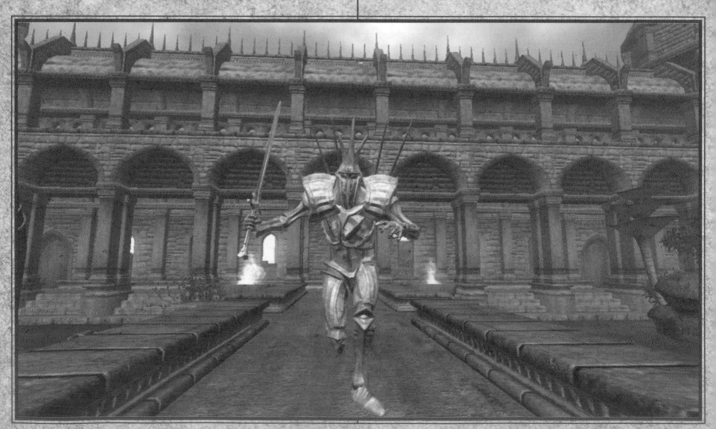

THE PRINCE OF MADNESS

No, it's not quite over.

Your journal now refers you to Haskill. This time, don't summon him. Always persnickety, Haskill won't discuss the matter outdoors amid the messy detritus of battle. You have to take up the benefits and duties of kingship within the Palace proper.

Those benefits are many but also limited. Most of them, "rooted in the magicks of the Isles," work only in Sheogorath's Realm.

You can enlist the Dark Seducer and Golden Saint who flank your throne to accompany you as escorts. These operate much like other fellow travelers: they follow you, wait for you, and you can just dump 'em.

Using the new Manipulate Weather spell, you can…well, manipulate the weather. You don't have control over which type of weather you get, but it is always one of five, each accompanied by a spell effect: fog (with a Detect Life enchantment), rain (which restores your Health), a storm (which boosts you Strength, Endurance, Agility, and Speed attributes by 20 points), snow (with 75 percent Chameleon and 50 percent Shield effects), and (rarest of the five) a torrential rain (with 30 percent Reflect Damage and Reflect Spell enchantments).

A second new spell called Sheogorath's Protection saves you from perilous situations. Invoke this spell when your life may be in danger. If you die while it's running, you are automatically returned to the Palace for repairs—at which time Haskill offers to zap you back to the place where you died.

By asking Haskill for "entertainment," you can summon a dancer. This young Imperial woman's name is "Dancer." She bows, dance around in front of your throne in a fashion that recalls Thadon (if you caught the half-pint Duke at his dance lessons in the Mania gardens), slinks around for 30 seconds, bows again, and return sto her original spot.

However, Haskill doesn't mention everything. Some omissions are obvious. The Court Healer now appears in the throne room at all hours. Simply ask her for healing and you get it free of charge. Sheogorath's fancy duds are lying right on the throne. Sheogorath's Regalia boosts your Personality and Luck attributes by 30 and 10 points, respectively, and your Speechcraft skill by 10. And you now are acknowledged as "Lord Sheogorath" (or just "lord") by a wide range of folks in the Isles.

But some omissions are less obvious. You can now fast-travel directly into The Fringe without making a stop at the Gates of Madness first. A *useable* souvenir of your exploits has appeared behind the throne: the leveled Sword of Jyggalag, on a pedestal opposite the door down to the Fountainhead, is a very nice (albeit un-enchanted) two-handed sword.

Nor does Haskill refer you back to the Sacellum Arden-Sul. This is a well-hidden perk. Revisit that temple, step into the flame you lit earlier in "The Cold Flame of Agnon" quest, and pick up a five-minute stat buff. On the Mania side, that amounts to 10-point boost in Intelligence and Willpower and a 10 percent resistance to Paralysis. On the Dementia, you pick up five-point boosts to your Speed and Luck attributes and four-point boosts to your Security and Sneak skills.

And your duties? An infinite supply of combat-oriented mini-quests! Ask Haskill about "Defend the Realm" and there's a 50 percent chance you are alerted either that creatures have appeared in the hamlet of Deepwallow, Fellmoor, Hale, Highcross, or Split, or that intruders are at The Gates of Madness.

You can either deal with the matter yourself or send a detachment of troops to handle it in your stead. In the case of enemies at The Gates, a third option—mentioned by Haskill in dialogue but not formally selectable—is to simply leave the matter in the hands of your new Gatekeeper. That works just fine.

In each case, you or your surrogates face five leveled critters or adventurers. The adventurers are bandits from Cyrodiil. The critters could include Elytra, Gnarl, Grummites, Hungers, and Scalons or Baliwogs. Send troops and you get 500 gold once the mission is complete.

Even though you've handed off the job, you still have to visit the community in question for the soldiers or Gatekeeper to complete the task.

Opt to handle it yourself, and you get 1,000 gold on your return—even if the Gatekeeper did all the work!

MISCELLANEOUS QUESTS

THE ANTIPODEAN HAMMER

There are a few ways to get into this big equipment upgrade.

If you've been through the Main Quest, or just explored on your own, you've no doubt happened upon two curious new substances in the dungeons—Amber and Madness Ore—and found no immediate uses for them.

These discoveries don't themselves set off the quest. But, if you're lucky, you also discover special molds, known as matrices, which are related to the two materials. There are 11 Amber and 11 Madness matrices: arrows, boots, bow, cuirass, gauntlets, greaves, helmet, shield, and sword for each, plus Amber warhammer and mace matrices, and Madness claymore and war axe matrices. On collecting your first matrix, you receive a vague journal entry identifying the mold as magical and reporting that someone in the Shivering Isles must know its proper use. "I should ask around," it says.

You can also get the quest seed by asking for rumors without the journal's prompting. Sooner or later, someone tells you that the smiths in the capital collect Amber and Madness Ore.

And you can bypass even this step by heading directly to one of the city's two arms dealers: Cutter's Weapons, in the Crucible district just north of the Museum of Oddities, or The Missing Pauldron, in the Bliss district between Common Treasures and Rendil Drarara's house. Cutter makes equipment from Madness Ore and Dumag gro-Bonk of The Missing Pauldron from Amber. Each gives you a document laying out the material requirements—from the maximum of five pieces for one cuirass to one piece for 25 arrows—and discloses that his/her mentor hid matrices throughout the Isles to absorb the land's innate magic. Find them, and the respective smiths can use them to manufacture a magical Amber or Madness Ore item.

However, the matrices aren't required to acquire Amber or Madness Ore gear. Each smith makes two classes of items: conventional ones, which require only the relevant raw material, and magical ones, which also require the appropriate matrix. Amber makes only light armor, and Madness Ore makes only heavy armor.

Is it worth it? Sure. These items have been specially set up as intermediate upgrades between rounds of new equipment acquired back in Cyrodiil. In other words, it's always better than what you currently have, but not as good as the stuff you can collect when you trigger the next round of leveled equipment back in Cyrodiil.

We'll start with the raw materials. You need 28 pieces of Amber and Madness Ore to have your suppliers make you one of everything. No special benefits come with the boxed set. We're just assuming you want to try out everything.

AMBER LOCATIONS

Amber is found in the following dungeons:

- **Blackroot Lair**: Hollowed Amber limb on the entry level, a hollowed Amber stump and limb on the Outer Encampment level, and a hollowed Amber limb on the Tunnels level
- **Cann:** Hollowed Amber stump on The Great Hall level, boss containers on the Amphitheater and Halls of Tranquility levels, and two hollowed Amber limbs and a boss container on the Arena level
- **Dire Warren:** Two hollowed Amber stumps, a limb, and a boss chest on the entry level, and a boss container and limb on the Subterrane level
- **Dunroot Burrow:** Hollowed Amber limb on the entry level, a boss container on the Bramble Halls level, a stump on the Kelp Fen level, and a limb on the Drone Tunnels level
- **Fain:** A hollowed Amber limb at the bottom, halfway between the shaft and the exit; a stump (nearby); a boss container (right next to the stump); and another boss container right at the top of the shaft.
- **Fetid Grove:** Two hollowed Amber stumps and two limbs on the entry level, and a stump on the Encampment level
- **The Fountainhead:** Provided the Main Quest mission "The Roots of Madness" is running or complete, you can find Amber in hollowed Amber limbs in the entry and Pool of Mania levels, and stumps on the entry and Pool of Dementia levels
- **Gardens of Flesh and Bone:** Provided the Main Quest mission "Rebuilding the Gatekeeper" is running or complete, you can find Amber in boss containers in the Natatorium of Wound Bled Tears and Caverns of Susurration levels
- **Knifepoint Hollow:** Hollowed Amber limb on the Chantry level
- **Knotbone Chamber:** Three hollowed Amber limbs and a stump on the entry level, and two limbs and a stump on the Juncture level
- **Knotty Bramble:** Two hollowed Amber limbs and a stump on the entry level, and a boss chest on the Lost Crypt level
- **Milchar:** Hollowed Amber limb on the Tieras level, and a boss chest on the Xetrem level

- **Rotten Den:** Hollowed Amber stump on the Deadfall level, and limbs on the Sanctum and Encampment levels
- **Swampgas Hole:** Two hollowed Amber limbs and a boss chest on the Chasm level, and a stump and boss chest on the Depths level
- **Vitharn:** Hollowed Amber limb on the Reservoir level
- **Xaselm:** Hollowed Amber limb on the Corpse Pit level
- **Xirethard:** Hollowed Amber limb on the Subterrane level

   In addition, you can find Amber in a boss container at Breakneck Camp east of Highcross, and loose in three locations: Jayred Ice-Veins' house in Passwall (three pieces on the bottom shelf against the west wall downstairs and one behind the candles atop the dresser upstairs), Shelden's house (three pieces atop the shelves on the left as you enter), and J'zidzo's house in Split (three in the Manic version). You can also acquire Amber, though less reliably, from the bodies of dead Gnarls—50 percent of the time from high-level Gnarls and 20 percent of the time from lower level Gnarls.

MADNESS ORE LOCATIONS

Madness Ore is found in the following dungeons:

- **Aichan Prison:** An Ore deposit and loose atop a chest in the southeast corner of the lower level
- **Blackroot Lair:** Boss containers on the Inner Encampment and Tunnels levels, and loose on separate tables in the Tunnels level's southeastern room
- **Cann:** Ore deposits on The Great Hall, Amphitheater, Halls of Tranquility, and Arena Substratum levels
- **Corpserot Passage:** Boss container (near the exit) and an Ore deposit
- **Fetid Grove:** Boss container on the Encampment level, with two pieces loose in a basket near the level's center (close to a boss and behind the barricades)
- **Howling Halls:** Provided the Main Quest mission "Symbols of Office" is running or complete, you find a boss container on the Antechamber level and loose Ore on a nearby counter in the southwest corner of Ciirta's sanctum
- **Knifepoint Hollow:** Ore deposit on the entry level and a boss container and Ore deposit on the Chantry level
- **Knotbone Chamber:** Ore deposits on the Juncture and Pipes levels, and loose on the Ruins level under the planks just east of the exit to the Pipes level
- **Knotty Bramble:** Ore deposit and boss container on the Lost Crypt level, and a boss container on the Hatchery level
- **Rotten Den:** Boss containers on the Precipice, Sanctum, and Hollow levels; Ore deposits on the Precipice and Sanctum levels; and loose in the coffin on the southeastern table in the Sanctum level's large northeastern room
- **Xaselm:** Ore deposit on the entry level
- **Xavara:** Boss container held by a statue in the dungeon's center and Ore deposit at the dungeon's far end

- **Xeddefen:** Boss containers and Ore deposits on both the entry and Fain levels, and loose beside a chest at the Fain level's northern extremity
- **Xedilian:** Provided the Main Quest mission "A Better Mousetrap" is running, there are boss containers on the entry and Halls of Judgment levels
- **Xiditte:** Boss container and Ore deposit on the Catacombs level
- **Xirethard:** Boss containers on the Depths and Subterrane levels, and an Ore deposit on the Depths level

   You can also find Ore in three stumps out in the wilderness: one along the exterior of The Fringe walls at water's edge, south-southeast of the Gates of Madness; one underwater below the roots of a mushroom tree southwest of the larger of the two islands in the bay north of the Madgod's Boot peninsula; and one under a natural stone archway on the grounds of Milchar. Plus, you can find it loose in three non-dungeon locations: Dulphumph gro-Urgash's house in Deepwallow (three pieces on a shelf on the left as you enter), Jayred Ice-Veins' house in Passwall (two pieces atop a food cupboard around the corner to the right as you enter), and Shelden's house in Passwall (two pieces atop the dresser on the ground floor's west side). You can also find it on dead Grummites   40 percent of the time on high-level Grummites and 25 percent on lower level Grummites.

MATRICES

Finally, the matrices. They are not common. Despite the vendors' remarks about their masters having hidden them, these molds don't appear in fixed locations. The chance that they appear in a relevant container is rarely more than 10 percent. Moreover, the lion's share of containers that can hold a matrix are in remote wilderness locations. The good news is that each of these repositories offers both a 10 percent chance at an Amber matrix and another at a Madness Ore matrix. If you shop for one matrix, you shop for both. These chests, urns, and stumps are found in the following regions.

NAMED LOCATIONS

- Four in Duchess of Dementia Syl's bedroom in Sheogorath's Palace: in the northwest corner, on the south side, against the east wall in the northeast corner, and in the southeast corner

- Two in the steward/servant bedroom in the House of Dementia proper: one at the foot of the bed and the other against the south wall

- In the southwest corner of the steward/servant's bedroom in the House of Mania

- On a raised platform in Blood Bay Camp, located on a peninsula northeast of the Main Quest dungeon Xedilian

- On the roof of the entrance to the Main Quest dungeon Howling Halls, and in the Alms Collection Chest at #8 on the map of that dungeon's Narthex level. The latter offers a shot only at Madness Ore.

- Squeezed in behind the entry structure for the Sufflex level of the Main Quest dungeon Milchar

- On the Milchar site also, but tricky to describe. Enter the ruin via the central archway on the north side of Overlook Road, descend the stairs, and make your way north around the west side of a small ruin, and then northeast through the stone archway. As you pass through, look east to see an urn up on a ledge.

- In a small ruin just east of the main entrance to the Main Quest dungeon Xaselm

- Beneath the bridge leading from Pinnacle Road to Xedilian

THE FRINGE (IN AND AROUND)

- Underwater, beside a cluster of Grummite Egg Mounds, southeast of the southernmost extremity of The Fringe

- At the water's edge, on the west coast of the northern of the two peninsulas northwest of The Fringe

- On a great root just east of the inlet formed by the two peninsulas on the coast northwest of The Fringe

- Just west of a mushroom tree sapling on a knoblike peninsula further south

- Underwater in the inlet just southeast of that peninsula

- Beneath the northern root of a mushroom tree on the mainland to the southeast

- On a rock overlooking the Emean Sea, on the west coast of the southern and smaller of the two peninsulas on the northwest coast of The Fringe

- Southwest of the Door to Cyrodiil, under a great mushroom tree at the center of a circle formed by five Grummite Egg Mounds

- Under a stone arch at the tip of the northern of the two peninsulas northwest of The Fringe

NORTH COAST

- On a stone platform off the northern tip of an island in an enclosed inlet northeast of the hamlet of Hale

- On a bier in a small ruin south of the dungeon Ebrocca (which is itself southeast of the hamlet of Highcross)

- High on a rock along the road to the Main Quest dungeon Brellach. It's on the east side of the path just before you reach the last stone arch.

EAST COAST

- In and around a small coastal ruin east of the dungeon Fain, on a stump and in an urn in the ruin itself, and in a chest just to the east

- Underwater just north of the base of a waterfall on the coast east of Runoff Camp, which is itself east-northeast of the entrance to New Sheoth's Crucible district

- Underwater, sandwiched between rocks, well off the coast east of Runoff Camp

- Underwater, sandwiched between rocks and Grummite Egg Mounds, well off the coast southeast of Runoff Camp

SOUTH COAST

- Two urns beside a statue of Sheogorath, on a stone platform south of the Low Road and south-southeast of Blackroot Lair

- Two urns in a ruined enclosure just north of Pinnacle Road, midway between Lost Time Camp and the Main Quest dungeon Pinnacle Rock. Be warned: it's occupied by three undead creatures.

- Underwater in the northeast portion of a coastal lake east of Corpserot Passage on the Madgod's Boot peninsula

- Beside a statue in a surface ruin on a small pond near the southern tip of the Heretics Horn peninsula, southwest of the Main Quest dungeon Howling Halls

- Underwater off the coast to the southeast of that ruin, atop a great rock

- Beside a statue on a stone platform out in the southern portion of the lake just east of Pinnacle Road and north of the Main Quest dungeon Xedilian

- Two urns partially submerged in a small ruin east of the previous location

- An urn and a chest, sandwiching an underwater rock just west of the tip of the Madgod's Boot peninsula

- Under a bridge on Pinnacle Road northeast of Lost Time Camp

- Mostly submerged in the south side of a pond southeast of Lost Time Camp. Beware the three Grummites to the east!

- Partially submerged in a small ruin on an island across the channel south of The Fringe

- Way out in the bay formed by the Madgod's Boot peninsula. It's underwater, among Grummite Egg Mounds, in a rocky corral crowned with mushroom trees and located south and slightly east of the previously referenced ruin

- Under a rocky shelf south-southeast of the corral mentioned above

- In a niche on a stone platform on the south side of a small pond just north of the dungeon Xavara. This is itself east of

Knotty Bramble—the dungeon from the Miscellaneous Quest "A Liquid Solution"—and south of the first Low Road bridge across the lake district.

- On a pedestal at the center of a templelike structure on the Madgod's Boot, located between Pinnacle Road and the dungeon Rotten Den. It's guarded by a pair of Mages.
- In a small cave midway down the eastern shore of the narrow lake south of the Main Quest dungeon Xedilian

IN THE INTERIOR

- Three urns just south of a small cliffside ruin south of the Main Quest dungeon Dunroot Burrow and northeast of Knifepoint Hollow
- South of The Low Road just before the final bridge to New Sheoth
- Underwater, beside a cluster of Grummite Egg Mounds, near the center of the large lake northwest of the Hill of Suicides
- Underwater, east of a large rock in a cluster of Grummite Egg Mounds, near the center of the eastern half of an odd-shaped lake west of the exit from the Main Quest dungeon Xirethard
- The western of two urns on a stone platform at the north end of the same lake—guarded by two Mages
- At the base of a ruined column northwest of the lake located to west of the Hill of Suicides

Whew. Okay, you've got a matrix or three and the necessary raw material. Make your way back to the relevant smith, make your selections, and glory in the results.

> **Armor enchantments:** Each piece carries a leveled enchantment that adds between 2–12 points to certain stats or your level of magical protection. The Amber Boots bump up the Acrobatics skill, while their Madness Ore counterpart boosts your Athletics skill. The Amber Cuirass bumps up your Agility attribute, the Madness Cuirass your Strength attribute. Amber Gauntlets add to your Marksman and Hand-to-Hand skills, while the Madness ones do Blade and Blunt. The Amber Greaves adjust your Speed attribute, the Madness Greaves adjust your Endurance attribute. The respective Helmets enhance your Intelligence and Willpower attributes, and the two Shields respectively reflect spells and damage.
>
> **Weapon enchantment:** Actually, they're all the same. The Amber and Madness Arrows, Bow, and Swords, the Amber Hammer and Mace, and Madness Axe and Claymore all have leveled Damage Health enchantments of 2–20 points.

And next? Continue collecting Amber, Madness Ore, and matrices, and trade them in for progressively higher-level versions of the two sets of equipment until everything tops out at Level 23. The best items are better than Daedric quality.

Madness Ore items can also turn up in the Miscellaneous quest "Ghosts of Vitharn." You can grab shields, axes, and a magic sword.

GHOSTS OF VITHARN

Sooner or later, you collect from rumors a report that the dead are walking in the ruined city of Vitharn. The resultant journal clarifies that Vitharn is far to the south, and you find a newly minted map marker on the south shore of the Madgod's Boot, over a region called Shallow Grave. Fast-travel to the dungeon Xiditte to the west, Backwash Camp to the north-northwest, or the Main Quest dungeon Xedilian to the northeast, and then make your way to this waterside ruin.

In the exterior, there are Fanatics fighting an eternal battle—with each other or with you. This is an easy way to lay your hands on axes and shields made from Madness Ore. (See "The Antipodean Hammer" earlier in this section. This is just a taste of what's going on inside.)

And how do you get inside? The great central door into the Bailey level is sealed with chains. However, there's a back door into the Sump level below the great tree in the southeast. This is a fairly conventional root tunnel system defended by three more Fanatics. Dive into the pool at the southeast end of the corridor to reach the root door to the Reservoir, then follow this southeast to the Keep entrance. Once inside, you're approached by the ghost of Count Cirion.

Tell him you didn't intend your presence to offend, and he asks for your help. Cirion explains that, centuries earlier, Vitharn was overrun by Fanatics and that his people have been cursed by Sheogorath to eternally relive their failures in battle. You're to break the curse by exploring what went wrong that day long ago and helping the ghosts correct their mistakes. The key mistake: Four guards failed to protect the lever that opens the gates. You perform four mini-quests in an effort to alter the course of events.

If you tell Cirion you've come to cleanse the place, he gets angry and curses you in turn. You're now locked in with the ghosts and have to sort out your mission without Cirion's instructions. However, this isn't much of a setback and you still get all the info you'd ordinarily receive, just from other characters.

Four people are out in the Bailey reliving the attack by four Fanatics. This courtyard can be reached from the Keep via three entrances: one off the dining room east of the hall where you encountered Cirion, one east of the chapel up the hall to the northwest, and one through a locked door (two to five tumblers) west of the Armory, which is located northeast of the dining hall. Watch them a bit if you like. The battle replays again and again. The Fanatics emerge from a sealed Reservoir door to the defenders' rear, cut down their opponents, and then use the Main Gate Wheel at the enclosure's center to open the exterior gate to the northeast. What can be done?

Three of the Vitharn defenders are handicapped by a lack of supplies and a personal agenda. You can deal with these problems in any order. We tackle them by proximity.

Start by using the north exit from other dining hall and head west. You quickly run into Desideratus Annius as he flees the courtyard. If he's already vanished, just wait until the scene recycles. He's the one with the agenda. Talk to him—if you don't, he quickly runs to the Keep door and vanishes—and he pleads that he must save his "betrothed."

Don't go looking for a woman. Talk to the priest Hloval Dreth (who's just to the west) about "Desideratus' Betrothed" to learn it's a freakin' doll. You can also sort this out by reading the inscription on his betrothed's stone in the little cemetery on the west side of the Bailey: "Beloved of Desideratus Annius, ragdoll to most."

But where's the doll? Return to the Keep dining room and follow the east hall north to the second sleeping area—a niche on the east side of the hall. Desideratus's Doll is on the lower of the two northern bunks. You can return it to him—he responds revealingly to the possibility of the doll's capture—but you have to retrieve it a second time.

There are two correct ways to use the doll. You can burn the doll—either in the brazier beside the guarded gate in the Bailey or in the one at the center of the Mausoleum. When you tell Desideratus about the cremation, he first says he throws himself on the Fanatics swords, the sooner to rejoin his betrothed. But when he comes back, he's hot for the Fanatics' blood, and he takes down one of the four attackers. Happily, his ferocity survives from iteration to iteration of the battle and you won't have to immolate the doll multiple times.

The other way to use the doll is to give it to one of the invading Fanatics. Just activate a Fanatic with the doll in your inventory. When you tell Desideratus what you did, he is so incensed that the Fanatics have his precious betrothed, that he goes into a frenzy. The results are the same as burning the doll.

Your next stop is with the priest Hloval Dreth. He doesn't have enough Magicka to assist the troops guarding the gate. You need to find a source. You can't see it, but he is cursed with Stunted Magicka. His dialogue gives a clue to his condition.

Luckily, there are a couple of sources nearby. One is in Vitharn's Mausoleum. The entrance is in the northwest corner of the Bailey. Descend the stairs and enter the niche directly to the south, then jump up onto either of the coffins and grab the Welkynd Stone under the arch against the south wall.

Return to Hloval and ask him about "Vitharn's Welkynd Stones." He's ticked that you've desecrated the stones but nevertheless happy to use them for their Magicka.

 You can loot the Mausoleum with impunity—notably, for the gems and gold nuggets in the east and west niches. But do it soon; you find it locked after the quest ends.

The other source of Magicka is in the Keep's chapel area. Return to the hall where you met Cirion and continue north and west. Just past the exit to the Bailey, push the button in the corridor's corner to open a section of the west wall in the chapel to the southwest. Within is a hidden study. In the middle shelf against the northeast wall, there is a magical Dagger of Depletion with a really nasty Damage Magicka enchantment that also absorbs Magicka when it strikes. Bring it to Hloval and he uses it on you! Either way, he's supplied with Magicka for future assaults and you receive another journal entry that a second Fanatic has gone down.

From Hloval's location, make your way south toward a sealed Reservoir gate, then make a U-turn north up the ramp to the gate controls and an archer named Althel. Talk to her. In addition to a good shrink, Althel needs arrows. A logical place to check would be the Armory—found down the hall that begins on the east side of the dining hall. But if you ask Armory chief Bat gro-Orkul about "Althel's arrows," he refuses to give them up. The Armory would be empty, he pleads.

Just take the arrows. Pick the leveled lock (one to five tumblers) on the Armory door, put yourself in sneak mode, round the corner to the south, and reach through the shelves to grab the sheath of 30 arrows from the table. Don't let gro-Orkul see you or he teleports you back to the Armory's front counter and relocks the Armory door. (If locked doors are not your best friends, use the key in the Keep hallway west of the dining room. It's on the round table between the two flights of stairs.)

Bring the arrows to Althel and ask about "Althel's arrows" again to deliver them. You soon see that a third Fanatic has fallen to Althel's attack. In future attacks, Althel always has arrows.

You won't have time to puzzle over the fourth guard. After the third Fanatic drops, a journal entry refers you back to Cirion. He failed Vitharn by running away from the battle. The Count appeals to you to take his helmet, with leveled Heavy Armor and Block enchantments, and defeat the last of the infiltrators, the Devoted Fanatic, to lift the curse. Return to the Bailey and wait at the Reservoir gate for him to appear. It is a tough fight; he's three levels above yours with leveled Madness Ore equipment—including a magic sword (which you can keep).

Once you've defeated the Devoted Fanatic, wait for Cirion to find you. The ghosts and bodies vanish in a swirl of light, the sealed doors lose their seals, the Mausoleum door is now impossibly locked, a thunderstorm breaks out, and you get a final journal entry that the Ghosts of Vitharn at last sleep in peace.

And, yes, you get to keep Cirion's helmet.

TO HELP A HERO

A standard retrieval quest. The item is a lost amulet. The would-be recipient is a former Knight of the Thorn named Pyke who visited the Isles for glory and stayed for love. You may have ventured into Oblivion to rescue some of Pyke's colleagues from this Cheydinhal chivalric order in "The Wayward Knight," a Miscellaneous Quest in *Oblivion*. If you start out with the amulet, you've got to find the owner. If you start with the owner, you go get the amulet. Simple, eh?

Generally. The latter's the easier route. Pyke, who lives in his girlfriend Zoe Malene's house in a little hamlet called Hale southeast across the water from the Main Quest dungeon Cylarne, gives you a general impression of where to find his jewelry: Grummites stole it as he was passing the Fetid Grove dungeon. He marks it on your map; the entrance is below a great tree on an island in the nameless lake southeast of dungeon Milchar, which is itself southeast of Hale.

It's not particularly hard. Watch for patrolling Grummites—eight of the 14 Grummites in the dungeon are on the move—and spike, worm, and spore traps. The quickest route down to the Encampment level is to make a left at the first junction and go straight at the second. However, this route puts you in a sinuous S-shaped trench (patrolled and trapped) and at some distance from your destination: a covered defensive position on high ground in the southern loop of the "S." A second Encampment entrance to the northeast puts you much closer to the chest containing the amulet, which has a leveled Fortify Speechcraft enchantment. You may even be able to sneak in and grab it with minimal combat.

Back in Hale, Pyke rewards you with his Thorn Shield—a nice enchanted item with leveled Fortify Block skill (5–23 points) and Reflect Spell (10–22 percent) enchantments. And that's that.

 Girlfriend Zoe is a something of a character. Check in with this odd painter after completion of significant milestones in the *Shivering Isles* Main Quest for her assessment of its artistic consequences. (Does she ever finish a painting?) After this small milestone, she's just happy to see Pyke happy.

If you find the amulet first, you can work backward to its owner using the inscription: "To Pyke, from Farwil." (That's Farwil Indarys, a royal pain in "The Wayward Knight" quest.) The rumor mill and overheard conversations place Pyke in Hale and supply the intelligence that he's living with Malene.

BRITHAUR

You pick up reports from the rumor mill that a shopkeeper named Earil is fed up with an incompetent thief named Brithaur. That rumor gets you a "Brithaur" topic and that, in turn, gets you the intelligence that Earil runs Earil's Mysteries and the suggestion that you follow up with the man himself.

The shop is in the New Sheoth's Crucible district just southeast of the Museum of Oddities. After you turn down Earil's weird offer to "place you on display," ask him about "Brithaur" and Earil enlists you to get rid of him. Provide proof that Brithaur's gone "and the reward is as good as yours."

In fact, you need to provide that proof only if you kill Brithaur. That's achieved most easily by ambushing this Level 4 character—one of the Shivering Isles' requisite obnoxious Wood Elves—while he's asleep at home between midnight and 8 a.m.

His house is at the foot of Crucible's main drag—just west of the main gate. Brithaur's here for breakfast, dinner, and bed (midnight to 8 a.m.). Pick the two-tumbler lock on the rear door to enter; otherwise, you find yourself operating in full view of the Dark Seducer guard near the city gate. Once Brithaur's dead, take his heart from his body and turn it over the Earil. In this case, your quest giver gives you 100–600 in gold—including a 33 percent bonus over and above what you get for the other two solutions. Brithaur's tombstone then appears in the northeast corner of New Sheoth Graveyard. "In the end, his last breath was stolen from him," reads his epitaph.

However, that's just the most direct of three solutions. By far the most involved is to have a little chat with Brithaur. Just wait for him to go out. From 2 p.m. to 4 p.m. he's at the Sacellum Arden-Sul. And beginning at 11 a.m., when not otherwise committed, he's set to wander for eight hours on a long tether anchored near either Earil's shop, Things Found, or Cutter's Weapons. In other words, he could be anywhere in the district. You won't actually find him stealing, but he does pop in and out of shops in a suspicious way.

Ask about "Brithaur" and discover he's in denial…until you bump his Disposition up to 65. Then he allows that he likes to collect "shiny things, valuable things" and that his collection is almost complete. He just needs five flawless pearls. You're expected to fill in the blanks.

It's good to meet you. The name's Fyke, and I welcome you to my humble home. Please, make yourself comfortable.

Fyk

This is not a small task. If the Main Quest mission "Symbols of Office" is running or complete, you find two loose flawless pearls in the rafters above Ciirta's sanctum in the Antechamber level of the Howling Halls. Another's on the ledge on the north side of Common Treasures in New Sheoth's Bliss district. Back in Cyrodiil, two pearls are on the Imperial City's Waterfront. They're in the chest of pirate captain Gaston Tussaud aboard the *Marie Elena*, which you visit in the Dark Brotherhood quest "A Watery Grave." And if you have the Vile Lair hideaway Deepscorn Hollow installed, collect the four hidden bags. Between them, they contain 24 guaranteed gems. With so many, there's a respectable shot at turning up a flawless pearl or two.

But let's assume you can't find all five pearls that way. Alas, in other Shivering Isles locations, the odds of them turning up are small (a little over 8 percent). Granted, there's a 25 percent chance you'll find a pearl in the wilderness and in Grummite container loot…but then only a 1-in-3 chance that pearl will be flawless.

The locations of the wilderness and the Grummite boss-level chests can be found under "The Antipodean Hammer," earlier in this section. The other containers that may contain pearls can be found in: Aichan Prison; Blackroot Lair with three chests on the entry level, two chests and a hollowed stump on the Channel level, and one chest each on the Outer Encampment, Inner Encampment, and Tunnels levels; Corpserot Passage with two chests and an urn; Fetid Grove with an urn and hollowed stump on the entry level and a chest on the Encampment level; Knotbone Chamber with a hollowed stump on the Pipes level; Knotty Bramble with two hollowed stumps on the entry level and two more on the Lost Crypt level; Xeddefen with a chest and urn on the entry level; and, provided the Main Quest mission "A Better Mousetrap" is running, Xedilian, with four chests on the entry level and four more in the Halls of Judgment.

In addition, there are four containers in the wilderness: a chest and urn under a rock shelf southeast of the northern of the two islands northeast of New Sheoth, another nestled against the south side of a rock just west of the same island, and one below the dock on the south side of the lake just south of the entrance to the Milchar site.

And, finally, there's the partly-buried urn hidden practically right under your nose—beneath a broken chest behind Sickly

Bernice's Taphouse. It's locked, too, wouldn't ya know. The key's required and it's not handy—it's on the roof of Cutter's Weapons on the north side of the Crucible district. Finding it takes you into an undocumented quest—which we cover in the "Freeform" section—so we'll settle here for just grabbing the key. The easiest way to get up there is to climb the stairs to the Palace district's highest landing and vault southwest to the nearest roof. Then jump again to the west and once more north. Here, on a stool, is the Sunken Urn Key.

Or you can go hunting for Baliwogs. They have pearls 20 percent of the time—Venomous Baliwogs 25 percent—but with the same limitations mentioned before. They're most plentiful in wet regions at Level 8 and below. In other regions, you're not guaranteed to find them at all times—they're mingled with other creatures—and in wet regions, beginning at Level 9, they're increasingly mingled with Scalons.

However, there are a number of spots where you can find all Baliwogs all the time:

- The Laughing Coast region north and northwest of Aichan, and at the base of a small peninsula southwest of the prison
- Just southeast of the triangular island east of The Isle of Flame
- In the inlets on both sides of the large knob on the north central coast, and in a third inlet in the northwest corner of that same knob
- In the Shallow Grave region of the Madgod's Boot, in an inlet just south of the cursed city of Vitharn and along the coast to the northeast
- West and south of The Isle of Flame
- In the channel just south of the tip of the Saints Watch peninsula, off that peninsula's north coast, at locations northwest and northeast of Brellach, and in the two inlets on the peninsula's eastern side
- Southeast of New Sheoth between the two northernmost of four small islands
- South of the western of those two islands
- Off the coast east of the Howling Halls
- In a small west-coast inlet just west of the Door to Cyrodiil in The Fringe

Once you delivered the pearls, Brithaur stops stealing and adopts a new anchor for his wanderings—near the base of the stairs leading up to the Palace.

A much simpler option—albeit one available to only an advanced character—is to flex your political muscles a bit. If you've either killed Syl in the Main Quest mission "Ritual of Accession" or completed the later mission "The Roots of Madness," you can talk to the Dementia steward, Kithlan, about "Brithaur." He tells you simply "it will be handled."

How? Check your journal: Brithaur is to be imprisoned. You need simply return to Earil once more and tell him about "Brithaur" to receive a reward of 75–450 gold.

However, as far as we can tell, Brithaur never actually goes to jail.…

FINAL RESTING

Hirrus Clutumnus wants to die.

You've figured this out already if you've listened to rumors or seen Hirrus standing wistfully at the edge of the high landing on the stairs that lead up from Crucible to the Palace (a three-story drop into an open sewer). He tells you so himself if you follow through on his proposal and meet him between 9 p.m. and 7 a.m. at the sewer grate just northeast of Crucible's southern entrance.

First, find him. Hirrus lives next door to Brithaur. He sleeps here from 10 p.m. to 6 a.m., he's at Sickly Bernice's Taphouse from 6 a.m. to 8 a.m. and noon to 2 p.m., and at the Sacellum from 6 p.m. to 8 p.m. When his time is his own between 10 a.m. and 4 p.m., he wanders Crucible. And every so often, he makes for that high landing. Worse case, just wait for him there.

Hirrus is one of those chronic depressive types. He finds life miserable in the Shivering Isles. "Everywhere I look, I see death, dying, and decay," he says.

But, for all his sadness, he's rather particular about just how he shuffles off this immortal's coil. He doesn't have the stomach for the consequences of suicide. (We explore these in the "Freeform" section.) He doesn't want to see his death coming. Should you take even vaguely threatening action in his general vicinity, he cowers and squeals for you to take him unaware. And, for your sake, he wants you to make his death look like an accident.

 Hirrus has already dabbled with suicide. Check out his house. On the ground floor is a bloody table with shears, calipers, and a hand scythe. Upstairs, in the southeast niche, there are writing materials laid out in the table and nine crumpled sheets of papers on the floor. None are readable… but what would this fellow be struggling to write, apart from a suicide note?

If you accept the quest, you can kill Hirrus anywhere and at any time—the only requirement is that he winds up dead—with the risk that the guards will get wind of the affair and treat it as murder. And, no, you can't talk him out of it or take him to Sickly Bernice's for a beer, or fix him up with your favorite Dark Seducer. Your best bet is to wait for him on the high ledge, give him a good shove by activating him, and let nature do the rest. It won't count as murder. Turn up the sound to hear his last words down below…and chat with the Dark Seducer guard (if she's around) for her take. Apparently this has happened a lot.

Or just tell him no. Of course, that way your only reward is a clean conscience.

If you kill Hirrus, take the key from his body. This doesn't show up on his person until he's dead. That gets you past his two-tumbler front door lock and one-tumbler upstairs lock and into the key-required jewel box atop the bedroom cupboard. Inside is a Ring of Happiness with leveled Feather (25–70 percent), Light (5–25 points) and Fortify Personality (4–10 points) enchantments, and a non-leveled Water Walking enchantment. Also Hirrus' will, which explains that the ring "made me feel odd—not myself." Which you'd think would be a good thing, no?

Afterward, there's a new stone in the southeast corner of the New Sheoth Graveyard with a dark inscription: "Hirrus Clutumnus never felt like he fit in anywhere. He fits in a coffin quite nicely, now."

TAXONOMY OF OBSESSION

This is a massive open-ended ingredients quest.

Have you visited Highcross? It's a pretty little community just over the Jesters Spine Mountains north of New Sheoth. Make your way north out of the Bliss district, take the side road to the east when you reach Frenzied Camp, and follow it north and then northeast.

When you arrive, seek out Mirili Ulven, who lives in the central house. She can be a bit hard to track down, as her research requires an elaborate schedule that takes her well out into the surrounding countryside—including the rock on the south side of the inlet to the north and the roots of a mushroom tree to the southwest. But you can always just hang out and wait for her to emerge from her house at 6 a.m.

Ulven's preparing an Encyclopedia Sheothia of the animals and plants in the Shivering Isles. You'd think she could use help in such a massive endeavor. But she's a difficult sort and if you ask after "Mirili's Research," she won't discuss it. Persuade her you're not an amateur by bumping up her Disposition to 60. She will supply a list of the 26 ingredients she requires.

If you have a more than passing interest in alchemy, you should be able to provide many of the ingredients on first acquaintance. You pick up 10 gold a pop for each sample—but for only one sample of each. Hence, it's wise to keep a real world list of what you've turned in so you don't waste your time.

INGREDIENTS

You may think this is one of those harvesting quests. Well, it can be—and we help you out with that approach in the following text—but that's the hardest way to do it. And while this is an intrinsically difficult quest, if only by virtue of its potential length, it doesn't have to be that hard. If you feel the journey is its own reward, you can go collect everything in the wild. But many of the items Ulven requires can be found in the Highcross metropolitan area (see the "Alchemy" chapter for more information on locating ingredient concentrations).

However, if you want to take the fast track, and have lost the needle on your moral compass, nothing starts you off faster than a timely burglary of Rendil Drarara's house in the northeast corner of New Sheoth's Bliss district.

No one tells you so, save Drarara himself, but he is a "chef extraordinaire." In his downstairs kitchen, you find more than half of Ulven's laundry list: Alocasia Fruit, Aster Bloom Core, Black Tar, Blister Pod Cap, Congealed Putrescence, Digestive

Slime, Flame Stalk, Fungus Stalk, Gas Bladder, Grummite Eggs, Hydnum Azure Giant Spore, Pod Pit, Screaming Maw, and Worm's Head Cap. (He also has sweetrolls, which come in handy in the Miscellaneous Quests "Falling Awake" and "The Coming Storm.") Drarara's cooks from 10 a.m. to 8 p.m., with no break, but at other hours he's either out or upstairs and his front door lock has just one easy-going tumbler.

Then it's just a matter of filling in the gaps. At Brithaur's House in the city's Crucible district, pick up Gnarl Bark, Hunger Tongue, and Swamp Tentacle (all the more easily if Brithaur's dead—one of the potential results of the Miscellaneous Quest "Brithaur".) In the Sanctum of Vivisection level of Xaselm, collect the Hound Tooth, Scalon Fin, Shambles Marrow, and Void Essence. The Elytra Ichor, Thorn Hook, and Withering Moon are found in Kishashi's House in Fellmoor. Then you just have to make a quick visit to Split to clear up the loose ends: Horkvir Bear-Arm's place (Dementia side) for the Rot Scale or either Urul gro-Agamph's or Jastira Nanus's place on the Mania side for Watcher's Eye.

Other locations with large supplies of ingredients include the second floor of the Bliss shop Common Treasures (11 ingredients from Ulven's list, with two more downstairs), Congregation Chambers level of the Howling Halls (nine ingredients), the Duke of Mania's quarters (eight), and the top level of Xiditte (seven). And you can always buy ingredients from Ahjazda at Common Treasures in New Sheoth's Bliss district. Sooner or later, she offers 20 of the 26 for sale—omitting only the creature-based Elytra Ichor, Gnarl Bark, Hound Tooth, Hunger Tongue, Scalon Fin, and Void Essence. (She does sell Shambles Marrow.)

CREATURES

Once you've turned in six ingredients, Ulven gets a new topic: "Mirili's Bestiary." Use it, and she starts you collecting critters. If you've reached at least Apprentice level in the Illusion skill (25), she sells you a command-creature spell (Ulven's Apprentice Command) for 500 gold that works on creatures up to Level 5. (When the skill hits 50 and 75, you can also buy Journeyman- and Expert-level versions for 1,000 and 2,000 gold that are effective on creatures up to levels 12 and 20, respectively.)

Baliwog: They're close by. Find at least two in the inlet down the steep slope north of Highcross—one near an island at the west end of the inlet, another northwest of the dock and, possibly, a third northeast of the dock. If you've reached Level 9, this last one could be a Scalon. Give it a close-up shot with Ulven's spell and the Baliwog follow you back to Ulven. A Detect Life spell would be a good idea, too, so you don't lose the critter in the tall grass. Watch the creature's health bar—it's now a timer—and keep applying the Command spell. (If it wears off in the presence of Runs-in-Circles and Bruscus Dannus, they'll probably kill it.) And run interference for it with any hostile creatures you encounter. Save your game along the way, as it's conceivable Ulven will accidentally kill the critter in her effort to capture it.

Delivery? That's a bit tricky. Ulven's doesn't always stop to recognize your achievement. The best bet is to be on-hand with your pet when Ulven goes out at 6 a.m. for her research. She should paralyze the creature and invite you into her house for your 20 gold reward. When you emerge, the Baliwog is in the walled enclosure in front of Dannus's house.

Elytra: Once you've collected 12 ingredients, Ulven invites you to retrieve one of these Shivering Isles spiders. Follow the path down toward the docks. At the fork, head south toward the undead dungeon Ebrocca. When the path turns east toward the site entrance, head west over the hill. You find a creature in the area—either an Elytra or a Gnarl. Each has a 50 percent chance of appearing. If it's an Elytra, follow the same procedure as with the Baliwog. This one winds up in a second pen behind Dannus's house—as does the Gnarl that follows below.

If a Gnarl turns up, your life just got a bit more complicated, as the other potential Elytra in the Highcross area—situated on high ground east of the fork on the path down to the docks—may already have been drawn out and killed when you brought back the Baliwog. Search southeast and east of the Mage treehouse known as Breakneck Camp, located northeast of Highcross, to find more. Or wait at least three days for the ones in the Highcross area to respawn.

Gnarl: When you hit 18 ingredients, the bestiary topic makes a comeback. Now Ulven wants one of these walking trees. Everything we've noted under the Elytra still holds here, as the Gnarl share these spawn points. Your reward this time is 120 gold.

Scalon: At 24 ingredients, you get one last beastly errand: retrieve this biggest and baddest of the Isles' aquatic monsters. If you've not reached Level 9, Ulven cautions that you're not yet "powerful" enough to tackle a Scalon. What she really means is that, as mentioned above, Scalons don't begin to appear in the Isles until you've reached that level and, by extension, that you need at minimum a Journeyman-level Command spell to take one in tow and the Expert spell if you've reached Level 19.

We mentioned your best source for Scalons in the Baliwog section above: the inlet north of Highcross. Beginning at Level 9, the spawn point northeast of the dock can generate a Scalon instead of a Baliwog—as can other coastal spawn points farther afield, including one at the great Scalon statue at the end of the peninsula northeast of Breakneck Camp. The hitch with these more distant locations is that, under the anesthetic of the spell, this monster moves s-l-o-w-l-y. On the attack, it's much faster, and a quick, if very dangerous, way to get it up the hill from the inlet is to just make it chase you and defer the Command spell until you're within sight of Highcross. Once Ulven subdues the critter, collect your reward of 195 gold to wrap up the animal portion of your quest.

THE MUSEUM OF ODDITIES

This is not a quest so much as an extra perk for thoroughness exhibited in other quests. Una Armina at the Museum of Oddities in New Sheoth's Crucible district pays you up to 350 gold for weird little things you find out in the game world.

She doesn't tell you about them in advance. However, once you've met with Armina, you can identify their potential as museum exhibits upon collection. So pop in for a chat when you have a second and take the tour—more fun after you've populated this mostly empty museum. She looks over your inventory for items that fit her museum's odd agenda and rewards you if you donate the ones that do. These items are then immediately placed on display. However, she only pays you for the first instance of each item—some are not unique—and won't purchase items you've stolen from the museum. You can return these to her though, with no questions asked.

The Oddities

Blind Watcher's Eye

The ingredient Watcher's Eye is found 80 percent of the time on the plants of the same name in dank dungeons like Knotty Bramble, The Fountainhead, Knotbone Chamber, Fetid Grove, and Dunroot Burrow.

But three plants hold an odd variation: a "Blind" Watcher's Eye—identical to the standard variety in all respects but name. One's on the Nexus level of the Main Quest dungeon Milchar, east-southeast of the entrance to the Grove of Reflection on the north side of a mound that's otherwise surrounded by Flame Stalk and Screaming Maw plants. Another is on the entry level of Knotbone Chamber, hanging on the west wall in a short north-south tunnel on the lower tier that connects the large central chamber to the southern one. And the third's on the Lost Crypt level of Knotty Bramble. It's the largest of the three Blind Watcher's Eye plants and is found on a little mound in a Grummite-guarded chamber on the west side of the level. Reward: 200 gold.

Dagger of Friendship

This enchanted knife heals those it strikes for 10 points. Alas, it also does 10 points of damage. Useless to you, but a nice exhibit for Armina, it's one of six items that turn up two percent of the time in a vast variety of containers, which we have lovingly and pathologically outlined below. The other items are the Hound's Tooth Key, Mixing Bowl, Ring of Disrobing, Soul Tomato, and Two-Headed Septim. Be warned: they can take a long time to appear. Reward for this item: 300 gold.

These six items can be found in the following containers:

Clothes Cupboards

These are on the second floor of the following buildings in New Sheoth's Crucible district:

- Brithaur's House
- Caldana Monrius's House
- Cutter's Weapons
- Hirrus Clutumnus's House
- Muurine's House
- Sickly Bernice's Taphouse (one in each of the three guest rooms)
- Things Found
- Ushnar gro-Shadborgob's House

Ditto for the Bliss district, where they're found in these spots:

- Amiable Fanriene's House (upstairs)
- Big-Head's House (upstairs)
- Books of Bliss (upstairs)
- The Choosy Beggar (two in one upstairs guest room and one in the other upstairs room)
- Common Treasures (upstairs)
- The Missing Pauldron (downstairs)
- Orinthal's House (upstairs)
- Rendil Drarara's House (upstairs)
- Thaedil's House (upstairs)
- Tove the Unrestful's House (upstairs)
- Duke of Mania's private quarters (two flanking the bed)
- Steward/servant bedrooms in both the houses of Dementia and Mania (two in the latter)
- The Palace
- Sanctum of Decadence, at the bottom of Dunroot Burrow (three)
- Congregation Halls level of the Howling Halls (two, both in the northernmost bedroom)
- Relmyna Verenim's bedroom in the Sanctum of Vivisection level of Xaselm
- Kiliban Nyrandil's quarters on the upper tier of the Halls of Judgment level of Xedilian

Chests

- Aichan Prison (one)
- On all five levels of Blackroot Lair (three on the entry, two on the Channel level, and one each on the Outer and Inner Encampment and Tunnels levels)
- On all five levels of Cann (two each on the Amphitheater and Halls of Tranquility levels and one each on the Great Hall, Arena, and Substratum levels)
- Corpserot Passage (two)
- Fain (one)
- Encampment level of Fetid Grove (one)
- Natatorium of Wound Bled Tears in the Gardens of Flesh and Bone (two)
- Congregation Chambers level of the Howling Halls (four in the apostles' southern bedroom, one in the northern)
- Chantry level of Knifepoint Hollow (three)
- Pipes and Ruins levels of Knotbone Chamber (one each)
- Lost Crypt level of Knotty Bramble (one)
- Tieras (two, with a third just outside the door)

- Nexus, Sufflex, and Xetrem (one each) levels of Milchar (with another on the west side of a little ruin east of the southern entrance to the Milchar site)
- Deadfall (two), Precipice (one), and Encampment (one) levels of Rotten Den
- Reservoir and Keep levels of Vitharn (one each)
- Xavara (two)
- Entry level of Xeddefen (one)
- Both levels of Xedilian (four each)

The chests also appear in these wilderness locations:
- Below the dock on the south side of the lake south of the dungeon Milchar
- At the back of an undersea cave southeast of the smaller of the two islands that are northeast of New Sheoth
- In another undersea cave southeast of Swampgas Hole, at the southern tip of the Heretics Horn peninsula
- In an underwater Grummite Egg patch on the southern edge of the map, west-southwest of Corpserot Passage
- Atop the high wall south of the entrance to the dungeon Xiditte (this one's hard to get!)
- In a ruin enclosure just off the north coast of the western of the two islands in the bay enclosed by the Madgod's Boot
- In a wealth of additional locations already noted above for the matrices under The Antipodean Hammer

Coffins
Coffins appear mainly in the giant undead dungeon Ebrocca, where you find four on the Descenia level, two on the Duwane level, thirty-three on the Sepechra level, and six in the hidden Crematorium. They also appear on the Sanctum level of Rotten Den (eight) and in Vitharn's Mausoleum (seven).

Hollowed Stumps
- Arena level of Cann (one)
- Entry and Subterrane levels of Dire Warren (three and one, respectively)
- Top four levels of Dunroot Burrow (two stumps on the first three levels and three in Bramble Halls)
- Fain (one)
- Entry (one), Conservatorium Corpusculum (three), and Caverns of Susurration (two) levels in the Gardens of Flesh and Bone
- Greenmote Silo (four)
- Entry and Cavities levels of Knotbone Chamber (two each)
- Nexus (two) and Sufflex (one) levels of Milchar
- All three levels of Swampgas Hole (three on the Chasm, two on the Burrows, and one on the Depths level)
- Subterrane level of Xirethard (one)

The hollowed stumps also appear in the wilderness at the following locations:
- On the trunk of a mushroom tree west of The Fringe
- West of another tree on a knob-shaped peninsula to the southwest corner of the map
- Beneath the northern root of a third tree southeast of the "knob"
- A ruined temple along the east coast, east of the dungeon Fain
- In a patch of Putrid Gigantea mushrooms on a slope just south of the easternmost Low Road bridges

Urns
- Descenia and Duwane levels of Ebrocca (four on Descenia and three on Duwane)
- Entry and Conservatorium Corpusculum levels of the Gardens of Flesh and Bone (one each)
- Ruins level of Knotbone Chamber (one)
- Lost Crypt level of Knotty Bramble (one)
- Xetrem level of Milchar (one)
- Deadfall and Sanctum levels of Rotten Den (one each)
- Keep level of Vitharn (one)
- Xavara (two)
- Entry level of Xaselm (three)
- Entry level of Xiditte (one)
- Subterrane level of Xirethard (one)

The urns also appear in the following wilderness locations:
- On the south side of a great column of rock that's south of a Grummite-defended tidal pool (the pool is southwest of the dungeon Xiditte)
- On the north side of a tower in the southwest corner of the Milchar site
- Underwater, southeast from Swampgas Hole, beneath the roots of a mushroom tree (two urns)
- Well out to sea—beside a rock east of the eastern island in the Shallow Grave region of the Madgod's Boot
- The eastern of the two urns atop a little shrine in the northeastern of the lakes that surround the Hill of Suicides (it's guarded by two Zealot Mages)
- Behind the southwest pillar of a little chapel (guarded by two or three Mages) at the center of the empty "lakelands" region that's south of the eastern portion of the Low Road (it's hard to give directions to this one, but it's near the southernmost of the three bays along the southeast coast, and just east of a mushroom tree)

Deformed Swamp Tentacle
You can find these in five wilderness locations:
- Two hanging side by side from a great rock just outside The Fringe—almost straight south from the Gates of Madness
- In the west branch of a rocky defile along Pinnacle Road south of Lost Time Camp

- At the east end of a large rock on the south side of a knob-shaped peninsula west of The Fringe's westernmost extremity
- On a large rock east of Pinnacle Road, southeast of the Main Quest dungeon Pinnacle Rock

Most of these are easy to get, but the first site requires a buffed-up Acrobatics skill. Reward: 180 gold.

Din's Ashes

This celebrated madman's remains are in a gilded urn on a set of shelves against the west wall in the secret Crematorium level of the dungeon Ebrocca—located southeast of the hamlet of Highcross.

Inside Ebrocca, beat down the ambushers (behind two secret walls on the second landing) and then follow the main corridor southwest and southeast until you see the floor opening and closing ahead of you. Eep! No, you don't have to go that way! In a niche in the southeast wall, you see two leather shields. Beneath the left one is a button. Push it to remove the wall to the northeast and expose a door. This is the Crematorium. Interesting place. We'll return to it in the "Freeform" section. However, your immediate purpose here doesn't extend beyond playing grab-ash (and possibly rearranging the bones of a unique skeleton called Bregor the Cremator). Oh, look inside the urn for a second prize: a Slaughterfish Scale Charm with Water Breathing and 25 percent Resist Disease enchantments. Reward for the Ashes: 200 gold.

Hound's Tooth Key

No, it doesn't open anything. For details on how to find it, see the entry for Dagger of Friendship. Reward: 120 gold.

Mixing Bowl

An alchemical mixing bowl. That doesn't sound so odd. Indeed, it seems perfectly ordinary when seen on the shelf upstairs—and Una seems unimpressed. For details on how to find it, see the entry for "Dagger of Friendship." Reward: a surprising 200 gold.

Mute Screaming Maw

Screaming Maw is found 66 percent of the time on 123 plants of the same name in the dungeons Aichan, Cann, Corpserot Passage, Dire Warren, Dunroot Burrow, Fain, Fetid Grove, The Fountainhead, Knotbone Chamber, Knotty Bramble, and Milchar.

But three plants are a bit different: "Mute" Screaming Maw appears identical to the big-mouthed variety in all respects save name.

One is in a root passage on the west side of Corpserot; it's right next to a standard Screaming Maw plant on the south side of the passage just west of where it enters the paved dungeon. Another's down on the Arena level of Cann; it's tucked in with three standard Screaming Maws in the western half of a room in the level's southwest corner. And the third is in the northwest part of the Bramble Halls level of Dunroot Burrow. It's beside a Root

Stalk and two standard Screaming Maws on the west side of a dead-end passage that squiggles west to one of the Felldew-bearing Elytra used to stave off withdrawal symptoms in the Main Quest mission "Addiction." Reward: 200 gold.

Pelvis of Pelagius

The hipbone of Pelagius III, Tamriel's mad emperor, has its own little shrine in the Congregation Chambers level of the Main Quest dungeon Howling Halls. Once you've climbed the stairs after dealing with Ra'kheran, use the north exit. The artifact is in a glass case on a table where the corridor turns east. The case has a leveled one- to five-tumbler lock. There's no key; pick it. Reward: 250 gold.

Ring of Disrobing

Anyone wearing it is forced to remove his or her clothes. It does work—on you and you alone. Yes, you keep your loincloth. And, no, Armina does not get even a little naked on her way to the display case. For details on how to find the ring, see the entry for Dagger of Friendship. Reward: A big fat zero.

Sheogorath-Shaped Amber

Technically the rarest item of the lot. There's a one percent chance it'll turn up in any container that holds Amber. Reward: 300 gold. It can appear in the following spots:
- Entry, Outer Encampment, and Tunnels levels of Blackroot Lair
- Great Hall and Arena levels of Cann
- Both levels of Dire Warren
- Entry, Kelp Fen, and Drone Tunnels levels of Dunroot Burrow
- Fain
- Both levels of Fetid Grove
- All three levels of The Fountainhead
- Chantry level of Knifepoint Hollow
- Entry and Juncture levels of Knotbone Chamber
- Entry level of Knotty Bramble
- Tieras level of Milchar
- Deadfall, Sanctum, and Encampment levels of Rotten Den
- Chasm and Depths levels of Swampgas Hole
- Reservoir level of Vitharn
- Corpse Pit level of Xaselm
- Subterrane level of Xirethard

Soul Tomato

This one's actually useful, hence the nice reward. It's a functioning Grand soul gem…in the form of a tomato. For details on how to find it, see the entry for Dagger of Friendship. Reward: 350 gold.

Two-Headed Septim

As in the coin named for the emperor Tiber Septim. For details on how to find it, see the entry for Dagger of Friendship. Reward: 150 gold.

Once you've delivered all 12 oddities, you get a journal entry confirming you've provided everything Armina needs. But take the tour again for some additional details on the stuff you've collected. (Din was a suicide and Armina apparently only displays the mixing bowl as a favor to you. You barely get any credit at all for the discoveries; at best, you're just "some intrepid adventurer!")

And pay special attention to the items already on display when you started this mission—notably the Ring of Desiccation. You'll be back here for one of them in the Miscellaneous Quest "The Coming Storm."

EVERYTHING IN ITS PLACE

This one's set in Fellmoor—a hamlet on the west coast of the Madgod's Boot, roughly half the distance from the junction of Pinnacle and Low Road to Xedilian. You hear about the community now and then in rumors, and it's mostly bad news—with the badness seeming to focus on the person of Cindawe.

Make the trek and chat with Khajiits Ranarr-Jo and Kishashi. They're either at their home just southeast of Relan's place or working out in the surrounding pools.

It's a brief chat—just enough to inform you that the cats are tinfoil-hats certifiable and don't trust you enough to reveal more. However, win over Kishashi and you gain Ranarr-Jo's trust as well.

Kishashi shows you one way. She's off to collect five pod pits. Collect them for her. If you don't have them, this is not a major endeavor. Fellmoor is Water Pod Pit City. Or, bump her Disposition up to 70. Either way, the Khajiit is happy and, when asked about "Ranarr-Jo's trust," gives you a spoon to show Ranarr-Jo that you're okay.

Bring the spoon to Ranarr-Jo and you get the story: Cindawe is "pure evil." Get rid of her—either by killing her or messing up her place. The latter so occupies this meticulous woman's time that she stays off the backs of the crazies in her employ. And you're to steal her notebook. Ranarr-Jo insists their boss has been "recording all our secret thoughts."

Ranarr-Jo is especially nuts on the subject of Cindawe. He watches her house from midnight to 4 a.m. daily. And on weekends, he stalks her from 9 a.m. to 9 p.m. Something bad was bound to happen here. Think of yourself as the instrument for making that something less bad than it might have been.

And Cindawe? Talk to her and the third worker, Relan, who's also a bit out there. You get the impression that, while the boss has a rough edge, she's nevertheless the only sane and reasonable person in Fellmoor. Does she deserve this shabby treatment? Probably not, but, if you want to complete the quest, it's your only option.

Killing's the harder route…but not as hard as you might expect. Cindawe's five levels above your own, but with nothing special in the ways of stats or equipment, and no spells at all. She's just a farmer.

The easier way, and more fun, is to trash her house; it's the one over on the east side of the settlement. Just wait until she goes out at 9 a.m., and pick the two-tumbler lock (or use a key pickpocketed from Cindawe) to get inside. Then start moving stuff around with weapon swings, spells, or dragging stuff around. Once you've displaced 16 or more objects, the job is done. Stick around to check out Cindawe's reaction; It's pitiable.

Then there's the journal. Take it off Cindawe's body once she's dead, or pickpocket it from her while she's alive. If you can get her Disposition up to 70, she even lets you look at it. Make sure to read it before you turn it over to Ranarr-Jo. Apparently Cindawe's mad as well—albeit in a more poetic way than the blatant style of the Khajiits. "I love this life," she writes, " but I hate the aftertaste. Like waking from a dream with someone's fingers in your mouth." At least she's kept it out of her interpersonal communications. Evidently only Cindawe has to listen to Cindawe's sad inner voice.

Of course, it's a serious betrayal of her trust to bring the book to Ranarr-Jo but, again, you don't have a choice. He rewards you with a magical version of the tin-foil hat: a Ring of Mind Shielding (with leveled Reflect Spell and Resist Magic enchantments of from six to 12 percent), and trade a randomly-selected skill book for the journal.

FALLING AWAKE

Amiable Fanriene is a Shivering Isles version of Chicken Little. The chicken thinks the sky is falling. Fanriene's more worried about walls—so obsessed with them, in fact, that he's unable to sleep at home.

MISCELLANEOUS QUESTS

When you find him cowering out of doors in the Bliss district, this exhausted Breton embraces your suggestion that he sleep outside. But where? He's seen people sleeping in the streets, but they're too close to the walls for his comfort. You're to find him a safe spot.

It's a matter of asking rather than looking. Start with those same street vagabonds. Bhisha, Bolwing, and Gloorolros—all found wandering in the Crucible district—suggest dealing with the beggar Uungor. Gloorolros wants you to get rid of Uungor; the other two indicate he's already planning to leave town.

Track Uungor down in the Bliss district. It's not difficult. He wanders, but you can always find him at the Sacellum from 8 a.m. to 10 p.m., near his bedroll in the northeast corner of the district's upper tier from 8 p.m. to midnight, and asleep there between midnight and 8 a.m. He confirms his intention "as soon as I can figure out how to leave without them noticing." (That "them" again.)

But while he's paranoid, Uungor's also rational, and the proposed swap of a bed indoors for one outside seems improbable to him. He says he doesn't trust you. Boost his Disposition to 70 to get him to change his mind, then tell Fanriene. He takes your deal and gives you a Burst of Might scroll, which gives you 100-point boosts in Strength and Endurance and a 100 percent Shield for five seconds each. After you complete the quest, they trade places—Uungor taking his meals and sleeping at Fanriene's place on the west side of Bliss, and Fanriene on Uungor's bedroll.

If persuasion isn't your thing, try the beggar Fimmion in the Bliss district. He helps you, but wants a sweetroll first. You may be able to buy one at The Choosy Beggar in Bliss or Sickly Bernice's Taphouse in Crucible. If not, drop by chef Rendil Drarara's house in Bliss. There are three sweetrolls on a shelf in the kitchen's northwest corner. Drarara's here from 10 a.m. to 8 p.m., with a two-hour prayer break at 2 p.m., but you can sneak the sweetrolls out or wait until the chef leaves the house or moves out of his kitchen. He's upstairs eating from 6 a.m. to 8 a.m. and 8 p.m. to 10 p.m., and out shopping at Common Treasures from 8 a.m. to 10 a.m. After you feed Fimmion, he reveals that Uungor's talk of departure is talk and that you're able to hasten his leave by returning Uungor's lucky glass grapes. Fimmion has these, and turns them over to you. Returning the grapes has the same effect as persuasion, and Uungor buys into the deal.

A LIQUID SOLUTION

Sickly Bernice

The proprietor of Sickly Bernice's Taphouse in New Sheoth's Crucible district says that she is dying. Your journal expresses gentle skepticism but suggests you hear her out. You can do so by asking Bernice about "cure." She understands from a dubious source that the cure is "aquanostrum" (aqua nostrum is "our water" in Latin), found around an ancient statue in a pool in the Knotty Bramble dungeon. She marks the place on your map and provides you a special flask for the purpose.

The entrance to this Grummite dungeon is beneath the roots of a great tree east of Pinnacle Road at the large lake's northwest corner. The pool you want is one level down in the Hatchery. On the entry level, your path west to the closest Hatchery entrance is blocked by roots. Make a long U-turn to the east, past a half-dozen Grummites and a spike trap, to reach a second entrance in the level's southeast corner.

When you emerge from the entry tunnel on the Hatchery level, you're on top on the statue with just three enemies within earshot: a Mage in the niche across the bridge to the west, a boss in the pool to the northwest, and an archer beyond the boss on the upper tier. Get the boss to come to you. You don't want to fight it in the water, where it regenerates, so use a ranged spell or arrow to get its attention. After you subdue the enemies, drop into the pool and approach the statue of a giant Grummite carrying a bowl of Withering Moon plants. You collect the liquid automatically. Alas, you also trigger two more Grummites near the level exit, up the ramp and tunnel to the north, and they come running. Watch out for the spore trap inside the tunnel entrance, too.

On the entry level, you're in the southwest corner on the other side of the roots that blocked your passage earlier. Use the pull pod on the hall's right side to peel back the roots, and you're outta here.

The Other Level

Knotty Bramble has a third level (Lost Crypt). You can reach this by heading southeast after you drop into the statue pool. Here the Grummite tunnelers have broken into a Zealot Mage tomb. You find two fresh Mage bodies on the biers. None of this is related to Sickly Bernice, but it's a nice side adventure—the focus being a seemingly inaccessible room at the tomb section's center.

Use the Grab button to drag the Mage in the tomb's northwest corner off the bier. This reveals a small button. Push it, and the west wall of the crypt opens. Open the two chests (one with a leveled lock of one to five tumblers) and two urns.

On the bier, the ebony dagger in the skeleton's hand is one of those replicas you may have encountered back in Cyrodiil. And the skull comes with a proper name: It belongs to one Lorenz Bog-Trotter. Take it. This pops up in a Freeform quest.

When you step into the eastern part of the crypt, nastiness ensues. The bodies on the biers in the corridor vanish—replaced by two live Zealot Mage guardians each a level above your own. They attack from opposite directions when you step back into the enclosing corridor. Take 'em out one at a time from the shelter of the crypt entrance.

Back at the taphouse, Bernice tells you you've saved her life. She gives you the Circlet of Verdure. This enchanted ring adds 2–12 points to your Endurance, boosts your Health by 10–35 points, and provides 10–60 percent Resistance to Disease and Resistance to Poison.

But the quest's not quite over. Four or five days after you save Bernice's life, pay her another visit. She asserts that she feels the "cold grasp of death" again and could you get some more aquanostrum for her? Nice of her to ask after the critters in Knotty Bramble have respawned. But sure, why not? You've done it once and it's the same this time—except your reward, which is now 75–450 in leveled gold.

WORK IS NEVER DONE

Ah. A clutter quest.

Drop in on Tove the Unrestful, who lives in the southeast corner of the New Sheoth's Bliss district. He asks "Do you have any yet?" You say "What the hell are you talking about?" or words to that effect.

Tove is looking for calipers and tongs for use in his construction of a "skyboat," which is in fact just a regular boat with a crazy skipper, and now you're looking for them, too. He gives you five gold for every one you deliver.

These things show up all over the place in junk loot along with shears, yarn, crystal balls, inkwells, quills, hourglasses, and so forth. We'd need a separate book to chart all their hundreds of potential appearances in clutter, so we're just going to mention the closest ones.

Calipers and tongs
Rumors
Skyboat

Tove the Unrestfu

Start in Tove's workroom upstairs, where he's building the boat. There are two sets of calipers and two sets of tongs on the bottom two shelves against the south wall. Don't worry; Tove doesn't recognize the stuff as his own.

Additional calipers ad tongs can be found in a whole range of locations. The quest's over when you deliver 100 items or when you get tired of visions of calipers and two different types of tongs infesting your dreams!

Interestingly, the final delivery can put you over 100. If you're a real min-maxer, make that final delivery a big one.

USHNAR'S TERROR

On the surface, this seems like a quickie—and it can be—but it's actually quite elaborate.

The rumor mill says there's an Orc in Crucible who's seriously afraid of cats. It's easy to just take that at face value. Perhaps you've seen Ushnar gro-Shadborgob wandering the streets with his dog—named, uh, Ushnar's Dog—and just figured him for a dog person.

Well, more precisely, gro-Shadborgob is scared to death of Khajiits. And no wonder: The beggar Bhisha the Khajiit follows him around all day. Bhisha says he just likes Ushnar's Dog. Talk to Ushnar about Bhisha, bump up his Disposition to 40, and he wishes out loud that "someone would just make him disappear."

Of course, there's disappearing as in "dead" and as in just disappearing from Crucible. You can bring about either of these situations—by heartlessly killing Bhisha somewhere out of the way, for instance, while he's asleep on his bedroll just west of Things Found. Or you can buy him off with 100 gold, in which case he removes to a spot in Bliss near the entrance to the Sacellum Arden-Sul. Alternately, coax up his Disposition. If you've completed the Main Quest, you have to get it to 70 before he bows to your demigod status and quits the district. If you haven't, a heady 90.

A fourth solution is less well advertised. After gro-Shadborgob has complained about Bhisha, but before you've acted on his information, talk to either Sickly Bernice at Sickly Bernice's Taphouse or Armina at the Museum of Oddities about the Orc. He visits the museum from 10 a.m. to 1 p.m. (even taking the tour!) and eats his lunch at the Taphouse from 1 p.m. to 3 p.m., so these women know a bit about him and can provide the some tidbits. Bernice says that his dog once tore apart a Khajiit who'd taken its food, and Armina says that the dog is trained to attack Khajiits. You can collect similar intelligence via the "Bhisha" topic from the beggar Gloorolros, who reports that Ushnar once tried to give Bhisha his dog's food to make the dog attack him.

That should give you an idea. Sneak into Ushnar's house—he's usually out with his pooch and the place is never more than nominally locked (two tumblers)—and steal some dog food either from the dog's dish against the north wall of the entry room or the food cupboard in the northeast corner. Then talk to Bhisha. You now have a third option: "Have some food. It's a gift from me."

We think this a rather cruel decision, as it preys on the beggar's hunger, and because you're giving dog food to a homeless guy, but it does work. The Orc's dog attacks the Khajiit. If it kills him, as is likely since it has almost twice the hit points, your job is done. If Bhisha somehow kills Ushnar's Dog, the Orc just gets a new one. This is a less than ideal situation as you no longer have tight control over the circumstances. The dog does indeed turn up in a couple of days and instantly renews its predecessor's attack on Bhisha—conceivably joined by Ushnar and any Dark Seducer guards in the neighborhood at the time. In that case, your quest giver may wind up dead, too, which fries your reward. "He asked to be buried with his beloved dog. Oh, well," reads Ushnar's epitaph in the New Sheoth Graveyard.

In any case, Bhisha eventually dies and a tombstone shows up in New Sheoth Graveyard for him as well. ("In memory of Bhisha. Killed because he loved dogs.") Tell the Orc about it. Ushnar doesn't care which solution you've adopted, but he's happy the cat's gone and vows to send you one of his old dogs as a reward. Depending where you are, it should be on the scene almost immediately. If not, stop by Ushnar's house in northeast Crucible to pick it up.

You're now the proud owner of Ushnar's Skinned Hound! This strange creature follows you loyally as long as it lives—even over great distances and difficult terrain. Go for a swim and it jumps in after you and does the doggie paddle. It fights for you if you're attacked. Its level is keyed to your own, but it never gets higher than Level 5. It's even kind of cute in its undead way—wagging its skeletal tail and cocking its skeletal head. And strange as it may be, you'll miss it once it's gone.

THE COMING STORM

The proprietor of Things Found, the Khajiit Ahjazda, expects the world to end soon and is laying in supplies so she's ready when an unspecified "they" come for her. (A number of folks in the Shivering Isles use this paranoid "they.") She asks you to collect three items that have eluded her: the Amulet of Disintegration, the Ring of Desiccation, and the Calming Pants.

Alas, she doesn't tell you where any of these things can be found. But you do get quest markers if you've made this your active quest, and two of the items come easily. If you've toured the Museum of Oddities during the quest of the same name, you already know the Ring of Desiccation is in an unlocked display case on the upper level. Pinching it should be beyond easy. And the Bliss beggar Fimmion has the Calming Pants. When worn, these boost your Personality attribute by eight points. As in the Miscellaneous Quest "Falling Awake," the little man has a sweet tooth and only a sweetroll, stolen most easily from Rendil Drarara's kitchen, is required to get him to seal the deal.

The Amulet of Disintegration is on Chatterhall level of the dungeon Milchar—reached only via the Tieras level, which is centered at the east edge of the site. Watch yourself in Tieras. The statue at the bottom of the second flight of stairs may be broken, but it's still trapped and a creature may be waiting (50 percent chance) behind a secret door east of the room at the bottom of the third. It's one of five to nine baddies—any one of which could be a leveled Baliwog, Elytra, Gnarl, or Scalon. However, you need to explore only a portion of the level to reach Chatterhall; they're not laid out toe to heel.

Chatterhall's an action-oriented puzzle. The amulet's in the urn at the middle of this large room. However, it's frozen shut. To thaw it out, raise the temperature by keeping fires burning simultaneously in the three braziers in the northwest and northeast corners and up on the dais on the south side of the room. Do this by swiftly grabbing the torch found on the southern brazier. This is a little bit tricky for a slow character, or one inexperienced with the Grab button, as the fires stay lit for 10 seconds and all go out again if you fail. If you can't quite make it, experiment with holding the torch as far in front of you as possible or throwing it ahead of you onto the final brazier. This may require some practice.

Once they're all burning in merry unison, you can open the central chest…and discover that the amulet is designed to disintegrate 10,000 points of its operator's armor and weapons. It's a scorched-earth policy for the End Times; Ahjazda explains later that she doesn't want "them" to get her stuff.

When you turn over all three items, Ahjazda rewards you with a new power called Ahjazda's Paranoia, which casts a high magnitude Frenzy spell. This is especially useful when fighting multiple enemies. It raises the target's aggression level and hence makes them attack folks they wouldn't attack ordinarily.

THE FORK OF HORRIPILATION

M'Aiq the Liar isn't the only weird Argonian who's emigrated from *Morrowind*. Big-Head is back.

You may recall this poor demented fellow from Sheogorath's quest in that game. You borrowed his Fork of Horripilation to battle a giant netch. And we're betting you didn't bring it back, either, because now Big-Head's taken up residence in a mansion just south of Rendil Drarara's house in New Sheoth's Bliss district and is looking for this lost possession with quiet desperation.

"It is gone," he says. "Gone, gone, gone. Taken from Big-Head, never returned."

Big-Head is at home in the morning. At noon, he's off to the Sacellum for two hours of worship. From 2 p.m. to 8 p.m., he hovers near Amiable Fanriene's house on the west side of town, seeking one or another of three mundane forks. Hey, we said he was desperate. And then he takes dinner from 8 p.m. to 10 p.m. at The Choosy Beggar.

Talk to him. He proposes that you recover the Fork for him, refers you to the beggar Bolwing, and supplies a charm that, surprise, looks just like a fork. As in *Morrowind*, Big-Head is obsessed with forks. In his house, there are find 15 standard forks, 15 pitchforks, 7 silver forks, and 5 fork cupboards, which each contain 4 forks that could be silver, pewter, or standard. If he dies, his epitaph in the New Sheoth Graveyard reads: "In memory of Big-Head. Completely Forked."

Bolwing sleeps from 10 p.m. to 6 a.m. in a little tunnel-like recess in the central section of Crucible's west wall, attends an early service at the Sacellum (7 a.m. to 9 a.m.), and wanders from 10 a.m. to 10 p.m. near the district's southern exit.

Now, you're probably not looking forward to talking to Bolwing. Madness has rendered this Crucible beggar inarticulate. He says things like: "Fribble! Just Fribble!" and "Rany Roo! Rany Roo!" and "Tell the daen! Tell the daen! Karn sky is relfing!"

But with Big-Head's charm—and to Bolwing's relief as much as yours—you can understand him just fine in this mission. Turns out the Fork's the focus of a battle between the Heretic and Zealot Mages and is located at Long Tooth Camp—in the Laughing Coast region north-northwest of the Gates of Madness, just north of Overlook Road at the point where it turns northeast toward Milchar.

Don't fast-travel there directly. If the quest is running, you turn up right in the middle of a battle between the three Heretics who occupy the camp and four Zealots who've just arrived from Hardscrabble Camp to liberate it. You very likely become a target for both sides, and that's no good.

Instead, fast-travel to Knotbone Chamber to the east or Wretched Camp to the north and then walk cross-country to Long Tooth. Watch from a safe distance in sneak mode as the battle plays itself out, then move in to clear out any survivors and reclaim the Fork. It's either in the unlocked jewelry box in front of a bust of Sheogorath on the top platform or one of the dead guys. Dressed up in the appropriate robe and hood, you can probably waltz in, grab it, and hustle out again. You've just "stumbled onto it," right? Just don't get too close to the resident Mage, lest he figure out you're not playing for the same team.

Where to find the robes? Kill a Heretic or Zealot Mage. The Heretics can be found here:

- Camp Tall Trees, just northeast of Long Tooth along Overlook Road
- Wretched Camp to the north-northeast
- Breakneck and Frenzied Camps
- Dreamwalk Camp, northeast of the dungeon Milchar
- Dungeons Cann and Fain, the latter shared with Grummites

Zealots turn up here:

- Backwash Camp north-northeast of Vitharn
- Camp Hopeful on Overlook Road north-northwest of Dunroot Burrow
- Puddlejump Camp on the southwest corner of the round lake just north of the Hill of Suicides region
- Entry level of Howling Halls before the Main Quest mission "Symbols of Office"
- Chantry level of Knifepoint Hollow
- Dungeons Rotten Den, Xavara, and Xiditte
- Shrines at the center of the lakelands out east-northeast of Xavara
- Shrine in the middle of the lake immediately northeast of the Hill of Suicides region
- Shrine northeast of Rotten Den
- The Bailey and Keep sections of Vitharn on the south coast of the Madgod's Boot—but only after the Miscellaneous Quest "Ghosts of Vitharn" has been completed.

Naturally, the Fork of Horripilation is useless. Did you imagine for a second it would be anything else? Equip it and a Fork's Wound spell kicks in and drains your Magicka. No, thank you.

Alternate approach: If the quest isn't running, the Fork is still at the camp—but now it's on the little table northeast of the bust. Then you can get the quest with the Fork already in hand.

Needless to say, either way, Big-Head's tickled pink and rewards you with useless spoken advice on the Alchemy, Blade, or Sneak skill. Happily, this translates into a one-point increase in whichever skill you select.

THE GREAT DIVIDE

In which the game finally gives you something to do in the very strange community of Split.

You probably already know something of its story from the rumor mill: There's two of everyone here—a Manic and Demented version of each the five settlers. But no one gives you an actual quest.

So how to get there? It's on the south shore of the lake south of the entrance to the Milchar site. The closest fast travel location is the Grummite dungeon Fetid Grove on the island in that lake. From there, a bridge leads to the south shore. The closest Main Quest locations are Milchar to the north-northwest and Knifepoint Hollow to the east-southeast. If you used Overlook Road to reach New Sheoth, Camp Tall Trees is just down the road to the west. And if you just want to walk, the quickest way is to follow the Low Road to the Hill of Suicides region. The road north here runs right into Split.

The first thing you notice is that, unlike the other rural communities, it's not a hamlet. It's a proper town with eight houses divided into two sub-communities— Mania to the north and Dementia to the south—with the archway serving as the dividing line. There's no obvious approach here, so just start chatting with folks about their lives. Most of them are out and about by 10 a.m.—with Mania's workaholic chief Horkvir Bear-Arm out as early as 8 a.m. to sweep the streets and till his garden.

You instantly learn everyone here hates having a double. "Why did I cross the road?" asks the Mania version of the Khajiit J'zidzo. "To avoid the other J'zidzo. That's no joke."

Whoever you speak to first refers you to leader Bear-Arm—that is, his or her side's iteration of Bear-Arm. Either reveals that the community's division has its origins in a Mage's experiment gone wrong. The Mage believed that everyone has a manic and a demented side, and present evidence suggests he was right. But the spell cast to test his theory split everyone into two people. And the people here aren't allowed to deal with their situation. But a stranger could deal with it. Say, you're a stranger.

Your options are limited. Conflict resolution is not on the agenda. The Manic Bear-Arm suggests you kill the Demented residents. The Demented Bear-Arm suggests you kill all the Manics. Each says he'll make it worth your while.

So which side do you kill, if you should decide to kill anyone at all? It's all a matter of taste. The rewards for backing Mania and Dementia are each based on the same formula (200–1,200 gold), and the characters on each side are identical in stats. However, there are some notable differences in equipment. While the only armed Mania resident is Bear-Arm, the Dementia version of Jastira Nanus packs a leveled longsword while the Dementia Urul gro-Agamph has an almost full suit of leather armor.

Ether way, before you start in, make sure you've announced your intentions to one or the other of the twin Bear-Arms. If you kill a Split resident without having first made this decision, you've blown the quest.

You can handle the actual killing a couple of ways. One is just to slaughter everyone in their beds. The Mania folks are all in bed by midnight and the Dementia folks by 2 a.m. Most of the doors are lightly locked. This way, you know who you're doing in.

Another is to target the community meals—held daily at 11 a.m. and 5 p.m. at picnic tables on the respective sides of the settlement. The Manic meals draw out four of the five residents—only Nanus is missing—and the Demented dinners three of the five. You can snipe the Dementia residents with virtual impunity from atop the mushroom tree sapling beside the road to the south. Bear-Arm has a bow and dagger, but he eats on his stoop some distance away, so no one fires back.

The Manic meals are a trickier affair. Bear-Arm is present for these—he shoots back—and only a Acrobatics expert or master can use the overhanging roots to reach stable snipers nests with clear views of the Mania table on the roofs of the Mania Urul gro-Agamph's and the Dementia Bear-Arm's houses.

Moreover, you can't just kill whoever turns up in the vicinity of the picnic table. Yes, generally speaking, you find Dementeds at the one and Manics at the other. But despite all the residents' talk about hating their doubles, there's a good deal of mingling on both sides of the fence. (The only two that don't mix at some stage are the two Bear-Arms.) So how do you tell who's who?

The Dementeds dress in darker colors, as befits their darker frame of mind. This is especially pronounced with gro-Agamph: The Mania version wears a dirty-white costume, the Dementia version dark leather armor. You may nevertheless have some trouble with the two J'zidzos, who can be distinguished only by the color of their trousers.

Moreover, the speeches of the Mania residents are generally upbeat—at worst, neutral—while those of the Dementia residents have a distinctly negative cast. The Mania Bear-Arm doesn't think there are enough hours in a day. His Dementia counterpart is a lazy slacker who stays in bed until noon, then sits on his stoop until 10 p.m. and seems to get tired just speaking. Only the Mania J'zidzo is a comic. The Dementia J'zidzo is just a terminally grouchy guy. The Mania gro-Agamph talks to you like you're a playful puppy. The Dementia one is obsessed with the size of your teeth and the prospect of being eaten. The Mania Jastira Nanus is a loon—always counting up or down—but a harmless loon. The Dementia Nanus is a sinister creature consumed with thoughts of corpses. She regularly presents you with detritus from the corpses she's found: rat meat, Gnarl Bark, Hunger Tongue, and Elytra Ichor. The Mania Atrabhi always talks about books, but doesn't carry one. She has a 50-volume library at home. The Dementia Atrabhi carries up to four books, but doesn't read them, and her speeches are always false.

Save your game after each successful kill. Each is acknowledged by a journal entry. If you've finished the Main Quest, don't bring your Saints and Seducer escorts in tow on this expedition. They don't seem to "get" it, and attack you mercilessly. Once the last resident of the targeted side keels over, return to the surviving Bear-Arm for your reward and to the others to soak up their reactions. J'zidzo has a new joke.

"How many J'zidzos can you fit in a breadbox?" he asks. "One! There's only one!"

BOOKS

There are 22 new books in the Shivering Isles, plus one from Cyrodiil with a new cover and a new price. No, none are skill books. The skill books in the Isles, all imported from Cyrodiil, are listed later in this section under "Skill Books."

You can buy these new books at Books of Bliss in New Sheoth's Bliss district and Things Found in the Crucible district. The former has 2–15 books for sale at any given time, but all 23 are on the shelves for your browsing or stealing pleasure. The latter establishment—kind of a junk shop—offers 2–6 books for sale, with just eight on the shelves.

Or check the bigger private libraries. The biggest is at Orinthal's house just across the street from Books of Bliss. (However, this library is missing the three rarest books in the Isles.) Other big collections can be found on the Congregation Chambers and Antechambers levels of the Howling Halls, in J'zidzo's house (Mania version) in Split, at The Choosy Beggar, the entry level of the Zealot Mage dungeon Xiditte, the Duke of Mania's quarters in the Palace, and Ushnar gro-Shadborgob's house in the Crucible district.

Here's a run-down on the books' contents and significance.

16 ACCORDS OF MADNESS

No real quest connections here, just some samples of your patron's wild history. These volumes recount contests of wits between Sheogorath and the Daedric lords Hircine, Malacath, and Vaermina. The three available volumes in this series are the rarest of the Shivering Isles books. There are seven copies of volume IX, eight of volume XII and nine of volume VI.

All three books can be found together in the library on the Congregation Chambers level of Howling Halls, in Books of Bliss in the Bliss district, and on the entry level of the dungeon Xiditte. In addition, you can find volume IX separately in Xavara (in a bookshelf atop a bier in a columned room almost straight north from the dungeon entrance) and Jayred Ice-Veins's

House in Passwall (on the little table behind the stairs). Volume XII appears separately in the Duke of Mania's quarters (in a bookshelf against the hall's west wall) and in the Vitharn's Keep (beside the magic dagger in the secret room off the chapel). And volume VI turns up in J'zidzo's House (Mania version) in Split and on a table in the northernmost room on the Catacombs level of Xiditte.

BARK AND SAP

The subtitle is *The Root System and Ecology and Culture of the Gnarl*. Which is indeed what it starts out to be, including persuasive explanation for the presence of Amber, before turning into a "clearly treasonous" rant against the root systems and belief in Sheogorath's omnipotence. No great surprise that the author wound up dead at the entrance to a root dungeon. This book is common.

THE BLESSINGS OF SHEOGORATH

The actual title is *The 13 Blessings of Sheogorath*. Ostensibly a series of blessings patterned after the beatitudes in the New Testament, it does double duty as a broad census of the neuroses that drive Sheogorath's realm. This book is common.

AN ELYTRA'S LIFE

The writer, one Karmelle, evidently lived with these Shivering Isles spiders much as Dian Fossey did with Africa's mountain gorillas. It sets up the Main Quest mission "Addiction," where you encounter docile, Felldew-bearing Elytra. This book is uncommon.

FALL OF VITHARN

A much more detailed account of the history of this realm on the south shore of Madgod's Boot than you get from Count Cirion in the Miscellaneous Quest "Ghosts of Vitharn"—which this book sets up. This book is all over the place.

FROM FROG TO MAN

An account of the life cycle of Grummites and Baliwogs. (Turns out a Baliwog is the beta version of a Grummite.) Not wholly accurate, as the author discounts tales of Grummite spell-casters. Evidently he's never visited Xedilian, the Hatchery level of Knotty Bramble, the lake southeast of Corpserot Passage, the coast southwest of The Fringe's Door to Cyrodiil, or the small pond at the southern tip of the Heretics Horn peninsula. Grummite Mages are guaranteed to appear in each location. This book is common.

GUIDE TO NEW SHEOTH

The actual title is *A Traveler's Guide to New Sheoth and the Shivering Isles*. It's a rose-colored view of life in the Isles, but with lots of useful tidbits, including a tip to the undocumented quest on the Hill of Suicides. Some old info: Abhuki has been replaced by Ahjazda as proprietor of Things Found. This book is all over the place.

HERETICAL THOUGHTS

This is an introduction to the Heretic Mages, who are found in surface camps and certain dungeons. It also mentions their robes, which can be used to fool them into thinking you're a fellow traveler. This book is common.

THE LITURGY OF AFFLICTION

The subtitle is *A Collection of the Writings of Vexis Velruan*. It is a dark account of experiments in pain that sets up Relmyna Verenim's own researches in Xaselm (which you encounter in the Main Quest mission "Rebuilding the Gatekeeper"). This book is common.

THE LIVING WOODS

Short, informative text on the Gnarl. Also contains the germ of the Miscellaneous Quest "The Antipodean Hammer." This book is common.

THE MADNESS OF PELAGIUS

Enjoyable biography of Tamriel's mad emperor. Sets up (in a broad sense) the Pelvis of Pelagius element of the Miscellaneous Quest "The Museum of Oddities." Identical in content to the book found back in Cyrodiil, this has a different cover and a different value (25 gold compared to 12 gold for the Cyrodiil edition). Curiously, the copy on the table in the "butterfly room" where you first meet Sheogorath chamberlain Haskill is the Cyrodiil edition. This book is common.

MYTHS OF SHEOGORATH

Similar to the *16 Accords of Madness* books, this collection charts three dark legends involving the Daedric prince. This is the most common of all Shivering Isles books.

THE PREDECESSORS

The subtitle is *Being an Examination of the Curious Ruins of the Shivering Isles and Their Terrible Significance For Our Future*. Alone among the Shivering Isles books, this one was written by a living character: Yngvar the Wanderer. (See "Yngvar the Doomsayer" later in this section for details.) It's basically a way for characters keeping a wide birth of the Main Quest to hear independently about the Greymarch. This book is common.

THE PROPHET ARDEN-SUL

The subtitle is *Volume II: The Sacellum*. That's the temple positioned between the Bliss and Crucible districts of New Sheoth. "It is the epicenter of a most interesting conflict," writes the unnamed author. "Two sides of the same coin [Mania and Dementia] vying for the favor of their god." You relight the Sacellum's Great Torch in the Main Quest mission "The Cold Flame of Agnon." Or you read here that it's supposed to burn in the temple's tower, and wonder why it isn't. This book is uncommon.

THE RAVINGS OF FENROY

Written on bed sheets and the cell floor in the bodily fluids of its demented author, this is included just for color: a touch of the realm's madness. But every so often, you may find it insightful. This book is rare, and can be found in Books of Bliss, Orinthal's House in Bliss, J'zidzo's House (Mania version) in Split...and in Inlet Camp!

SAINTS AND SEDUCERS

The actual title is *Sentinels of the Isles: A Treatise on Golden Saint/Dark Seducer Culture and History Within the Shivering Isles*. It sets up your two brushes with these Daedric warrior races in the Main Quest—first at Cylarne in "The Cold Flame of Agnon" and again at either Brellach or Pinnacle Rock in "The Helpless Army." This book is common.

THE SHIVERING APOTHECARY

One of most useful books around. The five potion recipes it contains serve well any adventurer. This book is all over the place.

THE SHIVERING BESTIARY

Ditto. Detailed rundowns on the Isles' nine critters. This book is all over the place.

THE STANDING STONES

Meaning the Obelisks that dot the Isles. This sets up a freeform campaign to shut them down. (See "The Obelisks" section later on.) Alas, the book doesn't actually reveal much about the great crystals—the author seems a few aces shy of a full deck—but it does contain this telling line: "They are waiting for their master to return." This book is uncommon.

WABBAJACK

Useless drivel that reads, in part: "Wabbajack. Wabbajack. Wabbajack." (That goes on for a bit, too.) Not much more than a reminder that Sheogorath's the fellow who supplied this clever toy (a potential dialer-down of nasty enemies) after you performed his quest in Cyrodiil. This book is uncommon.

ZEALOTRY

Alternate title: *Zealotry of Sheogorath*. This book sets up your encounters with Zealot Mages—arch-rivals of the Heretics—who dwell in dungeons and surface camps. Yes, you can fool them for a while by wearing their robes. And, no, regardless of what it says here, you can't join them and you won't find any Zealot robes left behind in settled areas. (The only loose Zealot robes are beside two skeletons in a niche in the north-central portion of the dungeon Xavara—presumably those of supplicants who were deemed unworthy.) This book is all over the place.

SKILL BOOKS

These are guaranteed to turn up on four occasions:

- Acrobatics: *The Black Arrow, vol. 1* appears in the Duke of Mania's quarters, on the top shelf of the southern of the two bookshelves against the hall's west wall. *Mystery of Talara* turns up atop a chest on a mountaintop that's west-northwest of the dungeon Dire Warren. Happy climbing!
- Sneak: *Sacred Witness* also appears in the Duke of Mania's quarters—on the bottom shelf of the northern of the two bookshelves against the hall's west wall.
- You get a random skill book (drawn from the full field of skill books) for turning in Cindawe's journal to Ranarr-Jo in the Miscellaneous Quest "Everything in Its Place."

This doesn't mean that's all you get; it's just that the other appearances are unpredictable. Stealth and combat-related skill books turn up 10 percent of the time in certain "boss"-level loot. The combat books appear in undead boss chests on the top three levels of Xaselm and the Sepechra level of Ebrocca; the stealth ones in Zealot Mage boss containers on the Congregation Chambers level of Howling Halls, the Chantry level of Knifepoint Hollow, the Lost Crypt level of Knotty Bramble, three Rotten Den levels (Precipice, Sanctum, and Hollow), Xavara, the Catacombs level of Xiditte, and the Depths and Subterrane levels of Xirethard. You can also find them in the wilderness—just below the overhanging rock south of The Fringe's eastern extremity (home to Deformed Swamp Tentacles required for the Miscellaneous Quest "The Museum of Oddities").

CRIME & PUNISHMENT

The justice system in the Shivering Isles is similar to the one back in Cyrodiil, but with a few significant tweaks.

One is the concept of "crime gold"—the accrued bounty on your head for all the bad stuff you've done. It doesn't carry over from Cyrodiil to the Shivering Isles or vice versa, with the pleasant result that a vacation in the Isles is the equivalent of "laying low." Of course, when you return to Cyrodiil, the bounty returns.

Naturally, you're responsible for bad acts committed in Sheogorath's realm. Act up in front of witnesses in New Sheoth and you find the guards right on top of you. Pay the fine. Depending on where you're picked up, you are either transported to a spot just southeast of the statue inside Bliss's north gate or to the middle of the Crucible district. Alternately, mess with the guards. Or do the time.

 You're not safe from the guards out in the countryside. Mania and Dementia are each patrolled by a two-woman team—Saints for Mania and Seducers for Dementia. The Saints march from New Sheoth's Bliss district to Highcross, then move on to Split, Hale, and the Gates of Madness before making their way back to Bliss. The Seducers move from their base at Pinnacle Rock to New Sheoth's Crucible district, west again to the Gates of Madness, and south to Pinnacle Rock again.

Jail's the biggest difference. The Isles don't have a dungeon for the general population. The one under the House of Dementia is evidently for Syl's personal enemies…or people she just thinks are her personal enemies. So if you opt for prison, you're zapped into…well, not a cell, exactly, more like a secret room either in Aichan on the Isles' northwest coast (if nabbed in Mania) or Corpserot Passage well down on the Madgod's Boot peninsula (if nabbed in Dementia). All your stuff goes into the evidence chest and you're left with a plain suit of clothes and the traditional lockpick. However, you won't need lockpicks in these prisons.

You can activate the bedroll at the back of your cell to run out your sentence. In that case, all your possessions are restored and you're free—with the same risks of stat damage as in Cyrodiil. You find yourself back in New Sheoth at the same locations where you'd be deposited after paying your fine. Or, you can push a button to open your cell door and make a run for the exit. In Aichan, this button's on the east wall in the northeast corner. In Corpserot Passage, it's on the north side of the pedestal on the west side of your cell. If you get out, all is forgiven. You don't have to worry about extra bounty for a jail break, as you do back in Cyrodiil.

In either case, you're well advised to first grab the contents of the urn in your cell. This contains a blade and blunt weapon, plus one or two food items.

So what do you say we make a run for it?

AICHAN

There are two distinctly different routes here—each loaded with traps. Once out of your cell, push the button on the base of the facing pedestal to open gates to the east and west. Step through either gate and it closes—not be opened again from this side.

The eastern path: In the first room, you have to get past three sets of crisscrossing spells from the six statues along the east and west walls. It looks harder than it is; just run down the middle and you find the spells easy to avoid. The traps in the next big room are a bit trickier, with disappearing sections of floor (and a dart trap below each section) added to the mix. Avoid the open floors by stepping between the columns to the east. And that's that. Pass though the gate and use the west door.

The western path: No problems here until you pass through a pair of broken dungeon walls, enemies begin to appear, and traps kick in: worms, spike, and spore. We think your best move is to run!

Either way, you reach a large hall with the evidence chest containing your stuff and a Golden Saint turnkey two levels above your own. You can kill her, but you don't *have* to kill her. Unlike her counterpart in Corpserot Passage, she doesn't patrol—but she wanders far enough from the chest that sneaking could work even at a low Sneak skill. The lighting's good here—which works both for and against you—and so's the maneuvering room.

The exit stairs to the south lead you past the cells of two "envious Grummites" who actually bow down in your presence. Alas, the two Grummite guards outside Aichan's front door do not. Sweet freedom!

CORPSEROT PASSAGE

This is pretty much a straight hack 'n' slash dungeon level.

If you got a crappy weapon from the urn in your cell, let's make it better. Turn right out of your cell and grab the iron longsword on the rock shelf in the neighboring cell. Hurry, too, since your passage has set off a visit by the Grummite guard just down the hall.

Once you've dealt with the guard, check out the cell where he was stationed for a second urn containing one or two healing items, and maybe a repair hammer as well. Beyond the door, head north up the root passage. There's a spore cloud trap at the top of the hall on the left, a stump with more healing supplies, a Grummite archer (his bow and arrows are invaluable), and a root gate. The pull pod is on the right. As you turn northeast, you come upon one the rarest plants in the game: the Mute Screaming Maw. Activate it; you can turn in this ingredient to the Museum of Oddities for a reward.

Now you're approaching a three-way junction. Another guard's just down the hall to the left. Switch over to your bow or spells to take him down from a distance—retrieve the arrows afterward if you use the bow—and retrieve additional supplies up the halls to the northwest and southwest. Edge

along the sides of the main hall on your way back to the southeast to avoid damage from the pit trap. Use the metal door opposite the root tunnel and make your way southeast. Here you find two additional Grummites—one of them an archer—and a choice of two paths. The root corridor in the southern corner of the sunken room to the southwest is the tougher route. The paths come back together at the northwest end of the northern of two wide halls populated by two archers and a melee fighter. These halls lead south to the exit.

Your exit from Corpserot Passage is trickier than that from Aichan. In the room atop the stairs are the evidence chest and prison boss—a Dark Seducer Turnkey. Unlike her counterpart in Aichan, the Seducer has fixed patrol routes to the northwest end of the room and the landing down the stairs to the northeast, so you can slip past her. However, the darkness here makes it tricky to identify her position—use a night-vision or Detect Life enchantment to play it safe. Make a quick exit to avoid getting entangled with the inbound Grummite summoned by your activation of the evidence chest. Your bounty is wiped clean. Note, too, that five Grummites are sited near the exit—one close by and four in the lake to the east-southeast.

Corruption at the Top

One last thing: Suppose you get in trouble with the guards after you've completed the Main Quest. Effectively, you're Sheogorath. It'd be a little weird for the guards to send Sheogorath to prison. So they don't. They're very polite. The guard says there's been a "misunderstanding" and gives you the option of accompanying her, which requires surrender of items you've "inadvertently borrowed," paying reparations if you've got the cash, or fighting, which the guard regards as a personal honor.

Accompany the guard and you wind up at one of two sites: the gate to the New Sheoth Graveyard if you were nabbed in Dementia, or a stone platform on Overlook Road up the hill north of New Sheoth if you were nailed in Mania. You've been inconvenienced rather than arrested—special treatment for the Shivering Isles' one true celebrity—but you still owe the bounty.

DRUG DEALER?

Skooma's in the Shivering Isles, too, in a very small way. You won't find it anywhere loose. But both of the J'zidzos in Split, Manic and Demented versions alike, have eight portions of this addictive drug on their person. Though they don't talk about it.

On the other hand, Caldana Monrius in New Sheoth's Crucible district barely talks about anything else. She's in a terrible way; she *always* has a "skooma" topic. Of course, you can just tell Monrius to get her own skooma—your only option if you don't have it. But if you're carrying the drug, you can give it to her—assuming the creepy role of her supplier.

The poor thing gives a pathetic cheer and even tries to pay you. Clearly, she's already sold or traded in almost everything of value. (Just check out her forbidding house just north of Muurine's place. Most of the time her payment is a useless item of clutter. Occasionally, it's either a potion drawn from the full potions list or a piece of jewelry.

Monrius's Disposition also soars 75 points, but to no clear effect, as she can't tell you anything else. If you question her in the Main Quest mission "The Lady of Paranoia," you still have to have Herdir torture her.

NON-QUEST DUNGEONS

AICHAN AND CORPSEROT PASSAGE

Situated respectively on the northwest coast and on the south coast of the Madgod's Boot peninsula, these are the prisons for Mania and Dementia. Aichan's got the traps, Corpserot the fighting. See the "Crime & Punishment" section in this chapter for details.

BLACKROOT LAIR

Initially, this big Grummite lair southeast of the Gates of Madness seems like a standard root-system dungeon—albeit one with a large number of patrolling enemies on the entry level.

But as you drop down to the Outer Encampment, Channel, Inner Encampment, and Tunnels levels, you find nine Gnarl prisoners and a total of 21 loose pieces of Gnarl Bark. The Grummites appear to be harvesting the stuff. It's an Alchemy hint of sorts. Grummites have an intrinsic weakness against fire, and a Journeyman alchemist can use Gnarl Bark to make Fire Shield potions.

Are we overreaching? Not really. The Grummites appear to be beasts, but (contrary to what you read in *From Frog to Man*) they're in fact semi-civilized creatures who practice magic, construct rudimentary shelters, and use common household items. If nothing else, this dungeon provides a better appreciation for their abilities.

CANN

This one's a kind of black comedy about bad communication.

In the Arena level of Cann, a deep dungeon at the western base of the Saints Watch peninsula, the Heretic Mages finally found a place to host an event they call the "Elaborate Spectacle." But it didn't come off as intended. It was a bloodbath. In fact, it's always been a bloodbath. The participants kill each other.

So what's the Spectacle *supposed* to be? Well, that's just the point. The two letters you find on the bodies of participants make it clear they have one understanding of its purpose (a brutal one). And the letter from a Mage to his brother suggests the Heretics have quite another.

Perhaps we should just start with the documents themselves. The Mage's letter is found among crumpled papers and gems beside a cupboard in the northwest corner of the arena portion of the Arena level. The easiest way down there is to make your way quietly northeast through the Great Hall to the Amphitheater and northeast again to the Arena entrance. You shouldn't have much trouble here—the deep darkness lends itself to sniping—and you have even less trouble if you first dress up as Heretic.

This letter contains the closest thing to the host's statement of intent: "Why would men given a week alone to write and feed on wine instantly set murderously upon each other rather than share a loving embrace?" writes the Mage. "We always believed that the Elaborate Spectacle would be the greatest public display of shared pleasure."

Sounds like an orgy, right?

So what went wrong? The participants' letters are down on the dark, Hunger-haunted Substratum level—reached via the gate at the west end of the arena floor. One's on the skeleton on the bed in the southernmost chamber, the other just inside the door of the room to the north. Both of these fellows think they're headed for combat, but one has doubts: "I think we might have got this whole thing wrong." He observes that their captors seem *scared* of them.

If the Heretics wanted these folks to enter into the spirit of the event, they had to tell 'em what it was about. Reading between the lines, the participants were kept in the dark and had to judge its purpose from their circumstances. And those circumstances did not encourage an optimistic view. Consider: The participants were kidnapped. They were fed what may have seemed like a last meal and given an opportunity to write what may have seemed like a last letter. And when you explore the Substratum you find their rooms equipped with practice targets and body bags. Confusing, to say the least!

DIRE WARREN

A sad story unfolds in a pair of journals on the Subterrane level of Dire Warren—a critter lair just west of the side path that links the dungeon Cylarne to Overlook Road.

Getting down there's a bit involved, and both journals are hard to find. They're in artfully concealed southwestern and northeastern sections of the level. On the entry level, turn left, right, and left again to reach the tunnel that takes you to the entry upper tier. Cross the trench using the bridge to the south and follow the passages east to a pool and south to the root door into the Subterrane.

Here you find a pair of large chambers. Drop into the trench on the east side of the western room. Don't climb the root ramp at its south end; rather, move south around the ramp and down the passage beyond. At its end, there's dead young woman sprawled on a rock, a bow called Ly'ssane, and a Diseased Scalon with three glass arrows in it. The young woman, Alyssa, is carrying 20 more arrows…and a journal.

This little book records her initial pleasure at this place, which she was introduced to by her boyfriend Traelius, and her increasing discontent as Traelius talks about this cave being their home. Alyssa begins to feel trapped and starts to explore. If her descriptions sound unfamiliar, it's because you haven't seen the couple's portion of the cave; they entered via a different door. At length, Alyssa leaves her boyfriend, only to break her leg in the attempt—or at the hands of the Scalon; it's not clear—and then dies crying for Traelius to rescue her.

Finding Traelius is tricky. Return north up the passage and follow the trench to the eastern of the two large rooms. On its east side is the waterfall Alyssa mentioned. However, there's no place for you to climb up where she climbed down. Instead, climb the root ramp in the room's southwest corner and follow the western shelf north to the northwest corner. Here you can use root-ends and protruding rocks to jump along the north side of the room and then south to the waterfall. Follow the stream east—it appears blocked, but you can get through—and the side corridor north to Traelius's quarters.

Don't expect to bond with him. A Heretic Mage boss in everything but name, Traelius turns hostile if you just show up in his cave. And yet, in view of Alyssa's death, it may seem wrong to just treat him like some anonymous Heretic Mage and kill him. Besides, he's two levels above your own, so that requires some hard work. If you're competently stealthy, you should be able to pickpocket the journal as Traelius sits on his stool. However, remove the creatures in the pool below the waterfall first. Otherwise, you're detected on approach.

The journal supplies a wrenching postscript: Traelius might have saved his girlfriend. In his last entry, he writes that "I still hear her voice now and then coming from the waterfall, but I know they are only echoes of memory."

Now, they really are.

EBROCCA

While tied by proximity to the Miscellaneous Quest "Taxonomy of Obsession," this big undead dungeon southeast of the hamlet of Highcross isn't technically a quest dungeon. After all, there are many other places you can come up with the ingredients that quest giver Mirili Ulven requires. This place has all kinds of things going on: a secret level with a cremator that turns bones into a new ingredient, an unusual vertical puzzle section, a unique boss who can resurrect himself, a third entrance up in the hills, and no fewer than *seven* documents setting up a story about the restoration of a family mausoleum. See the relevant section of the Miscellaneous Quests for details.

FAIN

We bet you've never survived a fall this long. This Heretic Mage dungeon north of New Sheoth features a spectacular descent to its lower tier via an esophageal tunnel. Just push the button on the pillar on the east side of the central dais to open the hole in the floor.

What's down there? Wait a moment before you take that long first step. A couple of documents up top suggest it's something out of H.P. Lovecraft's nightmares. *Gyub, Lord of the Pit*, in a glass case on the table north of the button, refers to the tentacles and "infinite maw" of this "Embryonic Prince." In addition, on the table in the southwest corner you find a letter that refers to the creature's delight when two "volunteers" are thrown down at the same time.

Ah, they're *messin'* with you. Upon arriving in the pool at the bottom, there's nothing more here than a little Baliwog colony. The boss is a Scalon if you've reached Level 7.

KNOTBONE CHAMBER

Up top, this dungeon along Overlook Road north-northwest of Xaselm is a critter lair: Baliwogs, Elytra, Gnarls, or Scalon (beginning at Level 9). Down below, it's a Grummite camp. And in the middle, on the Juncture level, it's a battle between the two tenants. South of the level entrance there are seven Grummites, at least four of them Mages, duking it out with five Elytra, including a boss, before the stairs of a long-buried structure. The Grummites slaughter the Elytra.

The buried structure is a clue to look deeper. On the short Pipes level, you get into the ruins. The Ruins level, slightly longer, is all pitched at an angle (and some of it is collapsing to boot). And the Cellar level, a small columned cavern, takes you back to the surface to the east-northeast of the top-level entrance.

No great supply of loot down here, however. In addition to a few containers, there's a scattering of loose gems and a pair of crude Grummite maces of some interest to a low-level character. These weapons don't normally turn up on Grummites until you reach Level 6.

XIDITTE

This Zealot Mage stronghold west of Vitharn on the Madgod's Boot peninsula offers a number of curiosities. On the desk in the Arbiter's (i.e. boss's) office on the entry level is a document called Arbiter's Log. Mainly, it charts infractions by followers—the typical punishment being a visit to "the pit."

What's the pit? Actually, it's right below the office. Push the button on the south side of the desk and a hole opens in the floor to the north. This drops you down to a door into the Catacombs level. Beyond, a cell with a five-tumbler lock. Obviously, you just want to take the stairs. (The other entrance is on the north side of the big room to the north.)

And then there are those five statues in a pair of adjacent rooms south of the cell. It's a puzzle. If you push the button on the base of the Hunger statue at the north end of the north room, chain lightning shoots south and strikes the Grummite statue. Use the control panel on the south wall up the stairs to the east to adjust the facings of the four Grummite statues so that each statue passes on the lightning to the next statue in sequence. Each of the four buttons here toggles a statue between its two facings. The lowest button operates the northern statue, the top the southern statue, the left the eastern statue, and the right the western.

For the lightning to reach its target, the northern statue must face southeast, the eastern statue west, the western statue southeast, and the southern statue south. Once everything's lined up properly, hit the button on the Hunger statue again. The lightning zaps between all four statues, then up the southern stairs to the fifth, immoveable statue. This statue redirects the lightning to the west—destroying the wall here and exposing a path to a Crystal Chest. Jump across three stone beams to reach the passage to the chest.

GEOGRAPHY

ROCK FORMATIONS

Follow the north coast east from the Golden Saints stronghold at Brellach to find a peninsula dotted with six tall spires of rock and, mingled with them, smaller spires with holes in them. The big ones look almost as though they've been purposefully stacked, and their arrangement suggests you're expected to use them as steps to jump to the top of the tallest. However, there's nothing up there except a nice view, and we're unsure if even Sheogorath could make the required jump. The formations aren't unique. You find them in even greater concentrations along Overlook Road north of Knotbone Chamber and outside the dungeon Cann to the southwest. However, standing alone as they do out on this peninsula, they're most distinctive at this location.

WATERFALLS

Some of the most spectacular waterfalls in the game can be found around Runoff Camp east of the New Sheoth. One is southwest of the camp, just east of the south gate into Crucible district, and two more on the coast to the east. You find other beauties dropping south from the lake just east of the dungeon Knifepoint Hollow, just west of Bliss's north gate, and two southeast and east-southeast of Puddlejump Camp on the south side of the lake just north of the Hill of Suicides region. There's also a small waterfall on the lower level of the dungeon Dire Warren.

VISTAS

Up for a little mountain climbing? You can see virtually the whole island from the lofty pinnacle up in the Jester's Spine Mountains—north-northwest of New Sheoth on the rough line between the dungeons Fain and Dunroot Burrow. There's a tall pedestal on the peak with a statue on top. Or try the one west of Dire Warren and north-northeast of Aichan. There's a chest and skill book up top. And while it's not exactly "mountain climbing," there's also a magnificent view all the way east to New Sheoth, from the rocks along the ridge road just south of Split.

HILL OF SUICIDES

A big freeform quest.

The Hill of Suicides is a great rocky outcropping located north of the Low Road between the dungeon Xaselm and Flooded Camp. There's a fast travel icon here, but no one alludes to a mission at this location until you retrieve a specific quest item.

In other words, there's a very good chance you won't hear about the mission *at all*.

But we're betting you eventually get curious about the site itself. Especially after both the Mania and Dementia versions of Horkvir Bear-Arm, from the Miscellaneous Quest "The Great Divide," tell you that suicide is against the law in the Shivering Isles. Along with Hirrus Clutumnus from the Miscellaneous Quest "Final Resting," they suggest the existence of the souls on the Hill is a miserable one. And if you stop in the hamlet of Deepwallow and chat with Erver Devani, he tells you his sister is among those souls. Follow up on the "Hill of Suicides" topic, and he explains that "It's where you end up if you don't die according to His [Sheogorath's] plan," and supplies his sister's name: Gadeneri. If you already have her skull, he instructs you to bring it to her on the Hill. That's the one reference to a quest.

So there is someone up there: ghosts. You find five "restless souls" spread across different tiers of this peninsula: Gadeneri Ralvel and Lorenz Bog-Trotter at the bottom, M'desi and

FREEFORM QUESTS

Salonia Viria higher on the slopes, and Limark up top. You can't talk to any of them or indeed interact with them at all. You need the appropriate skull in your inventory to bring peace to the skull's former tenant…and the skulls are scattered across the Isles.

Moreover, skulls are not exactly an uncommon item in these parts. There are dozens of them here—including 39 on two levels of the dungeon Xaselm, 18 in the home of the death-obsessed Jastira Nanus in Split, and 11 in the home of the savage farm-guard Relan in Fellmoor.

But that'd be too easy. The relevant skulls are all down in dungeons, and none are especially easy to find.

So what are you waiting for?

- **Gadeneri Ralvel's Skull:** We mentioned this one in passing in "Symbols of Office" in the Main Quest section. It's on the Chantry level of the Main Quest dungeon Knifepoint Hollow—atop a chest in a secret room directly east of the exit to the upper tier of the entry level. Slug your way through this Zealot Mage lair, light up the preternaturally dark room at level's end, and figure out where the heck they put the button to open the wall to the east. (It's on the north side of the base of the statue on the north side of the room.)

- **Lorenz Bog-Trotter's Skull:** This one is referenced in the Miscellaneous Quest "A Liquid Solution." It's in the Lost Crypt level of Knotty Bramble, on a bier in an enclosed crypt on the south side of the level. To get to it, you have to traverse the entry and Hatchery levels—dealing with Grummites en route—and then find a well-hidden button. This one's under the body on the bier in the northwest part of the corridor that encloses the crypt. Use the grab button to drag the body off…and prepare to be greeted warmly by living Zealot guardians when you emerge from the crypt if you trigger them by venturing into its eastern section.

- **M'desi's Skull:** It's three levels down in the Zealot Mage dungeon Rotten Den, atop a chest at the foot of a great Scalon statue in a large square chamber in the level's southeast corner, Oh, yeah: It's guarded by a Zealot Mage boss. Not fun. The entry, Deadfall level, finds you down in a trench and getting pelted by spells from the statues on the upper tier and jabbed by spike traps. On the Precipice level, make your way south, down one root ramp and up another, and then south again past the statue to the Sanctum entrance. This is a hub for the Hollow level to the east and Encampment level to the west. However, just drop down through a succession of three holes into the undead portion of our program and head east once you're out in the main hall. Also not fun: If you've reached Level 7, Shambles lie ahead in the room at the end of the hall, Skeletons if you haven't. But you're closing in. Climb the ramp here and head south through another spike-trapped root-system corridor to the boss, yet another spell-flinging statue, and the skull. Whew.

- **Salonia Viria's Skull:** It's at the foot of a Hunger statue in the south-central portion of the Amphitheater level of the big Heretic Mage dungeon Cann. On The Great Hall level, take the paved hallway to the north, rather than the root-system tunnel to the west, and follow this all the way east before slipping through the arch to the north toward the Amphitheater exit. This allows you to skip some of the more densely populated sections of the level. In the Amphitheater level, it's even easier: Keep heading east. You eventually see the room with a railing ahead of you. That's the one.

- **Limark's Skull:** It's on the Xetrem level of the Main Quest dungeon Milchar. You can get into this critter lair two ways: the separate entrance to the east end of the surface site or the one on the south side of the small Nexus level. The latter's more direct—Nexus is the fast travel destination—and also offers the simpler solution once inside Xetrem: south, up the stairs to the east, south again, and the skull's right in front of you. And so's a critter.

Return to the Hill of Suicides. Activate a ghost with the right skull in your inventory and it casts a Spirit Blessing spell on you before vanishing. This is a 20-minute, 100-point Fortify Fatigue spell. Don't turn in all the skulls at once. This is a nice benefit and you can get it five times over.

Once you've turned in all five skulls, you get a new Power: Risen Flesh. This works just like the Staff of Worms you win back in Cyrodiil at the end of the Mages Guild quests; it allows you to bring dead NPCs (not creatures) back to life and have them fight for you for 60 seconds—at which time they relapse into death.

INGREDIENTS

This section has been mostly pre-empted by the Miscellaneous Quests "The Museum of Oddities" and "Taxonomy of Obsession." In the former mission, curator Una Armina offers rewards for three of the rarest ingredients in the Isles: **Blind Watcher's Eye**, **Mute Screaming Maw**, and **Deformed Swamp Tentacle**. In the latter, Mirili Ulven sends you off to get more or less everything else. She doesn't send you to get **Ashen Remains**, but you can discover how to manufacture that ingredient while searching for loose ingredients in Ebrocca.

So what's left?

Just going by loose portions, **Hearts of Order** is the rarest of the omissions. While you've doubtless collected plenty of these from Knights of Order—the Knights around the Obelisks always have 'em—there's a single Heart that can be grabbed up elsewhere. It's on a table in the southwest corner of Ciirta's sanctum on the Antechamber level of the Howling Halls.

And, yes, the Hearts are indeed edible. But it's a non-standard ingredient that operates identically regardless of your Alchemy skill. If you munch on one, a pair of spells kicks in. Jyggalag's Ascendancy, which shows up under Active Effects as "Force of Order," boosts your Strength by 25 points and your Health by 50 for 15 seconds…and also invokes a second spell, The Boon of Order, that restores 60 points of lost Health. Eat a second heart while the effects of the first are active and all the effects, save for The Boon of Order, are cancelled.

Then there's **Bone Shard**. It always appears on dead Shambles, can appear on Grummite Mages, and can sometimes be purchased at Things Found in Crucible. However, if you haven't reached Level 9, when Shambles begin to appear, it's that much harder to find. There are exactly four portions lying around loose: two on the Descenia level of the dungeon Ebrocca (flanking the Watcher's Eye on the fountain near the entrance), and two on the alchemy table in the steward/servant's bedroom in the House of Dementia.

At Novice level, Bone Shard restores Willpower. At Apprentice, it has a Frost Shield effect. At Journeyman, it damages Magicka and, at Expert, Luck. And don't accidentally waste it while producing Ashen Remains in the Cremator Retort in the dungeon Ebrocca. That device accepts Bone Shard as a plain old bone.

Wisp Core can be harvested 25 percent of the time from 800-plus Root Stalk plants that grow almost exclusively in dungeons. However, just 10 portions are lying around loose: four in a bowl on an alchemy table on the Arena level of Cann, right near where you found the Mage's letter in the "Non-Quest Dungeons" section; three on plates on the bar at The Wastrel's Purse in Passwall; and three in a bowl on the dinner table in Jastira Nanus's House in Split (Mania version).

This ingredient restores Intelligence at the Novice level and has Burden, Light, and Chameleon effects at Apprentice, Journeyman, and Expert levels, respectively.

And the last of the new ingredients is **Smoked Baliwog Leg**. This staple of Shivering Isles cuisine can always be purchased at The Choosy Beggar in Bliss and Sickly Bernice's Taphouse in Crucible; poached in loose form from houses and businesses in New Sheoth, Passwall, Split, Deepwallow, and Fellmoor; swiped from cupboards; and even retrieved from dungeons. In fact, the biggest Smoked Baliwog Leg cache is on the Encampment level of Rotten Den, where it seems to be the main course in a Zealot Mage banquet. It restores Fatigue at the Novice level, has a Feather effect at Apprentice, restores Health at Journeyman, and at Expert level damages four times over the Fatigue it restored at Novice level.

Sometimes, it doesn't pay to know too much about what you're eating.

KILLING SHEOGORATH?

Nuh-uh. He's at Level 254. All his attributes and skills are 100. His Health, Fatigue, and Spell Points are all 10,000. Besides, he's not carrying anything except lettuce and yarn—presumably the same lettuce and yarn you used to get Sheogorath's quest at his Cyrodiil shrine. (And if you haven't done that yet, then they aren't.) And even if you were capable of killing him, the game won't let you; he's considered "essential."

Even so, given the experiences you may already have had back in Cyrodiil with Mehrunes Dagon, you may think the only good Daedra is a dead Daedra—even if the old dude doesn't look particularly "Daedric"—and thus feel inclined to poke your nutty patron with something sharp just on principle.

Have the presence of mind to save your game first. If you do try to hit the Madgod, you are very dead. Sheogorath won't give you a second chance. "You really shouldn't have done that," he says. "Enjoy the view." He then disables the player interface, teleports you to roughly the same altitude over the Isles at which you may have met the spirits of the crusading knight Pelinal and Ayleid baddie Umaril the Unfeathered in the Knights of the Nine quests…and then lets you fall onto a stone platform near the center of the Isles. He's right of course. The view is spectacular. You can see the whole Isle laid out below you, until…

All together now: *Ouch*.

Before you die, you may notice other bodies on the platform. You are not the first to receive this special attention. However, being dead puts a real crimp in further investigation. So, this time, don't take a swing at Sheogorath and instead seek out this Easter Egg on foot. It's northwest of New Sheoth on the south side of the hill north-northwest of the dungeon Knifepoint Hollow, which you explore in the Main Quest mission "Symbols of Office."

Along with four skeletons, a decomposed corpse, a silver dagger, and three potions, you come across an intact body labeled simply "Sheogorath's Punished." In its pockets, there's a Death Decree. The poor fellow was condemned to death for growing a beard! We suppose it competed with Sheogorath's own.

NEW SHEOTH GRAVEYARD

Stop in. It's not dangerous. The dead do not rise from their graves. But they do leave behind punchlines—and more of them than you may imagine.

It's easy to miss the cemetery's significance. If you visit it early in the game, there are eight tombstones: Vien Brenenus, Endarie, Helene, Meehn, Lob gro-Murgob, Ranesta, Blaise Sette, and Vivel Telaram. These folks are already dead when the game begins. Activate each stone to read its accompanying epitaph.

You may think this is just an Easter Egg—as indeed it is. But unless you make a practice of stopping here regularly, what may not be apparent is that an additional 23 stones can appear here. Two appear after the murder of Ma'zaddha and the execution of Muurine in the Main Quest mission "The Lady of Paranoia"—and the rest when other residents of New Sheoth's Bliss and Crucible districts die by your unforgiving hand.

These epitaphs all play off the personalities of the deceased. For instance, the inscription for the nymphomaniac proprietor of Books of Bliss reads: "Finally, Sontaire sleeps alone."

Some of this killing may occur semi-naturally over the course of the game. You're encouraged to kill four New Sheoth residents: the thief Brithaur in the Miscellaneous Quest "Brithaur," the assisted-suicide Hirrus Clutumnus in "Final Resting," the beggar Uungor in the Miscellaneous Quest "Falling Awake," and the beggar Bhisha in the Miscellaneous Quest "Ushnar's Terror." It's also possible that Ushnar gro-Shadborgob winds up dead if things get overheated in "Ushnar's Terror."

However, you have to put most of the others down without good cause. Save your game first. You wouldn't like the depopulated city. And remember, murder's a crime if you get caught. It often cuts you off from quests and colorful personal interactions. And it leaves this city feeling kind of, well, dead.

Plus, sometimes the actual killing is slightly taxing. Most personal weapons in the city are low-end. But Pad-Ei, the guest at The Choosy Beggar, is a level above you and has a leveled magic dagger. Museum of Oddities curator Una Armina, Things Found proprietor Ahjazda, and retired assassin Orinthal are all unarmed, but the first two are at levels 25 and 15, respectively, and Orinthal's one above your own. And Common Treasures proprietor Tilse Areleth is Level 10 with a leveled shortsword.

 You can't kill everyone. The game considers certain characters "essential." They can be beaten unconscious…and then dust themselves off and go back to what they were doing before they were so rudely interrupted. This includes the merchants Sickly Bernice, Cutter, and Earil in Crucible, and Dumag gro-Bonk in Bliss. Initially, it also includes Ma'zaddha and Muurine from the Main Quest mission "Brithaur," and Amiable Fanriene. However, Ma'zaddha and Muurine die during the Main Quest mission "The Lady of Paranoia" and completion of the Brithaur and Fanriene quests resets their respective statuses to non-essential.

Everyone else is fair game.

One character has alternate epitaphs. If the beggar Bhisha pays the ultimate penalty in the Miscellaneous Quest "Ushnar's Terror," he gets one that reflects the context of his demise ("Killed because he loved dogs."). If he dies under other circumstances, he's just "sweet, harmless Bhisha."

THE OBELISKS

There are 23 of these big crystalline formations in the Shivering Isles. You can't destroy them, but you can render them dormant.

When you arrive, all the Obelisks are inactive. Three go "live" and are then shut down by you directly in the course of two Main Quest missions: the one in Xeddefen's Great Chamber ("Retaking The Fringe") and the two on the lower tier of the grounds of Sheogorath's Palace ("The End of Order").

The other 20, scattered around the countryside, are tackled a bit differently. When you tune Xedilian's Resonator in the Main Quest mission "A Better Mousetrap," half these Obelisks are prepped for launch with the appearance near each of an attendant Priest of Order. (These are numbers 1–5, 10–12, 14, and 18 on the accompanying map.) In addition, Knights begin to patrol routes between most of these newly activated Obelisks.

When you actually enter the region around an Obelisk, the Obelisk goes "live"—its upper section rising and revolving on a stream of lavender energy—and spits out two Knights 25 seconds apart. Should you kill one these guards, it spawns another as a replacement.

This is the "Greymarch" you've been hearing about from Sheogorath. It advances as you progress through the early stages of the Main Quest. When you get the Chalice of Reversal in the Main Quest mission "Addiction," a priest appears at #13. When you leave Dunroot Barrow's Sanctum of Decadence, the Obelisk is directly to the east and the priest activates it as you watch.

When you actually deliver the Chalice to Thadon, Obelisks #6 and #19 join in on the fun. When you complete "The Lady of Paranoia," #7 and #16 come on and a second set of patrols is added. Once "The Cold Flame of Agnon" is lit at Cylarne, #15 comes on. Once you light the Great Torch at New Sheoth's Sacellum Arden-Sul, #8 and #20 are fired up as well. And selecting either side in "Ritual of Accession" adds the last two Obelisks—#9 and #17—and a third set of patrols.

Talking to Sheogorath at the end of the next Main Quest mission, "Retaking The Fringe," shuts down all Obelisks and Knight patrols—albeit only until you talk to the Madgod again to wrap up "Rebuilding the Gatekeeper." At this time, the power comes on again and all 20 Obelisks and patrols are restored. This is the Order's high water mark. The Obelisks and patrols are shut down once and for all when you finish "The End of Order."

Allied in spirit, if not substance, to the closing of random Oblivion Gates back in Cyrodiil, this task isn't entirely freeform. After you get the Main Quest mission "The Cold Flame of Agnon"—the first occasion on which the game puts you in close proximity to an Obelisk of Orders (#3)—Sheogorath orders you to destroy them and kill any nearby priests.

However, his order doesn't take the form of a quest. There are no journals and there is no overarching reward—save the obvious one of not having to periodically fight Knights of Order as you wander the Shivering Isles countryside. How you handle this, or whether you handle it at all, is entirely up to you.

FREEFORM QUESTS

What should you do? Strictly speaking, you don't have to do anything. If you wish, you can use detours and fast travel to avoid virtually all contact with these sites. But an early move against the Obelisks along your principal routes—Low and Overlook Roads in particular—makes good sense in the interests of convenience. And, of course, a concerted campaign to remove the Order's presence entirely nets you a lot of experience and loot.

Shutting these Obelisks down works just as it does during the Main Quest missions:

1. You need to insert three Hearts of Order. These can always be found on the Knights immediately around Obelisks and 50 percent of the time on Knights encountered elsewhere. There's a required four-second delay between insertions.

 Each Heart you insert also increases the production ceiling for a given Obelisk. Hence, if you pump in two Hearts, but are chased away before you can put in the third, the Obelisk now has a maximum of four Knight guards. It's now operating at its full capacity. A third Heart overloads it.

2. You want to put down the Obelisk's resident Priest—ideally right before or right after you insert the third Heart. See, the priests and Obelisks are inter-dependent: A live priest can restart a shut down Obelisk immediately upon his arrival at the Obelisk site, and a "live" Obelisk resurrects a dead priest after 25 seconds. Getting rid of the priest at this stage virtually ensures that the Obelisk is taken down before it can restore the priest.

We've mentioned there's no overarching reward for taking down all the Obelisks. But there is a long series of immediate rewards along the way. A Crystal Chest can be found near each Obelisk. These chests also appear in Brellach and Pinnacle Rock during the Main Quest mission "The Helpless Army," in the Catacombs level of Xiditte, and at certain wilderness locations (listed under "Wilderness Caches".)

Similar to a boss chest, these containers always hold a soul gem and might contain: gold (25 percent chance of 20–745 in leveled gold and a 50-50 shot at up to nine gold); a healing potion (50 percent chance); alchemical equipment, a scroll, and a magic or conventional weapon (25 percent chances); magic or conventional armor (10 percent shots at each); jewelry, a repair hammer, magic arrows, and a potion (all 10 percent shots). You need a Heart of Order to open each chest.

THE ROOFTOP CLUB

An odd little band of Crucible residents gets together on the roof of Sickly Bernice's Taphouse at night to stage mock battles.

Attendance varies, depending on the day of the week, but, initially, someone's up here between a little after 8 p.m. and 10 p.m. every night except Sunday. Drop by early in your stay and, at some point, you find Cutter, Ma'zaddha, Caldana Monrius, Muurine, and Ushnar gro-Shadborgob (and his dog) in attendance. If Ma'zaddha has already been killed and Muurine executed in the course of the Main Quest mission "The Lady of Paranoia," the club scales back its schedule to just Wednesdays and Fridays.

Watching is cool, but you can't join the group or participate in the fun. When you hit someone, it's for real. Talk to Muurine, Cutter, or gro-Shadborgob during these little parties and they instruct you to not interfere. "What we do here is our own business," says Muurine.

You can get a little more information about the society from a curious document called *Liturgy of the Duelists*. This can be found on four of the five club members—gro-Shadborgob is the exception—and in the locked box on the bar. Pick the three-tumbler lock or borrow the key from one of the members. This same Duelist's Key also unlocks the weapons chest against the roof's northeast railing.

These club rules do have a very liturgical timbre. But why? The first rule of Rooftop Club is to make you wonder what it's all about—especially in view of the involvement of two of its members in the conspiracy against Duchess of Dementia Syl. Are these folks just having fun, are they crazy like everyone else, or are they rehearsing for some nasty future event?

Yes, yes, and no. It's just another odd little thing in this supremely odd land.

SMALL ISLANDS

On three small islands, you find little Grummite encampments with a cauldron of skulls, totem poles, and one or two Grummites: on the western of the two islands off the coast southeast of Runoff Camp; northwest of the eastern of the two islands in the bay formed by the Madgod's Boot peninsula; and beneath the roots of a mushroom tree on an island on the map's south edge southeast of Corpserot Passage. The totem poles also appear on their own. (Typically, there's a signpost: "Grummites nearby.")

You come upon giant statues of Scalons on an island in the inlet northwest of the dungeon Cann and on a platform in the swampy lake east of Pinnacle Road and north of the dungeon Xedilian. (There's also one at the tip of the peninsula northeast of Breakneck Camp.) The statues themselves are just dead stone and can't be activated. However, it's interesting that, at Level Nine or higher, you find at least one live Scalon at each of these sites. Are they confused—like a beta fish looking into a mirror—or worshipful? Is there more to these hulking creatures than we imagine?

WILDERNESS CACHES

A range of caches large and small can be found in the wilderness. We've charted a lot of these in other sections, but here are the ones that have otherwise eluded us until now.

The boss-level Crystal Chests found at Obelisk sites (see "The Obelisks") have been sited at other locations as well. Each still requires a Heart of Order to open. These Crystal Chests can also be found:

- At the base of the waterfall at the northeast end of the lake west of New Sheoth's Bliss district
- Just east of the central portion of Sheogorath's Palace
- Just over the mountains southeast of Runoff Camp, which is itself east of New Sheoth
- Underwater, west of the bridge that leads across an inlet to the Isle of Flame
- Underwater, southeast of the eastern of the two islands south and southeast of Vitharn
- Beneath the roots of a mushroom tree on the Laughing Coast region of the Isles' west coast—roughly halfway between The Fringe and Aichan
- Beneath the roots of a mushroom tree on the east side of the triangular island just east of the Isle of Flame
- Just northeast of the square-shaped protrusion at the southern extremity of The Fringe
- In the bay formed by the Madgod's Boot peninsula—just off the north (inner) coast below the roots of a mushroom tree located south of the eastern of the two large islands in the bay

- In coastal waters just south over a hill from the southwestern extremity of the Low Road (the section between Hardscrabble Camp and Blackroot Lair where it curves around a hill)

And then there are the low-rent chests that turn up all over the Isles. These contain 1–10 gold, with a 75 percent chance of a piece low-end loot and a 15 percent shot at a lockpick. The "low-end loot" runs from pure clutter like crystal balls and scales to silver table items, animal pelts, jewelry, iron arrows, and gold and silver nuggets. Many of these are at camps, but two turn up:

- Just south of the rocks on the mountaintop southwest of Split and southeast of Obelisk #1. (See the Obelisk maps.)
- On a mountaintop west-northwest of the dungeon Dire Warren

YNGVAR DOOM-SAYER

"My message is actually one of comfort," insists Mr. Doom-Sayer. "The world is ending, and we can't do anything about it."

In truth, there's not a lot to say about Yngvar. He introduces himself as Yngvar the Wanderer, but this big shirtless Nord has acquired such a reputation as a proselytizer for Order's coming victory that he's won this moniker instead. He wanders from town to town with his silver battleaxe and leather leggings: from Highcross to Split, Split to Hale, Hale to the Gates of Madness, the Gates to Pinnacle Rock, Pinnacle Rock to Deepwallow, Deepwallow to Crucible, and Crucible to Bliss. You're bound to see him at some point. And his defining characteristic, apart from this cheerful pessimism, is his high level (10 above your own). This makes him an excellent road companion (albeit one beyond your control) should his destination also be your own.

And did you know he wrote a book? It's called *The Predecessors* and can be found in quantity at Books of Bliss, Orinthal's House in Bliss, and the Clanfather's quarters on the Sepechra level of Ebrocca, as well as singly at many other locations.

So how embarrassing it must be for him when the Main Quest ends and the world doesn't. "Order was supposed to destroy everything," he says. "It has always happened that way."

For the first time, Yngvar sounds frightened.

FREEFORM QUESTS

SHIVERING ISLES WORLD MAP DESCRIPTIONS

1. **Brellach:** The base for the Golden Saints. You reclaim it from the forces of Order in the Main Quest mission "The Helpless Army," if you replaced the Duchess of Dementia in the earlier quest "Ritual of Accession." Until that time, it is locked. Identical in layout to the Dark Seducer headquarters at Pinnacle Rock (from the Mania side of the same quest), its four levels are heavily populated with Knights and Priests of Order. Penetrate to the Font of Rebirth level and ring four chimes to shatter the crystal capstone that blocks the resurrection of dead Saints. Crystal chests are found on the Hall of Honor and Hall of Devotion levels.

2. **Cylarne:** Focus of the Main Quest mission "The Cold Flame of Agnon." Brellach belongs to the Saints and Pinnacle Rock belongs to the Seducers, but Cylarne is disputed territory. The Saints occupy the aboveground Altar of Rapture, and the Seducers occupy the underground Altar of Despair. Both altars have to be in the same hands in order for you to relight the Great Torch at the Sacellum Arden-Sul back in New Sheoth. To bring this about, you can help (or betray) either side. The dungeon consists of three levels: the main passage, defended in strength by the Seducers; the sparsely defended Underdeep; and the Altar of Despair situated between them. Before the quest starts, you can't get through the surface gates that lead to the opposing camps. There's decent loot here. The Ashen Remains in the urns on the Altar level is an ingredient.

3. **Hale:** A small settlement. You drop by Zoe Malene's house to see former Knight of the Thorn, Pyke, in the Miscellaneous Quest "To Help A Hero." Other residents are the poet Halion, who offers hints in verse, and clinically depressed spore farmer Talls-Tree-Falling, who offers unfailingly grim assessments of life on the Isles.

4. **Cann:** Five-level Heretic Mage dungeon that also has a fair population of Hungers. They are the only living creatures on the Substratum level. There are bosses and boss containers on the Amphitheater, Arena, and Halls of Tranquility levels. You can piece together a story here from three documents on the Arena and Substratum levels. And on the Amphitheater level, find Salonia Viria's skull, which plays into a Freeform quest on the Hill of Suicides. Beware of statue, dart, and floor traps.

5. **Highcross:** This is the focus of the Miscellaneous Quest Taxonomy of Obsession, in which you collect ingredients and critters for researcher Mirili Ulven. Many can be found or harvested in and around the hamlet. And residents Bruscus Dannus and Runs-in-Circles…well, let's just say they're eccentric!

   The fastidious Dannus has an anxiety attack if you handle certain of his household items in his presence, cleans up his house if you mess it up, and can collect a range of valuable items found in the hamlet and stow them in two special containers in his home. Runs lives up to her name: She dashes around Highcross's central stone pillar, sometimes stopping to make requests of you. You can give her gold coins, a pear, carrot, apple, poisoned apple (which kills her), and any of the eight types of lower-class shoes. "Ni-ni-ni-ni-ni-ni-ni-ni-ni-ni!" she cries. You were expecting gold?

6. **Breakneck Camp:** The most elaborate of the surface camps—it's like a Swiss Family Robinson tree house—this Heretic hangout includes a boss and boss chest. This is the exception rather than the rule. Most of these places have one or two regular Mages and low-end loot…and some are abandoned.

7. **Ebrocca:** Big undead dungeon with three entrances: this one (in the surface ruin), a second well to the south, and a third in the hills to the west. Potential source for some ingredients needed in the Miscellaneous Quest "Taxonomy of Obsession" in nearby Highcross. A secret level (Crematorium) can be found off the Descenia (entry) level. The cremator here reduces bones to the ingredient Ashen Remains, and Din's Ashes are needed for the Miscellaneous Quest "The Museum of Oddities." There's also a nasty pit puzzle in the vertical section at the end of the Descenia level.

   A boss (Clanfather Malifant) and boss chest are on the Sepechra level, where the large number of coffins makes this your best shot at obtaining certain hard-to-find items for the Miscellaneous Quest "The Museum of Oddities." (There's a lot of loot here!) You can also pull together a story about this place from seven documents found en route.

8. **Frenzied Camp:** Heretic Mage encampment. Good local source for ingredients needed in the Miscellaneous Quest "Taxonomy of Obsession."

9. **Dunroot Burrow:** This is the focus of the Main Quest mission "Addiction." You visit this five-level root-system dungeon to retrieve Thadon's Chalice of Reversal. En route, you become an addict yourself—taking Felldew to enter and harvesting more from the resident Elytra to prevent withdrawal.

   A boss and a boss container are on the Bramble Halls level. Spike, spore, and worm traps are on the Kelp Fen, Drone Tunnels, and Bramble Halls levels. The Chalice is in the care of three Felldew addicts in the Sanctum of Decadence at dungeon bottom.

10. **Camp Hopeful:** More like Camp Useless. It's abandoned. But even abandoned camps have bedrolls for road-weary travelers.

11. **Fetid Grove:** Pyke's Medallion from the Miscellaneous Quest "To Help a Hero" is in a chest down on the Encampment level of this two-level Grummite dungeon. There's also a boss and boss chest, plus spike, spore, and worm traps.

12. **Dire Warren:** This two-level affair is something of a critter hodgepodge. Up top, you find Baliwogs, Gnarls, Elytra, and Scalons (beginning at Level 9), and Baliwogs or Scalons—including a boss and boss chest—down below. But the main items of interest are the Mage Traelius and his late lady friend Alyssa, who are both on the Subterrane level. Get both sides of their story from their journals.

13. **Aichan Prison:** One of the two prisons in the Isles. This one's for Mania. The Dementia prison is Corpserot Passage at #51. You can opt to serve out your sentence by activating the bedroll, or push the button to open the secret door and find your way out. If you try to escape, make sure you take the contents of the Battered Chest in your cell. Your stuff is in a chest near the final exit.

14. **Wretched Camp:** Heretic Mage encampment.

15. **Camp Tall Trees:** Another Heretic Mage encampment.

16. **Split:** Once upon a time, there was a curious Mage. The curious Mage had an idea. He thought that everyone in the Shivering Isles had a happy side and a sad side. He tried to prove his idea with a spell, and so the curious Mage cast his spell on a hamlet currently known as Split. (Once upon a time, it must have been called something else.) And the curious Mage proved his theory, but not in the way he had planned. Each of the five people in town were divided into their two halves. Not literally, of course—that would be very messy. Each half was a full-fledged person, and the hamlet was renamed Split. But the halves didn't get along. Each was mad at the other, and wished the other were dead. And then a hero came to town and made it so.

17. **Knifepoint Hollow:** You visit the top level of this dungeon to find Dyus at the start of the Main Quest mission "Symbols of Office." At its end, he recreates Sheogorath's staff for you. It's a small level with one enemy—an undead boss—and a bit of loot. The bottom level, Chantry, is a Zealot Mage stronghold (with a boss and boss chest) that's unrelated to this quest, but it does contain Gadeneri Ralvel's skull, which plays into an undocumented quest on the Hill of Suicides. Watch out for traps, too!

18. **Fain:** Heretic Mages (including a boss) up above and Baliwogs (including a boss) down below. Way, way down below. There's a spectacular fall down a shaft—the longest we recall in any *Oblivion* dungeon level. Mercifully, there is water at the bottom. Documents up above suggest the presence of something big and toothy in the bottom lair, but that's just to scare the faithful. Watch for boss chests above and below and spike traps below.

19. **Puddlejump Camp:** Zealot Mage encampment.

20. **Long Tooth Camp:** The Fork of Horripilation is here. You return it to Big-Head in the Miscellaneous Quest of the same name. Also here to defend the Fork is a special contingent of three Heretic Mages (including a boss). On arrival, watch (or conceivably become enmeshed in) a battle between these folks and Zealot Mages from Hardscrabble Camp to the southeast.

21. **Knotbone Chamber:** Big critter dungeon. There's a critter hodgepodge on the Chamber and Cavities levels; Grummites (mainly Mages) fighting Elytra (including a boss) on the Juncture level; and Grummites on Pipes, Ruins, and Cellar levels. This dungeon is generally low on loot, but there's a good deal of Amber and Madness Ore up top.

22. **Bliss district:** The quaint, sun-dappled, upscale part of New Sheoth. We figure it's only a matter of time before condos go up on the current site of Uungor's bedroll. See the city map for details.

23. **Sheogorath's Palace** and the attached houses of Mania and Dementia, where Thadon and Syl hold court.

24. **Runoff Camp:** Zealot Mage camp with decent loot. Notably, the diamond, flawed diamond, flawed emerald, and jewelry box in the southwestern shelter. The camp takes its name from the streams that bracket the camp north and south on their way east to the waterfalls above the Emean Sea.

25. **Crucible district:** The scuzzy, open-sewer part of the New Sheoth. See the city map for details.

26. **New Sheoth Graveyard:** When someone dies in New Sheoth's Bliss or Crucible districts, a new stone is erected here in their memory—typically with a wisecrack as the epitaph. You may want to kill everyone in town just to read them all.

27. **Xirethard:** If you dug straight into the Main Quest on arrival in the Isles, this may actually be your *exit* from this three-level dungeon—the entrance being the secret one below a bust of Sheogorath in Syl's quarters in the House of Dementia. You use it if you opt to take out the Duchess in "Ritual of Accession," in which case you make your way through the trapped entry level to a confrontation with Syl and her Dark Seducer guards in the Depths level. The loot's okay on these levels—there's a murderously hard-to-reach boss chest in Depths— but if it's loot you're after, hit the Shambles-ridden Subterrane level for another boss chest and the Dark Chest of Wonders, which contains the immensely useful Ring of the Oceanborn.

28. **Flooded Camp:** Literally. The lone building in this abandoned camp has evidently floated off its foundation. There's nothing much here.

29. **Hill of Suicides:** Freeform quests. Ya love 'em, right? We got one for ya right here, pal. The five named skulls that turn up in various dungeons do have a use! See #4, #17, #39, #45, and #54—and also #36 for the one person who talks about it!

30. **Xaselm:** Once you've done in the Gatekeeper, Relmyna Verenim and pupil Nanette Don pack up their things and move from Passwall (#33) to the Sanctum of Vivisection level of this undead dungeon. You visit them here in the Main Quest when Sheogorath commissions you to construct a new Gatekeeper.

    It's also the location of a little side quest. Verenim is conducting horrific experiments on the effects of pain. You can get her to release her test subjects if you allow your psycho hostess to inflict stat-damaging pain on you. The Sanctum of Vivisection level is safe. The two above it, the entry level and Experiment Chambers, are not. The first is heavily trapped and well supplied in Shambles and creatures that could turn out to be Flesh Atronaches, Skeletons, or Skinned Hounds. The second has the latter creatures and a boss Flesh Atronach at the end. Look for boss chests in the Experiment Chambers and non-essential Corpse Pit levels.

31. **Xaselm secret entrance:** A number of dungeons have alternate entrances or exits—Fain, for instance—but this is the only one marked on the map. It's a shortcut to the Sanctum for use on your return from the Gardens of Flesh and Bone in the Main Quest mission "Rebuilding the Gatekeeper."

32. **The Gardens of Flesh and Bone:** You collect the special ingredients Verenim requires for the Main mission "Rebuilding the Gatekeeper" in this mostly undead dungeon. There are Hungers on the Caverns of Susurration level, and modest loot—save for the boss chest on the Caverns level. Watch for traps on the

entry level and in the Natatorium of Wound Bled Tears. The want of a key prevents you from entering the dungeon earlier.

33. **Passwall:** This hamlet in the shadow of the Gates of Madness is your second stop in the Shivering Isles. In the Main Quest mission "Through the Fringe of Madness," you collect information on how to take down the Gatekeeper from Nanette Don and Jayred Ice-Veins.

    The Wastrel's Purse, a combined tavern and shop, is open around the clock; no wonder proprietor Dredhwen is always pooped. She doesn't offer rooms, but buys and sells weapons, armor, books, ingredients, light sources, miscellaneous items, and potions, and has 300 in barter gold. (There are basic adventurer supplies here, including weak potions and Novice-level scrolls.)

    In "Retaking The Fringe," you return to help beat back waves of Knights of Order attacking Sheogorath's army. (More like a squad.)

    Note that everyone you meet here can turn up again later. Ice-Veins, your collaborator in the Gatekeeper affair, goes a-wandering on his own once you've opened the Gates of Madness. He may survive to see you again. And he may not, in which case you can try to track down his body. Relmyna Verenim and Nanette Don turn up at Xaselm for "Rebuilding the Gatekeeper." Shelden, the "mayor," is really just obnoxious comic relief, but you can rescue him (and whack the hypochondriac-turned-Priest of Order Sarandas) at Xeddefen in "Retaking The Fringe." And The Wastrel's Purse proprietor Dredhwen reappears in Passwall after you destroy the seat of Order power in The Fringe at the end of that mission.

34. **Hardscrabble Camp:** Zealot Mage encampment and a likely site for your first post-Fringe battle. It's right along the Low Road to New Sheoth. It's also the launch point for the Zealot assault on the Heretic Mage camp Long Tooth in the Miscellaneous Quest "The Fork of Horripilation." It has a bit more loot than other such camps, but most of it's just clutter.

35. **Blackroot Lair:** Baby's first Shivering Isles dungeon—if you're taking the Low Road from the Gates of Madness to New Sheoth, that is. And it's a big one: five levels of Grummites and their Gnarl prisoners, who begin to appear on the Outer Encampment level. To judge from the large supply of loose Gnarl Bark in here—21 pieces in total on the top two and bottom two levels—the Grummites are methodically harvesting the stuff. Why? Spells, we're guessing. You won't find them in this dungeon but, as you learn in Xedilian, the Grummites have Mages. Bosses and boss containers on the Inner Encampment and Tunnels levels.

36. **Deepwallow:** You pass through this hamlet en route to the Howling Halls in the Main Quest mission "Symbols of Office," but the game never expressly sends you here. The closest you get is after the Main Quest is complete and you begin to get randomly assigned "duties" to beat back critter attacks on various hamlets. So what's there to do here? Well, you can meet the Argonian Beelei, who worries about everything. There's Dulphumph gro-Urgash, who worries about Scalons—and who periodically searches for them on the peninsula to the north and the coast to the southwest.

If you've reached Level 9, Dulphumph should sight a Scalon at these locations off to the west and southeast, respectively. If attacked, this self-proclaimed "Scalon killer" will probably run away! And, finally, there's Erver Devani. He seems like another Shivering Isles crazy—he uses that paranoid "they" again—but in fact he's your entrée into a undocumented quest on the Hill of Suicides. If you have Gadeneri Ralvel's skull, he tells you to take it to her there.

37. **Howling Halls:** One of three stops in the Main Quest mission "Symbols of Office." You can treat this three-level base for Ciirta's cult as a dungeon—killing the apostles who live here—or reach an accommodation with renegade apostle Ra'kheran. Wearing an apostle's robes gives you free run of the place and enables you to easily supply three co-conspirators who carry out the required assassination on the Antechamber level. The Pelvis of Pelagius and ingredient caches on the Congregation Chambers level are helpful in the respective Miscellaneous Quests "The Museum of Oddities" and "Taxonomy of Obsession." Nice loot, too—especially in the Alms Collection Chest on the Narthex (entry) level and the boss chest in Ciirta's sanctum on the Antechamber level. Note that there's an impassable door on the entry level until the "Symbols of Office" quest kicks off.

38. **Xavara:** One-level Zealot Mage dungeon with an undead enclave at the far western end. There are bosses for each group and boss chests as well. (The loot's quite nice.) Watch for falling ceiling, statue, and floor traps in the deeper portions of the level.

39. **Knotty Bramble:** You visit this Grummite dungeon twice to retrieve a supposed cure for supposedly Sickly Bernice in the Miscellaneous Quest "A Liquid Solution." It's a fairly straightforward affair on the two quest levels, with a fair deal of Amber up top and a boss and boss chest in the pool down on the Hatchery level. However, the Lost Crypt level is tricky…and holds another of the skulls (Lorenz Bog-Trotter's) involved in the undocumented Hill of Suicides quest. Watch for spike and spore traps.

40. **Door to Cyrodiil:** The way out. You can use this at any time to return to that stony island back in Niben Bay.

41. **Xeddefen:** Ya gotta love a dungeon like Xeddefen. At the beginning of the game, this is a two-level Grummite stronghold with a boss chest on the entry level and a boss down on Fain. However, in the Main Quest mission "Retaking The Fringe," the Grummites are dead. Xeddefen expands to three levels—an obelisk and crystal chest can be found on the newly opened Great Hall level—and is occupied in strength by the forces of Order. The Knights are present on each of the three levels, but—surprise—you don't have to fight them all. If you're sufficiently sneaky, the three waves on the entry level will run on by to attack Passwall.

    And after you shut down the obelisk? It's a *different* three-level dungeon—one with a wealth of falling ceiling and collapsing column traps in the Great Hall and newly opened Felles and Fales levels. The place is coming down about your head. You can let the collapse do the fighting for you on these last two levels. No loot here, but loot in these levels should be the least of your concerns.

42. **Fellmoor:** In the Miscellaneous Quest "Everything in Its Place," you either kill (or deeply distress) Cindawe, who manages the Water Root Pod farm in this hamlet, at the behest of lunatic Khajiit worker Ranarr-Jo. Other residents: Kishashi, who is the instrument for winning Ranarr-Jo's trust, and the savage guard Relan, whose house is fairly littered with skulls and body parts.

43. **Blood Island Camp:** A camp occupied not by Heretics or Zealots, but Grummites! We suspect they aren't the original owners, as there are blood stains in the shelter and six bones beneath. The rest of the "island"—it's actually connected to the mainland in the west via a narrow isthmus—is notable only for a small ruin in the inlet west-northwest of the camp. The two partially submerged urns here each contain items useful in the Miscellaneous Quests "The Antipodean Hammer" (10 percent shots at Amber and Madness Ore matrices), "The Museum of Oddities" (2 percent shots at six items) and "Brithaur" (a roughly 8 percent shot at a flawless pearl).

44. **Swampgas Hole:** Three-level critter dungeon, with Baliwogs, Elytra, Gnarls, or Scalons (beginning at Level 9). No real surprises here: There's a boss down on the Depths level and respectable loot, with boss chests on the Chasm and Depths levels. Watch for spore traps here.

45. **Rotten Den:** Big Zealot Mage dungeon, with the Precipice level serving as a hub for the other four levels. On the Sanctum level, there's another of the five skulls (M'desi's skull) used in the undocumented Hill of Suicides quest. Watch for Zealots on Deadfall, Precipice (including a boss), and Encampment levels, plus a boss on the Sanctum level. There are also Shambles on the Sanctum (including a boss) and Hollow levels. Two boss chests are found on the Precipice level and one each on Sanctum and Hollow. Watch for traps throughout.

46. **Inlet Camp:** Abandoned camp, built over the water. A bit more loot than you'd ordinarily associate with such camps.

47. **Backwash Camp:** Zealot Mage camp.

48. **Vitharn:** A ruined castle where ghosts re-fight a lost battle again and again and again. In the Miscellaneous Quest "Ghosts of Vitharn," you correct their mistakes. The entrance to the Keep is sealed, but you can make your way in via the Sump beneath a tree to the southeast.

49. **Xiditte:** Two-level Zealot Mage dungeon. Tough crowd. An entry-level pit trap dumps you into a Catacombs level cell with a five-tumbler lock. There's a boss and boss chest down on the Catacombs level, too, plus a neat statue puzzle that opens the way to, of all things, one of Order's crystal chests.

50. **Lost Time Camp:** Abandoned.

51. **Corpserot Passage:** The Dementia prison. The Mania prison is Aichan at #13. If you are jailed in this happy land, you wind up in a secret room deep inside. You can opt to serve out your sentence by activating the bedroll or you can push the button to open the secret door and find your way out. If you escape, make sure you grab the contents of the Battered Chest in your cell. (You're in *jail*, son. You got *nothin'*.) All you stuff is in a chest near the final exit.

52. **Pinnacle Rock:** Take #1 and put "Dark Seducers" in place of "Golden Saints," and you pretty much have it nailed. In fact, since no one's watching anyway, let's do that: you reclaim this dungeon from the forces of Order in the Main Quest mission "The Helpless Army" if you replaced the Duke of Mania in the earlier quest "Ritual of Accession." Until that time, it's locked and the blue bikini girls are lookin' at ya funny. Identical in layout to the Saints headquarters at Brellach (Dementia side of the same quest), its four levels are heavily populated with Knights and Priests of Order. Penetrate to the Font of Rebirth level and ring four chimes to shatter the crystal capstone that blocks the resurrection of dead Saints. There are crystal chests on the Hall of Honor and Hall of Devotion levels.

53. **Dreamwalk Camp:** Heretic Mage encampment.

54. **Milchar:** There are four entrances to this sprawling dungeon. From west to east, there is Sufflex in the surface site's southwestern corner; Nexus, a hub for the three other entry levels east-northeast of Sufflex; Xetrem, southeast of Nexus; and Tieras, northeast of Xetrem. In the Main Quest mission "Symbols of Office," you use the Nexus entrance to reach the Grove of Reflection, where you claim a branch from the Tree of Shades. In the Miscellaneous Quest "The Coming Storm," you use the Tieras entrance to reach the puzzle level Chatterhall. The urn contains the Amulet of Disintegration. And in the undocumented Hill of Suicides quest, you use the Xetrem entrance to reach Limark's skull on that same level. This may make you wonder if there's something special down in Sufflex as well. Apart from some nasty traps, no.

    Most of the six Milchar levels offer the standard critter hodgepodge, with the following exceptions: the boss in Xetrem, two patrolling Elytra in Sufflex, and your own clone in the Grove of Reflection. The loot's just okay, with a boss chest on Xetrem.

55. **Gates of Madness:** Initially, the Gates of Madness (and the Gatekeeper who guards them) keep you penned inside The Fringe. Try as you might, you can't get over the surrounding wall. Once the Gatekeeper is dead, claim the keys to the Mania and Dementia gates from its body and enter the wider world to the east.

56. **Xedilian:** Xedilian is supposed to serve as a glue trap for adventurers, but it's been neglected since the advent of the Gatekeeper. The Main Quest mission "A Better Mousetrap" finds you making repairs to the dungeon's Resonator (which sends out a siren's song) and then testing out Xedilian's traps and tricks from a dungeon master's point of view on the upper tier.

    Xedilian offers up lots of Grummites and your first encounter with the Knights of Order. Lots of loot, too—including a boss chest on the Halls of Judgment level. You can get in here before the quest goes "live," but you can only explore a bit of the entry level.

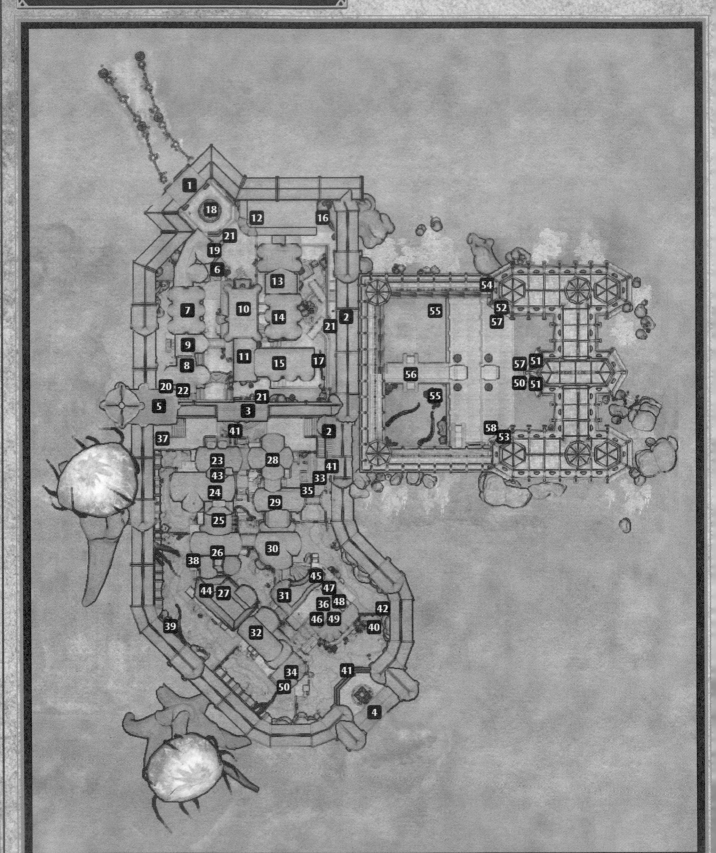

MAPS

1. Exit to Overlook Road.

2. Exits to the Palace district from Bliss (the northern district) and Crucible (the southern district).

3. This door links the Crucible and Bliss districts.

4. Exit to the Low Road.

5. Sacellum Arden-Sul: This temple operates around the clock, and can be reached both from Bliss and Crucible. You visit it three times in the Main Quest—once for instruction on how to replace the Duke of Mania or Duchess of Dementia in "Ritual of Accession," again for your confirmation once you've engineered the assassination of one or the other, and to relight the Great Torch in "The Cold Flame of Agnon." You also want to collect a daily blessing from the altar and, once the Main Quest is complete, step into the flame you lit in "The Cold Flame of Agnon" for a major perk. It's also a regular stop in the schedule of many residents, and an easy place to track them down. And there's more to see here than you may know: once the Great Torch is lit, the priests Arctus (for Dementia) and Dervenin (for Mania) each deliver one sermon a day.

6. Common Treasures: Proprietor Tilse Areleth buys and sells everything but spells from 8 a.m. to 8 p.m. She has 1,000 in barter gold. You can find soul gems here, Novice- and Apprentice-level scrolls, ammunition, torches, and repair hammers. There's also a lock: three tumblers, unlocked with the Common Treasures Key (carried by Areleth).

7. Amiable Fanriene's House: This fellow's worried the walls are going to fall down on his head. You find him a place to sleep outdoors (at #16) in the Miscellaneous Quest "Falling Awake." At that time, the beggar Uungor takes up residence here. As for the lock: two tumblers, unlocked by Amiable Fanriene's Key (carried by Fanriene).

8. Thaedil's House: Thaedil's a street entertainer—and not just because she says she's one. Follow her. You find her juggling balls at five locations around Bliss and then either moaning about her profession ("my mother pushed me into it") or acting like she's The Next Big Thing. The lock: two tumblers, unlocked with Thaedil's Key (carried by Thaedil).

9. Orinthal's House: A retired assassin, a statistics buff, and a book collector. He's at Books of Bliss from 2 p.m. to 5 p.m.—his house is linked to the store by a bridge—and there are 100-plus volumes in here. But what's with all the crumpled paper? The lock: two tumblers, unlocked with Orinthal's Key (carried by Orinthal).

10. The Missing Pauldron: Proprietor Dumag gro-Bonk has a part in the Miscellaneous Quest "The Antipodean Hammer." He can make armor and weapons from Amber. Gro-Bonk also buys and sells weapons, armor, light sources, and miscellaneous items. Plus he recharges magical equipment and repairs broken stuff from 8 a.m. to 8 p.m. He has 1,200 in barter gold. You can find enchanted armor for sale here beginning at Level 3. Locks: both four tumblers, unlocked by Dumag gro-Bonk's Key (carried by gro-Bonk).

11. Books of Bliss: Proprietor Sontaire buys and sells books from 8 a.m. to 8 p.m. She has 1,200 in barter gold…and, if you have a male character, a libidinous nature. "Spend one night with me, and I'll remind you why they say, 'Love hurts'," she says. No, you cannot indulge with Sontaire. On the other hand, if you have a female character, she tells you flatly that "the men around here are mine." The full run of Shivering Isles books are here, including the four that are hardest to find: the three volumes of *16 Accords of Madness* and *The Ravings of Fenroy*. Curiosity: She has breakfast with lunatic boat builder Tove the Unrestful (#16) at 6 a.m. Her current boyfriend? He doesn't sleep over…but he does have a copy of Sontaire's Key. As for locks: three tumblers, unlocked with Sontaire's Key (carried by Sontaire and Tove the Unrestful).

12. The Choosy Beggar: A tavern, open around the clock. Proprietor Raven Biter serves food and drink and will rent you a room for 20 gold. He also cautions you to stay away from his wife, Sheer Meedish (she's got a drinking problem). The third Argonian here, Pad-Ei, is a guest.

13. Rendil Drarara's House: Drarara's a chef. Meaning his kitchen is full of ingredients. Meaning it's a good place to steal ingredients for the Miscellaneous Quests "Taxonomy of Obsession," "Falling Awake," and "The Coming Storm." Locks: one tumbler, unlocked with Rendil Drarara's Key (carried by Drarara). The upstairs entrance is unlocked.

14. Big-Head's House: As in the loopy Argonian from *Morrowind*. He wants his Fork of Horripilation back, and you have to recover it in the Miscellaneous Quest of the same name. Lock: two tumblers, unlocked with Big-Head's Key (carried by Big-Head).

15. Tove the Unrestful's House: He's building a "skyboat" upstairs, and he needs tongs and calipers. He pays you five gold for each one you supply in the Miscellaneous Quest "Work Is Never Done." Lock: two tumblers, unlocked by Tove the

Unrestful's Key (carried by Mr. Unrestful). Possibly boyfriend of Sontaire at #11.

16. The beggar Uungor sleeps here…initially. In the Miscellaneous Quest "Falling Awake"—possibly with the aid of Fimmion (#17)—you convince him to trade places with Amiable Fanriene (#7).

17. The beggar Fimmion sleeps here. He has a role in the Miscellaneous Quests "Falling Awake" and "The Coming Storm"—*if* you provide him with pastries.

18. There is 10 gold in this fountain. You're not that desperate for cash, are ya?

19. On the ledge here, there is a flawless pearl. This can come in handy in the Miscellaneous Quest "Brithaur."

20. If you persuade the beggar Bhisha to quit Crucible in the Miscellaneous Quest "Ushnar's Terror," he sleeps here instead.

21. Golden Saint guards. The northern guard patrols the district from 6 a.m. to 7 p.m., the southern from 6 p.m. to 7 a.m. The one near the exit to the Palace patrols only the balcony—ending his round at a spot just west of Rendil Drarara's house.

22. Someone's idea of heaven: a little cache of booze…and a copy of *The Lusty Argonian Maid*.

23. Cutter's Weapons: Cutter's involved in the Miscellaneous Quest "The Antipodean Hammer." She fashions weapons and armor for you using Madness Ore. Open from 8 a.m. to 8 p.m., the shop sells weapons, armor, light sources, and miscellaneous items. It also recharges enchanted items and repairs busted ones. Cutter has 1,200 in barter gold. (She's also a member of the Rooftop Club—Crucible's version of Fight Club, staged at #36 on the roof of Sickly Bernice's Taphouse. See the Freeform section for details.) Locks: three and four tumblers, unlocked with Cutter's Key (carried by Cutter).

24. Museum of Oddities: This museum is itself an oddity, being that when you start your career in the Shivering Isles it's almost bereft of oddities. You rectify this situation in the Miscellaneous Quest "The Museum of Oddities," in which you find and sell 12 ultra-rare items to curator Una Armina. Una can also help you out in the Miscellaneous Quest "Ushnar's Terror." Lock: three tumblers, unlocked with Una Armina's Key (carried by Una). This key also unlocks two display cases on the museum's ground floor. The door on the upstairs balcony is unlocked.

25. Earil's Mysteries: Shopkeeper Earil's complaints about Brithaur put you in the Miscellaneous Quest named for that incompetent thief. Earil buys and sells books, ingredients, alchemical equipment, spells, magic items, and potions from 8 a.m. to 8 p.m. There are Novice- and Apprentice-level scrolls, magic jewelry, and soul gems in his inventory. Earil has 1,000 in barter gold. Locks: three tumblers, unlocked with Earil's Key (carried by Earil).

26. Things Found: Proprietor Ahjazda gives you the Miscellaneous Quest "The Coming Storm." She buys and sells books, alchemical equipment, miscellaneous items, magic items, and potions between 8 a.m. and 8 p.m. (Her inventory's kind of junky, as the rumor mill reports.) She has 1,000 in barter gold. She also sneaks around the district from midnight to 4 a.m.—presumably looking for the three items at the heart of her quest. Lock: three tumblers, unlocked with Ahjazda's Key (carried by Ahjazda).

27. Ma'zaddha's House: Until you find him dead here, Ma'zaddha's a contact in your Main Quest mission ("The Lady of Paranoia") to uncover a plot against Duchess of Dementia Syl. There's a smoking gun pointing to ringleader Muurine in a cabinet upstairs. (He's also a member of The Rooftop Club.) Locks: two tumblers, unlocked with Ma'zaddha's Key (carried by Ma'zaddha).

28. Ushnar gro-Shadborgob's House: Gro-Shadborgob's fear of Khajiits is the foundation for the Miscellaneous Quest "Ushnar's Terror." He is out much of the day, trailed by his dog…with the beggar Bhisha trailing the dog. Lock: two tumblers. No key.

29. Caldana Monrius's House: Rooftop Club member and Skooma addict. The latter pretty much governs all her interactions with you…and probably accounts for the empty feel of this big dark house. Lock: two tumblers, unlocked with Caldana Monrius's Key (carried by Monrius).

30. Muurine's House: Ringleader in the conspiracy against Duchess of Dementia Syl. You pry out her confession in the Main Quest mission "The Lady of Paranoia," and she pays with her life in the House of Dementia dungeon (#53). Muurine is also a member of The Rooftop Club. Lock: two tumblers, unlocked by Muurine's Key (carried by Muurine).

31. Sickly Bernice's Taphouse: Bernice sends you off to the dungeon Knotty Bramble (twice!) to find a cure for her illness in the Miscellaneous Quest "A Liquid Solution." She also helps you out in the

MAPS

Miscellaneous Quest "Ushnar's Terror." Bernice sells food and drink and will rent you a room for 20 gold.

32. Hirrus Clutumnus's House: This guy wants to die. In the Miscellaneous Quest "Final Resting," you give him a colorful send-off…

33. …ideally from this landing on the way to the Palace. However, you first have to meet him at #40.

34. and 35. Brithaur's House: You need to kill this thief, jail him, or just get him to knock off his stealing in the Miscellaneous Quest "Brithaur." If you opt for killing, this is the place. If you get him to move on, he makes #35 the focus of his wanderings, rather than the shops. Locks: two tumblers, unlocked by Brithaur's Key (carried by Brithaur).

36. The Rooftop Club holds its duels here.

37. The beggar Gloorolros sleeps in a little cave here. He can direct you to Uungor in the Miscellaneous Quest "Falling Awake."

38. The beggar Bhisha sleeps here initially. He can give you a hand in the Miscellaneous Quest "Falling Awake." In the Miscellaneous Quest "Ushnar's Terror," if you persuade him to leave Crucible, or buy him off, he relocates to #20 in the Bliss district.

39. And the beggar Bolwing sleeps in a little cave here. He helps you out in the Miscellaneous Quest "The Fork of Horripilation."

40. In the Miscellaneous Quest "Final Resting," you meet Hirrus Clutumnus here.

41. Dark Seducer guards: There are three of them. The northernmost of the three patrols the district from 6 a.m. to 7 p.m., the southern from 6 p.m. to 7 a.m. The one on the landing of the Palace stairs can comment on Hirrus Clutumnus's "accident" at #33.

42. A sunken urn…beneath a smashed crate. You find gold, jewelry, three bottles of Fellmoor Spore, one bottle of Fellmoor Swamp Wine (the best in the Shivering Isles), three sweetrolls, two portions of Congealed Putrescence, a 25 percent shot at a pearl, a crystal ball, bouquet, and yarn. (The last three must have come from the crate!) Alas, the urn is locked, and you need the key on the rooftop stool at #43. And that requires vaults from #33 to #29 to #24.

43. The key to the sunken urn at #42.

44. A Ring of Light and fur gauntlets atop a chimney.

45. Two portions of Scales.

46. Two clubs, a rusty iron war axe, and a dagger.

47. A chest containing another club and three items from leveled lists that incorporate iron and steel weapons and light fur and leather armor.

48. The Rooftop Club bar: Wine, beer, and mead…and a box with a bit of gold, a bit of clutter, and a document called *Liturgy of the Duelists*.

49. Two potatoes, two bottles of mead, and an orange.

50. A Feather potion (amid what appears to be the remains of a bird).

51. Entrance to Castle Sheogorath: Your effective base of operations during the Main Quest, you get most of your missions here from Sheogorath. This throne room also contains the entrance to the dungeon The Fountainhead, which you explore in the Main Quest mission "The Roots of Madness." Once the Main Quest ends, you can enlist Golden Saint and Dark Seducer escorts here, receive the ministrations of the court healer, and watch a dancer perform.

52. Entrance to the House of Mania: You visit the Mania court at least twice during the Main Quest: during "Addiction," your quest to recover Thadon's Chalice of Reversal, and "Ritual of Accession," should you decide to off the Duke of Mania.

53. Entrance to the House of Dementia: A similar story here. The first visits come during the Main Quest mission "The Lady of Paranoia," when you investigate a plot to kill Syl. The second set of visits comes should you decide to plot against Syl yourself in "Ritual of Accession." A third visit's also possible if you finish the Main Quest before you take on the Miscellaneous Quest "Brithaur." In that case, talk to Dementia steward Kithlan about the thief and he says he'll see that Brithaur's jailed.

54. Secret entrance to the Greenmote Silo. You tail Mania steward Wide-Eye here and then visit this dungeon in search of greenmote if you opt to take out Thadon in Ritual of Accession. Note that the entrance is on the lower level of the arcade.

55. These two inert obelisks go "live" during the final Main Quest mission "The End of Order" and start pumping out Knights of Order. You have to shut both down to trigger the appearance of Jyggalag…

56. …here. Beat him and you're done!

To enable the Knights of the Nine quest line, you simply have to stay out of the city of Anvil for five seconds. (If you're resuming a game in Anvil after installing the expansion, leave the city and then return.)

Then ask anyone about "Rumors" and you'll learn that something terrible has happened at that city's Chapel of Dibella. The messages will vary a bit, depending on where you are and whether the NPC is male or female, but you'll put it all together easily. The chapel staff has been wiped out by unknown attackers. Apparently no one saw a thing. A prophet showed up a day or two later, and is carrying on about "the end of the world" and calling for the return of a "holy knight." Some debate whether he's a holy man or just a crazy man, but in Anvil he seems to be winning converts.

Obviously, a trip to that Gold Coast city is in order. You'll discover on arrival that you have two new topics: "Anvil Chapel attack" and "Prophet." Asking about either one nets you the initial quest—"Pilgrimage"—and the other updates the journal. You'll be pointed to the chapel and the prophet preaching across the street. (The church is southeast of Anvil's main gate, and you can see its tower rising behind the Fighters Guild.)

PILGRIMAGE

You'll find a city guard on the chapel steps. He'll urge you to stay out unless you have a strong stomach, confess his own bafflement over how the murders could have escaped the watch's notice, and suggest that "Maybe that Prophet is right. Some kind of unholy doom visited upon us."

Step inside, if only to satisfy a morbid curiosity. The healer Laralthir, priestess Dumania Jirich, and priest Trevaia are all dead. The pews have been knocked about. Fires burn at the rear of the chapel. And on the floor around the central altar are strange runic words written in blood. You can't interpret them yourself.

Once you're done in here, cross the street to the garden and speak to the Prophet. He discloses that the attack on the chapel is "only the beginning." It marks the return of the vengeful Ayleid sorcerer-king, Umaril the Unfeathered—defeated (but not utterly vanquished) by the crusading knight Pelinal Whitestrake 3,000 years earlier.

If you'd like some background on Pelinal, revisit the chapel, take a key from one of the bodies—after all, no one's watching you except the gods—and look in the Chapel Hall for a new set of books called "The Song of Pelinal." Volume 2 is on a little table against the north wall of the central room. Volumes 3–8 are on a bookshelf in the storage/dining room to the south, and Volume 1 on the table in the same room. You'll learn about this Alessia companion's roots, deeds, and his terrible end.

(You'll also find complete sets of "The Song" at the Southern Books in Leyawiin, and later in the game at the fleshed-out version of the Priory of the Nine; almost-complete sets in the Mystic Archives at the Imperial City's Arcane University (missing Volume 1) and the Chapel Hall of Bruma's Great Chapel of Talos (missing Volume 5); and a largely complete set in the Chapel Hall of Chorrol's Chapel of Stendarr (missing Volumes 3, 6, and 8).

The Prophet also translates the Ayleid runes around the altar—"By the eternal power of Umaril, the mortal gods shall be cast down"—and reveals that you'll need the help of those Divines and the lost "Crusader's Relics" to stop him. Volunteer to quest for the relics, and the Prophet asks if you're a "worthy knight."

It's not as simple a question as it appears. Say "yes" and you'll get a fair number of unique replies depending on where you are in the game. (There are two replies for different stages of the Main Quest—one after you've saved what's left of Kvatch, the other after the defeat of Mehrunes Dagon—and one for completing each of the faction quest lines.) But you want the quest, so be a humble knight and say "no," and the Prophet points you to "the Pilgrim's Way." You're to pray at the wayshrine of each of the Nine Divines on the map he provides, and then wait for a sign.

This may take you a good while, as none of the shrines appear on the standard game map—you can't fast-travel directly to the sites—but if you've explored a good bit of the map, you should be able to fast-travel near most points and reduce your legwork. Note that you don't have to pray at the particular shrines listed on the Prophet's map—any shrine to the same god will work. (There are two or three to each god scattered across Cyrodiil. Again, you'll find a full list of wayshrines in the Freeform Quests chapter.)

The nearest fast-travel locations are as follows:

- Akatosh (south of Bruma): Fast-travel to Toadstool Hollow (at the junction of the Orange and Silver roads) and head straight west.

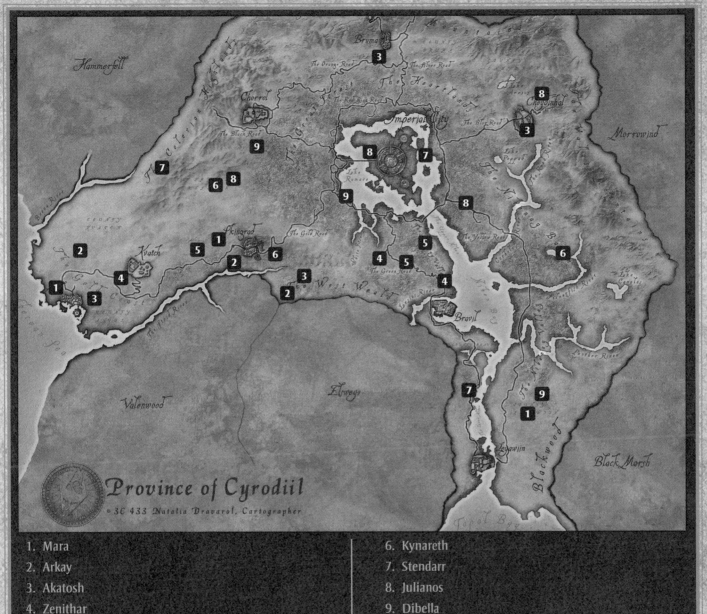

Province of Cyrodiil

© 3E 433 Natalia Dravarol, Cartographer

1. Mara	6. Kynareth
2. Arkay	7. Stendarr
3. Akatosh	8. Julianos
4. Zenithar	9. Dibella
5. Tiber Septim	

- Arkay (west-northwest of Kvatch): Fast-travel to Bleak Mine and head east-southeast.

- Dibella (south of Chorrol): Fast-travel to Fort Carmala and head northeast.

- Julianos (southeast of the Imperial City): Fast-travel to Cracked Wood Cave and head west-northwest along the Yellow Road.

- Kynareth (in the middle of nowhere, east-northeast of the nameless lake north of the Silverfish River): Fast-travel to Mackamentain and head east-southeast.

- Mara (west of Skingrad): Fast-travel to Cursed Mine and head northwest.

- Stendarr (between Bravil and Leyawiin): Fast-travel to Sheogorath's Shrine and head east-southeast.

- Talos (south of the Imperial City): Fast-travel to Hircine's Shrine and head east-southwest, or to Fort Variela and head west-northwest.

- Zenithar (north of Bravil): Fast-travel to Flooded Mine and head south.

There should be no major surprises here. (Well, no surprises that don't attend every cross-country jaunt.) Simply activate each shrine to receive its blessing(s)—identical with the ones listed in the Freeform Quests chapter under "Wayshrines"—and an attendant journal entry.

However, if you go about this task on foot, it's conceivable that you'll happen onto another questing knight. Sir Roderic and his squire, Lathon, first appear on the Green Road, north of the Ayleid ruin Wenyandawik (which is itself northwest of Bravil).

Talk to them. Roderic's making the rounds of the shrines, too, and invites you to travel with them on an informal basis. (Read: You have no control over their movements.) Not a bad idea if you have a new character and are feeling lost and skittish. The knight's a fair escort—set at your own level and equipped with heavy armor and a long blade. (Lathon's a couple of levels below yours and in plainclothes.)

Once the chat ends, they'll start their own pilgrimage—setting off toward the ridge to the east-southeast and Zenithar's shrine beyond—and will eventually visit all nine shrines. (If you don't run into them, they won't start this trek until yours is complete.)

With or without Roderic, once you've tackled the ninth shrine, you'll learn you've cleared away any Infamy (needed to equip any of the Crusader's Relics you'll be collecting during this quest line) and gained a new Greater Power of "Pilgrim's Grace," which fortifies all eight attributes by 10 points for 300 seconds. Your journal pops up again here to advise you to pray and wait for a vision.

Actually, no more prayer is required. You just have to wait a few seconds. You'll be teleported to airliner altitude over the Imperial City. A spectral Pelinal appears—no less pissed-off for the passage of three millennia—and points you to a shrine built upon the spot where he fell.

And then you're back on Nirn—right where you were before you left terra firma.

THE SHRINE OF THE CRUSADER

You don't need return to the Prophet after this mission, but that doesn't mean you shouldn't at some point just to hear him speak—he'll make sermons for 15 hours a day irrespective of whether you're talking to him or not—and get his takes on recent benchmarks in the quest line.

The Shrine of the Crusader is located in a dungeon under the southeast corner of Lake Rumare—just north of the bridge that separates the lake from the Upper Niben. Memorial Cave to the north Fatback Cave to the west, Shinbone Cave to the

southeast, and Fort Alessia to the south-southwest are roughly equidistant fast-travel locations. You'll find the entrance to a new Ayleid ruin called Vanua against the east bank.

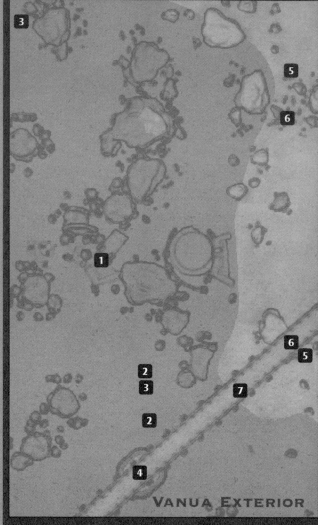

VANUA EXTERIOR

1. Entrance to Vanua.

2. Clams. There's a 75-percent chance that each clam will contain a pearl. At levels one or two, that pearl will be flawed. By the time you reach Level Nine, there's a 50-50 shot that the pearl will be without flaw.

3. A slaughterfish. Maybe. (25 percent chance.)

4. The bridge on which the Red Ring Road crosses the Upper Niben.

5. A mudcrab. Probably. (75 percent chance.)

6. A Nirnroot plant--useful in the Miscellaneous quest "Finding Your Roots." (Note that the southern one is under the Niben bridge, not on it.)

7. A Khajiit highwayman.

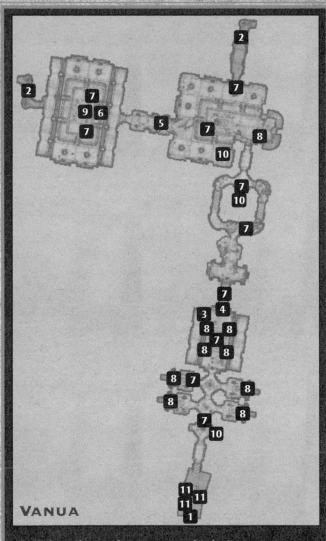

VANUA

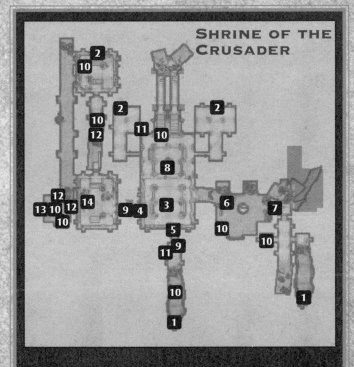

This isn't a shrine; it's a tomb. Eleven leveled undead creatures (including a boss) roam Vanua's dark halls. Just spill 'n' spell your way north-northeast, collecting those nice Magicka-restoring Welkynd Stones (eight on this level), and push the block on the west wall to open the secret door. Then it's clear sailing to the Shrine of the Crusader…though you may wonder if you're missing out on something. (You are. The big room at the end of the level has an upper tier and three enemies inaccessible from this level. You'll run into them on the way out.)

1. Exit to the southeast corner of Lake Rumare.

2. Entrances to the Shrine of the Crusader. (You'll use the eastern one on your way in, and the western on your way back out.)

3. The button on the wall here …

4. … opens the secret wall here.

5. This remotely-operated closed gate isn't quite so easy to open. You won't trigger it until you liberate the Helm of the Crusader in the Shrine of the Crusader.

6. Undead boss: Depending on your current level, this could be anything from a ghost up to a lich.

7. Undead creatures: This could be anything from a skeleton at low levels to a wraith at high ones. In any case, it'll be a lot less nasty than the boss. (Note that the one near the entrance to the Shrine is on a lower level than appears here.)

8. Welkynd stones: These restore your magicka.

9. Boss chest.

10. Standard tomb chest.

1. Entrances to Vanua: The one in the southeast corner is where you'll appear on your way into the dungeon. The one in the southwest is the one you'll use on the way out.

2. Entrances to The Lost Catacombs: Bit confusing, isn't it? You'll use the northwest entrance on your way into the Catacombs, and either of the other two on your way out.

3. The remains of Sir Amiel. Search them to read his journal. At a minimum, take his key which lets you out of this room, and his ring, which lets you into the cellar of the Priory of the Nine. (You'll also find a Knights of the Nine shield and a fine steel longsword nearby.) The key unlocks gates …

4. … here …

5. … and here. #4's the one you want to use now. #5's your way out once you have the Helm.

6. When you reach this point, the big stone …

7. … here will descend to block your exit. For better or worse, you're trapped in here until you recover the Helm.

8. The Helm of the Crusader. Take the Helm to fulfill your quest and open the gate at #5 on the Vanua map.

9. Undead creatures: these won't appear until after you retrieve the Helm.

10. Undead creatures.

11. A chest containing one or two Restoration-related items.

12. The standard tomb creatures chest.

13. Kind of an Easter egg. This room can be reached only in the room to the east via the gap high in its west wall. You can reach that gap by jumping from atop the broken column ...

14. ... here!

Same deal in the Shrine of the Crusader proper: 10 scattered undead baddies. Beat 'em down, jump up through the hole in the west wall, cross a room that looks very like the Imperial Subterrane from the starter dungeon…and discover that an immoveable boulder now blocks the door behind you. No turning back.

But better to come. Drop down through the hole on the room's west side and inspect the skeleton in the middle of the room. This is Sir Amiel—a Shrine-seeker in ages past. Your journal suggests you search his body for clues.

Sir Amiel

Sure enough: Amiel has a journal of his own that identifies him as a member of a holy order called the Knights of the Nine, places the Knights' former base in Cyrodiil's West Weald region, and reveals that Pelinal's cuirass is in that Priory and his helm in the Shrine. While you're pawing through his stuff, grab Amiel's ring, key, fine steel longsword, and Knights of the Nine shield. You'll need the ring to open the way to the Priory's cellar.

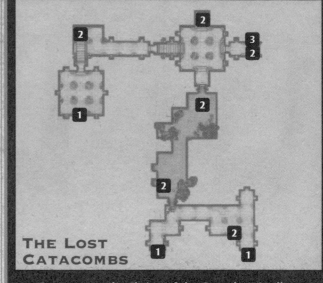

THE LOST CATACOMBS

1. Entrances to the Shrine of the Crusader. You'll enter the Catacombs via the door to the northwest. You'll leave it by either of the two to the southeast.

2. The same leveled undead creatures from Vanua and the Shrine.

3. Standard tomb chest.

And you'll need the key to unlock the gates to the west and south. The southern gate takes you into a new section of Vanua—where, for the time being, you'll find yourself stopped by a remotely-operated gate with no obvious remote trigger. The western leads to another hole in the wall, a sandy north-bound passage, and the door to the Lost Catacombs—which, in turn, is a straight shot back to two doors into the Shrine of the Crusader. Both lead to the Helm of the Crusader.

Go ahead, put it on. It'll be either Light or Heavy Armor, depending which skill is higher. If those skills are identical, it'll be Heavy. Either way, it comes with leveled Restoration skill and Personality attribute boosts, and supplies a new Lesser Power called "Serene Beauty," which allows you to Calm characters of up to Level 25 for 10 seconds.

And that's that. So how to get out of here? Backtrack to where you found poor Amiel. (Or simply hop over the railing to the south.) Now use the south exit and make your way back into Vanua. The remotely-operated gate that was closed is now open. Alas, the room that was empty is now populated with three undead enemies—one of them the boss. Kill 'em, run from 'em, bellow at 'em like Brendan Fraser in "The Mummy." We don't care; just get through the open gate into the upper tier of that big room we wondered about earlier. Drop down to the lower level, take the southern exit, and then swim until you see the bridge over the Upper Niben.

PRIORY OF THE NINE

As mentioned above, Sir Amiel's journal establishes that the Cuirass of the Crusader was kept in the Priory of the Nine, in the wilds of the West Weald. That's our next stop.

And we do mean wilds. The priory's in that broad empty space along the Elsweyr frontier between the Ayleid ruin Silorn and Fort Black Boot. (However, the closest fast-travel location is the Ayleid ruin Nornalhorst to the north-northwest.) Make sure you're well equipped with healing supplies and magic before you set out. You've got some fighting ahead of you.

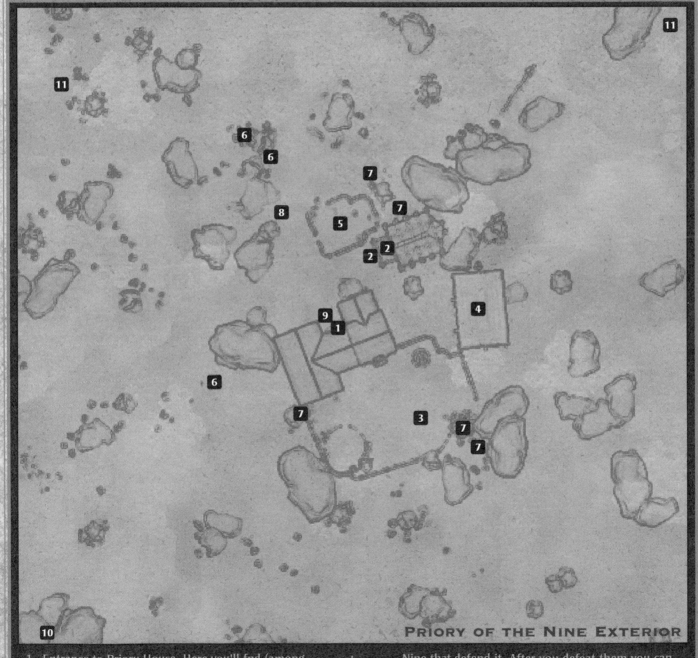

PRIORY OF THE NINE EXTERIOR

1. Entrance to Priory House. Here you'll fnd (among other things) the Undercroft, home to the Cuirass of the Crusader and the eight spirits of Knights of the

Nine that defend it. After you defeat them you can get your next four quests here.

2. Entrances to Priory Chapel. Site of your final meeting with the Prophet (in "The Blessing of Talos"), and the launch point for the final quest "Umaril the Unfeathered."

3. Archery range: You'll find knights practicing their marksmanship here from dawn to dusk. (Thedret and one of the generic knights even practice at night! Medic!)

4. Stable: Initially, it's empty. However, when you return to the Priory for "The Faithful Squire" quest, you'll find three horses quartered here. One belongs to Lathon, but you're free to use the others.

5. Ingredient garden: You'll find 15 lettuce plants, 42 carrots, 13 ginsengs, eight Dragon Tongues, eight flaxes (including the two outside the entrance) and two fennels. Avita Vesnia and Brellin look after the plot.

6. You can also find two other ingredient-bearing plants in the immediate area around the Priory. One is Nightshade (eight plants) ...

7. ... and the other Columbine (11 plants). South and northeast of the Priory, the latter is mingled with additional Flax plants. (All told, there are seven more of these in the Priory area.)

8. When you return to the Priory by fast-travel, you'll appear here.

9. Thedret, your self-appointed second-in-command, addresses the assembled knights here after your return from final Knights quest "Umaril the Unfeathered."

10. Random Oblivion Gate: Whether you'll find anything here depends on what stage you've reached in the Main Quest when you enter the area. (See "The Oblivion Crisis" section for details.) But if you've completed the "Dagon Shrine" segment, the gate will open.

11. A forest creature: Depending on your level, this could be anything from a harmless deer to a troll (at Level Eight), a spriggan (at Level 13) or brown bear (at Level 16).

The sense of emptiness endures when you arrive at the priory. Clearly, no one has lived here for a very long time. True, the altar in the chapel still works its magic and there's a shabby bed for sleeping and a couple of new books ("Shezarr and the Divines" and "The Adabal-a") upstairs in the Priory house. But that's about it. And there's no ready evidence of conventional underpinnings (i.e. cellar doors) in the house or chapel.

But remember that Amiel's ring is an unconventional key for what must be an unconventional door. As it happens, you can activate the design (nine diamonds in a circle) in the southwestern section of the ground floor. It transforms into a flight of stairs. At the bottom, the door to the Priory cellar. And in the northwest corner of the cellar, the door to the chapel's Undercroft. That's the Cuirass of the Crusader on the opposite wall.

Gulp.

You may find here you've bitten off a bit more than you can digest. When you enter the Undercroft, the spirits of eight dead Knights appear in a circle. Sir Amiel approaches you and growls that, to prove your worth, you'll have to best each dead knight in combat.

No small task! In short order, you'll face Sir Gregory, Sir Casimir, Sir Ralvas, Sir Henrik, Sir Calus, Sir Juncan, and Sir Torolf (all three levels below your own), plus Sir Amiel (one level below yours). (One knight, Sir Berich, about whom we've heard a bit, isn't in attendance. More on him later.)

There's a good deal of room to maneuver here, so use it, but no opportunity to retreat. (The exit is now blocked by the same kind of magic shield that protects the Cuirass.) Hence the need for healing supplies. Work around the ghosts' innate resistances—disease, frost, and poison—to win all eight battles and the barriers protecting the Cuirass and the Undercroft exit vanish and you can claim the armor for your own. It comes with leveled boosts to your Restoration skill and Health and Resistance to Normal Weapons. Your journal then suggests you talk to the Knights to locate the remaining artifacts.

Six remain. The ghosts know the locations of four.

Sir Casimir

Casimir puts you onto the Gauntlets of the Crusader and gives you the quest "Stendarr's Mercy." The gloves slipped from that knight's hands in Chorrol's Chapel of Stendarr after Casimir struck dead a beggar and was himself cursed. ("Heavy as stone, they would not move," he says.) You'll have to prove to Stendarr that you are worthy to lift them. He advises you to seek guidance from the chapel's priests.

Sir Ralvas

Ralvas gives you the quest "The Path of the Righteous" and sends you to Leyawiin's Chapel of Zenithar to claim the Mace of the Crusader. There, you'll undergo a test in which faith will supposedly be your guide. (Talk to Ralvas about "Zenithar" as well for an oblique hint: Zenithar's and Kynareth's realms are connected. In other words, what you get from the one might help you in the other.)

Sir Henrik

Henrik offers the quest "Wisdom of the Ages." He reveals that he found the Shield of the Crusader and brought it to Fort Bulwark (located near the Black Marsh border in southeast Cyrodiil) only to die defending it there.

Sir Juncan

And Juncan puts you onto the Boots of the Crusader. They're guarded by the god Kyanareth, and again you'll have to be tested and prove yourself worthy. In the quest "Nature's Fury," he sends you off to a shrine west of the Imperial City to speak to that god's priests.

Once you've gotten all four quests, you'll get another journal advising you to return to the Priory once they're complete.

But which task should come first? We've introduced them in the order you fought these knights, but, with one caveat, they can be completed in any order that best suits to your needs and talents. The caveat: You'll have to do "Nature's Fury" before "The Path of the Righteous."

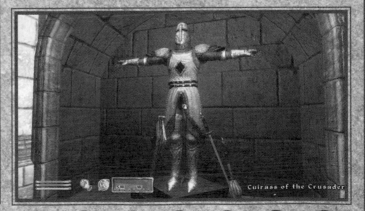
Cuirass of the Crusader

There's a significant benefit in the Undercroft that none of the knights mentions. The armor stand from which you collected the Cuirass of the Crusader serves as a free repairer, recharger *and* re-leveler for *all* Crusader relics—weapons included. Simply activate it for the option to place, or retrieve all or one (via "Swap") of the relics. The re-leveler function is especially nice: If you picked up the Helm (for instance) at a low character level, but are now at a high one, put it on the stand and then take it back. Its enchantments have been reset to your current elevated level.

NATURE'S FURY

The Kyrnareth shrine isn't marked on the map (meaning you can't travel there directly), but it's west-southwest of the Imperial City—closest to Haynote Cave to the south (just west of the Gold Road where it turns east to join the Red Ring Road) and Breakneck Cave to the northwest.

Avita Vesnia

Talk to priestess Avita Vesnia about "Boots of the Crusader." She'll point you to a "Grove of Trials" in the forest to the west and remind you to "fear and respect Nature and all Her creations."

Make directly for the grove. (In fact, it's a clearing near some big rocks). It isn't far. When you find it, you'll get a journal entry and, seconds later, a bear (identified as "Forest Guardian") will lumber onto the scene and attack you.

Just let it do its thing. Don't fight back, and don't leave the grove. (If you do, you'll have to take the test again while everyone else is playing outside.) The bear eventually lumbers off and you'll receive a follow-up journal alerting you to the appearance of a cave entrance in a big rock to the northwest.

Kynareth's Grotto leads down into an underground grove with two giggling spriggans…and the Boots of the Crusader on a bier at its center. They're equipped with a leveled Fortify Restoration enchantment, and when you pull 'em on you'll see a fleeting reference to an effect called "Woodland Grace."

Spriggan

If you stop by the shrine again for some post-quest acknowledgment from Ms. Vesnia, you're out of luck. She's vanished and her absence doesn't register with the two remaining priests.

But she's not gone from the game. Zap back to the Priory. She's there. She's had vision from Kynareth and now she wants to be a Knight of the Nine.

You can tell the lady to shove off (in which case she says she'll stick around anyway for a second opinion) or welcome her to the Order. If the latter, she'll head downstairs to the cellar and return as "Sir Avita," decked out in Knights of the Nine regalia. Now you can question her about the boots, and you'll get a sense of that "Woodland Grace" effect mentioned earlier: "It is said the wearer has the blessing of Kynareth upon him, and will not come to harm from creatures of the forest."

As it happens, you're also all fixed up to go ahead with the quest "The Path of the Righteous."

THE PATH OF THE RIGHTEOUS

Fast-travel to Leyawiin's West Gate, make your way east to the front of the nearby Great Chapel of Zenithar, and enter.

Carodus Oholin

Here you'll be buttonholed by Carodus Oholin, who's heard of your exploits. He's come looking for the Mace of the Crusader as well and, like Ralvas, messed up the test. He can't help you with it directly, but supplies the same oblique hint about a Zenithar-Kynareth link you may have received earlier from that knight.

Tomb of Saint Kaladas

Make your way down to the Undercroft and activate the Tomb of Saint Kaladas at its west end. You're teleported to "some sort of dark void" (says your journal) where you can see the Mace off in the distance.

If you're wearing the Boots of the Crusader from "Nature's Fury," you'll also learn that a glowing path leads to the Mace and that the Boots are vibrating and "seem to have have some connection to the mystical path."

In other words, ya done good. Follow the glowing path, grab the Mace, and before you know it you're back in the chapel

Undercroft. Equip it: It has leveled Fire Damage and Turn Undead enchantments and gives you a new Ability—Crusader's Arm—that fortifies your Blunt skill by 10 points.

 If you're not wearing the Boots…well, let's just say the water smells like dirty diapers and you're in need of a paddle. Faith or no faith, there's no way to reach the Mace and the only reward for stepping off into starry space is a landing back in the Undercroft. Do this three times and you'll get a journal suggesting another artifact might help.

You've got the Mace, but you're not quite out of the woods. When you re-enter the main body of the church, you'll hear weapons being drawn and see the flash of combat spells from the nave above. Like Anvil's Chapel of Dibella before it, Leyawiin's church has been invaded by three of Umaril's followers. This time, you get to fight them. They're a heretofore-unseen type of Daedra called Aurorans—Dremora-like creatures with significant resistances to magic and Shock Damage and equpped with Crude Ayleid Battle Axes.

 However crude, the axes bring a pretty penny should you collect and sell them.

Why Daedra? Umaril was an Ayleid king. Weren't the Ayleids elves? They were indeed. But remember your history from Volume 3 of "The Song of Pelinal." (There will be a quiz.) The Ayleids were allied with the Daedra god Meridia and Meridia's Auroran warriors were summoned to the defense of the White-Gold tower. (Umaril himself is part-Ayleid and part-Daedra.)

Happily, this chapel is well defended—not only by the local clergy but a knight with at least half of Pelinal Whitestrake's equipment (you) and a prospective knight (Oholin). Hence, the battle against these leveled foes shouldn't last long.

Once the last Auroran's lights go out, you'll be approached by an excited Oholin, who pledges himself to your cause. You can tell him to get lost (talk to him again if you change your mind), or welcome him to the order—in which case he marches off to get better equipment and vanishes when he leaves the chapel.

After a few hours, you may begin to wonder if he's coming back. Not hardly. Oholin has already removed to the Priory and exchanged his gear. If you drop by again, you may even find him chatting with Avita Vesnia.

WISDOM OF THE AGES

Recovering the Shield of the Crusader from Fort Bulwark on the east edge of the Black Marsh swamps is probably the most difficult of the four middle quests.

If you've explored this remote region—possibly for the Miscellaneous quest "Finding Your Roots"—you can fast-travel either to Fieldhouse Cave (the closest location) to the northwest, Onyx Caverns to the south-southwest, Fort Teleman to the north-northeast, or Fort Doublecross to the west, and then wade through the muck and mire.

You can get by mainly on your wits in the other relic missions. This one, however, requires a fair amount of fighting. You'll find a pair of hostile Conjurers in the surface ruin and 12 more—including two bosses—and a minimum of two Daedra (and probably many more that will be conjured in combat) on the first two of the three levels within.

Also, this dungeon is not a straight shot down to the Shield. The whole place is something of a puzzle.

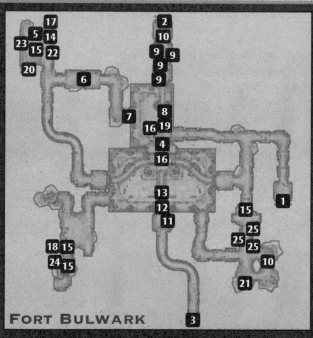

FORT BULWARK

1. Exit to fort exterior.
2. Entrance to the prison level.
3. Entrance to the puzzle level. (You'll use this on your way out of the dungeon. It's inaccessible on your way in.)
4. Gate: You'll find it closed. Opening it requires first turning a handle ...
5. ... here. This opens a second gate ...
6. ... here, which allows you to reach a second handle ...
7. ... here. Activate it to open the gate back at #4 and lower the drawbridge ...
8. ... here. Whew.

9. A pressure-plate puzzle. Step on the plates marked with a "9"—left, middle, right and left—to open the gate ...
10. ... here!
11. On your way out (via #3), it's a lot easier. Just activate the handle here ...
12. ... to open the gate here ...
13. ... and lower the drawbridge here, and you're home free.
14. Conjurer Adept (i.e. boss).
15. Conjurer.
16. Daedra. This could be anything from a Stunted Scamp up to a Storm Atronach or Xivilai at Level 22 and up.
17. The boss's chest. Also, look nearby for the Conjurer's Note, which supplies a hint for getting past the puzzle at #9.
18. A standard conjurer's chest.
19. A chest of containing one or two healing items.
20. Two torches in a barrel.
21. Two daggers (plus some unreadable crumpled papers on the floor).
22. A pair of shortswords.
23. Most of a suit of iron armor: a helmet and two pairs of gauntlets (on shelves) and cuirass and boots (on the floor).
24. Most of a set of alchemy equipment—along with a bit of Redwort Flower. (The Domica Redwort Flower from which this comes is especially plentiful in the area around the fort.)
25. Dart traps. They get even worse on the next level.

On the top level, skip the northernmost passage (a dead-end) and move south and west at first opportunity to an old wooden door. Cross the large room beyond—the one with a raised drawbridge to the south—to a second such door and head north (passing a remotely operated gate to the east) to a little Conjurer camp.

Ignore their summonings and take on the Conjurers themselves. Then turn the handle in the floor against the north wall to open the closed gate you just passed. Also read the note on the desk in the northeast corner, with special attention to its reference to the gate to the lower levels: "Make note of the candles along the walls if you would pass through."

Pass through the gate you just opened and turn the handle beyond to lower the drawbridge in the room to the east. Now, retrace your steps to the big room and make your way through the gate in the north wall and across the now-lowered drawbridge beyond.

Just past the drawbridge, you'll find a closed gate and 12 pressure plates arranged in four rows of three. You need to hit the right four plates (one from each row) to open the gate.

A couple of methods will work. You've already found a hint in one of the Conjurer Notes: "Make note of the candles along the walls."

For there are candles here: one to the left of the first rank of pressure plates, two to the right of the second, three to the left of the third, and one to the left of the fourth. The number of candles reflects how many plates you need to tick off from the candles to find the right plate.

The other method: The correct pressure plates *sound* different from the others. Stepping on the right one will be accompanied by a low noise of stones grinding and locking into place. The correct sequence is: left pad, middle pad, right pad, left pad. The gate opens. The door beyond leads to the second level.

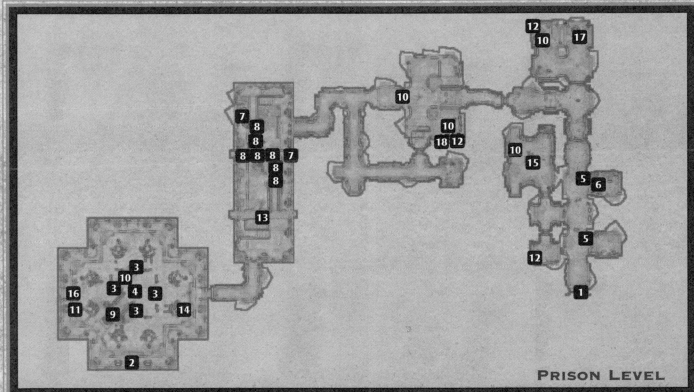

PRISON LEVEL

1. Entrance to the fort entry level.

2. Entrance to the puzzle level. Or, rather, to a passage leading to the exit (not shown).

3. You say #2 isn't there? That means the secret wall hasn't been opened yet. You'll need to adjust these four statues so that they're looking at the circular plate on the floor ...

4. ... here! Then the door appears, and you'll be on your way to a nastier puzzle.

5. You can turn these handles to open the adjacent cells.

6. Sir Thedret: This knight was captured by the Conjurers while himself questing for the Shield of the Crusader. Free him and he'll provide a clue to the puzzle at numbers 3 and 4 and turn up at the Priory of the Nine and act like he freakin' owns the place. (If you don't free Thedret, he'll still appear at the Priory and join the Order after the "Wisdom of the Ages" quest is complete. But he'll have slightly different dialogue: "You do not know me," he begins, "but you have saved me.")

7. These switches lower the respective nearby drawbridges.

8. Unfortunately, the lowering of the first of the two sets off this veritable crapstorm of dart traps. These can be traversed with a bit of care – just follow behind the darts as they fire sequentially and you can avoid taking any damage.

9. Who gets to stand in front of the statue of Julianos? Why, the prison's Conjurer boss, naturally.

10. Conjurer.

11. Boss chest.

12. The standard Conjurer chest.

13. A chest containing one or two healing items.

14. A sack containing four food items.

15. The implements of torture around this brazier include a mace and dagger.

16. The shelves here contain a complete set of alchemical equipment, three Ironwood Nuts, two Bog Beacon Asco Caps and Bonemeal.

17. On this table, you'll find a flawless topaz, a ruby, eight gold and a Conjurer's Note—a report on the uncooperativeness of the prisoner Thedret (#6).

18. On these shelves, you'll find a diamond (in a bowl on the top shelf) and another complete set of alchemical equipment.

You'll find yourself in a prison of sorts, with cells to east and west. Use the handle on the floor to open the second cell to the north and speak to the prisoner, Sir Thedret. He was questing after the Shield when he was captured by the Conjurers, and imprisoned when he refused to help them reach the artifact.

Sir Thedret

Thedret's a future Knight of the Nine. Alone among the knights, he joins your cause automatically once he's freed. (You'll find him later at the Priory.)

But he can help you right away: He's done some research on the fort and kept running into the phrase: "When the eyes of the Guardians are upon you, Julianos will show you favor." And with that, Thredret makes for the exit.

It appears you released him none too soon. A note on the table in the corner room to the north reveals that Thredret hasn't told the Conjurers squat and had at most a week remaining before his frustrated captors put him to death.

The passage to the west descends into a watched chamber— some fighting is inevitable here—and then twists west again to the long north-south one. Climb the stairs at its north end, head south and turn the handle to lower the first of two drawbridges. Then turn east and turn a second handle against the wall to lower the second bridge to the south. And beware—as you approach the bridges, you'll trigger a series of dart traps which fire sequentially down onto your path. Wait for the first set of darts to fire, then run to the second handle (out of the line of fire). Once the second set have finished firing, you can run the rest of the way in safety.

At the south end of the room, the passage turns west again to a large chamber with five statues—one tall one up on the dias (the god Julianos) and four smaller ones arranged in a square around a circular plate on the floor below. These are the "Guardians" referenced in the texts Thedret mentioned earlier.

Conjurer

Trouble is, they're all looking in different directions. You'll need to use the handles at the base of each statue to turn them so they're looking at the central circular plate. This'll require two pulls at the handle on the statue to the west, four on the one to the south, one on the one to the east, and one on the one to the north. Once this is done, all the fires go out at once and a door opens in the room's south wall. Beyond, a passage winds down to the entrance to Fort Bulwark's bottom level.

PUZZLE LEVEL

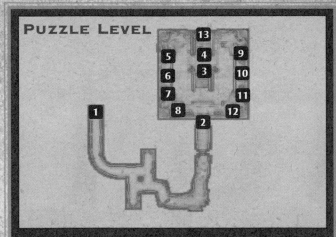

1. Entrance to the prison level.

2. Once the puzzle starts, this door is locked and remains so until the puzzle's complete.

3. Pressure plate: Stand on it with an item taken from the big chest at #4 in your inventory, and look around the room. Above one of the eight chests against the east and west walls, you'll see the image of the item that chest should contain. (Alas, it's never the one in your inventory!)

4. Big chest: The idea here is to place eight items taken (one at a time) from this chest into the appropriate chests along the walls.

5. Rodgar's gem goes here.

6. His skull goes here.

7. His hammer goes here.

8. His book goes here. (It's not readable, by the way; none of Rodgar's stuff can be used.)

9. Rodgar's stone goes here.

10. His helm goes here.

11. His goblet goes here.

12. And his sword goes here.

13. Once the items in #5 through #12 are in place, a door opens here. The passage beyond leads to a room (not pictured) where you'll find the Shield of the Crusader. Take the Shield and secret doors open in the northwest and northweast corners. These lead to a passage to the entrance to Fort Bulwark's entry level. (It leads to #3 on that map.)

Here, a corridor loops south and then north to a large chamber. Advance up the stairs in its center to get a journal entry that you've found a puzzle or trap, and that you'll have to sort out its meaning to reach the Shield. And, by the way, the wooden door you opened to get here? It's now locked, and you don't have the key.

Along the east and west walls are eight statues, with a chest at the base of each. At the top of the first flight of stairs, in the room's center, is a larger version of the chest, with a pressure plate just to the south.

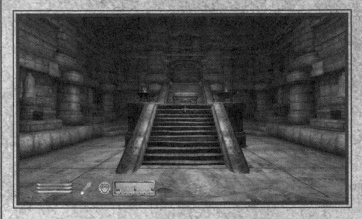

The big chest contains an item. It'll be different each time you enter the level, but it's always a Miscellaneous item called Rodgar's something-or-other: his book, his gem, his goblet, his hammer, his helm, his skull, his stone, or his sword. Whatever the item is, take it.

You should sort out pretty quickly that you have to match eight items to the eight statue chests. The game gives you a little help in figuring out which item goes with which chest. Stand on the pressure plate *with one of Rodgar's items in your inventory* and look around the room. You'll see that an image has appeared above one of the statue chests representing what it should contain.

However, that help is never geared to the particular item you have at a particular moment. In other words, the game doesn't tell you where things go; it just steadily narrows the field of places where you can put them. You'll make the process much easier if you draw yourself a little map showing which images have appeared over which chests.

Choose correctly, and item is removed from circulation, the chest glows whitely, and the statue above it turns around. Choose incorrectly, and the statue chest is emptied out and a new item can be claimed from the big chest.

In other words, you're going to do a lot of trial-and-error placements and running around, but each subsequent match will be easier than the one before it.

Here's where Rodgar's stuff should be stowed. In the east wall chests (from north to south) place his stone, helm, goblet, and sword. In the west wall chests, from north to south, place his gem, skull, hammer, and book.

Once all eight items have been matched to their chests, the lights go out, the entry door unlocks, and a new door opens at the top of the stairs. Head north. Atop a bier in a large room, you'll find the Shield of the Crusader (with a leveled Reflect Spell enchantment), a half-dozen potions, four Restoration scrolls, and a bit of gold. Take the shield and the lights go out here as well and doors open in the north wall to the east and west.

Shield of the Crusader

 This isn't an escape hatch, but a short-cut. You'll find yourself in the previously-inaccessible southern section of the fort's top level. Use the switch to open the gate and lower the drawbridge to the north, and make your way east and north to the exit.

If you like, explore the southeast part of the level, which we skipped on our way in. (Just watch out for the dart traps near the south end of the entry corridor.) It provides easy access to a little Conjurer hideaway in the level's southwest corner, with nominal loot and evidence of recent excavations. Evidently, the Conjurers were so desperate to find the Shield that they'd started digging randomly for it!

STENDARR'S MERCY

Fast-travel to Chorrol's south gate and make your way northwest to the Chapel of Stendarr. You'll find the Gauntlets of the Crusader at north end of the nave, surrounded by candles and flowers. Activate them and you'll find that, regardless of your actual Strength, they're too heavy to lift.

Gauntlets of the Crusader

Speak to new priest Areldur about "Gauntlets of the Crusader" to learn that the curse of weariness that Stendarr placed on Casimir has been passed down to his descendant Kellen. Kellen has come to Chorrol from Hammerfell in hope of lifting the curse. You'll find him resting in bedroom on the west side of the Chapel Hall. (He's exhausted. Kellen only sleeps, sits and eats.)

Areldur

He also has lots of time to think, and he suspects Areldur knows more about the curse than he reveals; he hears guilt in the priest's voice. "Why would that be?" he asks. He pleads with you to persuade him to open up.

Kellen

Return to Areldur and ask him about "Kellen." Coax his Disposition above 70, and learn he knows how to lift the curse. He just doesn't have the strength of character to do it himself. (Hence the guilt.)

The solution: Someone else must take over the curse from Kellen. If not Areldur, you?

You can return to Kellen and either report what you've learned—his Disposition jumps 10 points—or lie that there's no cure. (Kellen sees through the lie, and his Disposition drops five points.) Or you can act straightaway: Activate the altar and pray for the power to lift the curse. You'll be given the temporary ability to "Lay Hands" on Kellen. (This is a Lesser Power that allows you restore 10 Fatigue points.) Return to Kellen's room directly and use the Power on him.

He's a changed man. He feels like running. In fact, he does run around the Chapel Hall. In fact, he doesn't stop there; he's off to see the world! And, in fact, for the rest of the game you'll find him traveling Cyrodiil on Mondays, Wednesdays, and Fridays. At any given time, he might be bound for Anvil's The Count Arms, Bravil's The Lonely Suitor Lodge, Bruma's Jeral View, Cheyndinhal's Bridge Inn, Chorrol's own The Oak and Crosier tavern, Leyawiin's Three Sisters Inn, or Skingrad's West Weald Inn.

Areldur's changed as well. Initially, he seems bewildered by your selfless act. ("Why would you do such a thing?") Then he turns the question inward and asks why he didn't do it himself—and, if he can't, what business has he acting as a priest? He'll leave the chapel and then make his way out Chorrol's south gate. Is he…?

He is. Areldur is the newest candidate for the revived Knights of the Nine. Talk to him at the Priory. Let him into the Order and he'll make the same equipment trip to the cellar that your other recruits have made. Tell him to get stuffed, and he'll stick around in the hope you'll reconsider.

And you? You've changed, too—taking over the Curse of the Consumed, a Damage Fatigue effect that will leave you panting like a dog after the smallest exertion.

Can you remove the curse? Eventually, yes, but you're going to have to suffer under it for a while. (Otherwise, it wouldn't be much of a curse!)

However, you can counter it with other magical effects. For instance, you can buy novice- and apprentice-level Fortify Fatigue spells from Ungarion at A Warlock's Luck in Bravil or Edgar Vautrine at Edgar's Discount Spells in the Imperial City's Market District. (If you have the Spell Tomes plugin installed, and you're lucky, you can also learn these spells from two of those special books.) You can create Restore Fatigue potions—no fewer than 31 ingredients (typically, food) have this as their primary effect—and a more advanced alchemist can create Fortify Fatigue potions using Wormwood (primary effect) and Flour (tertiary effect).

Or, finally, you can hunt up the game's one built-in item with a Fortify Fatigue effect: The Fortify Fatigue Pants found on a desk on the ground floor of the Mystic Exporium in the Market District.

In any case, you can now pick up and equip the Gauntlets of the Crusader. They have a leveled Fortify Restoration skill enchantment and a heady, non-leveled 50-percent resistance to disease. And they'll also add to your repertoire a new Lesser Power called "Merciful Touch" that restores 50 points of health, a touch spell that will come in very handy when in battle with your knights later on.

THE FAITHFUL SQUIRE

Not a quest so much as a housekeeping mission.

On your return to the Priory, after finishing the last of the four quests given by the ghost knights (whatever order you did them in), you'll find the place fairly packed. In addition to the already inducted and prospective knights waiting around, you'll find Geimund and Gukimir, a pair of Nord brothers from Skyrim, who want to sign on with the Order. Tell either of them "OK" or "Get knotted" and it'll take for both. You know the routine by now, yes?

 Cute touch: You can hear about these guys *waaay* before they actually show up. Any time between the end of the "Priory of the Nine" quest and the end of the quest line, male Nords and Orcs who aren't at the Priory or in Skingrad may report that two brothers passed through the latter location in search of the Priory. (In fact, it's possible – although unlikely – to run across them actually travelling from Skyrim to the Priory at any time after your first knight has joined up.) Same story with the Bosmer recruit Brellin late in the quest line when talking to male elves in Bravil during the same period.

Thedret is here as well; he's already suited up. And, surprise, joining them is Sir Roderic's squire, Lathon, who you may have met back in "Pilgrimage."

Lathon reports that Roderic is dead.

That knight completed his own pilgrimage and received his own vision. But it was different from your cloudtop meeting with spirit of Pelinal. Instead, he met Berich, the missing ninth Knight of the Nine, and returned to tell his squire they must put him to rest. But in his effort to find the evil Berich's remains—and the Sword and Greaves of the Crusader—Roderic fell in Underpall Cave at the hands of its powerful wraith guardian.

Lathon managed to get out of Underpall with the Greaves of the Crusader, which he presents to you. This leg armor has leveled Destruction and Restoration skill boosts—as well as adding a new Lesser Power. "Blessing of the Eight" permits you to erect a 20 percent Shield for 60 seconds.

 At this point, you'll also pick up a cumulative benefit from all this nice armor you've acquired, called "Holy Aura." Along with "Woodland Grace," you'll find this Shield effect packaged in "Active Effects" under the curious wrapper "Umaril's Bane." More on this later.

The sword's another matter. The wraith used it against Roderic, and Lathon says it may have been turned to evil purposes. If so, it'll have to be "reconsecrated" on the altar of Arkay. (If you'd like some background about Berich's switch to the Dark Side, return to the Priory chapel Undercroft and consult Caius and Amiel.)

No surprise that Lathon wants to sign on as Knight as well. And once he's suited up, his behavior is a little different than the others. (You can only talk to them at this stage.) He's your companion on the next mission: "The Sword of the Crusader." You can order him to follow you (which he does by default) or wait.

Have him wait a little while. There have been some changes at the Priory, and what you learn can trigger a pair of informal mini quests.

You now have a blacksmith down in the cellar. Sergius Terrianus is a pal of Thedret. His repair service isn't free, but he's cheap and you don't get much more local than your own basement. And he never sleeps.

Did you notice that the furniture has been upgraded a second time to provide for a full house of knights? The first, modest upgrade occurred after you completed the first of the four quests received from the knights' spirits. Now that all four are complete, there's a big old dining room table downstairs, 10 single beds upstairs, plus a big cozy one for you in the northeast room. Three horses have been installed in the stable out back. (The Paint horse belongs to Lathon, and stealing it is a crime. However, while the Bay and Chestnut horses are associated with new arrivals Gukimir and Geimund, they're not owned by them and are yours for the riding.)

The Priory really comes alive with this many people around. Routines vary a great deal, but at some point during the day, everyone takes three-hour shifts at melee-combat practice in the Priory house cellar, a single meal and prayer in the Chapel before bed at midnight.

In addition, Areldur, Brellin, Gukimir, Carodus Oholin, and Thedret practice archery on the range just north of the Priory house. Brellin and Avita Vesnia tend the vegetable garden beside the Chapel. (You'll find mainly Lettuce and Carrot plants here, but also Dragon's Tongue, Fennel, Flax, and Ginseng, with Nightshade and Columbine plants in the area around the Priory.) Gukimir and Geimund, connected at the hip, spar together in the cellar. And Vesnia, Oholin, and Thedret like to read in the library upstairs. (If you're wondering where the Priory's copy of Volume 8 of "The Song of Pelinal" has gone, wait until Thedret's asleep and search him.)

Naturally, the knights cross paths while going about their business, and may stand around gossiping about relics you've recovered…or express impatience that they have to wait for Umaril to strike. So it's appropriate that, beginning now, you may learn from general chatter from Imperials about an attack on Bravil's Great Chapel of Mara.

It's not just talk. Visit that city. Triggered automatically at the end of "Nature's Fury," this attack recalls the slaughter in Anvil all over again. You'll find the priestesses Chana Mona and Uravasa Othrelas, the healer Marz and the commoner Olava the Fair dead—the last of these in the Great Chapel Hall—with bloody runes again written around the central altar, pews scattered, and the Chapel Hall dining room destroyed.

You can't prevent the attack and you're not expected to respond to it. After four missions spent accruing equipment, it's just a timely reminder of what the Relics are all about: the defeat of Umaril.

The other side trip: Lathon mentioned that the knight and his squire went back and forth across "Colovia" (presumably, the Colovian Highlands) in search of information about a noble family called "Vlindrel."

Again, that's not entirely an idle reference. Let's suppose you're the suspicious sort and don't want to take on the squire as a knight until you've retraced his steps and substantiated his story.

Well, it turns out there's a good-faith basis for Roderic's search. Read the book "The Knights of the Nine." (You'll find it in chapel halls in Bravil, Bruma, Chorol, Leyawiin, and Skingrad; at Southern Books in Leyawiin; and on the second floor of the Mystic Archives at the Imperial City's Arcane University.) It calls Berich "the scion of one of the great noble families of Colovia."

In addition, until you recover the Sword of the Crusader—see the next quest—passers-by in Bruma and Chorrol will mention that Lord Vlindrel's ghost haunts the road between those cities. (No, you can't find it. The creature doesn't leave Underpall Cave on your watch.)

 There's an almost invisible event in the game's background. Shortly after this housekeeping quest begins, the Prophet quietly packs up, bedroll and all, and quits Anvil. No one mentions his absence, but it doesn't last long. Can you be in any doubt about where he's headed?

THE SWORD OF THE CRUSADER

When you're ready, speak to Lathon and have him follow you outside the Priory. He'll head for the stable and mount his Paint horse. Then lead him to Underpall Cave—north of the Orange Road a little more half the distance from Chorrol to Bruma.

Unlike other Knight of the Nine dungeons, this cave and its underground keep exist independent of the Knights of the Nine quest line. (Check out "Non-Quest Dungeons" in the Freeform Quests chapter for some details.) However, two levels of the five-level dungeon have been tweaked for "The Sword of the Crusader."

A word or two on Lathon before we start in. Generally, he's a useful companion and eager combatant. For instance, he'll carry a torch, and if you get off-track—easy to do in this big place—he'll mention that this isn't the path he followed with Roderic. And the Redguard can hold his own in one-on-one battles against the cave's undead inhabitants.

However, that said, Lathon may run in and start whacking irrespective of the overall danger. And since he can easily join his former master in death in Underpall, you'll need to be careful with him. Heal him up on a regular basis, and leave him behind in situations where he's at risk. (You can read Lathon's health just as you would that of an enemy in combat.)

If you don't already have a targeted healing spell, the recent depletion in the number of Cyrodiil healers may make acquiring one slightly tricky. Seek out Isa Raman at Bruma's Great Chapel of Talos, Orraggra Bargol at Chorrol's Chapel of Stendarr, Tumindil at Skingrad's Great Chapel of Julianos and Avrus Adas in Leyawiin's Great Chapel of Zenithar (if he survived the Auroran attack). Your new "Merciful Touch" Power will also work nicely.

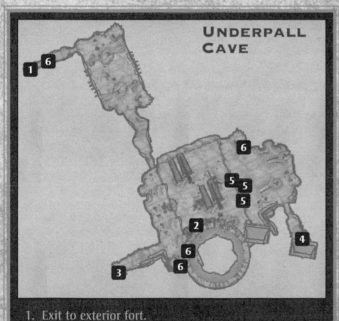

UNDERPALL CAVE

1. Exit to exterior fort.
2. Entrance to Underpall Keep.

3. Entrance to Underpall Keep - South Wing.
4. Entrance to Underpall Keep - North Wing. Note that these two Wing doors are on high ground, inaccessible from the cave floor below. You'll have to go through the Keep itself. (And you don't need to visit them at all. Your destination is in the Reflecting Chamber level.)
5. Skeleton archers.
6. Standard tomb-creatures chest.

This doesn't have to be a long trip. Cross the pit near the entrance and head southeast to Underpall Keep. The Keep has two wings, which can be entered to the northeast and southwest, but leave them alone. Instead, from the Keep entrance, do a U-turn to the west and south and follow the passage southeast. Beyond the double doors, you'll find a cave-in trap and two baddies and, further southeast, the entrance to the Reflecting Chamber.

UNDERPALL KEEP

1. Entrance to Underpall Cave.
2. Entrance to the Reflecting Chamber.
3. Entrance to the Keep's North Wing.
4. Entrance to the Keep's South Wing.
5. Zombies! One for sure, and as many as three more at this location. The chances each of these three will appear are 75, 50, and 25 percent, respectively. In other words, odds are this will be nasty.
6. Not much chance of this zombie turning up. (Just 25 percent.)
7. Two skeleton archers and a cave-in trap. We humbly suggest you advance just far enough through the door to the north to set off the traps, dumping the rocks on the idiot skeletons, and then back off.

8. A skeleton melee fighter ...

9. ... and a skeleton archer in close support.

10. A skeleton or, at Level 19 or higher, a lich.

11. A mudcrab or, more likely, a rat.

12. Depending on your level, this could be anything from a skeleton or ghost to a lich or wraith. And there's a 20-percent chance it could just be a plain old rat.

13. Same story as in #12 ... except there's a 50-percent chance this critter won't appear at all.

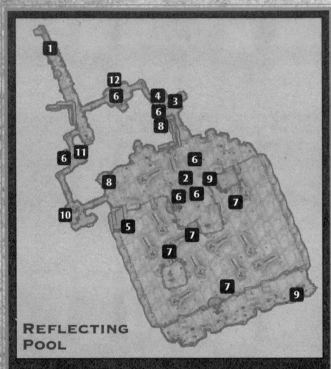

REFLECTING POOL

1. Entrance to Underpall Keep. In the Knights of the Nine quest "Sword of the Crusader," when you enter the level with the newly-knighted Lathon in tow, he'll take over the lead here. (If you're exploring the "vanilla" Oblivion, note that #2, #3 and #4 won't appear.)

2. The Wraith: Or Lord Vlindrel to you young people. Slap him around with something lethal and take his sword to complete the first stage of "Sword of the Crusader." Now the blade just needs a holy Wash 'n' Wax at Cheydinhal's Great Chapel of Arkay.

3. Tomb of Lord Vlindrel: Nothing too amazing in here. Just the standard Knights of the Nine cuirass and shield and regular chainmail for the rest.

4. Sir Roderic's body. Again, nothing here that'll blow you away—just Roddy's standard unenchanted heavy armor and sword and perhaps a repair hammer or two.

5. Necromancer boss: Nothing to do with Berich Vlindrel or the Sword of the Crusader. This baddie ruled the roost in Underpall before the Wraith's arrival—it was here in the unexpanded edition of Oblivion—and survives its departure. Unless you gotta problem with that ...

6. Undead buddies of the Wraith? Summonings of the Necromancer boss? All we know is, they turn up 75 percent of the time, they're dead (unless they turn out to be rats) and you may want to make them deader.

7. Slaughterfish. (Half the time.)

8. Standard tomb chest.

9. Big lake. There's gotta be something down there. Yup. Right here. (Note that the chest in the southeast corner, beside a coffin lid, has a leveled lock with one to five tumblers.)

10. Coffin.

11. A chest containing one or two Restoration-related potions.

12. A standard Necromancer chest.

When you enter, Lathon takes point and leads you southeast and then northeast. Here you'll find a small chamber containing Roderic's body and the tomb of Lord Vlindrel (i.e. Berich) lit by a shaft of light from above. (You won't find anything unusual in either.)

You might want to leave Lathon here, for the door to southeast leads to the great wraith—a creature either fixed at your level or one above it. (However, even if you're just starting out, it will always be at least Level Six.) It has Frost Damage and Silence spells; the ability to absorb your health and damage, your Strength and Endurance; all the standard resistances of the ethereal undead (disease, frost, normal weapons, and poison) and it can float above the giant underground lake that occupies much of this level. And, in a twist unique to high-level enemies in Knights of the Nine, Sheogorath's Wabbajack staff won't work on it!

Lord Berich Vlindrel

However, you can beat the wraith to its second death handily with the Mace of the Crusader or any number of other magical weapons that do Fire Damage.

Afterward, grab the Sword of the Crusader. It comes with leveled Fire Damage and Damage Magicka enchantments. But your journal confirms that, as Lathon speculated in "The Faithful Squire," it has been "desecrated" by the wraith and should be reconsecrated at the Great Chapel of Arkay in Cheydinhal. Report your success to Lathon, who sets off for the Priory to report the good news.

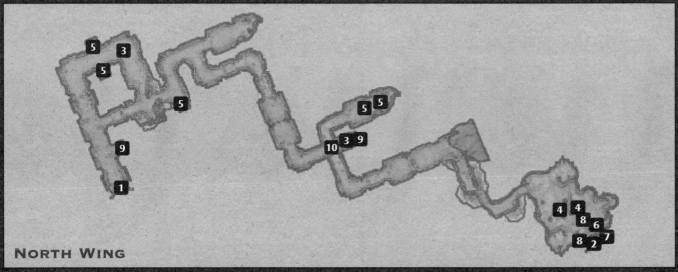

NORTH WING

1. Entrance to Underpall Keep.

2. Entrance to Undercave Cave.

3. Skeleton archer.

4. Probably a tomb creature or a rat. (There's a 75 percent chance one or the other will appear.) Note that some of these locations can be the source of more than one critter.

5. The same critters from #4, but with a 50-50 chance of appearing. Ditto, also, on the more-than-one-critter thing at certain locations.

6. There's just a 25 percent chance this creature will appear. But if it does, there's a 50-percent chance it will be a vampire. (There's a 1-in-3 chance it will be another undead creature and a 1-in-6 chance it'll be a leveled beast.)

7. Boss-level coffin.

8. Standard tomb chest. The one beside the exit to Underpall Cave has a leveled (one- to five-tumbler) lock.

9. Standard healing-supplies chest.

10. A hole in the floor—directly over a spike trap.

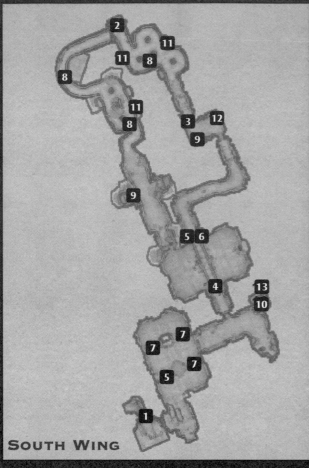

SOUTH WING

1. Entrance to Underpall Keep.
2. Entrance to Underpall Cave.

3. Locked gate. You can pick it—the leveled lock has two to five tumblers—or just look at the ground. The Underpall Gate Key's right in front of the gate!

4. The first of six sets of pressure plates. The bridge is paved with 'em. Stepping on either plate in a set triggers a swinging mace trap, with the first mace coming in from the west, the second from the east and so on. Solution: Don't step on the pressure plates! Instead, walk along the bridge abutments. Or coax a skeleton archer at the far end of the span into stepping on the plates. Woo-hoo. Problem solved. (Note that there are two paths to the exit from the bridge. The one that starts down in the northwest corner of the bridge room is probably tougher.)

5. Actual skeleton archer. He's here all the time.

6. Probable skeleton archer. He's here 75 percent of the time.

7. Theoretical skeleton archer. He's here 25 percent of the time.

8. This is a skeleton, too—unless you're Level 19 or higher. Then it's a lich.

9. #8 all over again, but with a 75-percent chance the skeleton-or-lich will appear.

10. Rat or mudcrab.

11. Coffins.

12. Gotta love those standard tomb chests.

13. A sack containing healing potion and a grain sack that yields an ingredient. (Could be rare, could be run-of-the-mill.)

You can use this man-splitting sword even in its corrupted condition. However, we advise against it. If your Infamy is 1 or less, you'll be saddled with Lord Vindrel's Curse. Not only won't your Magicka regenerate for the duration of the curse, but until the sword is reconsecrated, you'll be entirely at the mercy of fire, frost, magic, poison, and shock damage, with 100 percent weaknesses against each. So, Mr. Perverse, if you gotta use it, fast-travel to Cheyndinhal's East Gate pronto to get the sword fixed and don't do anything else in the chapel until you do. Run to the altar, activate it, and re-arm yourself with the cleaned-up sword. (The reconsecration also removes the curse.)

Why run? Because the chapel's under attack by three leveled Aurorans. They've already killed the healer Ohtesse and the pilgrim Errandil, and started writing the usual bloody runes around the altar, but haven't yet done in Gruiand Garrana or Hil the Tall down in the Chapel Hall. (Given opportunity, they will.) This time, you're just in time.

When the third Auroran drops, you'll get a journal entry urging your return to the Priory to consult with your knights on the destruction of Umaril.

In fact, you'll be consulting with a visitor.

THE BLESSING OF TALOS

Again, not a quest so much as a few last-minute administrative maneuvers.

When you reappear on the Priory's front lawn, you'll be approached immediately by Thedret. He says the Prophet has arrived and is addressing the knights in the Chapel. "You should speak to him at once."

Enter the chapel and you'll find eight knights and prospective knights arrayed on five benches, with a seat saved for you up front. Speak to the Prophet. He'll offer extravagant praise for your accomplishments and say it's time to put down Umaril, who can be found at Garlas Malatar. You'll meet those knights you've judged "worthy" at this new Ayleid ruin on the Abecean Sea northwest of Anvil.

You'll need a blessing from god Talos to follow Umaril into the spirit world upon the death of his body and destroy his spirit as well. You don't have to make another long trip to get it. The Prophet, who apparently has Talos's Power of Attorney, bestows it himself. This Lesser Power comprises the god's blessing (which runs for 30 seconds) and 20-point boosts to your Strength and Endurance (60 seconds) at the expense of your Speed and Agility, which are drained by 15 points for the same period. (The blessing also removes the curse of weariness that you picked up in the "Stendarr's Mercy" quest.)

And, with that, all inducted knights will storm out of the chapel and head off for Garlas Malatar—both on horseback and on foot, leaving you, the Prophet, Brellin, and any knights you've deemed "unworthy" alone in the chapel.

Brellin?

Sitting in the back row, this Akatosh follower from Silvenar is late to the party but not too late to join in the fun. Sign him up—the more the merrier—and he'll rush off to the Priory cellar for his equipment and then rush off in pursuit for his comrades. (Really, there's no point in holding anyone back at this stage.) At your convenience, join them.

UMARIL THE UNFEATHERED

The closest fast-travel location to Garlas Malatar is Crowhaven—a vampire lair north-northwest of Anvil which you may have visited in the Miscellaneous quest "Origin of the Gray Prince." Make your way west-southwest from this hilltop ruin and you'll find your troops lined up near the east end of a bridge leading out to the Ayleid outpost.

Talk to the any of the knights, and you'll be given a choice: Launch the attack or wait for your signal. You can't give the assault any additional "special handling" so just give the go-ahead. Everyone charges off again to slaughter the two leveled Aurorans in the exterior ruin and the first four of up to 21 on the topmost of Garlas Malatar's three levels.

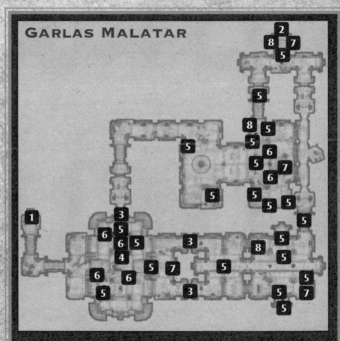

GARLAS MALATAR

1. Exit to the exterior ruin.
2. Entrance to the Ceysel level.
3. Closed gates. Your troops will gather nearby. You'll open all three gates by activating the stone block ...
4. ... here. (You'll also find a standard "Restoration" chest from #8 nearby; we couldn't fit in another number on the bier!) Your troops will then take off north and east and do their best to fight their way into the Ceysel level (reached via #2).
5. Aurorans.
6. Welkynd Stones.
7. Standard Conjurer chest.
8. Standard "Restoration" chest.

Now, the results of these battles are not scripted, and your mileage may vary. But if you've inducted all eight available knights, things should go smoothly on this level. They'll clear the passage down to the large room to the east and then wait at three remotely-operated gates—two up the stairs to the east and one in the north wall.

A ballsy way to play this not to let anyone into the Order that you don't have to admit—i.e. Thedret—and then tackle Garlas Malatar as a duo!

Push the stone block atop the northern of the two biers in the center of this room. All three gates will open simultaneously. Your troops go charging off again in three parties—the northern one consisting of the swordsmen Areldur and Lathon and the archers Avita and Carodus, and the eastern ones of the brothers Geimund and Gukimir and Thedret and Brellin, respectively. (The two eastern parties quickly reunite, as the passages rejoin beyond the gates.)

Ordinarily, we're not a great fans of dividing our forces, but the knights should meet with success again—killing off many of the remaining Aurorans on the level. Don't be worried if they get ahead of you and then you can't immediately find them; they've moved into the ruin's second level, Ceysel, where you'll find them waiting at a pair of gates.

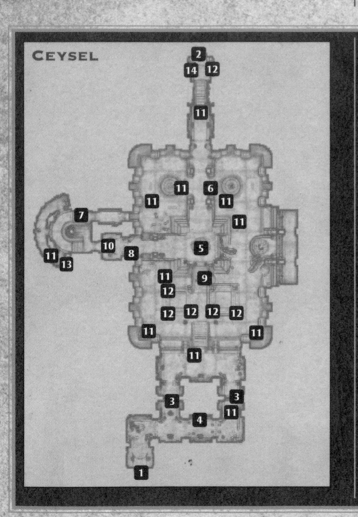

1. Entrance to Garlas Malatar's entry level.

2. Entrance to Carac Abaran. This is protected by a forcefield. You'll have to first destroy the Orb at #5 to reach it.

3. Closed gates. Press the button ...

4. ... here to open them. Your assembled knights will then pound down into the big room to the north— where they'll run into trouble. Enemies that go down don't stay down.

5. The trouble comes from this Orb. To destroy it, you'll have to truck your way around the high platform, through the entrance ...

6. ... here, then up the stairs ...

7. ... here and activate it. Boom: Time stands still. Enemies go away. Allies go away. Forcefield at #2 go away. Player go north.

8. This button raises a staircase ...

9. ... here. (To no real effect. Your knights won't attack the Orb in your stead.)

10. Orb guardian. (Really just a standard Auroran, though.)

11. Other standard Aurorans.

12. Welkynd Stones.

13. Standard Conjurer chest.

14. Standard "Restoration" chest.

We suggest you stay right with one of the parties. Reasons? 1) You'll help them survive. 2) They have not killed all the Aurorans on the level. Triggers scattered through the level key on the player's presence—not that of your knights. Hence, if you explore independently after your troops have passed through—and they move fast—you may find yourself generating enemies your pals are unavailable to help put down.

When you catch up to the gang, check everyone's health and heal up any who need it. Then push the block in the north wall between the two gates. Everyone takes off into the big room to the north and starts fighting the Aurorans around the central

promontory—this time, without much success. The folks in here are strangely durable. They go down, all right, but then they get up again…and again…and again.

Naturally, this is a losing proposition for your knights, who have no such resurrection ability. Is there a way to level the playing field?

You betcha. Atop the promontory is a great glowing orb rather like the Sigil Stones atop the citadels in Oblivion. You may hear your troops yelling about as the source of the

Aurorans' power. Bypassing these resilient enemies, make your way quickly north and west around the promontory, climb the stairs, and activate the Orb to destroy it. (The button beside your path raises a flight of stairs that leads up to the Orb from the battlefield below.)

Activating the Orb doesn't simply turn off the resurrection effect. It stops time itself—pieces of the orb are frozen in the air—and somehow in the process turns off everyone and practically everything in the level. (Well, except for the shield that blocks retreat to the gates to the south.) Your enemies and allies have vanished. So has the forcefield to the north. Now you can make your way across the bridge to Carac Abaran and the endgame.

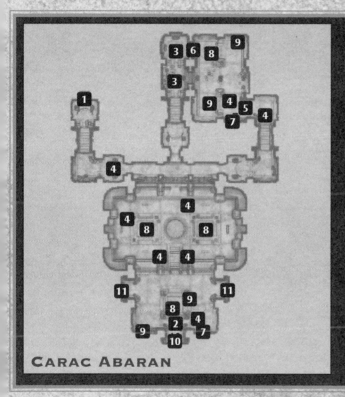

CARAC ABARAN

1. Entrance to Ceysel.

2. Umaril. Smite him.

3. Though there's pretty much one type of Auroran baddie in this final level, we've noted them down as both #3s and #4s. Why? Because during the "Umaril the Unfeathered" quest, you'll face just two of his minions. They're the #3s, and they're waiting behind Door #6.

4. On the other hand, if you come back to Garlas Malatar later on, you'll face everyone else on this level who didn't show their nasty faces the first time around. These are the #4s.

5. Trigger point for the opening of the secret door ...

6. ... here! (And here comes trouble.)

7. Boss chest.

8. Standard Conjurer chest.

9. Standard "Restoration" container.

10. Three Welkynd stones.

11. Varla Stones.

Here, it's just you and the enemy. And not many of the enemy at that. You'll face just two Aurorans (who charge through a secret door) and the big bad guy himself.

At the bottom of the dungeon, step into the large dark room. A blaze of light appears to the east and west, stairs begin to rise to the north and an Auroran-like figure appears at the top. Umaril. Classic.

On the surface, Umaril's a scary guy. He carries a claymore with leveled Damage Fatigue and Shock Damage enchantments, and his Lesser Power "Mortal Light" has Shock Damage and Damage Magicka effects. And he's impervious to Shock Damage himself and has a 33 percent resistance to Magic.

And yet the battle may seem surprisingly easy. A few swipes with the Sword or Mace of the Crusader and Umaril is gone, gone, gone.

A couple of things account for this. 1) Remember we mentioned a cumulative effect called "Umaril's Bane" a ways back? Now it comes into play: Umaril's Strength, Agility, and Luck attributes take 60-point hits and his Blade skill a 50-point hit when he faces the player. Is it any wonder he goes down like a sack of potatoes? 2) The Sword and Mace of the Crusader are designed to do extra damage specific to Umaril. (After all, these are the weapons that did him in once before.)

But remember: Umaril's not gone for good. You've robbed his body of life, but his spirit lives on. Grab his sword and the Varla Stones from the east and west niches (use one to recharge your weapon, if need be), heal up and invoke the Blessing of Talos. A cloud seems to form around you and then, in a burst of light, you're teleported to that same cloudy plain far above the Imperial City where you met Pelinal near the beginning of our story.

Yes, that's the spirit of Umaril up ahead. This combat won't be so easy—Umaril's Bane never kicks in here—but you've got the same Umaril-clobberin' weapons in your pockets. A few more choice swipes connect and you'll start to fall back to Nirn…to reappear in the central circle in the Undercroft of the Priory's chapel with a journal entry that Umaril is now "utterly destroyed."

Bring on the rewards. Amiel steps forward, offers heartfelt thanks and farewell, and says you can receive a blessing from each of the dead knights by praying at their respective tombs. In each case, this gets you a five-point boost in one of seven attributes. Activate Amiel's tomb for Akatosh's blessing (Strength), Caius's for Stendarr's (Personality), Casimir's for Mara's (Endurance), Gregory's for Dibella's (Personality again), Henrik's for Julianos's (Intelligence), Juncan for Kynareth's (Speed), Ralvas's for Zenithar's (Luck), and Torolf's for Arkay's (Willpower). Each of these benefits runs in perpetuity until you activate another tomb and swap the blessings.

And with that, the knights are gone—all but newcomer Sir Berich. This is Berich as he was before evil claimed him. You can elicit some details on his descent into that grim state, and his thanks for his redemption.

Step into the Priory basement, and you'll run into Thedret. Amazed, he reports that you vanished in Garlas Malatar, were found apparently dead beside Umaril's corpse and interred secretly here for fear of what the Order's enemies might do if they learned the truth. Then he rushes off to tell the others that there's a living ghost in the basement. (If he only knew.)

Follow Thedret topside, where he'll speak to the knights assembled outside the Priory—at once a victory speech and a herald of the homecoming of the "Lord Crusader" (your new title).

Congratulations. Umaril is undone. The Auroran threat has been beaten back. And you have a hell of a suit of armor.

But you're not quite done.

EPILOGUE

Is your full band of knights present for Thedret's speech? This is your first opportunity to see which of them survived their final battle in Garlas Malatar. (Thedret can't die in those battles, but all the others can.) And if you don't pick up on it here, keep an ear peeled. When talking among themselves, the knights take up a range of post-quest topics—among them their memories of any lost knights.

Note that there are now nine knights under your command, including at least one new one, called simply "Knight of the Nine," drawn from a pool of eight generic characters: three Imperials, two Nords, a Redguard, an Orc, and a Dark Elf. If any named knights died in the assault, they'll be replaced by generics as well.

Upon request, any one of these knights will now follow you in your adventures. Handling is similar to that in other quest lines that bestow this privilege: You can order the knight to follow you, wait for you or get out of your sight. When you consider all the characters you can have following you—a Mages Guild appentice, a Dark Brotherhood acolyte, an Atronach Familiar (if you have the Frostcrag Spire plugin installed), and now a Knight of the Nine, you can throw quite a wild little party.

Which knight should you take with you? Some are worse than others. The named male knights are best; all but one are one level above yours. (The exception is Lathon, the squire-turned knight, who's still two levels below.) By contrast, the one female, Avita Vesnia, is at your own level. But they're all better than the generic knights (three levels below yours) that replace them when they die. So take good care of your comrades.

Finally, let's tie up a few loose ends:

The Prophet? Gone; left no forwarding address. Last seen in the Priory's chapel, he vanished from the game when you struck down Umaril's physical form in Garlas Malatar. He does not reappear somewhere else.

The desecrated chapels? The dead staffers are replaced and the damage repaired the moment the final Knights of the Nine quest ends. At Anvil's Chapel of Dibella, you'll find a healer named Amragor and a priestess named Selene Duronia and at Bravil's Great Chapel of Mara, a healer named Beem-Kiurz and a priest named Eris Senim.

At Cheydinhal's Great Chapel of Arkay and Leyawiin's Great Chapel of Zenithar, where you headed off the Auroran attacks (and which can thus exhibit a variety of results), things are handled a little differently. If Umaril's minions managed to kill the priest Hil the Tall or crusader Gruiand Garrana at the Cheydinhal chapel, they'll be replaced by Esbern and Inius Colus, respectively. If they took out the priest Avrus Adas in Leyawiin, he'll be replaced by Aron Verethi.

Garlas Malatar? The time-stop effect in the Ceysel level has run its course and the door between Ceysel and Carac Abaran is unlocked again. The latter level is also a lot tougher than when you visited it earlier, with eight more Aurorans added to the mix. As in other dungeons, the enemies here respawn and you can return to clear the place out.

And does anything more happen at the Priory? Not really. It's quiet. The surviving knights will sometimes make enthusiastic noises about other missions—listen for amusingly dated references to Daggerfall and Morrowind here—but they never act on them, and sink into their old routines.

However, a bit of excitement occurs should you enter the region just southwest of the Priory after you've completed the Main Quest mission "Dagon Shrine." You'll trigger the appearance of an Oblivion Gate.

But, of course, that's a whole other story.

DOWNLOADABLE CONTENT

MEHRUNES RAZOR

Firthan Andoren
Andoren Manor, Godsreach
Mournhold, Morrowind

For your immediate Attention:

Advisor Andoren; my apologies for the nature of this letter, but I fear that King Helseth's initial appraisal of the threat posed by Frathen Drothan may have been premature. You know well my trust in the judgement of the King, but I have learned new, disturbing details which may give him cause to re-consider the decision to ignore this matter.

As expected, Drothan has received no support from the Great Houses, but has gathered strength in the form of mercenary soldiers. I realize King Helseth anticipated this, but I do not believe he anticipated Drothan being able to hire so many. My sources are still attempting to discern where this unexpected wealth is coming from. We have yet to rule out the possibility of funding from within Morrowind's borders.

We also have interviewed several scholars with whom Drothan has been in communication during recent months. His interests seemed keenly focused on Mehrunes Razor. Drothan went to great lengths to keep his academic contacts separate, and now that they have been cross-referenced, we're becoming convinced he has a chance at recovering the artifact. Worse, we suspect he's going to try and recover it from an excavation site within Cyrodiil borders.

I need not remind you of Morrowind's tenuous relationship with the Empire. While Drothan may not stand a chance against the Legion, possessing the Razor may give him courage enough to try. If that happens, I'm not sure even I could convince Ocato and the Council of your innocence in the matter. I implore you, re-visit the matter at the Royal Palace, a pray send word that the good King Helseth intends to resolve the matter internally. The Oblivion Crisis has caused arguably greater turmoil in Cyrodiil than any other province. Drothan is the last matter I wish to trouble my superiors with at this time.

With the utmost respect,
Philea Nielus
Office of the Imperial Ambassador
Ebonheart, Vvardenfell

The Daedric Quests don't include one from Daedric prince Mehrunes Dagon. Not a surprising omission. As the game's principal bad guy, the Lord of Destruction is doubtless preoccupied with his Main Quest conquest of Tamriel. Wouldn't you be? Identifying you as his opponents' key instrument, Dagon would be reluctant to strike any bargain that materially improved your chances of prevailing. And Brother Martin would probably think twice before using an artifact extracted from his enemy.

In any case, this big quest nicely fills that gap: It sends you off into a huge new dungeon in the eastern Niben region in search of a Dagon-related Daedric artifact known as "Mehrunes Razor."

Naturally, you're not the only one looking for it.

One note before you start: If you've reached the "Blood of the Daedra" segment of the Main Quest, in which you have to collect a Daedric artifact for Martin, the Razor won't do. You'll have to retrieve one of the other 15. See the Daedric Quests chapter for details.

If you're starting a new game, "Unearthing Mehrunes Razor" begins when you enter the Imperial Sewers. A journal entry suggests you explore Sundercliff Watch for clues to the location of a lost Ayleid city called Varsa Baalim in which the Razor is said to be hidden. (If resuming a game, the journal will appear at that time.)

Linking to the game map from the journal, you'll find this old keep on your map on a hill to the east of Lake Canulus. However, you can't travel directly to the location; you'll have to find it in the game world first. That's a long haul, and a much quicker trip if you've already visited Abandoned Mine (to the north-northwest); Fort Cuptor (on the lake's southwest shore); Lost Boy Cavern (to the west-northwest); or even Malada from the Miscellaneous Quest "Nothing You Can Possess" (to the north-northwest).

SUNDERCLIFF WATCH

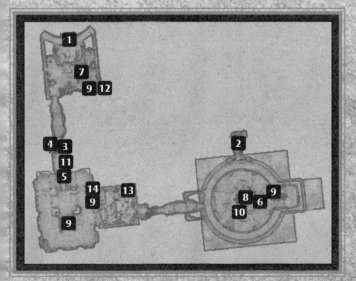

1. Exit to the surface and Sundercliff Keep.
2. Entrance to Sundercliff Village.
3. A guarded door. You'll need the password to get it open.
4. You'll find that password ("Chimer") here—in a Small Diary in a knapsack propped against the stool.
5. Drothmeri Steward: On his body, you'll find a note to the steward from head honcho Frathen Drothan. Lots of helpful hints here.
6. Can you sneak past this sleepy recruit on the upper level?
7. Or backstab this patrolling Drothmeri soldier? He'll start his rounds here and set off toward the door at #3.
8. On the other hand, this soldier'll be tough to avoid. His patrol path takes him upstairs to the steward at #5.
9. These troops could be either soldiers or the weaker recruits.
10. A veteran soldier—and your biggest problem on this level.
11. On this table, you'll find the Steward's Registry (a run-down on Drothmeri dispositions), as well as gems and gold.
12. A bit of loot: a chest, shield, arrow and, up on the wall, a grain sack. You'll run into this "bandit" chest a number of times in the dungeon. It'll always contain gold, but could also hold a a lockpick, silver nuggets, a repair hammer, an arrow, a stealth-related potion or a scroll. (There's a 15 percent chance of the lockpick appearing and 20 percent chance for the others.) So always look. Every so often, you'll find a big score.
13. Another bandit chest and a big food sack.
14. You'll find a healing potion in this sack.

The surface keep is undefended. You'll find the door to the interior on the south side. Within, you'll quickly come up against a pair of Dark Elf "Drothmeri" soldiers. Kill them and move south to an old wooden door. (You shouldn't have much trouble with most of the soldiers and recruits—so long as you engage them individually. The soldiers range from one level above your own to four below it, and the recruits are all five below it.)

You'll find an abandoned knapsack on the stool beside the door. The small diary it contains supplies the first guess about what's going on here: An army is being mustered at the keep under the leadership of a certain "Drothan," and his semi-literate cousin's diary mentions Drothan's own journal is in his "cabin"—though not where the cabin can be found. (It's a couple of levels away in the Sundercliff Commune.)

The password the diary contains is of immediate use: Try the door and a voice calls, "Who gathers stormclouds over Nirn?" Say "Chimer" and you're in. The Dunmer steward and soldier beyond are not exactly happy to see you, so, uh, kill them, too, and have a peek at the Steward's Note on the former's body and the Steward's Registry on the table. The latter just puts some firm evidence behind your journal's guess about the army, but the former is a font of information: It puts a name to this Drothan (Arch-Mage Frathen Drothan), suggests the army is out of neighboring Morrowind (the reference to Morrowind King Helseth), alludes to big plans, makes another reference to the journal in Drothan's cabin, mentions the capture of an assassin, and also a foray through an unspecified door. (Also, be sure to scoop up the nice gems on the table.)

Crossing the bridge beyond (and setting off a fair amount of havoc with the troops below), descend the stairs to an east-bound passage and two final enemies. See if you can gun down the veteran soldier ahead of you at a distance; at your level, or one above it, he's the only significant combat issue on this level. Then descend to the camp below and head north into Sundercliff Village.

SUNDERCLIFF VILLAGE

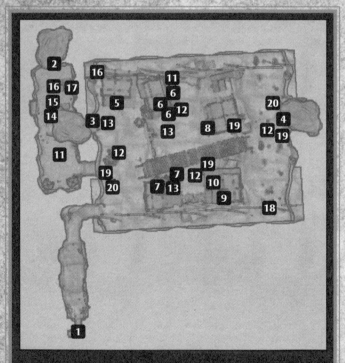

1. Entrance to Sundercliff Watch.
2. Entrance to Sundercliff Commune (lower level).
3. Entrance to Sundercliff Commune (upper level).
4. Entrance to Sundercliff Forge (upper level).

5. Entrance to Jail. Within, just to the left as you enter, you'll find an imprisoned Morag Tong assassin. Your options: 1) Release him. He'll make his way into the Commander's Quarters in Sundercliff Commune (see #4 on that map) and try to kill the Drothmeri Commander. And being that he's eight levels above yours, and the commander only two, the odds are pretty good the assassin will succeed. That'll make your job of obtaining the enchanted bezoar in the commander's charge much easier. Then he'll relocate to the Inn of Ill Omen on the Green Road northwest of Bravil. 2) Surrender to temptation and kill the assassin yourself for his nice suit of enchanted armor. Other loot in the Jail: a pair of repair hammers near the fire. Item of interest: The Jailor's Note on the table in the corner, which intimates the assassin has stuck the sought-after "writ" authorizing the execution where the sun don't shine. (All we can say is that it's "soiled." Um, can we not talk about this any more?)

6. Entrances to the Recruit Barracks. (The northern entrance is on second floor, middle entrance is via trapdoor in roof and southern one is on the ground floor.) Home to three Drothmeri recruits, this place could be empty—the guys take melee-weapon training at the west end of the level—or you could find them asleep or at table. Loot: Healing supplies in two sacks downstairs and a chest upstairs.

7. Entrances to Canteen. (Western entrance is on the second floor balcony; eastern is on the ground floor.) One or two soldiers or recruits. Loot: Twelve loose food items, two food barrels, two torch barrels and a pair of bandit chests.

8. Entrance to Soldier Lodgings. Within, one to three soldiers or recruits. Loot: a pair of gems and some gold found on and around a table on the ground floor, a locked (one- to five- tumbler) jewelry box on the second floor, two bandit chests (one on each floor), a dozen loose food items and two food barrels.

9. Entrance to Private Attic. Here, behind a leveled one- to five-tumbler lock, you'll find an unfriendly Argonian or Khajiit worker and possibly a Drothmeri trooper (who could be anything from recruit to veteran). Also a plateful of gems up in the rafters!

10. Trainer: This veteran can typically be found instructing the recruits from #6 in the training room at the level's west end.

11. Patroling Drothmeri soldier: There are two of these in the village exterior. Can you eliminate them James Bond style without someone raising the alarm? The one at the Recruit Barracks follows a route with waypoints that include the village entrance, the

mine entrance at #4 and a position south of the Barracks down in the pit. The one in the training room to the west makes for the mine entrance at #4.

12. Drothmeri soldiers or recruits.

13. See #12. However, there's a 50 percent chance these particular troopers won't appear.

14. A pair of Keen Edge potions. (They fortify the Blade skill by 15 points for 30 seconds.)

15. Two iron warhammers.

16. A chest of healing supplies.

17. Two iron daggers and two iron longswords.

18. A sack of healing supplies (on top of the practice target).

19. Hutch: These are storage sheds. All they're guaranteed to contain is food, but you've a good chance of finding something else as well: a potion, gold, a weapon or even heavy armor.

20. A barrel of torches. (Well, two torches, anyway.)

Drop down the passage into a huge cavern that's home to an old mining camp. Restored by Drothan's troops, it consists of five buildings: Barracks, Private Attic, Canteen, Soldier Lodgings, and Jail.

You can skip most of the buildings—low-level battles and loot—but you'll be back and forth through the Village a couple of times in the course of your mission, so at a minimum clear out the half-dozen or so scattered soldiers and recruits in the exterior. (In addition, a veteran can be found training three newbie troopers from the Recruit Barracks in the large room at the west end of the lower level. However, this area is separate and discrete from the village proper, and he's not an immediate issue.)

The exception is the Jail on the upper level in the village's northwest corner. The single cell is just left from the door. The leveled lock has three to five tumblers. The Morag Tong assassin within has no dialogue, but you can set him free or kill him for his nice enchanted Morag Tong armor and Soiled Writ of Assassinaion. (He's been sent to do in Drothmeri commander Telani Adrethi, whose name has already popped up in the Steward's Note.)

Heartlessly, we vote for killing him. Not at all easy; he's eight levels above your own. But it's worth the effort: Each piece of his armor carries leveled enchantments. The boots fortify your Acrobatics and Sneak skills. The cuirass fortifies your Agility attribute and add to your resistances to magic and normal weapons. The gloves boost your Luck attribute and your Security skill. The greaves punch up your Speed a bit and add a Feather effect. And the cowl adds to your Marksman skill and adds a Detect Life effect. What's not to like?

Then again, you can let the assassin go. He'll set off for the Sundercliff Commune to exercise his mandate. If he succeeds, it'll make your job of claiming the bezoar much easier. If he doesn't, it'll make claiming that nice armor from his corpse

much easier. (If the assassin escapes the dungeon with his life, you can find him later hiding out at the Inn of Ill Omen on the Green Road south of the Imperial City.)

You might also want to poke your nose into the Private Attic just east of the Canteen—with a one-tumbler lock and a hostile Argonian or Khajiit laborer and possibly a Drothmeri trooper. (It's got some great loot on a plate on the cross-beam above the bed: six gems, including two flawless diamonds!)

Here, our path branches. There are three exits from the Village. The one in the east wall of the village's upper level leads to the Sundercliff Forge. The others—at the north end of the training room at the west end of the lower level, and the west wall of the upper level just south of the Jail—lead to Sundercliff Commune. We suggest you hit the Forge now, as it'll save you a trip later.

SUNDERCLIFF FORGE: UPPER LEVEL

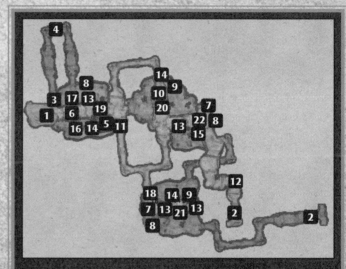

1. Entrance to Sundercliff Village.

2. Entrances to Sundercliff Mines. Note that you'll have to pass through the Mines to reach the Forge's lower level. (The west entrance is the exit from the Forge's upper level and the east one the entrance to the lower.) You can't move directly from the top to the bottom of the Forge until you open the secret door at #3; the holes you'll find on the upper level have been carefully blocked. Note, too, that much of the lower level (displayed with a dark tint) lies directly beneath the upper. That can make this map a bit confusing. In places where an enemy or item on the lower levels appears to be on the upper one, we'll point it out in the text.

3. Secret door: Operated by a pull-cord on the north side, this is an escape hatch from the lower Forge back to Sundercliff Village.

4. But the escape hatch has a hitch: When you reach the hairpin turn in this passage, you may trigger the spawning of up to three new enemies just inside

Sundercliff Village. If survival here is a near thing for you in this dungeon, you may want to consider backtracking through the Mines instead.

5. Forgemaster's Tent: Here you'll find one of the enchanted bezoars needed to enter the Excavated Ruins from Sundercliff Commune. And if you try to poach it without first sending the Forgemaster to meet his forger, you'll also find inside the tent another trigger point that sets off an ambush. (There's also a boss-level chest here patterned on those from Marauder lairs: a combat potion for sure, gold likely, repair hammers and jewelry possible and the really nice magical stuff as iffy as usual.)

6. The Forgemaster: He's on the lower level, he's a boss, and he's got some really nice magical equipment. And while we're on the subject of nice stuff, over his head is a bucket. And suspended above the bucket is a diamond.

7. Apprentices: Two of them, also on the lower level. One's a suck-up, the other a renegade, as you'll learn if you read their personal correspondence. (See #9.) However, this doesn't have an impact on their survival instincts. (Note that each has a repair hammer close by.)

8. Forges: One for each smith, and all three on the lower level. No, they don't do anything—unless you walk on them, in which case they flame your idiot ass for six points of fire damage.

9. The correspondence mentioned in #7. One apprentice rats out his co-worker. The other tears into his boss—and raises an interesting question. Just how is Arch-Mage Frathen Drothan paying for all this? By magic—as you'll discover when you perform a thorough search of his quarters in the Sundercliff Commune.

10. Just two Drothmeri soldiers patrol the upper level, and a stealthy character can easily avoid this one. He makes his way from here ...

11. ... to here.

12. This one's trickier—being that his whole route (from here to a position above the #7 to the northwest) follows a fairly narrow passage.

13. Argonian and Khajiit laborers: There are three on the lower level, one on the upper (the southernmost of the four), and they're as hostile as their brothers in the Mines.

14. The only containers on this level are three food barrels—each on the bottom level and each a bottomless source of food and drink.

15. There's enough equipment in here for an army. <grin> Iron boots—11 pairs of 'em—are laid out here on two tables.

16. Two claymores, two longswords, iron greaves and another pair of boots.

17. Three daggers and a repair hammer.

18. Four short swords on two weapon racks.

19. Finally, do you remember the diamond over the bucket above the Forgemaster's head back in #6? There are four more like it. Above this one are three iron nuggets.

20. Above this bucket is a flawed emerald.

21. Above this one are 12 iron nuggets. (If you could only turn iron into silver. Hmmm.)

22. And, finally, this bucket comes equipped with a sapphire and another iron nugget.

Kind of a tricky level. Without regular reference to your map, it's easy to walk in circles in the small maze that comprises its initial section. And some of the information the map supplies may seem to contradict that of your own senses.

To wit: A short way down the west-to-east entry corridor from Sundercliff Village, the map pictures an entrance to "Forgemaster Tent"…only there's no such entrance at that location. In fact, there *is* an entrance, but on a lower level of the Forge that's accessible only via the Mines. You're currently on the upper of two discrete levels and face a fair trek before you can claim the prize the Forge contains: one of the two enchanted "bezoars" needed to open the way into Varsa Baalim.

You're in no real danger as you enter the level. This area is patrolled only by two Drothmeri soldiers four levels below your own. Just make two left turns and a right you'll find yourself at the mine door.

SUNDERCLIFF MINES

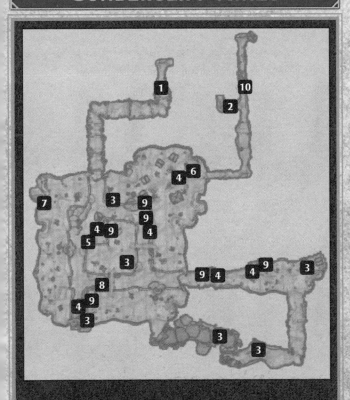

1. Entrance to the upper level of Sundercliff Forge.
2. Entrance to the lower level of Sundercliff Forge.
3. Patroling Drothmeri soldiers. It's tricky, but their movements provide a stealthy character with the opportunity to avoid detection. The northernmost of the six moves to the mine's central island. The soldier already on the central island moves to the northwest corner of the southern island. The soldier on the platform in the mine's southwest corner heads north to a second platform just south of the passage from the level entrance. The easternmost

soldier moves to a position down the corridor to the west. Finally, the western of the two soldiers in the southeast part of the mine moves west up the hall to a storage platform. And the eastern soldier moves west to a position near the western soldier's original spot.

4. Of course, the six hostile laborers—two Khajiit, two Argonian and two more that could be either—make this task a bit tougher!
5. Another Drothmeri soldier, but with no fixed patrol route.
6. This could be a soldier or a recruit.
7. A hoe in a barrel. Nothing special about it at all. Honest.
8. Just above the bucket, you'll find a ruby!
9. Iron nuggets.
10. Cave-in trap.

Follow the corridor south and west to the lower level of a large two-tiered chamber where you'll quickly find yourself under attack both by the Drothmeri and the Khajiit and Argonian mine workers. The latter are all three to five levels below your own, but armed with the not-insubstantial Rockpick Hoe. (They're also infected with the new disease called "Tunnel Cough," which drains your Sneak skill.)

Speaking of rock-picking, note that you'll find a lot of iron ore nuggets in this area. Twenty-four lie loose about the level and more can be extracted from 11 veins. The loose ones include eight pieces in bowls in the northeast corner of the room, two more suspended above the bucket above the nearby wagon and five more across a bridge in the northwest corner. Can you do anything with them?

Sure. This is apparently how Drothan is financing his army. They have their own innate value (5 gold), but you can enhance it using Transmutation scrolls you'll find later in Drothan's cabin. So take a few in hand…as well as the ruby you'll find suspended above a bucket hanging on the south side of the room.

An eastern loop in the mine's southeast corner takes you up to the second tier—more Drothmeri soldiers here—and you'll use rock bridges to the north and then east to reach a little camp in the northeast part of the level. In the east wall, you'll find a corridor that leads north to the entrance to the lower level of the Forge. (Watch out for a cave-in trap just after you reach the door.)

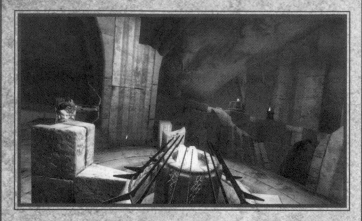

You're now in a previously inaccessible section of the Forge slightly east of where you entered the Mine. The passage wiggles west to a blacksmith's forge—attended by a Weapons Apprentice (one level above your own) and a handful of workers leaking in from the east.

We shouldn't have to tell you this, but no, do not walk on the forge. Flames boil up and you will catch fire and take damage. However, do read the Apprentice's suck-up note to the Forgemaster, in which he rats out another apprentice you've yet to kill. It's beside "Manual of Arms" on the table.

The north exit loops east and west to a second forge. Here you'll find the Armor Apprentice (a level below your own), a load of iron boots and, sure enough, on the table to the north, a letter home in which he raves about the insane pay and does indeed bad-mouth his employers. ("I figure we'll end up deserting soon, just as soon as we've gotten as much pay as we

can without actually following this addled madman into battle.") Graduates of *Morrowind* will take pleasure in the letter's in-jokes. (The writer's girlfriend is working as an exotic dancer at Desele's House of Earthly Delights in Suran.)

Finally, the passage turns west to a third forge, the Forgemaster Tent and the Forgemaster himself. He's just a level above yours, but he's equipped to the Nines—including a leveled amulet that boosts Armorer, Blunt and Heavy Armor skill and Strength attribute, and a leveled smock that adds to his Fatigue points and his resistance to normal weapons. Those make him a fairly tough customer, and provide you with a nice reward when he finally goes down—to say nothing of the enchanted bezoar and the gems you'll find on the table in his tent. (Not to mention Tamriel's favorite smutty book, "The Lusty Argonian Maid," under his bed.)

You can also nip into the Forgemaster's tent, without killing him first, and swipe the bezoar. But you'll trigger an ambush and he'll come at you in the tent.

There's a little extra here, too: When you entered the Forge's upper level, did you look down through the occasional holes in the floor? If so, you probably saw what appeared to be gems in the buckets below. Now you're within easy reach of the buckets and can liberate the contents. Striking the bucket in the Weapons Apprentice's room releases 12 iron nuggets. Hitting the one in the Armor Apprentice's forge gets you a flawed emerald. And bashing the two buckets above the Forgemaster's room releases, respectively, a diamond and three iron nuggets.

All that's left to do now is leave. Just follow the uphill passage in the north wall of the Forgemaster's room, pull the cord at the end to open a secret door, and you'll find yourself right beside the door back to Sundercliff Village.

However, in climbing this passage, you've set off a trigger and may find upon returning to Sundercliff Village that your passage through the Forge has not gone unnoticed. You may be hit with up to three newly-spawned enemies the moment you step through that door. Then again, there's a 50-50 chance that each of those soldiers or recruits won't appear. So maybe you'll get lucky!

1. Entrance to Sundercliff Village (lower level).

2. Entrance to Sundercliff Village (upper level).

3. Entrance to Frathen Drothan's Quarters. You'll stop in here mainly to read Drothan's journal, but the place merits a proper burglary: for the Varla stone, the potions, the soul gems, the gold and not least for the Transmutation scrolls in an intimdiatingly-locked secret closet. (You'll find the key in The Nefarivigum when you find Drothan.)

4. Entrance to Commander's Quarters. Here, you'll have put a beatdown on the commander (if the assassin from the Village's jail hasn't done so already) and claim one of the two enchanted bezoars that opens the path to Varsa Baalim. Decent loot, too—including a Telekinesis scroll, six gems, a jewelry box and a boss-level chest. This last is guaranteed to contain a weapon and a modest amount of gold, with a good chance of extra gold, small chances of a magic weapon, stealth-related potion, jewelry and three lockpicks and still smaller ones of magic armor, a stealth skill book and two soul gems.

5. Entrance to Yeoman Barracks: Non-essential. You'll have to fight off a soldier or recruit, and then you can grab anything that isn't nailed down. This includes two gems, a silver shortsword, an iron bow and four arrows and two gold—plus whatever you can scrounge out of a bandit chest and food barrel.

6. Entrance to the Veteran's Lodge: Ditto on the non-essentiality, but tougher, as here you face a vet and possibly two more troopers who could be either soldiers or recruits. Your main reward: a Marauder boss chest that's only guaranteed to contain combat potions and probably leveled gold ... but if you're

lucky will contain a little bit of everything. Also, a bandit chest, iron gauntlets, torches and a range of grub.

7. Entrance to the Excavated Ruin.

8. The two pedestals you'll activate to place the enchanted bezoars liberated from the Forgemaster and the Drothmeri commander.

9. An archery trainee.

10. An Argonian gardener . . . who actually does garden. (See # 22.)

11. Patrolling Drothmeri soldiers. The one on high ground moves to the front porch of Drothan's house and across the central trench to the entrance of the Yeoman Barracks. The one just outside the Veteran's Lodge moves to the platform just south of the bridge across the chasm.

12. Drothmeri veteran.

13. There's a 50 percent chance this soldier or recruit will appear.

14. A Conjurer's chest. Inside, gold for sure, with small chances of a soul gem, potion and scroll and smaller ones of an ingredient, gem or a piece of alchemical equipment.

15. A sack containing a healing potion.

16. A chest containing one or two items of Restoration-oriented loot.

17. A sack containing four food items.

18. A bandit chest containing gold—with very small chances of a lockpick, silver nugget, repair hammer, arrow, scroll or a stealth-related potion appearing as well.

19. A barrel containing two torches.

20. A hutch—just like the ones back in Sundercliff Village.

21. A bottomless barrel of food.

22. A little potato patch—which the gardener at #10 will till with his rake ... if you don't scare him off first.

23. An iron battleaxe.

Which way in? It doesn't make much difference. The upper and lower routes converge on the south side of the central trench and, either way, you'll wind up fighting the same two or three Drothmeri troopers.

There are two important structures here: the Commander's Quarters and Frathen Drothan's Quarters on the north side of the chasm.

Drothan's is the eastern of the two. As mentioned in the Steward's Note, he's not home and the journal is on his desk. Read it to learn he's entered Varsa Baalim to find an undescribed "Nefarivigum," which guards Mehrunes Razor. The door has been sealed behind him. But enchanted "bezoars"—stony masses found in the innards of animals—have been left with Adrethi and the Forgemaster that would enable you to unseal the door and follow him. You've already found one of these. The other should be right next door.

That's not all. Read the "Treatise on Ayleid Cities" on the bookshelf to the left of the desk. (Purchased from Jobasha's book shop in Vivec, says the receipt on the bottom shelf!) It provides background on the fate of Varsa Baalim—infected by a vampire, engulfed by madness and finally by the mountains—and a bit more about the nature of the "Nefarivigum." (It's an "unknown trial of worth.")

And check out the false wall just to the left of the bookshelf. If you can line up the five tumblers, you'll find seven scrolls of Transmutation. (Two more can be found on the table across the room.) If the lock is beyond your talents, just wait a bit. You'll find the key later on.

Highlight the scrolls in your inventory. "Transmute mineral"? Why's Drothan messing around with minerals?

 If you use a transmute scroll without any ore/nuggets, you waste the scroll, and these are the only ones you'll find.

For profit. You've stumbled onto how the wizard is financing his army. Effectively, the spell kicks any mineral one step up the monetary food chain. Try it with one of the iron ore nuggets—either the ones on the table or the ones you brought with you from the Mine. It'll turn it into silver. If you use it on a silver nugget—there aren't any lying loose in Sundercliff—it'll turn to gold. And if you use it on the gold nugget from the table, it converts it to cash. Fifty gold coins are added to your inventory. (However, note that a transmuted mineral cannot be transmuted a second time.)

Finally, you'll find two Trichobezoar Extract potions on the shelves. Presumably this is a happy byproduct of the extraction of the two bezoars: a Cure Poison potion that also includes full poison resistance for five seconds.

Let's go get that other bezoar. Sad to say, Commander Adrethi *is* home and, at two levels above your own and decked out in leveled heavy armor, puts up a good fight. (Unless, of course, you set the Morag Tong assassin free back in the jail—in which case the commander's probably a mangled heap on the floor.) You'll find the bezoar on the nightstand upstairs, and get a journal that you're ready to tackle the enchantment on the door to the Ayleid city.

The entrance just south of the Veteran's Lodge leads to the sealed door. You'll face a veteran and possibly a Drothmeri soldier or recruit here. Then simply activate each of the pedestals flanking the door to place the bezoars, and the filmy shield over the door vanishes. Activate the door and step into the darkness of Varsa Baalim.

Some Communal odd and ends: The other two buildings—the Yeoman Barracks on the south side of the trench and the Veteran's Lodge west of the lower entrance—are nonessential unless you're hard up for loot. In the former, you'll fight a Drothmeri soldier or recruit and find a silver shortsword and two gems on a little ledge on the south wall. At the latter, you'll take on two veterans—one outside and one in—and possibly one or two soldiers or recruits within. With a little luck, you'll find good loot in the boss-level Marauder chest downstairs.

And did you check out the Argonian gardener working in the little potato patch east of the Commander's quarters?

EXCAVATED RUIN

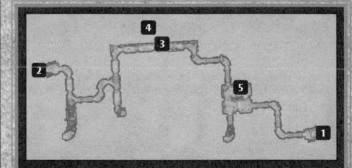

1. Entrance to Sundercliff Commune.

2. Entrance to Varsa Baalim.

3. A diamond, ruby, rock, pickaxe and candle on the windowsill. That's much it it in terms of loot. Unless you collect bones.

4. Don't get all worked up over the ruins to the north. They're just for show. You can't get out there. But do watch the little scene unfold on the wall just north of the window. It is a grim preview of life and death in Varsa Baalim.

5. An iron dagger.

Not much to say, as nothing much happens here. No puzzles, no enemies, not much loot. It's just an antechamber for the city proper. Drop down three flights of stairs to a room partly filled with bones and then three more to the door to Varsa Baalim. Along the way, in a long east-west hallway, you'll find a diamond, a ruby, and a pickaxe on a window sill, and get a dark glimpse of huge ruins to the north. If you look carefully at the ruins you may witness a Drothmeri soldier getting chased by a couple of vampires. (No, you can't get out there to inspect them, and you can't get around the blocked passages.)

Closer to the exit, you'll find several splashes of blood. It looks fresh.

VARSA BAALIM

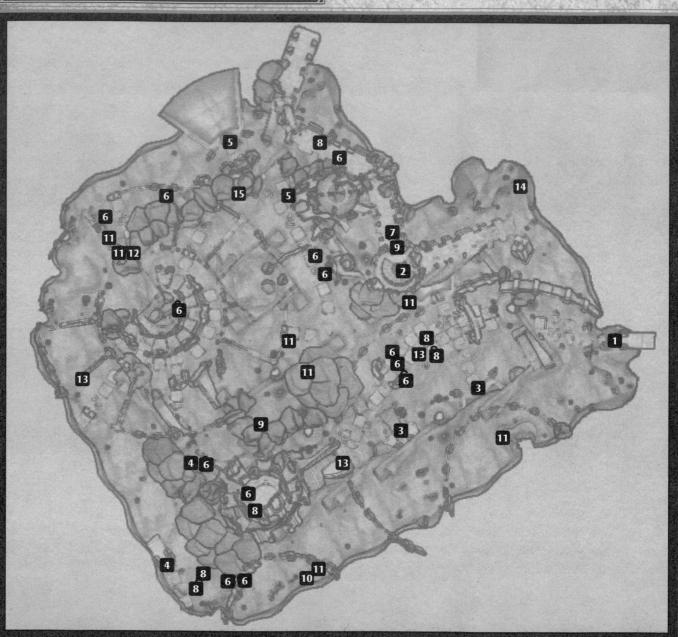

1. Entrance to Exacavated Ruin.

2. Entrance to The Nefarivigum.

3. Entrances to Cava Arpenia. Non-essential. Contains two vampires, the body of a dead veteran, a standard vampire chest (see #11), a sack of gold and an iron dagger.

4. Entrances to Cava Beldameld: You'll have to pass through this house en route to The Nefarivigum. You won't tarry long. One vampire; no loot.

5. Entrances to Cava Marspanga: Again, you'll have to traverse this house, where you can witness (or, to your significant risk, participate in) a battle between three vampires and three Drothmeri soldiers. You'll

find two standard vampire chests (see #11) and also a fine iron longsword (near the dead Drothmeri veteran).

6. Vampires!

7. A vampire Patriarch or Matriarch.

8. Drothmeri soldiers.

9. A boss-level vampire chest. Both are guaranteed to contain gold, but a good roll can net you a ton of stuff—everything from magic equipment to a skill book to soul gems. (The chest to the southwest requires some jumping to reach, and has slightly better potential loot.)

10. A chest containing one or two Restoration-oriented items.

11. Standard vampire chest. Gold for certain, with a small shot at a repair hammer, a smaller one at a lockpick and smallest at a gem, ingredient, armor, arrow or potion.

12. An iron bow and arrow. Oddly, this is the only loose loot item in the city exterior that isn't associated with a dead Drothmeri soldier. To wit:

13. These are the Drothmeri veterans who are already dead when you enter the city. (i.e. It doesn't include any casualties of the battles you watch.) Search 'em for loot, and look for their weapons nearby.

14. Dead Drothmeri recruit: Beside his corpse, not a sword, but a quill—a clue to search the remains for An Undelivered Letter to the recruit's brother. It's a harrowing account of the expedition into the city and a further clue: bad guy Frathen Drothan has fled deeper into the ruins.

15. Mortally wounded Drothmeri veteran: Though that's really just a technicality. By the time he lands at the base of this cliff, he's dead.

On entry, you'll get a journal: "There's no telling what I may encounter here; I must be on my guard."

What you'll encounter here, mainly, is vampires. As predicted by the treatise you found back at Drothan's place, the ruined city is fairly thronging with them. The Drothmeri detachment that followed Drothan into this hellhole is being decimated. Watch from the relative safety of the high ground near the entry area as three vampires wipe the floor with two veterans.

And that's the best way to deal with Varsa Baalim in general: Watch from a safe distance whenever possible. Sneak (or use magical concealment), stay hidden, allow the two sides to fight each other, and then move against the weakened survivors. Just running in and killing everybody here—vampires and the Drothmeri survivors both—works for us, too, but that's whole lot of killing. Not counting any casualties in the vampire/Drothmeri battles, there are 13 vampires in the exterior city—including a "boss"—and another six in the three houses.

And, besides, the only character in Varsa Baalim you need to kill is Drothan himself …and he's already moved on to the Nefarivigum.

Your route through the city should be pretty self-evident. You can skip the first house (Cava Arpenia), but you'll have to pass through the second (Cava Beldameld). When you exit on the other side, watch a second battle and make your way northwest along the west edge of the city. When you run out of path, drop down to the east and head northeast to Cava Marspanga. Inside, let the third battle run its course. After you exit on the other side, head northeast, use the ramps formed by the ruins to climb atop the wall and follow the top southeast and then south to the entrance to The Nefarivigum…and the vampire "boss" who guards the entrance. He/she is either at your level or two levels above it.

Loot: There are 10 containers scattered across the ruins— including two "boss"-level chests. These are guaranteed to contain only gold, but the right roll can nail you everything from a skill book to a magic weapon. One can be found near the Patriarch or Matriarch.

The other is the prize in a jumping puzzle. It's in a raised area, surrounded on three sides by high rocks, just northeast of the entrance to Cava Beldameld. However, the open side of this enclosure is beyond the reach of even the most accomplished acrobat, and you'll have to use the nearby walls as launch pads to reach it.

There's also a dead Drothmeri recruit lying in a dark corner near the entrance to the Nefarivigum with an undelivered letter on him that recounts the last moments of his life.

THE NEFARIVIGUM

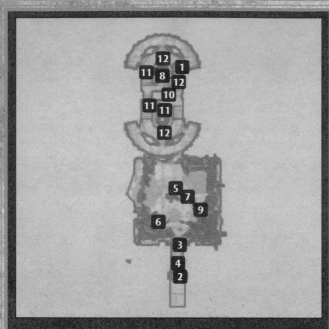

1. Entrance to Varsa Baalim.

2. Entrance to the Forgotten Tunnels. (You'll need to grab Mehrunes Razor before you can reach this door.)

3. Closed gate. If you're strong enough, you can force it open. Or you can eat the heart of Dagon's champion at #6. Hey, is there any mayo?

4. This wall lowers once you've got the Razor.

5. Frathen Drothan: The mastermind behind the plot to seize the Razor and invade Cyrodiil. Yeah, you need to whack him. You also should take his enchanted hood and robe—and the closet key will help if you mean to backtrack to his quarters in the Sundercliff Commune.

6. Msirae Faythung: Dagon's champion. Your dinner. Sort of. You'll have to beat Faythung, or you'll have to eat his heart. Either one'll open the way to the Razor, but the heart part pounds you with nasty aftereffects.

7. Drothan's Field Journal: The arch-mage's thoughts on getting the gate to the Razor open. ("Eating the dead guy's heart" didn't occur to us unaided.)

8. Boss-level chest: Gold's a given, and there's a good chance of extra gold. Not so good are the chances of a magic weapon, stealthy potion, jewelry or three lockpicks. Smallest of all are the chances of magic light armor, a Stealth-related skill book and two soul gems.

9. A bottle of cheap wine and a pair of sacks containing, respectively, four food items and a healing potion.

10. Another sack with a healing potion.

11. The entry stairs was the scene of a final battle between the Drothmeri and the vampires. Only Drothan survived. These are dead veterans ...

12. ... and these the dead vampires. (Note that one of these is on a level lower than it appears on the map.)

Lots of dead bodies down here—both vampire and Drothmeri—and your first job is to add one more to the pile. In the room at the bottom of the satirs, you'll find Frathen Drothan standing beside by the frozen form of Msirae Faythung. (More on him in a bit.)

Tough battle. Drothan's four levels above yours and equipped with a raft of Battlemage spells—not to mention a Bladeturn Hood (with leveled Resist Normal Weapons, Reflect Damage, and Shield enchantments) and Spellturn Cloak (with leveled Resist Magic, Reflect Spell, and Spell Absorption enchantments). So it's in your best interests to make the fight as short as possible—say, a nice backstab with an enchanted weapon followed up by a high-level combat spell—provided you've got the health points to absorb the blowback.

 In addition to the nice equipment, you'll find Drothan's Key on his body. This opens that five-tumbler closet with the Transmutation scrolls back at his quarters in Sundercliff Commune.

On to Mehrunes Razor. This plays out a few ways.

You'll find Drothan's Field Notes beside his bedroll on the east side of the room. He has found a way to make the Razor appear, but the gate that leads to the weapon is blocked "and I dare not risk force lest the gate is trapped. The notes *suggest* that the way to the Razor is eating the heart of Dagon champion Faythung, but notes that the late wizard thought there might be another route.

We're not crazy about the idea of eating anybody's heart—plus, we had a big lunch—but this is in fact an easy path. Activate Faythung's body, remove the "beating heart" and chow down.

Oh, and keep your distance from Faythung, who'll wake up and come after you. Ordinarily, this would be a real concern—the champion's three levels above your own, with a leveled Daedric war axe and Dremora armor—but he's not going far without a damn heart, is he? Just backpedal and wait him out. (You can't loot his body afterward, and the axe crumbles in your hands.)

But it does work. The gate in the south wall is now open, and the rear wall has descended to reveal the entrance to The Forgotten Tunnels. (This small cave, inhabited by some combination of rats and mudcrabs, is an escape hatch that deposits you in the calm waters of Lake Canulus. And, no, you can't poach the Razor by entering the Nefarivigum through the back door.)

Approach the Razor to collect it. You'll get the quest's last journal entry. It describes the artifact as "a potent daedric dagger which has a chance to instantly destroy an opponent." That chance, based on the player's Luck attribute, is no better than 10 percent. (More likely, a good deal lower.) And the other 90 percent of the time, it's still a nasty little blade with a leveled Disintegrate Armor spell.

Unfortunately, munching on the heart carries with it an effect called "Cannibal Consumption." Your Infamy rises by four points. You've caught a new disease: Cannibal's Prion, which drains your Intelligence and Agility. And if you aren't already a vampire, you've caught Porphyric Hemophilia. Serves you right for eating a heart in a freakin' vampire lair.

If you don't want to deal with all this, simply belly up to the gate and activate it. You'll be asked if you want to defy Dagon and force your way through. Say "yes."

If your Strength is more than 90, bingo: The gate rises. And once again, Dagon's champion gets medieval on your ass. This time round, he's a much more creditable opponent, and you'll either have to beat him down or make your escape.

If your Strength is 90 or less, busto: The gate stays in place. Dagon's champion does his thing. However, by the time the battle's over, the gate has opened. The Razor is yours. You're done.

The Orrery

You couldn't reach the Orrery in the original release of Oblivion. The big room off the lobby of the Arch-Mage's Tower at the center of the Imperial City's Arcane University was all locked up. It's still locked, but with The Orrery downloadable content (DLC) you can find your way inside and receive a nice reward or two in the process.

If you're starting from scratch with this expansion installed, you'll receive a journal entry upon leaving the Imperial Sewers. (If not, you'll receive it upon resuming play.) You've found a "Note from Bothiel" inviting you to liberate five Dwarven artifacts—two cogs, a coherer, a cylinder and a tube—hijacked by bandits now thought to be at Camp Ales north of Kvatch.

You may recall that Dwarven artifacts—among the "it" items in Morrowind—were pretty much absent from Oblivion. And, sure enough, these five were being imported from that neighboring province to permit repair of the Imperial City's broken Orrery—a working model of the solar system.

No need to trot down to the Arch-Mage Tower's lobby to see Bothiel (the Orrery caretaker) just yet—though, if you do, she tells you she'll pay handsomely for the artifacts' return.

Make directly for the Ales camp. Up a hill in the wild country well north of ruined Kvatch, it's sandwiched between Fort Hastrel (to the west), Shattered Mine (to the south-southwest), Mongrel's Tooth Cave (to the east-southeast) and the Ayleid ruin Varondo (to the northeast). Any of these intermediate fast-travel destinations should cut down on your footwork.

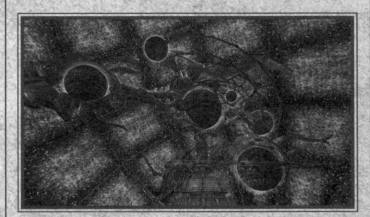

Before you installed The Orrery, the camp was occupied by an ordinary bandit or dog. He's still around, but now has been joined by the first of five "Bandit Carriers." These low-level bosses, who hold the artifacts, include two Redguards, two Imperials, and a Nord—all one level above your own, with boss-level blunt weapons and fair skill at using them. They can be deadly if you have a lower-level character. If you have trouble, keep a discrete distance and use a bow or magic.

From the body of this first one, take the first of the two cogs and an "Undelivered Letter" reporting that the remaining artifacts have been scattered to four camps: Dagny's, Brotch, Bodean, and Varus. The locations will now be highlighted on your map.

You just have to give four repeat performances—any order will do—and you won't have far to go. The camps are all within fairly easy walking distance of this central location: Dagny's to the southeast (southwest of the Ayleid ruin Talwinque); Brotch to the northeast (northwest of Echo Mine); Bodean to the southwest (southwest of Brittlerock Cave); and Varus to the west (southwest of the Ayleid ruin Niryastare). At Dagny's Camp, you'll locate the coherer; at Brotch, the second cog; at Bodean, the cylinder; and at Varus, the tube.

Once you have all five artifacts in hand, you'll get another journal entry instructing you to pay Bothiel a visit. Zap back to the Arcane University and talk to her to deliver the artifacts. You'll receive 100 to 3,000 gold as your immediate reward. Bothiel then marches off into the Orrery...and the door remains locked. What gives?

There's more to come. Bothiel just needs a little time to make the repairs. Wait until the next day and you'll receive a journal reporting that the Orrery is functional again, that you now have access and can receive powers from it based on the current phase of the planet Nirn's moons.

In the dark room beyond a Dwarven door, you can admire the great whirling mechanism overhead and climb either flight of stairs to activate the Orrery console on the second level. When you do so, the two moons will appear at the console's center—probably with a portion of each highlighted in pale blue. This reflects the moons' current phase (one of eight—reflecting the moons' actual phase at the time). Activate the console again to receive the Greater Power associated with that phase.

Each of these powers can be invoked once per day. It lasts 60 seconds and adds 20 points to one of your attributes while stealing 20 from another. The phase and its associated power changes every three days. Activate the console again after a change for the option to change the power.

Here's the cycle of the moon's phases and appearance, along with their related powers and effects:

Magic users won't receive much benefit from these Powers. Apart from Secunda's Brilliance and Will, they're geared more to the attributes of fighters.

Full	The moons in the console are entirely dark.	Masser's Might	+20 Strength, -20 Speed
3/4 Waning	Right-hand slivers of the moons are lit	Masser's Grace	+20 Agility, -20 Endurance
1/2 Waning	The right halves of the moons are lit.	Secunda's Will	+20 Willpower, -20 Intelligence
1/4 Waning	All but left-hand slivers of the moons are lit.	Seunda's Luck	+20 Luck, -20 Personality
New	The moons are entirely lit.	Masser's Alacrity	+20 Speed, -20 Strength
1/4 Waxing	All but right-hand slivers of the moons are lit.	Secunda's Magnetism	+20 Personality, -20 Luck
1/2 Waxing	The left halves of the moons are lit.	Secunda's Brilliance	+20 Int., -20 Willpower
3/4 Waxing	Left-hand slivers of the moons are lit.	Masser's Courage	+20 Endurance, -20 Agility

WIZARD'S TOWER

Frostcrag Spire is a spectacular new house—a palace, more like—with a few interesting features attached.

And did we mention it's free?

If you've just started a game with the expansion installed, you'll take delivery of the deed and key to Frostcrag Spire shortly after entering the Imperial Sewers. (If you're resuming a game, the journal reporting this event pops up immediately afterward.)

This majestic wizard's tower is well up in the Jerall Mountains almost straight east from Bruma's eastern gate. You can fast-travel there directly if you wish.

Upon entering the tower's antechamber, you'll find a book, "Frostcrag Spire Memoirs," atop something that looks every much like an atronach's hand. (A nice bit of foreshadowing.) Reading the book will snag you another journal—which informs you that you can dress up the place at the Mystic Emporium in the Imperial City's Market District—and a run-down on the tower's "many wonderful inventions."

But one thing at a time.

A few seconds after you exit the book, the north wall will glow blue and then roll aside to reveal the main body of the tower. Here you'll find two teleport pads and, atop the ramps to the north, three altars: one for enchanting items, one for building spells and the third for creating an Atrronach Familiar.

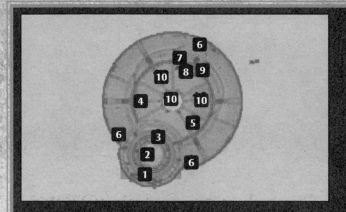

1. Exit to the tower exterior.
2. An atronach's extended hand—supporting the useful book "Frostcrag Spire Memoirs." (Read it: Among other things, it contains instructions on how to furnish the place.)
3. The entrance to the tower proper.

4. Teleport down to the Vault.
5. Teleport up to the Living Area.
6. Library areas.
7. Altar of Spellmaking: Requires Magetallow Candles to operate. (They're available at the Mystic Emporium in the Imperial City's Market District.)
8. Atronach Altar: Used for summoning one of three types of Atronach: Flame, Frost or Storm.
9. Altar of Enchanting: Again, requires Magetallow candles to operate.
10. Atronach summoning spots. (From left to right: Storm, Frost and Flame.)

Right now, none of the altars work. The Spellmaking and Enchanting altars each need Magetallow Candles for power and the Atronach Familiar Altar requires Fire Salts (for a Flame Atronach), Frost Salts (for a Frost Atronach), or Void Salts (for a Storm Atronach). We'll tackle these in a bit.

The eastern of the two teleporters takes you up to the Living Area. Here you'll find:

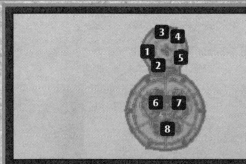

1. Teleport down to the Main Level.
2. This bookshelf is home to a nice magic ring (in the jewelry box on top) and a skill book.
3. Exit to the tower's balcony—which has teleport pads to every exiting Mages Guild and the Arcane University.
4. Alchemy Lab: A special Alchemy table that temporarily raises your Alchemy skill by 15 points for as long as you're standing beside it.
5. Teleport up to the tower roof.
6. Ingredient garden. Here you'll find the mushrooms ...
7. ... and here mostly flowering plants ...
8. ... while this section is given over to plants that appear in Oblivion.

• Another teleport pad taking you to the top of the tower, where you can take in a breathtaking view of the Jeralls to the north, Bruma to the west and the countryside to the south.

• An indoor garden dense with dozens of ingredient-bearing plants in 29 varieties:

8 Bloodgrasses	6 Milk Thistles
4 Cairn Boletes	1 Morning Glory
7 Dragon's Tongues	4 Nightshades
4 Elf Cup mushrooms	1 Nirnroot
3 Emetic Russula mushrooms	2 Pumpkin Vines
4 Flaxes	5 Rice Plants
6 Ginsengs	10 Spiddal Sticks (another domesticated edition of an Oblivion plant)
2 Goldenrods	5 Steel-Blue Entoloma mushrooms
9 domesticated samples of the vicious Harada plants from Oblivion (of three different types)	4 Stinkhorn mushrooms
1 Lady's Mantle	6 Strawberry Bushes
4 Lady's Smocks	5 Tinder Polypore mushrooms
6 Lilies of the Valley	8 Tobacco plants
7 Mana Blooms	4 Wisp Stalks
2 Mandrakes	7 Wormwoods

The Rice Plant is new to the game: Its ingredient—surprise: rice!—can be found loose in *Oblivion* but you couldn't harvest it yourself. Now you can.

Chorrol, and Bravil mages guilds. (Needless to say, the pad for the Kvatch guild is non-functional. That guild is now a smoking hole in the ground.) The central pad deposits you just outside the door to Arch-Mage's Tower at the Arcane University.

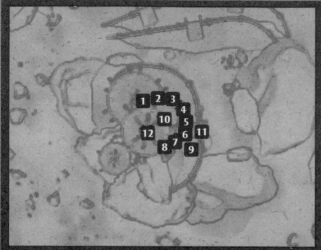

1. One of the nice things about the Spire is its built-in rapid-transit system. On this balcony off the second-floor bedroom, you'll find nine teleport pads. Eight of them work. This particular one goes to the Skingrad Mages Guild …

2. … while this one to the Anvil Mages Guild …

3. … and this one to the Bruma Mages Guild.

4. This pad would have sent you to the Kvatch Mages Guild. But ever since the Daedra attacked Kvatch, the Kvatch Mages Guild has been pretty much a raging bonfire. Do you want to be teleported into a raging bonfire? We didn't think so.

5. This pad works. It'll send your atoms whizzing over the Jeralls to the Imperial City's Arcane University (where the Mages Guild has its headquarters).

6. Teleport pad to Cheydinhal Mages Guild.

7. Teleport pad to Leywiin Mages Guild.

8. Teleport pad to Chorrol Mages Guild.

9. Teleport pad to Bravil Mages Guild.

10. Entrance to the Spire's second level. (Bedroom, special Alchemy table, ingredient garden.)

11. The tower's main entrance. A Storm Atronach would look very intimidating right here, wouldn't it?

12. Observation Tower.

• An exit onto a northeastern balcony, where you'll find nine teleport pads—their destinations including (from west to east) the Skingrad, Anvil, Bruma, Cheydinhal, Leyawiin,

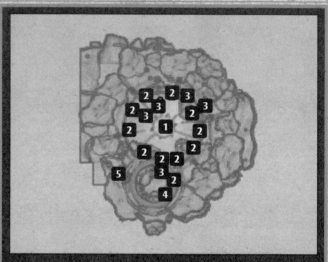

1. Teleport up to the tower's Main Level.

2. Containers. Fill 'em up with good stuff from your travels.

3. Vault Guardians: These imp bosses—they're five levels above your own—are mostly for appearances. (No one actually tries to loot the Vault.) Then again, an enterprising wizard could kill them for imp gall. (They respawn.) However, they'll attack you if you attack them, so you might want to enlist some help. (See # 5.)

4. Wine collection. This includes a bottle of Shadownbanish wine for the Settlement quest "A Venerable Vintage" and the best wines from the Tamika and Surilie Brothers vineyards, which may come in handy in the Master Trainer quest for Alchemy.

5. Tombstones! What kind of wizard would you be if you didn't have someone magical buried in the basement? Activate Rindsey's to get "Daedric Lava Whiskey" (a potion with effects that include the summoning of a Dremora Lord!) and Lennasaan's for a nice daily blessing.

Finally, the western teleporter drops you down to the Vault. That's the tower's cellar—currently empty, as indeed is much of the tower. What can you do about populating it?

Fast travel to the Imperial City's Market District. Go straight and, at the cross street, hang a right. The Mystic Emporium is just west of Slash 'N Smash in the little arcade on the right side of the street. Within you'll likely find proprietor Calindil and a new NPC named Aurelinwae.

The latter will sell you pricey bills of goods for the Spire's Alchemy Lab and Bedroom (both in the Living Area), Library (on the Main Level), and Vault areas—along with two even pricier boxes of Magetallow Candles. You'll pick up another journal entry once you've paid for everything in her keeping. (Make sure you bring a nice chunk of change. All this will run into the neighborhood of 14,000 gold.)

And the Atronach salts? Aurelinwae sells the ingredients that fuel the Atronach Altar—as do numerous other ingredient vendors—but you'll have to be Level Nine to buy Fire or Frost Salts and Level 20 to buy Void Salts.

Alternatively, you can find the Fire and Void Salts in containers in Conjurer lairs and in Oblivion, but only if you've hit Level Seven (for Fire) or Level 17 (for Void). (Frost Salts turn up sparingly in "Mythic Enemy" lairs beginning at Level 13.)

Finally, you can harvest salts from the remains of dead Atronaches…but finding live Atronaches to make dead may be an issue. Flame Atronaches appear only in leveled encounters beginning at levels 5 to 9, Frost Atronaches at levels 10 to 15 and Storm Atronaches at levels 16 to 20 (depending on the location). (Exception: One Storm Atronach can be found lumbering around at all player levels. It appears on the second level of Sandstone Cavern northeast of Kvatch at the end of the Settlement Quest "The Sunken One.")

Or, if you're already Arch Mage of the Mages Guild, you can place one portion of a given salt in the special chest in your quarters atop the Arch-Mage's Tower at the Arcane University and generate additional ones.

Really low-level characters will have to pinch salts from a handful of locations where they're lying around loose:

Fire Salts
- Skingrad, on a shelf on the upper floor of the Mages Guild
- Imperial City, on a shelf on the lower level of the Palace Library
- Bruma, on adjacent shelves in Honmund's House

Frost Salts
- Leyawiin, on a bottom shelf in the Mages Guild's laboratory
- Bruma, at the bottom of a smaller book shelf right next to the one with the Fire Salts in Honmund's house
- Bruma, on a middle shelf in the cellar of Brotch Calus's house
- Skingrad, on a table at All Things Alchemical, and on a corner shelf in the cellar of the West Weald Inn

- Imperial City's Arcane University, on a scale atop a desk on the ground-floor of the Lustratorium and two atop a desk on the second floor of the Praxographical Center
- Market District, on a shelf in the cellar of the Mystic Emporium

Void Salts
- Leyawiin, atop a shelf on the second floor of The Dividing Line
- Skingrad, on a plate on an alchemist's table in the cellar of the West Weald Inn
- Bruma, on a bottom shelf in the cellar of the Mages Guild
- Bravil, on a little stone shelf off a pillar in the Castle Bravil dungeon Wizard's Grotto (from the Thieves Guild quest "Arrow of Extrication"), and beside the Night Mother's skeleton in the crypt below the Lucky Lady statue (from the Dark Brotherhood quest "Honor Thy Mother").

All done? Then jet back to the Spire to see what's changed.

It is fairly transformed. In the near corners of the main ground-floor chamber, and atop the ramps, you'll find an expansive library—albeit one without skill or rare books, and with multiple copies of almost everything in the collection. Near the easternmost shelves, you'll also find an alchemist's worktable complete with mortar and pestle, retort, calcinator, alembic, and a pair of soul gems. (Note that this is not the special Alchemy table referenced in the lobby book. We'll get to that in a bit.)

Simply activate the enchanting and spellmaking kiosks atop the ramps with the Magetallow Candles in your inventory to fire up these altars. Then they'll operate as usual. No need to join the Mage's Guild now to access these useful altars!

And the Atronach Familiar Altar? Activate it and you'll be invited to create a Flame, Frost or Storm atronach. If you have the appropriate salts in inventory, the big critter will appear immediately in one of the three respective circles on the floor below.

Speak to it. Like other followers you may have encountered in the Arena, Dark Brotherhood and Mage's Guild quest lines, you can boss it around in a basic way, telling it to follow you, stay in place or rejoin the ether (at which time you can cook up another). Have it stand guard outside the tower or follow you in your adventures; it's just the elemental, clobberin'-time touch your little party needs. The creature is set at your own level—up to Level 12 for the Flame, 18 for the Frost, and 22 for the Storm—and if you've killed an Atronach, you already know they can be tough in a fight.

Teleport up to the Living Area. We've already seen the garden and the rapid-transit system, but some neat subtleties have been added—the most conspicuous being the Alchemy Lab just across the room. It's not just for making magic; it's magical in and of itself. Stand next to the table and a temporary effect called "Alchemical Brilliance" kicks in—raising your Alchemy skill by 15 points. You'll also find a bed, a smattering of ingredients, an Alchemy skill book ("A Game at Dinner" on the top shelf of the bookshelf), a rare book ("The Argonian Account, Book 4"), two poison potions, lesser and petty soul gems…and in the jewelry box atop the bookcase, a significant magic ring (Pentamagic Loop) that raises your Conjuration, Destruction, Illusion, Mysticism, and Restoration skills by five points each for as long as you wear it.

Finally, down in the Vault, you'll find 29 containers, seven imp guardians, and a respectable wine collection. The containers contain mainly household junk, but you can always toss it and use the chests and barrels for your own goodies. And the 32 wine bottles include one sample of the Shadowbanish wine you'll need in the Settlement Quest "A Venerable Vintage" and two each of the best wines from the Surilie Brothers and Tamika vineyards, which will be helpful in the Master Trainer quest for Alchemy.

And in a dark recess, against the wall southwest of the teleport pad, you'll find a pair of tombstones—marked "Rindsey" and "Lennasaan."

Activate them. The former nets you a one-time sample of Rindsey's "Daedric Lava Whiskey"—a potion that paralyzes the user for 10 seconds while doing a mite of Fire Damage, restoring 20 points of health and summoning a Dremora Lord. The latter grants a three-pronged daily blessing: temporarily fortifying your Personality attribute by 10 points for your Speechcraft and Mercantile skills by 15.

Ah. There's no place like home.

You may already know that there's a disused cavern beneath Castle Anvil. It's not hard to find. A secret passage leads down from the castle proper to an impassable door leading to "Smuggler's Cave." And if you wade around to the castle's sea side, you'll find a wooden door with a five-tumbler lock in the cliff face.

Beat back the tumblers and you'll find yourself in a dark hole with some low-grade but useful loot on high ground around a watery pit.

The Dunbarrow Cove plugin adds a large cave off this small one. Just as Frostcrag Spire is designed as a new home for a wizardly character, so Dunbarrow Cove is set up for a stealthy one.

Only this time, you'll have to fight for it.

If you're starting a new game, you'll learn about the new cave in a journal entry right after the death of the emperor. (If you're resuming a game, it'll pop up at that time.) The journal reports a great battle in Anvil Bay between the celebrated pirate Torradan ap Dugal and the (future) first Count of Anvil, and implies that the pirate captain escaped. Now rumors are abroad that Captain Dugal took refuge in a hidden cavern beneath the castle and that his "final resting place" may have been discovered.

Follow the new map marker to Dunbarrow Cove just south of Castle Anvil. On arrival, you'll get another journal reporting on your discovery of the cave (just across the water to the north) and pressing you to explore it. (The door at the end of the castle's secret passage is still impassable, but the seaside door, marked by a pair of Water Hyacinths, is unlocked.) Once inside, the entrance to Dunharrow Cove is just northeast across the pool, up the ramp and around the corner.

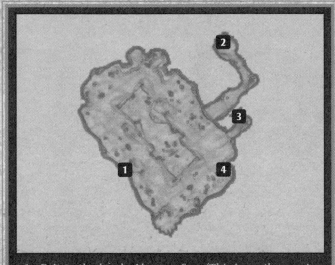

1. Exit to the lovely Abecean Sea. (This is on the cave's lower level.)
2. Entrance to Dunbarrow Cove.
3. Entrance to Castle Anvil—specifically, the Dining Hall. However, note that this door requires a key. And to acquire the key, you'll have to beat down the Cove's undead pirates and then furnish the Captain's Cabin.
4. Lots of "clutter" in this cave, but this one chest contains something useful: the Security skill book "The Locked Room."

In the deep darkness just beyond the second door, you'll get another journal confirming you've found the remains of Dugal's ship (The Black Flag) and crew, but noting you'll have to put down that skeletons that populate the place before you can turn it to your own uses.

That's not a small venture. The Cove proper contains six Red Sabre skeletons (fixed at your own level): three guarding the gangways around the Black Flag, two down on the top deck of the ship itself, and one guarding a little jail reached by a passage in the northeast corner of the upper level. (The ship's lower decks are empty of skeletal pirates, but you'll find a pair of gold nuggets and some booze.) And Cap'n Dugal, whose cabin is a quick right from the entrance and then left down the gangway, is six levels above your own and armed with one in a series of progressively nastier leveled cutlasses.

When the last pirate drops, you'll get another journal reporting that the place is a freakin' wreck—skeletons not being the best housekeepers—and referring you to Dahlia Rackham on the good ship Clarabella for help converting the Cove into "a suitable base of operations."

So make your way back out to the sea and then north to the Anvil docks. The Sea Tub Clarabella is the southern of the two

ships in port. First mate Rackham can be found in the cabin at the rear. Speak to her about "Dunbarrow Cove Upgrades" and she'll offer to set you up with a fence, fletcher (an arrow-maker), security expert, spymaster, or supplier (1,000 gold each), or upgrade your quarters for 500 gold.

Each purchase nets you a journal update. Read 'em all, and you'll have a better idea what to expect when you get back to your hideway. And once you've bought all six upgrades, you'll get a further entry: You can send your pirate pals out of missions. They'll return a week later with your cut of their loot.

Back in the Cove, you'll find quite a few changes.

For one, it's much brighter and no one is waiting to cut you in half. The Captain's Quarters is now your quarters. Inside, you'll find a bed, a steel cutlass, five lockpicks, a wanted poster for the "Gray Fox"—reading it starts the admission process for the Thieves Guild—and, at the foot of the bed, a captain's chest containing a Smuggler's Key that opens the impassable door to the castle out in the Smuggler's Cave. Finally! You can use this to burgle the castle with a minimum of fuss.

Out in the Cove proper, you'll find most of your new hires.

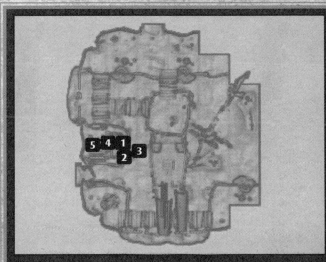

1. Cap'n Dugal: Your first task here: Defeat this mighty skeleton. (The pirate captain is six levels above your own.)
2. The Captain's Chest: The second: Visit the Sea Tub Clarabella on the Anvil docks and get the Cove spruced up. Once you fix up this cabin, you'll find in the chest the key to the door at #3 on the Smuggler's Cave map. And when your pirate buds start plundering, this is where your cut of the loot appears upon their return.
3. The Captain's Journal: The four volumes are scattered on the floor here. Read 'em all. 'Tis a good tale!
4. A steel cutlass, five lockpicks and a poster of the Gray Fox. Reading this last one kicks off the Thieves Guild quest line.
5. Exit to Dunbarrow Cove.

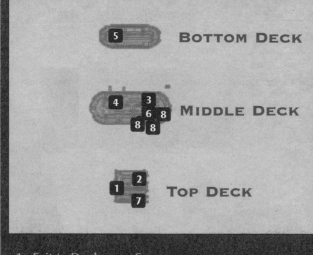

1. Exit to Dunbarrow Cove.
2. Trap door down to the ship's middle deck.
3. Ladder up to the ship's top deck.
4. Trap door down to the ship's bottom deck.
5. Ladder up to the ship's middle deck.
6. Jak Silver: Your supplier, and the last of yer scurvy mob. Silver sells Miscellaneous items and potions and will train you up to 75 in the Speechcraft skill between 10 a.m. and 11 p.m.
7. Two gold nuggets, three bottles of mead (on the floor nearby) and two of ale.
8. A modest stash, including a silver bow and dagger and an open chest of silver pitchers and vases. We're sure they were all acquired for a fair price on the open market. (Arr.)

The fence Khafiz and his pet boar Bacon are based in that little jail down the passage in the Cove's northeast corner. From 10 a.m. to 11 p.m., he'll buy your stolen goods with his 1,500 in barter gold—you don't have to belong to the Thieves Guild to use him—and he'll train you up to 75 in Mercantile skill at any hour. (Note that, after his shift, Khafiz heads topside for three hours for chow and can be found sitting on the deck of the Black Flag.) It's conceivable you'll find Khafiz (and other vendors) on station at odd hours as well but you can count on him pulling a minimum 13-hour shift every day.

The arrow-maker, Melliwin, can be found testing bows and enchanting arrows between 9 a.m. and 9 p.m. near the archery targets in the Cove's southeast corner. She'll sell a variety of arrows, bows, and twangy spells—she does buy them as well, but with only 100 in barter gold—and will train you up to 75 in the Marksman skill. (She'll head off for dinner on the Black Flag at 9 p.m.)

The security expert is Tahm Blackwell. From 8 a.m. to 8 p.m., you'll find him just around the corner west of the Cove entrance near the gangway to the Captain's Cabin. He sells books and Security-minded spells, and potions—again, he'll buy as well, but with just 100 in barter gold—and train you up to 75 in the Security skill. He marches off to eat at 8 p.m.

Kovan Kren is the spymaster. Between 7 a.m. and 8 p.m., this Dark Elf typically is found across the gangway just east of the Cove entrance. He'll train you up to 75 in the Sneak skill and sell armor, books, clothing, sneaky spells and potions…and buy them with the same 100 gold as practically everyone else. The most active of the Cove vendors—you'll sometimes find him practicing his swordplay on the wooden target here—Kren is naturally the hungriest and breaks for lunch for an hour at noon and for three for dinner at 8 p.m.

Finally, one deck down in the Black Flag, you'll run into supplier Jak Silver. He'll sell a variety of potions and Miscellaneous items (i.e. lockpicks)—not to mention train you up to 75 in Speechcraft—but, again, he has just the usual 100 in barter gold. (Nearby, you'll find some weapons and armor—among other things, a silver bow, dagger, arrows and spoons, glass arrows, and seven lockpicks—and on the bottom deck containers to store additional loot.

You'll also find three upstanding citizens fellows wandering the Cove: the Imperials Zedrick Green and Scurvy John Hoff, and the Argonian Yinz'r. Talk to any one of them and tell him "I want you to head out and plunder."

All three pirates (but none of the vendors) immediately take off to do their piratey thing. You can't follow them but wait a week and they'll return. You'll get an update that your cut of the loot can be found in the captain's chest—the one at the foot of the bed in the Captain's Cabin. (This cut is geared to your current level: 100 gold for each level, up to 2,000 at Level 20.) And after your boys have rested for a day, you can send 'em off again. Not a bad way to make a living!

VILE LAIR

Frostcrag Spire is for wizards. Dunbarrow Cove is for thieves. Deepscorn Hollow? Designed for evil guys.

If you're starting a new game, you'll hear about the Hollow right after entering the Imperial Sewers. A "mysterious message" reports that you've inherited this underground lair. (If resuming a game, you'll learn about the lair at that time.)

Check that know-it-all map of yours. The Hollow is under the western of the two islands in Topal Bay—just off the coast southeast of Leyawiin—and you can fast-travel there directly.

Ignore the covered well and ruined house. Simply step off the island's south shore, swim into the hollow log on the bottom, and unlock the door at its north end. (You received the key at the same time as the mysterious message.) Beyond the door, continue north along the passage until you surface in a dimly lit room—rather like a ruined monastery—where you'll get a journal entry on your discovery of a forgotten diary. Reading the diary (an account of a foiled plot by vampires to take over the Dark Brotherhood) will get you another entry: You can restore the Hollow to its dark grandeur by dealing with Rowley Eardwulf at the Wawnet Inn, located in a small settlement just west of the Imperial City.

You'll want to do that pretty quickly. Unless you're a reluctant vampire looking for a quick way out of The Un-Life, without the upgrades, there's currently not much going on in this rambling four-section lair.

However, that said, you will find a place to sleep—the double bed in the east room of the Bastion, which is itself north of the Cloister, which is in turn west of the Hollow proper. You'll find nominal storage space. You can extract a little loot. (Shoot the well bucket with an arrow or spell to scatter 21 gold coins.) You'll find a hidden mainland exit—behind the big tree west of the north end of the rope bridge to the island.

And if you don't want to go through the huge Miscellaneous quest "Vampire Cure," you can take a huge shortcut here—one described in the diary. Make your way west up the stairs to the Cloister and then south down the stairs to a room with a pool and obelisk at its center. In the room's northeast corner, activate the intruding rock vein (Purgeblood Crystal Formation) to receive Purgeblood Salts. Now drop into the pool and, with the salts in inventory, activate the Font of Renewal.

~Poof~ Vampirism gone. That simple.

The Wawnet Inn is the first building to the north on the mainland after crossing the bridge west of the Imperial City. (You may have dropped in here to talk to proprietor Nerussa for the Settlement Quest "A Venerable Vintage.") Rowley's around—on the stairs to the second floor unless he's eating. Apart from a modest selection of weapons, this crabby-looking Breton will sell you seven bills of goods to populate your new home-away-from-home—along with a "Dark Minion" and "Ichor of Sithis."

This will be an expensive proposition. Even if your Mercantile skill is through the roof, expect to spend a total of at least 15,000 gold for the Minion and Ichor and decoration of the Deepscorn Bedroom Area, Cattle Cell, Dining Area, Garden of Venomgrowth, Storage Area, and Study. When you've picked up everything, you'll get an acknowledgment from your journal. Scoot back to the Hollow to witness its transformation.

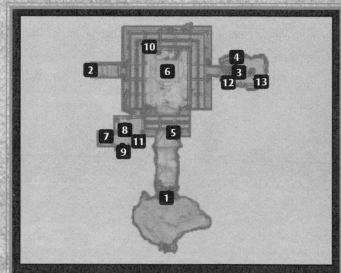

1. Underwater exit to Topal Bay.
2. Entrance to Deepscorn Cloister.
3. Dark Minion: Once you get the lair all fixed up (at

the Wawnet Inn west of the Imperial City), you'll enable this wandering assassin.

4. Dark Minion's Loot Chest.

5. Grewyn's Journal: Found on a stool under a flawed gem, this book serves up the Hollow's history and functions and also provides instructions to get it up and running. (Many of the descriptions that follow assume you've already done so.)

6. Garden of Venomgrowth: The plants here are geared to the production of poisons. And if you shoot the bucket above the garden, you'll be rewarded with a shower of gold coins.

7. Greywyn's Poison Supply: A chest of 12 leveled poison potions.

8. This "armory" chest could contain some fair loot.

9. Two jewelry boxes.

10. Greywyn's First Cache: one of the four hidden loot bags.

11. A claymore.

12. A fine iron bow and a raft of arrows...

13. ... with more arrows in and around the target here.

If you enter the lair by the water route, the first thing you'll notice is the garden. Imagine the one in Frostcrag Spire turned on its side; every ingredient that can be harvested here has negative effects. You'll find the following:

5	Elf Cup mushrooms	6	Nightshades
4	Fennel plants	10	Stinkhorn mushrooms
6	Ginsengs	5	Wisp Stalks
5	Milk Thistles	3	"Chokeberry Vines"
2	Morning Glories		

The Chokeberry Vine is new to the game, and not surprisingly yields an ingredient called the Chokeberry. This isn't a conventional ingredient. Rather, it's a variation on the poison apple introduced in the Dark Brotherhood quest line. If someone eats one, they die. You just have to make sure the intended victim doesn't have anything else available to eat.

East of the garden, the cave where you found an empty chest earlier has been, uh, fleshed out. (This is your Dark Minion's bedroom.) You'll now find a bed, some containers, an archery range, a Fine Iron Bow and a raft of arrows, and a woodsy painting that seems to consist partly of human entrails!

In addition, a nice range of loot can be found in your upgraded storage chamber just west of the water passage, including a claymore (atop an open chest), Greywyn's Poison Supply (a chest of poison potions hidden behind two crates in the western niche), and a splash of gold and jewelry.

Depending on the time of day, you may also run into the Dark Minion himself in this region. This sinister hooded figure, who wanders the Hollow on an elaborate schedule from 5 a.m.

to midnight, will do your bidding for the asking. Simply speak to him and say, "Murder in the name of Sithis." He'll immediately make for the ladder to the Hollow's mainland exit and vanish. (You can't follow him on his assignment.)

A few days later, the Minion will return by the same entrance and you'll get a pop-up message on his success or failure. If he succeeds, your Infamy rises one point—you ordered the hit, after all—and he'll deposit the loot in the Victim's Loot Chest in his quarters. Look for leveled gold, jewelry, magic armor, armor, magic, and conventional weapons, soul gems, and stealth and poison potions.

Grab what you like when you like; it's in the Minion's room, but it's your chest. Unlike some loot chests in the game, this one doesn't get flushed between missions. And once the loot has been deposited, the Minion's immediately available for duty again, with no rest period required (unlike the lazy pirates of Dunbarrow Cove).

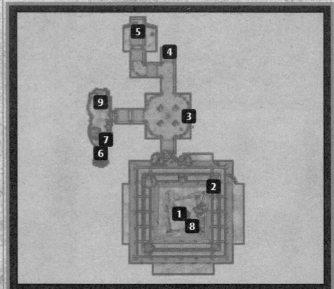

1. Font of Renewal: A quick route out of vampirism—provided you have Purgeblood Salts mined at ...

2. ... three locations in this corner.

3. Entrance to Deepscorn Hollow.

4. Entrance to Deepscorn Bastion.

5. Ladder up to trapdoor on mainland.

6. Deepscorn Prisoner: If you stick with vampirism, the anonymous monk here is "cattle" for your bloodsucking pleasure.

7. Another of the four hidden sacks.

8. And another.

9. A Leyawiin town guard shield.

We've already touched on the key feature of the Cloister to the west—a lightning-quick cure for vampirism—but what if you like being a vampire? In that event, you'll find something here to sustain you. Down the stairs west of the central room is a small enclosure with cast-off skeletons, an official Leyawiin shield, and an unlocked cell. Its lone occupant, "Deepscorn Prisoner," is vampire "cattle." He sleeps 24 hours a day and a vampire character can feed on him.

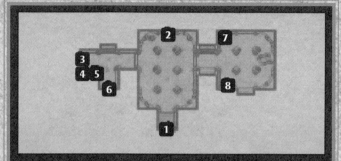

1. Entrance to Deepscorn Cloister.

2. Entrance to Deepscorn Shrine.

3. On this shelf, you'll find the Sneak skill book "Sacred Witness" (on top of the bookshelf) and a Great Detect Life scroll (on the bottom shelf).

4. The Marksman skill book "The Gold Ribbon of Merit" (on the floor).

5. On this shelf, you'll find the Alteration skill book "Sithis," the unique book "Opusculus Lamae Bal ta Mezzamortie," the valuable book "Dwemer History and Culture," iron gauntlets and helmet, a pearl and three gold coins.

6. And on this one, you'll find the Light Armor and Hand to Hand skills book "Rislav the Righteous" and "Immortal Blood," the unique book "Manifesto Cyrodiil Vampyrum," the rare book "Fragment: On Artaeum," Chameleon and Absorb Health scrolls.

7. A jewelry box.

8. On the desk and adjacent bookshelf, you'll find a full set of alchemical equipment and the ingredients Daedra Heart, Daedroth Teeth, Minotaur Horn and a Nirnroot.

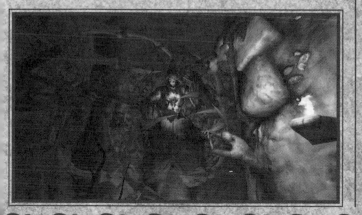

The Bastion north of the Cloister serves as the Hollow's dining room and study, but it's really all just loot, right? The big prize is in the east chamber: In Greywyn's Armoire, you'll find Raiment of the Crimson Scar—armor equipped with leveled Fortify Agility, Speed, Sneak, Marksman, and Blade and Reflect Damage enchantments.

This room also contains a padded coffin for sleeping, a complete set of alchemical equipment and a raft of ingredients—including the only loose sample of nirnroot in the game.

Be sure to check out the book shelves in the western part of the Bastion for the Marksman skill book "The Gold Ribbon of Merit" (on the floor between two bookshelves), the Sneak skill book "Sacred Witness," and the Alteration skill book "Sithis" (on the bookshelves themselves), plus the Hand-to-Hand skill book "Immortal Blood" and Light Armor skill book "Rislav the Righteous" (respectively within and atop a bookshelf in a niche just to the east). You'll also come upon two conventional but unique books: "Opusculus Lamae Bal ta Mezzomortie" (atop the shelf that contains "Sithis") and "Manifesto Cyrodiil Vampyrum" (right beside "Rislav"), which respectively lay out the roots and rules of the vampires—as well as Absorb Health, Chameleon, and Detect Life scrolls.

And if you're ever hard up for cash—after all, this place didn't come cheap—there's a jewelry box in the east chamber and load of silver place settings in the central room.

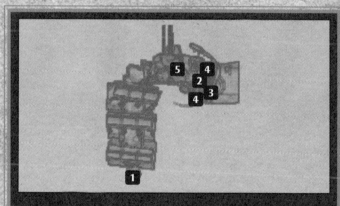

1. Entrance to Deepscorn Bastion.

2. Ichor Basin: Fill it with the Ichor purchased at the Wawnet Inn and then activate it. If you have an Infamous character, you'll get a nice (or nasty, depending on your point of view) daily blessing tuned to your level of Infamy.

3. Unusual Box: Within, the Crimson Eviscerator—an enchanted blade.

4. Nightshade plants.

5. Greywyn's Final Cache: one of the four hidden loot bags.

Just north of the Bastion stands the Shrine of Sithis. Here's where that expensive Ichor comes into play. At the base of the stairs, you'll find a creepy monument to Sithis. Activate the Ichor Basin at its feet. It will fill with the nasty liquid. Activate it again, and, if your Infamy exceeds your Fame, you'll receive a major daily blessing. (If you're famous instead of infamous, you're be admonished to "recant your honorable nature"!)

 The most basic of these—Call of Sithis, for an Infamy of up to 20—cures disease, restores all eight attributes and both restore and fortifies your health. We like.

The beauty of the Ichor Basin is the more evil you become, the better the blessing gets. If your Infamy is more than 20, but not over 50, you'll get Scream of Sithis, which steps up the Fortify Health benefit and adds Agility and Sneak boosts to the mix. If your Infamy's more than 50 but not over 90, this is replaced by Lament of Sithis, which ratchets up the Agility, Sneak, and Fortify Health boosts. And if it's over 90, it's Death Knell of Sithis. All three of those effects are improved once again, with a nice Chameleon effect thrown into the bargain.

Look around a bit, too. On the right side of the altar, you'll find an Unusual Box. Within, a Crimson Eviscerator—a nifty one-handed blade with leveled Absorb Strength, Damage Health, Damage Magicka, and Weakness to Poison enchantments. And you'll find six portions of Nightshade in the water.

We're done…and yet not quite done. There's a kind of Easter egg here. Former Hollow operator Greywyn hid four "loot caches" in the Hollow. Can you find them all?

The first is easy if you have a torch. Back in the entry area, northwest of the garden, you'll see a stalagmite. Beside it is Greywyn's First Cache. Within, you're guaranteed to find leveled gold, jewelry, a ring, and four gems.

The second and third caches are in the Cloister—the second underwater just south-southeast of the Font of Renewal, the third tucked away in the near eastern corner of the "cattle" cell. The second contains about half the gold of the first, but two rings, three items of jewelry, and six gems. The third has a bit more gold than the second: two rings, two jewelry items and eight gems.

Greywyn's Final Cache is in the Shrine. This one's hiding in plain sight—sandwiched between rocks below the waterfall about halfway down the north side of the stairs. This bag holds the most gold of any of the caches, and also includes four gems and a piece of magic jewelry. Nice bit of change when you put it all together.

Now we're done. Never mind all this hero nonsense…it's time to go and do naughty things.

HORSE ARMOR

You may recall that, in the original release of *Oblivion*, the Chestnut Handy stables outside the Imperial City had no horses for sale. Orc proprietor Snak gra-Bura had eaten them.

For all we know, Ms. gra-Bura is still eating horses, and is just being a touch more selective. But now, with the Horse Armor downloadable content (DLC), her stable does have something to sell.

Ride
Armored Paint Horse

If you begin a new game with the DLC installed, you'll receive a journal entry immediately after the death of Tamriel emperor Uriel Septim. (If the game's already underway, the journal should appear immediately after you resume play.) It refers to your finding a notice from Ms. gra-Bura—effectively a free-with-this-ad coupon for horse armor.

The "Horse Armor Note" that appears in your inventory reminds you that the stable is located outside the Imperial City. (It's just west of the west gate, in fact—an easy trip for an adventurer fresh from the stink of the Imperial Sewers.)

Just enter the stable building with the note and tell the hungry lady orc that "I'm here about the horse armor." What Ms. gra-Bura offers you depends on what you already have;

1. If you don't own a horse—and no, stolen ones don't count—tell her "I want horse armor, and a horse too" and then choose either of the first two follow-ups. She'll supply an old (and, we presume, inedible) nag fitted out with steel armor. It'll be waiting for you outside the stable.

   Now, this isn't the greatest horse in Cyrodill. It's more like the floor model—even armored, it has the same hit points as an un-armored Bay horse—and you may want to wait to cash in on this offer until you have a more respectable beast beneath you.

   However, if you're just looking for something serviceable to get you over to Weynon Priory, you can't argue with "free."

2. If you already own a horse, Ms. gra-Bura will give you a choice of steel or elven armor.

   This horse (which doesn't have to be physically present) can be any of the five types of store-bought horses, the paint horse that Prior Maborel donates to the cause on your initial visit to Weynon Priory or the great black steed Shadowmere (which you'll acquire in the course of the Dark Brotherhood quests). Just step outside, and there it is.

Either way, armoring your horse is a good idea. After all, the creature is at once your boon companion and your ride—not to mention a sometimes-sizeable investment—and an armored horse is much tougher to kill. Armoring Bay, Chesnut, Paint, and Black horses in each case doubles the horse's hit points. Fitting out a White horse almost doubles them—they rise from 400 to 750—and even the mighty Shadowmere gets a 50-percent HP bonus (from 500 to 750). The horses' other stats remain unchanged.

A few fine points:

If you own more than one horse, the armor purchased will attach to the last horse you rode. Hence, if you want to armor each of your horses, you'll have to ride each in its turn and return to the stable after each ride.

If an armored horse dies, the armor does not survive its death. Hence, you'll have to buy a replacement horse from the stable at which the original horse was purchased and then return to gra-Bura for the replacement armor. Which will now cost 500 gold.

Armored Black Horse

Once you've used the coupon in either of the above situations, you can come back and swap out the armor for the other type (again, for 500 gold).

Are there more of those free-horse-armor coupons lying around? There are not.

SPELL TOMES

This expansion adds to *Oblivion* a new kind of document called a "Spell Tome." Each of these 280-plus special volumes allows the player to learn a particular spell.

Found exclusively in containers and on the bodies of enemies, the Tomes turn up where you'd ordinarily find scrolls and function much like skill books. Read a Tome, and you'll be given the option to add its attached spell to your spell list. Agree, and it appears there immediately for your casting pleasure. And the book remains in your inventory afterward. It retains value and you can sell it as you would a used skill book.

Many of the spell effects will be familiar from store-bought spells, but others are either new—for example, the "Summon Bear" effect from the Pride of Hirstaang tome was previously a Power accessible only to Spriggans—or appear in new combinations or with new ranges, durations, and intensities.

The spells run the gamut—ranging from Aundae's Apprentice (which boosts the Willpower attribute by 10 points and Blade, Mysticism and Destruction skills by five for 30 seconds while exposing the player to Sun Damage), to Karstaag's Breath (Paralysis for five seconds and 10 points of Frost Damage for 10), to Orum's Aquatic Escape (15 seconds of Invisibility, Night Eye, and Water Breathing), to Superior Bound Armor (which simultaneously binds a cuirass, boots, gauntlets, greaves, and helmets to the player for 40 seconds).

SPELL TOMES

Spell Name	Spell School	Level	Effects	Cost	Tome Name
Defensive Boost	Alteration	Apprentice	Fortify Light Armor 5pts for 30sec on Self Shield 15pts for 30sec on Self	57	Defensive Boost Tome
Shieldwall	Alteration	Apprentice	Fortify Heavy Armor 5pts for 30sec on Self Shield 15pts for 30sec on Self	57	Shieldwall Tome
Mara's Grace	Conjuration	Journeyman	Light 40pts in 15ft for 30sec on Target Turn Undead 30pts in 15ft for 30sec on Target	123	Mara's Grace Tome
Pride of Hirstaang	Conjuration	Expert	Fortify Strength 5pts for 30sec on Self Resist Frost 30pts for 30sec on Self Summon Bear for 30sec on Self	271	Pride of Hirstaang Tome
Chilling Touch	Destruction	Novice	Frost Damage 4pts for 5sec Weakness to Frost 25% for 5sec	24	Chilling Touch Tome
Choking Grasp	Destruction	Novice	Drain Health 35pts for 3sec on Touch	25	Choking Grasp Tome
Decaying Taint	Destruction	Novice	Damage Health 2pts for 5sec on Target	21	Decaying Taint Tome
Electrifying Spark	Destruction	Novice	Shock Damage 3pts for 5sec on Target	23	Electrifying Spark Tome
Elemental Flare	Destruction	Novice	Fire Damage 5pts on Target Frost Damage 5pts on Target Shock Damage 5pts on Target	25	Elemental Flare Tome
Flammable Touch	Destruction	Novice	Fire Damage 4pts for 5sec on Touch Weakness to Fire 25% for 5sec on Touch	25	Flammable Touch Tome
Freezing Shard	Destruction	Novice	Frost Damage 3pts for 5sec on Target	22	Freezing Shard Tome
Searing Flare	Destruction	Novice	Fire Damage 3pts for 5sec on Target	22	Searing Flare Tome
Soul Grasp	Destruction	Novice	Damage Health 3pts for 3sec on Touch Soul Trap for 3sec on Touch	23	Soul Grasp Tome
Spark Touch	Destruction	Novice	Shock Damage 4pts for 5sec on Touch Weakness to Shock 25% for 5 sec on Touch	25	Spark Touch Tome
Decaying Bolt	Destruction	Apprentice	Damage Health 3pts for 6sec on Target	44	Decaying Bolt
Electrifying Bolt	Destruction	Apprentice	Shock Damage 5pts for 6sec on Target	55	Electrifying Bolt Tome
Electrifying Touch	Destruction	Apprentice	Shock Damage 6pts for 6sec on Target Weakness to Shock 50% for 6sec on Touch	54	Electrifying Touch Tome
Elemental Bolt	Destruction	Apprentice	Fire Damage 9pts on Target Frost Damage 9pts on Target Shock Damage 9pts on Target	55	Elemental Bolt Tome
Freezing Bolt	Destruction	Apprentice	Frost Damage 5pts for 6sec on Target	52	Freezing Bolt Tome
Freezing Touch	Destruction	Apprentice	Frost Damage 6pts for 7sec on Touch Weakness to Frost 50% for 7sec on Touch	61	Freezing Touch Tome
Kindling Touch	Destruction	Apprentice	Fire Damage 6pts for 7sec on Touch Weakness to Fire 50% for 7sec on Touch	62	Kindling Touch Tome
Searing Bolt	Destruction	Apprentice	Fire Damage 5pts for 7sec on Target	61	Searing Bolt Tome
Strangulation	Destruction	Apprentice	Drain Health 70pts for 3sec on Touch	62	Strangulation Tome
Decaying Burst	Destruction	Journeyman	Damage Health 7pts for 6sec on Target	130	Decaying Burst Tome
Electrifying Burst	Destruction	Journeyman	Shock Damage 10pts for 6sec on Target	133	Electrifying Burst Tome
Elemental Burst	Destruction	Journeyman	Fire Damage 15pts on Target Frost Damage 15pts on Target Shock Damage 15pts on Target	108	Elemental Burst Tome
Freezing Burst	Destruction	Journeyman	Frost Damage 10pts for 6sec on Target	126	Freezing Burst Tome
Frostbite	Destruction	Journeyman	Frost Damage 12pts for 6sec on Touch Weakness to Frost 75% for 6sec on Touch	121	Frostbite Tome
Hangman's Noose	Destruction	Journeyman	Drain Health 130pts for 3sec on Touch	137	Hangman's Noose Tome
Lightning Touch	Destruction	Journeyman	Shock Damage 12pts for 6sec on Touch Weakness to Shock 75% for 6sec on Touch	127	Lightning Touch Tome
Mark of Fire	Destruction	Journeyman	Fire Damage 1pt in 15ft for 30sec on Target	75	Mark of Fire Tome
Scorching Touch	Destruction	Journeyman	Fire Damage 12pts for 6sec on Touch Weakness to Fire 75% for 6sec on Touch	123	Scorching Touch Tome
Searing Burst	Destruction	Journeyman	Fire Damage 10pts for 6sec on Target	128	Searing Burst Tome
Arctic Touch	Destruction	Expert	Frost Damage 30pts for 6sec on Touch Weakness to Frost 100% for 6sec on Touch	366	Arctic Touch Tome
Decaying Blast	Destruction	Expert	Damage Health 16pts for 6sec on Target	375	Decaying Blast Tome
Electrifying Blast	Destruction	Expert	Shock Damage 20pts for 6sec on Target	324	Electrifying Blast Tome
Electrocuting Touch	Destruction	Expert	Shock Damage 30pts for 6sec on Touch Weakness to Shock 100% for 6sec on Touch	384	Electrocuting Touch Tome
Elemental Blast	Destruction	Expert	Fire Damage 25pts on Target Frost Damage 25pts on Target Shock Damage 25pts on Target	209	Elemental Blast Tome
Freezing Blast	Destruction	Expert	Frost Damage 20pts for 6sec on Target	308	Freezing Blast Tome
Immolating Touch	Destruction	Expert	Fire Damage 30pts for 6sec on Touch Weakness to Fire 100% for 6sec on Touch	370	Immolating Touch Tome

SPELL TOMES

Spell Name	Spell School	Level	Effects	Cost	Tome Name
Mara's Wrath	Destruction	Expert	Fire Damage 3pts in 15ft for 30sec on Target Turn Undead 35pts in 15ft for 30sec on Target	388	Mara's Wrath Tome
Searing Blast	Destruction	Expert	Fire Damage 20pts for 6sec on Target	312	Searing Blast Tome
Touch of Death	Destruction	Expert	Drain Health 250pts for 3sec on Touch	316	Touch of Death Tome
Blink	Illusion	Novice	Invisibility for 5sec on Self	20	Blink Tome
Enhanced Visibility	Illusion	Novice	Light 10pts in 30ft for 30sec on Target	19	Enhanced Visibility Tome
Night Form	Illusion	Journeyman	Fortify Sneak 10pts for 30sec on Self Invisibility for 30sec on Self Sun Damage 2pts for 50sec on Self	100	Night Form Tome
Orum's Aquatic Escape	Illusion	Journeyman	Invisibility for 15sec on Self Night-Eye for 15sec on Self Water Breathing for 15sec on Self	114	Orum's Aquatic Escape Tome
Thunderclap	Illusion	Journeyman	Paralyze in 20ft for 1sec on Touch	142	Thunderclap Tome
Fenrik's Welcome	Illusion	Expert	Chameleon 100% for 5sec on Self Open Average Lock on Target	210	Fenrik's Welcome Tome
Karstaag's Breath	Illusion	Expert	Frost Damage 10pts for 10sec on Touch Paralyze for 5sec on Touch	378	Karstaag's Breath Tome
Baltham's Insight	Illusion	Novice	Detect Life 150pts for 5sec	24	Baltham's Insight Tome
Llivam's Reversal	Illusion	Expert	Reflect Spell 15pts for 20sec on Self Spell Absorption 10pts for 20sec on Self	338	Llivam's Reversal Tome
Aundae's Aura	Restoration	Apprentice	Fortify Willpower 10pts for 30sec on Self Fortify Blade 5pts for 30sec on Self Fortify Mysticism 5pts for 30sec on Self Fortify Destruction 5pts for 30sec on Self Sun Damage 1pt for 30sec on Self	50	Aundae's Aura Tome
Berne's Aura	Restoration	Apprentice	Fortify Agility 10pts for 30sec on Self Fortify Sneak 5pts for 30sec on Self Fortify Hand to Hand 5pts for 30sec on Self Fortify Acrobatics 5pts for 30sec on Self Sun Damage 1pt for 30sec on Self	50	Berne's Aura Tome
Quarra's Aura	Restoration	Apprentice	Fortify Strength 10pts for 30sec on Self Fortify Blunt 5pts for 30sec on Self Fortify Hand to Hand 5pts for 30sec on Self Fortify Heavy Armor 5pts for 30sec on Self Sun Damage 1pt for 30sec on Self	50	Quarra's Aura Tome
Disease Resistance	Restoration	Journeyman	Resist Disease 50pts for 20sec on Self	149	Disease Resistance Tome
Leech Vitality	Restoration	Journeyman	Absorb Health 10pts on Touch Absorb Magicka 20pts on Touch	64	Leech Vitality Tome
Magicka Vortex	Restoration	Journeyman	Absorb Magicka 10pts for 5 sec on Touch Stunted Magicka for 30sec on Touch Weakness to Magic 25pts for 30 sec on Touch	140	Magicka Vortex Tome
Resist Paralysis	Restoration	Journeyman	Resist Paralysis 20pts for 20sec on Self	69	Resist Paralysis Tome
Resist Poison	Restoration	Journeyman	Resist Poison 50pts for 20sec on Self	149	Resist Poison Tome

Don't expect to find a Tome right away. Sorry. None appear in fixed locations. Like so many things in the game, they're tuned to the player's current level. Moreover, the odds of finding one vary according on the spell level of the Tome and the type of container in which it can be found.

However, those odds are much better in chests, and your best shot is searching boss-level chests in Necromancer, "Mythic Enemy" and Conjurer lairs.

CREDITS

BETHESDA SOFTWORKS

Written By
Peter Olafson

Additional Writing
Jeff Browne
Joel Burgess
Erik Caponi
Brian Chapin
Jeffery Gardiner
Kurt Kuhlmann
Al Nanes
Mark Nelson
Bruce Nesmith

Screenshots
Matthew Carofano
Dane Olds

Editors
Pete Hines
Bruce Nesmith

Production Coordinator
Jeff Gardiner

Maps and Layout/Design Work
Lindsay Muller
Mike Wagner

The Elder Scrolls® IV: Shivering Isles™ **Created By**
Bethesda Game Studios

Oblivion **Executive Producer**
Todd Howard

Special thanks to: Our friends and families, everyone at Bethesda Softworks, Bethesda Game Studios, and ZeniMax Media, Inc.

PRIMA GAMES

Product Manager
Mario De Govia

Editor
Rebecca Chastain

Copy Editor
Jill Ellis

Guide Design
Marc Riegel

Guide Layout
James Knight

Manufacturing
Suzanne Goodwin